W9-DBD-329

Guide to Military Installations

Guide to Military Installations

6th Edition

Dan Cragg

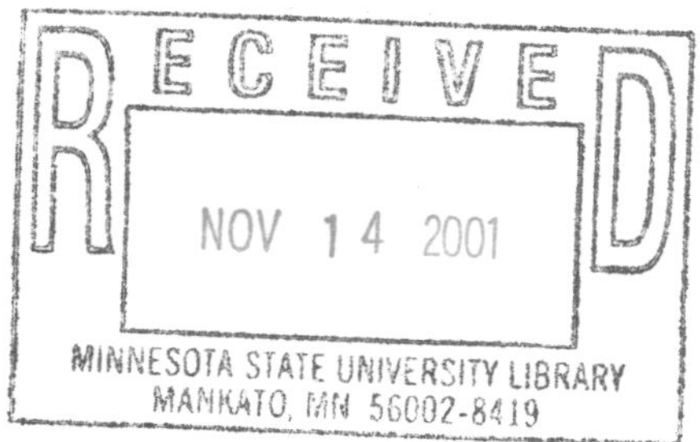

STACKPOLE
BOOKS

Published by
STACKPOLE BOOKS
5067 Ritter Road
Mechanicsburg, PA 17055
www.stackpolebooks.com

Cover design by Wendy A. Reynolds

Printed in the United States

Sixth Edition

10 9 8 7 6 5 4 3 2 1

Library of Congress Cataloging-in-Publication Data

Cragg, Dan.
Guide to military installations / Dan Cragg.—6th ed.
p. cm.
Includes index.
ISBN 0-8117-2781-5 (alk. paper)
1. Military bases, American—Directories. 2. United States—Armed Forces—Facilities—Directories. I. Title.
UA26.A2 C723 2001
355.7'023'73—dc21

2001020961

The National War College at Fort McNair in Washington, D.C. U.S. ARMY PHOTO

Contents

Preface

Welcome to the sixth edition of Guide to Military Installations.

What a difference a decade makes. When ten years ago we started work on the third edition of this guide, the world was a much different place than it is today. Back in 1991, the units that had fought in the recently concluded Gulf War were on the verge of redeployment to their home stations and the troop reductions in Europe were just getting started. In 1991, the Department of Defense had 1.9 million men and women under arms: 710,000 Army, 570,000 Navy, 194,000 Marine Corps, and 510,000 Air Force. Today that force is down to 1.3 million: 479,000 Army, 373,000 Navy, 172,000 Marine Corps, and 360,000 Air Force.

Of today's force, 1,132,000 are deployed in the United States and its territories, while the remaining 252,000 personnel are deployed overseas, afloat (45,000) and ashore, in a total of 139 different countries. By far the largest overseas deployment is still in Germany, with 65,000 personnel, 50,000 of whom are Army. This is down from over 200,000 in 1991. Next is Japan with 40,000 personnel (5,800 Air Force, 19,000 Marines, and 13,000 Navy) followed by Korea with 35,000 (26,000 Army).

Totally unforeseen a decade ago was the deployment of American troops to the Balkans in 1995. Today the 5,800 American military personnel still in Bosnia-Herzgovina have taken on the mantle of a semipermanent garrison. Interestingly, at press time the plan to replace troops in the Balkans on a rotational basis through 2001 includes significant numbers of reserve component personnel, principally members of the Texas Army National Guard's 49th Armored Division, Virginia's 29th Infantry Division, and Pennsylvania's 28th Infantry Division. Separate units from Georgia, Indiana, Mississippi, North Carolina, and Oklahoma are scheduled to participate. This will represent the largest overseas deployment of reserve personnel since the Gulf War.

So the contribution of the 1.35 million men and women in the reserve components to our national defense is vital. This is not to discount the more than 700,000 Department of Defense civilian employees, all of whom are important members of the military communities described in this guide.

On 31 December, 1999, the United States officially withdrew from the storied Panama Canal Zone, ending nearly a century of operations there.

This guide was compiled from unclassified materials, most of which were obtained directly from the installations. The author and the publisher strive to make this guide as complete as possible; any installations not included here either have very small military populations or chose not to participate. In this new release of the guide, we have striven to include more remote and temporary locations. We have also provided, where available, the addresses of the World Wide Websites established at various installations. The user should understand, however, that information in that medium frequently changes its location within the web or is discontinued without notice.

In this new edition, we've tried to capture both the facts and the temper of these rapidly changing times for the U.S. military. When we put the fifth edition to press in 1997, the U.S. armed forces were adjusting to the aftereffects of the base closures and realignments that started in 1989, with the end of the Cold War. Since the Clinton administration, our armed forces have significantly downsized and that has been reflected in the number of closures and mission reduction at many of our installations. Things stabilized to a degree after Congress refused to consider more closures until after the national elections in November 2000, which has given a reprieve and breathing space to commanders and troops alike.

The guide is divided into two general sections, domestic and overseas, with a third section consisting of maps showing the location of each installation by service, both domestic and foreign. States and countries are arranged alphabetically, and under these are the installations, arranged alphabetically by military service. At the end of each entry is the address of the official to contact for more information, and the domestic entries also offer a commercial telephone number, as well as the installation's World Wide Web address, where provided.

Each entry contains information regarding the installation's history and mission; facts on housing, schools, and personal and recreational services available there; and something about the local area. As with the previous editions, we have excluded details on topics such as transportation of household goods and automobiles, travel pay and allowances, and so on. Those who need such information should contact the appropriate service representatives.

Although designed primarily for the use of active-duty and retired military personnel, Department of Defense civilian employees, and their families, this guide is also intended to serve as a valuable tool for anyone who travels. Most military installations in the United States are to some degree open to the public, and a side trip to a military post can prove a worthwhile diversion for John and Jane Public on their annual family vacation. Besides, all these installations belong to the American taxpayers, and where security restrictions do not apply, they should feel free to stop by and see how their money is being spent.

Active-duty personnel are authorized access to morale and personal support services at any Department of Defense installation anywhere in the world. Retired military personnel are generally authorized the same access in the United States, depending on availability; overseas, the rules may be different, so travelers should check with the overseas commands they will be visiting. Members of the general public visiting any military installation should always check with the security personnel at the main gate before proceeding onto the grounds.

To the many public affairs officers who made this guide a reality, we offer our humble thanks. We wish we could thank each of you personally, but that would entail a list several hundred names long. Please accept our thanks and know that they are sincere.

PART I

United States Installations

ALABAMA

Air Force

MAXWELL AIR FORCE BASE

Education is their business at Maxwell Air Force Base, home of the Air University, the Air Force's largest complex of professional schools, including the Air War College, the Air Command and Staff College, the Squadron Officer School, and the Air Force Senior NCO Academy. In addition to its educational functions, Maxwell also has jurisdiction over Gunter Annex, just across town, home for the Air Force Standard Systems Group.

History. First established in 1918 as Wright Field (because in 1910 Orville Wright chose the site to establish a flying school), the installation was renamed in 1922 to honor 2nd Lt. William C. Maxwell, a native of Atmore, Alabama. Maxwell was killed in an air crash in the Philippines. The Air University was established at Maxwell AFB in 1946, and today it provides educational services for more than 500,000 airmen annually.

Housing and Schools. More than 1,600 sets of family quarters are available between Maxwell and Gunter. Temporary housing is available to families moving in with permanent-change-of-station orders. Temporary housing in motels is available but becomes relatively expensive when the stay is two weeks or more. A couple of the motels have kitchenettes or efficiency apartments, which cost from $150 to $225 per week (prices are subject to change). You are required to check with billeting before making any off-base arrangements.

Maxwell operates an elementary school (kindergarten through sixth grade) on base, while older children are bused to Montgomery schools. Both Maxwell and Gunter operate child-care centers. Associate's, bachelor's, and graduate degrees in eighteen majors are offered on base through Troy State University in Montgomery, and Auburn University offers three doctoral degree programs at Maxwell. The University of Alabama offers a master's degree in military history.

Personal Services. Medical care is provided by a four-floor, intermediate-sized referral facility at the USAF Regional Hospital, Maxwell. An excellent commissary and base exchange are available, with branches at Gunter Annex. Officer and NCO open messes are also available.

Recreation. Recreational facilities are plentiful. Maxwell offers two 18-hole golf courses and a sixteen-lane bowling center, as well as gymnasiums and a recreation center. For the outdoorsman, fishing is available at several places on the installation, particularly in the two lakes near the base picnic area and in the Alabama River, which borders the base on the northeast. The on-base family camp is open year-round and offers six camper sites with hookups and three tent sites, as well as fishing, hiking, tennis, and appropriate equipment.

Maxwell operates the Lake Pippin and Lake Martin recreation areas. At the Lake Pippin site, located on Choctawhatchee Bay on Florida's northern Gulf Coast near Niceville, there are thirty furnished trailers, a playground, picnic areas, swimming areas, and boat rentals. At Lake Martin, 50 miles northeast of the base, there are 10 trailers and 50 camper spaces, a playground and a picnic area, fishing, camping, an aero club, swimming, and boating. Both sites are open year-round.

The Local Area. Maxwell AFB is about two miles northwest of Montgomery's business district. Montgomery is the third largest city in Alabama and has a population of over 180,000. It was at Montgomery in February 1861 that the Confederate States of America was formed and Jefferson Davis took office as its president. Snow and ice are a rarity at Maxwell, which is situated in the famous Sun Belt of the Deep South.

For more information, write to 42nd Air Base Wing Public Affairs Office, 50 LeMay Plaza South, Maxwell AFB, AL 36112-6334, or call (334) 953-1110. Home page: *www.au.af.mil.*

Army

FORT RUCKER

The steady whop-whop-whop of helicopter rotor blades forms a backdrop to the normal cadence of life at Fort Rucker, the "Home of Army Aviation." Every soldier and every civilian who works there is in some way dedicated to the mission of keeping flying soldiers ready to fight with the ground troops as a part of the Army's modern combined-arms team.

History. Occupying over 64,000 acres in the southeastern Alabama countryside, Fort Rucker opened in 1942. Named after Confederate general Edmund W. Rucker, a Tennessee native, Fort Rucker became involved in Army aviation in August 1954, when the U.S. Army Aviation School moved there from Fort Sill, Oklahoma. The post's population today is approximately 19,000, with more than 8,000 active-duty personnel and 3,800 family members.

The rolling and wooded countryside around Fort Rucker is well watered by lakes and streams, and with its proximity to the Gulf of Mexico, military anglers find it a paradise of fresh- and saltwater fishing. The climate is mild, and snow and ice are rare. By early April, the noonday temperatures on post are usually in the low eighties, but breezes from the Gulf, ninety miles to the south, and frequent rainfall moderate the summer nights.

Housing and Schools. There are over 1,500 sets of family quarters at Fort Rucker, and guest-house facilities are available. The post also has 50 mobile home lots. There are approximately 300 bachelor quarters and over 470 rooms for temporary-duty personnel.

There are two on-post schools for dependent children in kindergarten through sixth grade. The schools also offer services for mildly mentally handicapped, learning-disabled, speech-impaired, and gifted students. Child-development services provide special care for all age groups and offer full-day, part-day, preschool, hourly care, and family child-care services for children from six weeks to twelve years old.

Military personnel interested in further educational opportunities are offered programs conducted on post by Troy State University and Embry-Riddle Aeronautical University. Enterprise State Junior College and George C. Wallace State Community College offer courses on post, as well as in nearby communities. The Alabama Aviation and Technical College is located in nearby Ozark.

Personal Services. Medical care is provided by the modern, seventy-two-bed Lyster Army Community Hospital, which provides care to more than 50,000 people. Its various outpatient clinics average more than 17,000 visits a month. The commissary offers 27,000 square feet of sales space with a meat market and a deli. The exchange has a shopping mall, complete with a one-hour photo shop, a flower shop, and various food emporiums.

Recreation. The Lake Tholocco Outdoor Recreation Office offers military personnel and their dependents over 600 acres of water for fishing, swimming, and waterskiing, with boats and canoes for rent at nominal fees. The Fort Rucker Florida Recreation Area, on Choctawhatchee Bay between Freeport and Niceville on State Highway 20, contains fifteen two-bedroom house trailers and twenty campsites with electric hookups. In addition, the information, tour, and travel office at Fort Rucker provides information and makes reservations for military recreation areas, sells tickets to all types of popular events, and has discount tickets for places such as Walt Disney World.

Fort Rucker's NCO and officers club systems provide a full range of services, including on-post catering, dining and banquet rooms, and party, conference, and seminar areas at the main officers club and the Lake Lodge. There is also an Olympic-size swimming pool at the main officers club.

The Local Area. Fort Rucker is situated approximately ninety miles south of Montgomery, the state capital, and thirty miles northwest of Dothan. The towns of Enterprise, Daleville, and Ozark are just west, south, and east, respectively. Fort Rucker is an hour-and-a-half drive from the Gulf of Mexico and about three hours from Mount Cheaha State Park, the highest point in the state.

For more information, write to Headquarters, U.S. Army Aviation Center and Fort Rucker, Attention: Army Community Services, Building 9204, Fifth Avenue, Fort Rucker, AL 36362-5033, or call (334) 255-9339/2887.

Soldiers Marching at Redstone Arsenal, Alabama U.S. ARMY PHOTO

REDSTONE ARSENAL

It's a long way from Peenemunde on the shores of the Baltic, where the Germans developed their V-1 and V-2 rockets during World War II, to Huntsville, Alabama, but over 100 German scientists made the trip—via Fort Bliss, Texas—in 1950. Among them was the noted Wernher von Braun, who later played a significant role in America's space program.

History. Created in 1941 to make conventional toxic chemical ammunition, Redstone's involvement in the space age began early in 1949 and continued in 1950, when the Army moved its missile experts there from Texas. Today the arsenal is home to the U.S. Army Aviation Missile Command (AMCOM), which oversees the research, development, engineering, testing, procurement, production, and logistical support of the Army's aviation missile and rocket systems. To do this job, the installation supports a daily working population of nearly 13,000 people—10,000 civilian workers, 1,400 active-duty military personnel, and 1,222 family members.

Housing and Schools. Redstone has 638 sets of family quarters in two- and four-bedroom units. Bachelor housing consists of air-conditioned brick barracks for enlisted soldiers in the lower grades and more than 100 rooms for senior NCOs and officers. The installation also has newly renovated guest lodging facilities.

Dependent children attend schools in Huntsville. There are a nursery and a preschool on post. The University of Alabama, Alabama A & M, and Oakwood College offer college courses for adult education.

Personal Services. Medical and dental care at Redstone are provided through the Fox Army Health Center. There are a post exchange, a commissary, and the usual morale and support activities.

Recreation. The northern Alabama climate offers mild winters and humid summers with long spring and fall seasons, making outdoor recreation possible all through the year. The installation's 38,000 acres include many lakes, ponds, and streams open to fishing. Redstone also has excellent hunting for waterfowl, small game, and deer. Boating and camping are also available, and the Redstone Recreation Center offers programs that cover a wide range of interests, from amateur photography to bowling.

The Local Area. Huntsville, situated on a northern bend of the Tennessee River, is a thriving modern city of 171,000 inhabitants and is keyed to the pulsating life of the space age. Located in the Alabama mountain lakes section, Huntsville is conveniently close to one of the foremost resort areas in the South. Chattanooga, Tennessee, is to the northeast, and Birmingham is to the south, on Interstate 65.

For more information, write to U.S. Army Aviation Missile Command, Attention: AMSAM-PA, Redstone Arsenal, AL 35898-5020, or call (256) 876-1461. Home page: *www.redstone.army.mil.*

Coast Guard

MOBILE AVIATION TRAINING CENTER

History. In 1966, the vacant 232-acre Air Force Reserve facility located at Mobile's Bates Field was acquired by the Coast Guard for the purpose of establishing there a standardized pilot training program. In December 1966, Air Station Mobile was officially commissioned with the transfer of HU-16E Albatross aircraft from Biloxi, Mississippi, and the establishment of fixed-wing and rotary-wing pilot training units.

In 1969, the Helicopter Icebreaker Support Unit (IBSU), now known as the Polar Operations Division, was established at Mobile and the installation became known as the Aviation Training Center. Today the 500 active-duty and civilian personnel of each of the eight divisions of the center—operations, training, polar operations, aviation engineering, medical, comptroller, services, and facilities engineering—work together to support Coast Guard missions worldwide. HU-25A Guardian aircraft stand on alert in support of 8th Coast Guard District missions, such as search-and-rescue and enforcement of maritime laws. HH-65A aircraft from the Polar Operations Division deploy on Coast Guard icebreakers to the ends of the earth, where they fly scientific, logistical, and occasionally search-and-rescue missions. The training division provides initial and recurrent training to Coast Guard pilots. The Aviation Training Center is the largest air unit in the Coast Guard.

Housing, Schools, and Personal Services. While there is no family housing onboard the center, temporary lodging is available in the form of visiting officer and enlisted units that are available by reservation. One-room off-base apartment rentals start at $250 per month; two-bedroom units range from as little as $375 a month to as much as $700. A security deposit plus first and last months' rent are usually required upon signing a lease.

Dependent children attend one of the ninety-five public schools in Mobile County. College-level courses are available from many sources.

The center has a large grocery annex and a Coast Guard exchange with a service station and barber and beauty shops. A swimming pool, tennis court, and racquetball court are available, as are equipment and boat rentals and a base picnic area. A full-service medical clinic is also available.

The Local Area. The Aviation Training Center is located at Mobile Municipal Airport, six miles west of Interstate 65 along Airport Boulevard. Downtown Mobile and Mobile Bay are about eight miles east of the center.

The modern city takes its name from a French trading post—Fort Louis de la Mobile—established nearby in 1702. Today Mobile is the second-largest city in the state of Alabama and a thriving seaport town on the Gulf of Mexico, situated on the west bank of the Mobile River, where it enters Mobile Bay. With a population of over 200,000, Mobile offers plenty of historical, cultural, and recreational activities for everyone, including the celebrated Azalea Trail, a 37-mile flower-lined drive.

For more information, write to Commanding Officer, USCG Aviation Training Center, Attention: Public Affairs Branch, Mobile, AL 36608-9682, or call (334) 639-6428.

ALASKA

Air Force

EIELSON AIR FORCE BASE

What do oil, Dr. Henry Kissinger, and Gen. "Chappie" James all have in common? Eielson Air Force Base, for one thing. They were all drawn together in 1975 when President Gerald Ford stopped at Eielson and delivered a speech on the merits of the fledgling Alaskan Oil Pipeline. Pump Station No. 8 of that line is only ten miles south of the base. Add to that the fact that Eielson has the only combat-ready forward-air-control squadron in Alaska, and you have quite a combination.

History. Eielson was known simply as "Mile 26" when it opened in 1943, because it was the site of a U.S. Army Signal Corps telegraph station exactly 26 miles from Fairbanks that provided a link with Valdez, Alaska. During World War II, Eielson served as a storage area for excess Lend-Lease aircraft on their way to Russia, and Russian airmen were stationed there to take possession. On 4 February 1948, Mile 26 was redesignated Eielson Air Force Base in honor of Carl Ben Eielson, a famed arctic pioneer and aviator. Today the base is home for the 354th Fighter Wing whose pilots fly the F-16 Fighting Falcon and the OA-10 Thunderbolt II. The wing's primary mission is to provide close-air support and forward air control for Army ground forces in Alaska. Approximately 2,700 active-duty personnel, their 4,300 dependents, and 620 civilian employees call Eielson home.

Housing and Schools. There are 1,200 sets of family quarters at Eielson, but space is usually very limited from May to September. The base also has accommodations for 730 single and unaccompanied military personnel. Local housing is expensive. One-bedroom apartments average $650 to $700 a month; efficiencies average about $450, plus utilities. The average rent for a two-bedroom apartment is $700 a month, but rents as high as $900 are not uncommon. Utilities average $50 to $200 a month. Three-and four-bedroom units can be found for anywhere between $1,000 and $1,500 per month. Variable housing

Aerial Refueling near Eielson Air Force Base, Alaska USAF PHOTO

allowance is available to personnel living off base, and a cost-of-living allowance is paid to all personnel to offset the high cost of housing in Alaska.

The Fairbanks North Star Borough School District operates three elementary schools, one junior high school, and one senior high school on base for children residing on Eielson. A preschool and a child-care center are also available. The University of Alaska–Anchorage, University of Alaska–Southeast, and Wayland Baptist University offer many undergraduate courses on base, and La Verne University offers classes leading to a master's degree in business management.

Personal Services. Medical care at Eielson is provided by the 354th Medical Group clinic staff, with referrals to Bassett Army Hospital at Fort Wainwright for care beyond the clinic's capability. The base exchange stocks over 140,000 items, and the commissary offers shoppers a complete selection of groceries.

Recreation. Recreational facilities include a twenty-lane bowling center, gymnasium, three tennis courts, auto and wood hobby shops, and a recreation center. A ski lodge is located four miles southeast of the base. The Birch Lake Recreation Area, about 35 miles south of Eielson, offers cabins, trailer pads with or without electric hookups, tent sites, a marina, a lodge, and a picnic area. The site offers camping, boating, hiking, and picnicking from Memorial Day through Labor Day.

The Local Area. Fairbanks is located 26 miles north of Eielson and sits 110 miles south of the Arctic Circle. The greater Fairbanks North Star borough boasts a population of more than 79,000 permanent residents. In June, the sunlight shines a maximum of 21 hours and 40 minutes, and in December, a bright day sees the sun shining 3 hours and 47 minutes. The average low temperature in January is minus 19° F, and the average high in July is a balmy 70° F.

For more information, write to 354th Wing Public Affairs Office, 3112 Broadway Avenue, Unit 15A, Eielson AFB, AK 99702-1895, or call (907) 377-3148. Home page: *www.eielson.af.mil.*

ELMENDORF AIR FORCE BASE

Elmendorf Air Force Base lies farther north than Helsinki, Finland, and is almost as far west as Hawaii, but it lies in the northern suburbs of Alaska's largest city, some 1,400 air miles from Seattle. With a population of over 250,000, Anchorage has almost 50 percent of the total population of the state of Alaska.

History. Elmendorf began as an airfield called Fort Richardson. In November 1940, the field was designated Elmendorf Field after Hugh M. Elmendorf. In March 1951, the Army relocated its garrison to the new Fort Richardson on the southeast side of Anchorage, and the installation came under the authority of the Air Force. Today the base's 13,000-square-acre expanse is home for the 11th Air Force, 3rd Wing, and other commands. Approximately 6,700 active-duty personnel, 10,300 dependents, and 1,150 civilian employees call Elmendorf home.

Housing and Schools. There are more than 1,500 sets of family quarters at Elmendorf. Bachelor housing consists of 68 bachelor officer quarters, 40 units for senior NCOs, and spaces for 1,100 billets in organizational housing (better known as barracks). There are also 100 temporary lodging units available.

The base has three elementary schools, kindergarten through sixth grade, and a special-education school. High school programs are available off base. A main child-care center and four auxiliary centers, as well as numerous family day-care providers, are located on the installation. Education services for adults include a number of college programs from Chapman College, University of La Verne, University of Alaska, Alaska Pacific University, Wayland Baptist University, and Embry-Riddle Aeronautical University.

Personal Services. Medical care is available from the 3rd Wing Medical Group, a modern, seven-story, 75-bed medical facility offering 16 specialty clinics. Services and facilities available on base include a commissary with 7,000 line items, a complete exchange complex with numerous concessions, a package liquor store, a 60,000-volume library, enlisted and officers clubs, and the Galaxy Cafeteria, located in the base passenger terminal, which is open 24 hours a day.

Recreation. Recreational facilities include an eighteen-hole golf course, a forty-lane bowling center, hobby shops, a base theater, and many athletic programs. The base also has several lakes where boating, fishing, and other water sports are available.

For more information, write to Public Affairs Office, 3rd Wing, Elmendorf AFB, AK 99506-2530, or call (907) 552-1110.

Home page: *www.topcover.af.mil.*

Army

FORT RICHARDSON

Fort Richardson is truly in the Alaska that millions of Americans dream of visiting—a wilderness that begins right on post, where moose freely roam. Only a brief drive from the post is the center of the port city of Anchorage (population 250,000). Fort Richardson occupies 71,000 acres and is situated on the northeast side of town, adjacent to Elmendorf Air Force Base. Rimming the city to the east are the Chugach Mountains.

History. Named in honor of Brig. Gen. Wilds P. Richardson, a pioneer explorer in Alaska, Fort Richardson was originally located on the site of Elmendorf AFB from 1940 to 1941 and moved to its present location in 1950. The post is home to the U.S. Army, Alaska (USARAK), headquarters, and to elements of the 172nd Infantry Brigade (Separate), which has forces at both Fort Richardson and Fort Wainwright. The primary unit at Fort Richardson is the 1st Battalion, 501st Parachute Infantry Regiment, which has the distinction of being the Army's oldest airborne battalion, as well as the only Army airborne battalion, in the Pacific Theater. The post is also headquarters for the Special Troops Battalion and Headquarters, U.S. Army Garrison.

These units assist USARAK in its mission of commanding and controlling U.S. Army forces in Alaska and providing the services, facilities, and infrastructure to support power projection and training to rapidly deploy U.S. Army forces from Alaska in the conduct of contingency operations within the Pacific Theater and elsewhere as directed.

The post supports a population of approximately 2,100 military personnel, 2,900 family members, and 1,300 civilian employees.

Housing and Schools. There are about 1,300 sets of family quarters, ranging in size from detached houses for colonels and higher-ranking officers to duplexes for field-grade officers to four- and eight-plex housing for other grades.

An excellent education-services plan offered through the Fort Richardson Education Center includes a basic-skills education program, a high school completion program, and college programs on post and at local college campuses. Three on-post elementary school facilities are available for dependent children through the Anchorage School District. Students in grades seven through twelve are bused to nearby junior and senior high schools. Child-care facilities, including certified home-care providers and centers for infants, toddlers, and preschoolers, are available on post. Before- and after-school care is available for children through sixth grade. A diverse youth-services program—which includes rock climbing, whitewater rafting, and ice fishing—is also offered for school-age children and teens at the youth center.

Personal Services. On-post medical care is provided through outpatient facilities only; inpatient hospital care is available at nearby Elmendorf AFB. A new Joint Military Mall on Elmendorf AFB, featuring a commissary, AAFES exchange, clothing sales, numerous vendors and large food court, serves the shopping needs of post residents. Fort Richardson's shoppette provides convenience items and video rentals.

Recreation. Fort Richardson offers an excellent outdoor recreation program. The largest activity is the Seward Resort, located on Resurrection Bay 129 miles south of Anchorage, where people enjoy mountain climbing, hiking, boating, and fishing. The Black Spruce Army Travel Camp for recreational vehicles, located near Otter Lake on Fort Richardson, offers electrical and water hookups, dump facilities, showers, a washer and dryer, and a children's playground.

Otter Lake Recreation Area is five miles from the main post and covers a total of 2,900 acres (the lake covers 99 acres). The on-post outdoor recreation center offers a skeet and trap range, as well as an archery range. Buckner Physical Fitness Center offers weight training, aerobics, intramural sports, karate, swimming, and other sports activities. The post also has golf and ski courses, an auto crafts shop, and an arts and crafts shop.

The Local Area. The Anchorage area has a mild climate, with summers comparable to those in Seattle or San Francisco. On the shortest day of the year, there are a little more than five hours of daylight, and on the longest day, the sun shines for more than 19 hours. During the summer months, it is possible to enjoy a wide variety of outdoor activities, such as flying, camping, hunting, fishing, and hiking. Winter activities include skiing, ice skating, snowmobiling, and ice fishing.

For more information, write to Public Affairs Office, U.S. Army, Alaska, Attention: APVR-RPO, 600 Richardson Drive, Fort Richardson, AK 99505-5900, or call (907) 384-1536/2072. Home page: *www.usarak.army.mil.*

FORT WAINWRIGHT

"Above all, keep your chin down, eyes in the pan, knees bent, and dig-shake, dig-shake, dig-shake," advises a prospector's guide to gold panning in Alaska. There is gold in Alaska, in more ways than one, and for some soldiers an assignment to the 172nd Infantry Brigade (Separate) at Fort Wainwright may be a golden opportunity to participate in a challenging and exciting experience in one of the world's most spectacular natural wonderlands.

History. Fort Wainwright is located just east of Fairbanks along the Chena River, some 350 miles by road north of Anchorage and 1,500 miles northwest of Dawson Creek, British Columbia, Canada, along the Alaska Highway. Named after Gen. Jonathan M. Wainwright, Medal of Honor winner, defender of Bataan against the Japanese in the Philippines in World War II, the post began its existence in January 1961, when Ladd Field was transferred to the Army and renamed Fort Wainwright.

Housing and Schools. Approximately 1,900 units of family housing are available for all grades. Off-post apartment rentals run from about $545 a month for a one-bedroom unit to as much as $960 for a three-bedroom unit; utilities can run as high as $260 a month, depending on the time of year.

Dependent schooling is conducted through the Fairbanks North Star School District and includes one elementary school and satellite middle school on post. Fort Wainwright offers many ways for soldiers and their family members to broaden their formal education. Off-duty courses are offered through the University of Alaska, Central Texas College, and University of LaVerne.

Personal Services and Recreation. Fort Wainwright offers a complete range of community services, from the 60-bed Bassett Army Community Hospital and large commissary and post exchange to a 23,000-volume library and an 18-hole golf course. Recreational facilities also include a bowling alley, hobby shops, tennis courts, an indoor pool, and two gymnasiums.

Brown, grizzly, and black bears, as well as moose, may be hunted in season on designated areas on post, and fishing is excellent throughout the state. (The limit on post is 15 fish per angler per day.)

The Local Area. At Fort Wainwright, the temperature may dip to minus 65° F in December, when the days are mostly dark, with only brief periods of light, and the ground does not begin to thaw until April.

In summer months, when temperatures often reach into the 90s, the post's information, ticketing, and registration office schedules many interesting trips for military personnel and their dependents at very reasonable prices. These include excursions into the Arctic Circle and Denali National Park, via the Alaskan Railroad. Birch Lake, on the Richardson Highway, is run by the Recreation Services Office at Eielson Air Force Base and offers swimming, fishing, waterskiing, camping, picnicking, and boating.

Personnel planning to drive to Fort Wainwright from the lower 48 may do so on the Alaska Highway, which is 1,520 miles long between Dawson Creek, British Columbia, and Fairbanks. Depending on road conditions and weather, the drive may take up to seven days, so those making this trip should be prepared.

For more information, write to Public Affairs Office, Building 1555, Room 118, Fort Wainwright, AK 99703-5000, or call (907) 353-6701. Home page: *www.wainwright.army.mil.*

Coast Guard

KODIAK COAST GUARD INTEGRATED SUPPORT COMMAND

Coast Guard Integrated Support Command Kodiak is located on Kodiak Island, Alaska. Kodiak Island is approximately 235 air miles south-southeast of Anchorage, Alaska.

History. The Coast Guard took control of the Naval Air Station there in April 1972. The station was originally built during World War II to help protect Alaska from Japanese invasion. Today the facility is home to Air Station Kodiak, Communications Station Kodiak, Loran Station Kodiak, Electronic Support Unit Kodiak, Marine Safety Detachment Kodiak, North Pacific Regional Fisheries Training Team, and the cutters Storis, Yocona, Ironwood, and Firebush. In addition to the Coast Guard, the Naval Special Warfare–Kodiak Detachment is located there. There are approximately 1,100 active-duty personnel, 3,400 family members, and 47 civilian employees on Kodiak.

Housing and Schools. Housing is available on base for both enlisted and officer personnel. There are currently 454 enlisted housing units in use, 83 officer housing units, and 127 barracks rooms for unaccompanied personnel. There is a newly remodeled and refurbished forty-six-room guest house available for temporary lodging. Contact the guest house manager for reservations or information at (907) 487-5446. Child-care services for infants through preschoolers is available on base in the Child Development Center (CDC). Information on in-home child-care providers is also available in the CDC. The Petersen Elementary School is located on base. Middle schools and high schools are located in town. The University of Alaska–Anchorage, Kodiak College, provides a two-year degree program in town. Educational services are also provided by the Coast Guard Education Center.

Personal Services. Medical and dental services are available at the Rockmore–King Clinic on base for routine and urgent care. Emergency and extended care are provided by Kodiak Island Providence Medical Center and at Elmendorf Air Force Base Hospital in Anchorage. Specialty care is provided at either Elmendorf Air Force Base or Madigan Medical Center in Seattle. A commissary, exchange, and Coast Guard dining facility for all hands are available, along with two convenience stores that provide the essential goods and goodies. A gas station, pizza parlor, on-base shuttle bus, uniform store with dry cleaning and tailoring services, furniture shop, and beauty salon round out the service sector.

Recreation. Recreational facilities include a bowling alley, the Billiken Movie Theater, a teen center, baseball fields, a gym with a pool, an auto hobby shop, a wood shop, and a ceramics shop. Kodiak is a hunter and fisherman's paradise. Salmon, halibut, deer, and bear are plentiful, as well as hundreds of miles of four-wheeler and hiking trails.

The Local Area. Kodiak Island lies in the Japanese Gulf Stream, which makes the weather conditions wet with moderate temperatures. Average annual rainfall is about seventy inches. Winter temperatures average in the 30s, and summer temperatures average in the 60s. The town of Kodiak, population 10,000, is about eight miles from the base. The people of the community are very friendly and supportive of the Coast Guard. Transportation to the island is available via aircraft and ferry. There are two museums, two state parks, and a wildlife refuge area.

For more information, write to Commanding Officer, USCG Integrated Support Command, Attention: Public Affairs, P.O. Box 195014, Kodiak, AK 99619-5014, or call (800) KODIAK2 or (907) 487-5525, ext. 275. E-mail: *dcallahan@cgalaska.uscg.mil;* Home page: *www.ptalaska.net/~isckod.*

ARIZONA

Air Force

DAVIS–MONTHAN AIR FORCE BASE

The first Europeans to come to Tucson were lost. That was back in about 1535, and they were the survivors of the ill-fated Navarez expedition to Florida. With Davis–Monthan Air Force Base now firmly anchored in the city of Tucson, airmen looking for an assignment (or just visiting) should have no trouble finding the place.

History. Davis–Monthan is named after two Air Corps officers who died in separate aircraft crashes. Lt. Samuel H. Davis died in a crash at Carlstrom Field, Florida, in 1921; Lt. Oscar Monthan died in a crash near Honolulu, Hawaii, in 1924. The Army Air Corps established an airfield at Davis–Monthan in 1927. Today Davis–Monthan is home for the 355th Wing, 12th Air Force, the Aerospace Maintenance and Regeneration Center, and other tenant units. The 355th's mission is to provide worldwide deployable combat-ready A/OA-10 forward-air-controller support and EC-130 H and E command, control, and communications countermeasures capability. Davis–Monthan today is home to 5,500 active-duty personnel, 7,000 family members, and 1,300 civilian employees.

Housing and Schools. More than 1,200 units of family housing are available at Davis–Monthan. Temporary lodging for families is provided for permanent change-of-station personnel on a space-available, day-to-day basis. Over 100 trailer spaces are also available.

Elementary schooling is available on the base for children from kindergarten to sixth grade, and a child-care center is also maintained on base. The base education office offers college courses through Park College, Troy State University, Embry-Riddle Aeronautical University, Chapman University, and Pima Community College.

Personal Services. Medical care is provided by the 35-bed 355th Medical Group. This facility has a staff of over 500 and serves a community of 60,000 people. The base exchange carries over 40,000 items on display in a 29,000-

square-foot sales area. The base commissary serves approximately 55,000 customers a month.

Recreation. Recreational facilities available on base include an 18-hole golf course, a 20-lane bowling center, eight tennis courts, and a base swimming pool. Also available are a gymnasium, hobby shops (wood, auto, and ceramic), and both NCO and officers clubs. Davis–Monthan has two picnic areas and a skeet range.

The Local Area. With over 300 days of sunshine a year and clear, unpolluted air, Tucson is a fine place for outdoor activities. The city's residents own thousands of swimming pools, and there are 17golf courses open year-round. Tucson, with a population of nearly 700,000 people, has 80 parks, all of them with some kind of recreational facilities.

Tucson is surrounded by mountains. The Tortolitas and Santa Catalinas are to the north, the Tucsons are to the west, the Rincons are to the east, and the Santa Ritas are to the south. Mount Lemmon, in the Santa Catalinas, is more than 9,100 feet high.

Phoenix is about 105 miles north of Davis–Monthan, and Nogales and the U.S.–Mexican border is about 60 miles south of the base.

For more information, write to Public Affairs Office, 5275 E. Granite Street, Davis–Monthan AFB, AZ 85707-3010, or call (520) 750-4717. Home page: *www.dm.af.mil.*

LUKE AIR FORCE BASE

Luke Air Force Base is named after the first airman to earn the Medal of Honor, Lt. Frank Luke, Jr., a native of Phoenix. In action over France in 1918, he destroyed eighteen enemy aircraft in just seventeen days. Forced to make an emergency landing behind enemy lines, he defended himself from capture until he was gunned down by German soldiers. It is entirely fitting that this base, known as the "Home of the Fighter Pilot," is named after this hero.

History. Opened in 1941, Luke today occupies 4,197 acres twenty miles west of Phoenix. There are over 20,000 people at Luke: 6,000 active-duty and reserve personnel, 1,500 civilian employees, and over 12,000 dependents. The base is now home for the 56th Fighter Wing, which trains aircrews in the F-16 Fighting Falcon. About 2.7 million acres at the Barry M. Goldwater Air Force Range are available to Luke pilots for aerial maneuvers.

Housing and Schools. There are 874 base housing units at Luke and over 40 transient living quarters that may be reserved by families traveling on official change-of-station orders.

There is one civilian elementary school adjacent to the base (kindergarten to sixth grade) and numerous elementary, junior high, and senior high schools close by. College courses are available on base from a variety of institutions. These include Golden Gate University, Grand Canyon College, Arizona State University, and Embry-Riddle Aeronautical University.

Personal Services. The 56th Medical Group hospital is a complete medical-care facility that maintains forty beds for inpatients. Located on base are a large exchange store, a commissary, a number of concessions and snack bars, and officers and NCO clubs.

Recreation. Recreational facilities include a bowling center, a gymnasium, hobby and craft shops, three swimming pools, a recreational center, a skeet and trap range, a riding stable, and tennis courts.

The Local Area. The city of Phoenix offers much in the way of culture and recreation for personnel stationed at Luke. The 150-acre Papago Park Desert Botanical Garden and the Phoenix Zoo, located in the Botanical Garden park, are major visitor attractions in the city. The city also offers many museums and galleries, as well as horse and dog races, horse shows, and professional sports. The community boasts many fine parks, especially South Mountain Park, with 15,000 acres affording picnicking, horseback riding, and hiking.

For more information, write to 56th Fighter Wing/PA, 7383 N. Litchfield Road, Luke AFB, AZ 85309-1534, or call (602) 856-5853. Home page: *www.luke.af.mil.*

Army

FORT HUACHUCA

A proud Buffalo Soldier greets you as you enter the main gate at Fort Huachuca, and this is fitting; of more than seventy frontier cavalry posts established by the U.S. government in Arizona during the 1800s, Huachuca is the last one to host active Army troops. *Buffalo Soldier* was a nickname given to black cavalrymen by the Plains Indians, and the veterans of the 9th and 10th Cavalry Regiments brought the name with them when they were assigned to Fort Huachuca in the early 1900s. Huachuca's Buffalo Soldier is nine feet tall and made of bronze, a fitting monument to this group of American soldiers.

History. Fort Huachuca (the name comes from an Indian word that means "place of thunder") was established in March 1877, when Capt. Samuel Marmaduke Whitside and two companies of the 6th Cavalry were ordered to build a post in the foothills of the Huachuca Mountains. In 1886, the fort was Gen. Nelson A. Miles's headquarters and forward supply base for his campaign against Geronimo and his Apache warriors. It was men from Huachuca's B Troop, 4th Cavalry, who chased Geronimo in 1886 and finally brought him to bay after five months and a 3,000-mile pursuit throughout southeast Arizona. Today, Fort Huachuca's 73,000 acres are home for the U.S. Army Intelligence Center and School, the U.S. Army Information Systems Command, the Joint Interoperability Test Center, the 11th Signal Brigade, and other specialized units. The post has a permanent population of almost 7,550 military personnel, 5,700 civilian employees, and over 11,000 dependents.

Housing and Schools. Fort Huachuca boasts 1,900 family quarters. There are 230 quarters available for temporary-duty personnel, 2,000 barracks rooms for single soldiers, and 34 guest houses.

The post operates three elementary schools, as well as a child-care center. Besides the full range of testing and MOS-related skill programs, the Army Education Center offers college-level courses on post from Cochise College, the University of Phoenix, and Western National University.

Personal Services. On-post facilities include a modern and well-stocked commissary and post exchange and the Raymond W. Bliss Army Community Hospital, a thirty-bed facility offering a full range of inpatient and outpatient medical care.

Recreation. The post offers an extensive outdoor recreation and equipment-loan facility, including four campgrounds. Hunting and fishing are permitted on post in season. The area's moderate climate (snow falls only occasionally in winter, and the average annual rainfall is only 20 inches) is conducive to outdoor activities year-round.

The Local Area. Fort Huachuca is bordered on the east and north by the town of Sierra Vista (population 37,000). Surrounded by beautiful mountains (sierra), the view (vista) is entirely unobstructed by the smog that often plagues other cities. Sierra Vista is situated on the broad and level plain of the San Pedro Valley at an altitude of over 4,600 feet. The town is 75 miles southeast of Tucson and 180 miles from Phoenix. Tombstone is a 25-minute drive east of Sierra Vista, and Nogales, Arizona, and the Mexican border are 65 miles to the southwest. A bit farther away is the Grand Canyon, 79 miles north of Flagstaff.

Fort Huachuca is sometimes called the "best-kept secret in the Army," because the area combines the best of small-town and metropolitan living, plus southwestern informality along with a moderate cost of living.

For more information, write to Public Affairs Office, Attention: ATZS-PA, U.S. Army Intelligence Center and Fort Huachuca, AZ 85613-6000, or call (520) 533-1285.

YUMA PROVING GROUND

History. The U.S. Army has been at Yuma since 1850, when it established a hilltop fort across the Colorado River from the city in what is now Imperial County, California. This was later supplemented by a Quartermaster Depot that served as a supply base for forts throughout the Southwest. The present Yuma Proving Ground (YPG) began as Yuma Test Branch and Camp Laguna in 1943. Today it covers over one million acres, or 1,300 square miles, in the southwestern portion of Arizona. It consists of extensive ranges and test facilities, where experts test weapons, munitions, aircraft armament systems, and air delivery systems, as well as all sorts of military equipment for desert warfare. Research and development activities are conducted for all military services and numerous friendly nations. Yuma is often referred to as America's premier test and proving facility. Interestingly, only the Support Detachment is actually assigned to the installation—all the other units are tenants. YPG is the home of the Military Freefall School, a component of the Special Warfare Training Group.

Housing and Schools. There are 285 sets of family quarters at YPG, and a 10-room guest facility is operated there for transients. Quarters are available immediately to three months.

An elementary school is operated on post—James D. Price Elementary School, (520) 329-4279/4280—as is a day-care center. Adult education is offered through the YPG Education Center. On-post associate degree programs are available, and undergraduate and graduate education is located on a college campus 10 miles from YPG. The Marine Corps Air Station located in Yuma also provides educational programs. An Army Learning Center located at YPG rounds out a solid academic resource base at the installation.

Personal Services. The U.S. Army Health Clinic, YPG, provides emergency and routine medical service to soldiers, their families, and retired personnel. Persons requiring hospitalization are referred to the Yuma Regional Medical Center or to Fort Huachuca, Balboa Naval Hospital in San Diego, or William Beaumont Hospital at Fort Bliss, Texas. Space-available dental care is offered for dependents and retired military personnel.

YPG has a commissary and a post exchange, and if you can't find what you want, special orders and use of the neighboring Marine Corps commissary are definite options. The exchange operates several concessions, including a service station. The facilities at YPG are complemented somewhat by those at the Marine Corps Air Station, Yuma, on the south edge of town, adjacent to the Yuma International Airport. YPG has a delicatessen, a pizza shop, an arts and crafts center, a library, a leisure-travel office, a thrift shop, a gas station, a credit union, and a community club.

Recreation. Recreational facilities include a swimming pool, a six-lane bowling center, a post theater, a gymnasium, and a recreation services boat dock at Imperial Dam, three miles from the main post on the Colorado River. Sporting equipment, such as trailers and camping equipment, is available for rent at the Morale Support Supply Office on post.

The Local Area. Although the climate in this part of Arizona is very dry, with less than three inches of rain per year, fishing is great in the Colorado River. There are a number of excellent camping and fishing sites locally, including Laguna Dam, Mittry Lake, Imperial Dam, Senator's Wash (not named after a political scandal!), Squaw Lake, and Martinez Lake, where bass, catfish, and bluegill are abundant.

Yuma, with a metropolitan population of more than 60,000, has one of the finest winter climates in the country, with the average temperatures in the 70s and sunshine an average of 96 percent of the time. There are numerous historical points of interest in and around the city, including the old Territorial Prison, Fort Yuma, and the border towns of San Luis (23 miles south) and Mexicali (55 miles south). In Old Mexico, 75 miles south of San Luis, is the Sea of Cortez or Gulf of Lower California, with a wide expanse of clean, white beach offering fishing, surf casting, clam digging, and swimming. Europeans first came to the site of present-day Yuma with the Spanish explorer Hernando de Alarcon in 1540. The name Yuma is said to derive from the Spanish *umo,* meaning "smoke," after the huge fires once built by local Indians attempting to induce rain.

For more information, write to Commander, U.S. Army Yuma Proving Ground, Attention: STEYP-PA, Yuma, AZ 85365, or call (602) 653-6189. Home page: *www.yuma.army.mil.*

Marine Corps

YUMA MARINE CORPS AIR STATION

History. Marine Harrier, Skyhawk, and Phantom jets have been a familiar sight streaking over the bombing and gunnery ranges adjacent to Yuma Marine Corps Air Station (MCAS) in the southwestern Arizona skies since the Marine Corps took over the former Vincent Air Force Base in 1959. Originally authorized in 1928 by President Coolidge (a native Vermonter), the 640 acres that originally comprised Yuma was devoted to air training. One can only speculate what Hernando de Alarcon, the first white man to see the area, would make of the changes that have occurred there since he visited in 1540.

Today the station occupies over five square miles and is home and workplace for approximately 5,000 permanently assigned military personnel. During the course of an average year, units deploying to Yuma for training account for another 10,000 personnel and 900 aircraft accommodated at the station. Aircraft flying from Yuma MCAS use 2.8 million acres (an area equal to the state of New Jersey) of training ranges, all within ten minutes' flying time of the station's 13,300-foot main runway. Today Yuma MCAS is home to Marine Air Group (MAG) 13, a tactical air-combat unit flying the AV-8B Harrier II fighter aircraft. All of this makes Yuma the Marine Corps's busiest air station and the naval service's third busiest.

Housing and Schools. There are more than 800 sets of family quarters at Yuma. The waiting period for quarters depends on the rank of the sponsor and can stretch from as few as four months for an enlisted person to eight months for some officers. There are, however, about 100 mobile home parks available in the civilian community, and the station also operates a temporary lodging facility with 36 units and a 13-unit hostess house.

Dependent children attend local schools. A child-care center is operated on the station, and on-base educational facilities cover the full range of opportunities for improvement in vocational military skills, as well as off-duty pursuit of college courses. Instruction is available from Arizona Western College, Northern Arizona University, Southern Illinois University, and Webster College.

Personal Services. The quality of life onboard the station is enhanced by a full range of commissary and Marine Corps exchange operations. Medical and dental care are provided by on-base clinics. Inpatient and specialty medical care are available through civilian sources or the Naval Regional Medical Center in San Diego.

Recreation. The special services office operates a vigorous recreational activities program for the personnel at Yuma. These include a twelve-lane bowling alley, a gym, tennis courts, swimming pools, stables, athletic and camping gear issue, hobby shops, a skeet club, and officers, staff NCO, and enlisted clubs.

The Local Area. Yuma, a city of 60,000 people, is a beautiful town with a dry and delightful climate, especially during the winter months. Annual rainfall is less than three inches, but the town is surrounded by water in the form of canals and small lakes formed by the Colorado River. This gives the angler and water sports enthusiast much opportunity to engage in these pastimes most of the year. The sun shines at Yuma an estimated 96 percent of the time.

The surrounding area has many interesting places to see, and there are many activities to participate in, from greyhound racing to gun shows to rodeos. Every summer, one may enter the annual inner-tube race on the Colorado or just stand on the riverbank and watch the courageous contenders float by. Historic Fort Yuma and the notorious Yuma Territorial Prison and Museum are favorite tourist attractions, as are the state parks and many recreational lakes in the immediate vicinity. And of course, Mexico is only 11 miles from Yuma, with San Luis, Mexico, only 23 miles south of Yuma.

For more information, write to Public Affairs Office, P.O. Box 99113, Yuma, AZ 85369-9113, or call (520) 341-2275.

Home page: *www.usmc.mil/baseguide/yuma.*

ARKANSAS

Air Force

LITTLE ROCK AIR FORCE BASE

History. When the first airmen came to Jacksonville, Arkansas, in 1955, there were no quarters ready for them at the base, so the local people put them up. In 1952, a Little Rock citizens' committee began raising the money needed to purchase the first 6,000 acres of land required for the base's construction, and eventually this land was donated to the U.S. government by the citizens. Arkansas congressman Brooks Hays personally turned the first shovel to begin construction on the base housing. Military personnel have always been cordially welcomed at Little Rock.

Today the base is home to some 4,700 active-duty personnel, their 5,500 family members, and 1,300 civilian employees. The host unit is the 314th Airlift Wing, which has the dual mission of worldwide airlift and airlift crew training to conduct tactical air operations globally.

Housing and Schools. There are over 1,500 units of family housing and more than 800 enlisted units on the base. Transient lodging is limited to seven VIP units, 180 units for visiting officers, and another 144 for enlisted personnel. There are also 24 spaces available for RVs on the base.

There is an elementary school on the base and a child-care center. The base education center offers schooling for adults from various universities and colleges to include Arkansas State University, University of Arkansas, Embry-Riddle Aeronautical University, Harding University, Hendrix College, Park College, Philander Smith College, Pikes Peak Community College, and other institutions.

Personal Services. Medical services are provided by the 20-bed hospital operated by the 314th Medical Group. There are a very large commissary, an exchange, and a shoppette available on base.

Recreation. Recreational facilities at Little Rock are excellent. Among the many offered are a gym, the eighteen-hole Deer Run Golf Course, a twenty-four-lane bowling center, a twelve-bay automotive hobby center, a saddle club, a sports and fitness center, and a wood skills center. In the culinary arts arena, the Airlifter's Club offers a generous menu for members and guests, while Champs Pizza and Subs provides singular gustatory service to hungry airmen. Little Rock also has two lakes where fishing and canoeing are allowed. A family camp is conveniently situated near the lakes.

The Local Area. Jacksonville, just outside the base, has a population of about 30,000. The base is located about 20 miles northeast of Little Rock, the state capital. Metropolitan Little Rock operates 19 parks and a 200-acre zoo. The climate is temperate, with an average mean temperature of 61° F. Snow is rare and precipitation is usually in the form of rain, which averages approximately 48 inches a year.

For more information, write to Public Affairs, Little Rock AFB, PSC Box 2400, AR 72099-4399, or call (501) 987-1110.

Home page: *www.littlerock.af.mil.*

CALIFORNIA

Air Force

BEALE AIR FORCE BASE

What do the Army Camel Corps and Beale Air Force Base have in common? Gen. Edward Fitzgerald Beale. During the administration of Franklin Pierce, Beale, then an Army officer, suggested to Secretary of War Jefferson Davis that the Army's transportation problems in the Southwest could be alleviated by importing camels from North Africa to act as beasts of burden. The idea was tried, but the Army lost interest and Beale went on to a successful career in business.

History. Opened in 1942, Camp Beale was home to the Army's 13th Armored Division, which trained infantry and tank crews on its 86,000 acres. Although reduced to 23,000 acres when acquired by the Air Force, today Beale is one of the largest bases in the Air Combat Command. The base is home to the 9th Reconnaissance Wing, which flies U-2S and T-38 aircraft, and to more than 3,400 military personnel, 4,000 family members, and a civilian workforce of more than 1,300 people.

Housing and Schools. There are over 1,400 units of family housing available at Beale, plus a mobile home park that can accommodate 140 trailers. The housing area is situated about 10 miles from the flight line, in the foothills of the Sierra Nevada. Temporary lodging is available for visitors and newly assigned personnel.

Two elementary schools for children in kindergarten through sixth grade are operated on the base, and a child-care center is available there as well. Educational opportunities for adults are offered through California State University, the University of Southern California, and Chapman College, all of which conduct on-base classes.

Personal Services. On-base services include a medical clinic, a base exchange, a commissary, and complete banking facilities.

Recreation. Recreational facilities at Beale range from hunting preserves to family garden plots. The sports-minded will find a gymnasium, a 16-lane bowling center, swimming pools, a nine-hole golf course, and a fine intramural sports program. A recreation center, arts and crafts and hobby shops, and an on-base picnic area are also offered. The base has many lakes and streams well stocked with fish, and small-game hunting on the base is very good for pheasant, duck, quail, rabbit, and dove.

The Local Area. Beale lies just 10 miles west of the twin cities of Marysville and Yuba City, which have a combined population of 50,000. Lake Tahoe and Reno are not far to the east, and the Oroville State Recreation Area is less than 40 miles north of Marysville. The climate in this area offers long, hot summers with little humidity, and the winters are relatively mild. In the summer months, striped bass weighing up to 50 pounds may be caught in the local rivers.

For more information, write to Public Affairs Office, 590 C Street, Beale AFB, CA 95903-5300, or call (916) 530-8889. Home page: *www.beale.af.mil.*

EDWARDS AIR FORCE BASE

With a wooden propeller attached to its nose to disguise its real propulsion system, the Bell XP-59A, America's first jet aircraft, arrived at Edwards Air Force Base in September 1942 and made its first test flight there on 1 October 1942. On 14 April 1981, the space shuttle Columbia landed there, another important first in the base's long and exciting history.

History. Edwards began its official existence in 1933, when it was used as a bombing range for the Army Air Corps, and in 1937, Air Corps gunnery and bombing maneuvers were held there. Known initially as Muroc Army Air Field and later as Muroc Air Force Base, the installation was named in 1949 in honor of Capt. Glen W. Edwards, a native of California who was killed in a test flight of the "flying wing" experimental bomber in June 1948. Today Edwards's 301,000 acres are home to the Air Force Flight Test Center and 3,500 military personnel, 5,400 family members, and 7,200 civilian employees.

Housing and Schools. Edwards has over 1,800 sets of government quarters spread throughout eight separate housing areas. Unaccompanied personnel are housed in one-bedroom, apartment-style units for officers and dorms for enlisted people. The base has three elementary schools and two secondary schools. The education services center offers college courses from Cerro Coso Community College, Chapman College, the University of Southern Illinois, California State University, Embry-Riddle University, and the University of Phoenix.

Personal Services. The personal services and facilities available at Edwards include the 95th Medical Group's clinic, a commissary, a base exchange with many concessions, such as the Colonial Inn cafeteria located near the flight line and a service station, and family support and child-development centers.

Recreation. Recreational facilities include a 20-lane bowling alley, a gym with an enclosed swimming pool open year-round, and an 18-hole, par 72 golf course. Officers and NCO clubs are located on base, as are a library, a theater, a skating rink, a variety of hobby shops (auto, ceramics, and wood), stables, aero and rod and gun clubs, and a community center. A 35-channel cable TV package is available.

The Local Area. Edwards AFB is located about 20 miles east of Mojave and eight miles west of Boron, sandwiched between the small communities of Lancaster, thirty-five miles to the south, and California City, 20 miles to the north. In the bigger picture, Edwards is 100 miles northeast of Los Angeles, 90 miles northwest of San Bernardino, and 80 miles southeast of Bakersfield. The climate there is dry, and the weather is generally clear. Temperatures average around 100° F in the summer and 40° F in winter, but the humidity is low; about four inches of rain fall there in an average year. The base is situated in the Antelope Valley, one of many such valleys in the Mojave Desert area, and is at an elevation of 2,300 feet.

For more information, write to Public Affairs Office, 15 Teager Boulevard, Edwards AFB, CA 93524-1225, or call (661) 277-3510. Home page: *www.edwards.af.mil.*

LOS ANGELES AIR FORCE BASE

Los Angeles Air Force Base is located in El Segundo, three miles south of Los Angeles International Airport. It is not like a conventional air base, because little of a conventional nature goes on there. Los Angeles AFB is a key installation in the space-development program.

History. The base was dedicated in July 1964, and today is home for Air Force Materiel Command's Space and Missile Systems Center, with the mission of strengthening our national defense through the full exploitation of space. Los Angeles AFB occupies about 100 acres of urban-industrial real estate and employs 1,419 military and 990 civilian personnel. The adjacent Aerospace Corporation employs over 3,000 workers.

Housing and Schools. Housing is located nineteen miles south of the base at the Fort MacArthur Annex. The 299 officer and 275 enlisted town houses and renovated field-grade homes are in high demand, with a waiting time of about nine to twelve months. Temporary living facilities and visiting quarters are available at Fort MacArthur. Housing off base is very expensive: Two-bedroom apartment rentals begin at $750 per month.

Dependent children attend schools off base. Adult education is offered on base by several colleges, and more than 100 colleges and universities are situated in the greater Los Angeles area, giving servicemembers a wide variety of choices.

Personal Services. Medical care at the base is provided by the 61st Medical Squadron, but patients are seen there by appointment and emergency services are not available. Definitive medical care is provided by local civilian hospitals or the Naval Hospital in San Diego. A large commissary is located on base, and a base exchange operates there with a main store, a flower shop, a laundry and dry cleaner, a service station, and other concessions. Officers and NCO club facilities are also offered.

Recreation. Recreational facilities include a gymnasium, hobby shops (auto and arts and crafts), and a recreational supply checkout facility where camping, athletic, and water sports equipment are available.

Los Angeles AFB is divided into two areas. Area A has restricted access; Area B, where most of the base morale and support facilities are situated, is open to the public.

The Local Area. Although there is little to see at the base itself, the local area abounds with sights and attractions. Fort MacArthur provides a pool, a picnic area, and an unparalleled view of the Pacific Ocean. Tourist draws in the area range from skiing in the local mountains to sunning on the beaches. Disneyland and Universal Studios tours are prime attractions. The weather is very nice during the early spring months, but from June to September the smog associated with the Los Angeles area can be very unpleasant, as can the traffic, which sometimes transforms the freeways into parking lots.

For more information, write to Space and Missile System Center Public Affairs Officer, 2430 E. El Segundo Boulevard, Suite 4049, Los Angeles AFB, CA 90245-4587, or call (310) 363-1110. Home page: *www.laafb.af.mil.*

MCCLELLAN AIR FORCE BASE

(Note: McClellan Air Force Base is scheduled to close in the summer of 2001.)

McClellan Air Force Base occupies 3,763 acres of land ten miles northeast of Sacramento and is home to more than 2,080 active-duty personnel, their families, and 7,511 Department of Defense civilian employees. The key words at McClellan are maintenance and logistics. The Air Logistics Center has responsibility as system manager for aircraft such as the A-10, the F/EF-111, and the F-117A (Stealth fighter).

History. The base began life in 1937 as the Sacramento Air Depot but was renamed later that year in honor of Maj. Hezekiah McClellan, a pioneer in the charting of Alaskan air routes and aeronautical experiments, who was killed while flight-testing an aircraft near Centerville, Ohio, in a crash on 25 May 1936.

Housing and Schools. There are over 600 family housing units at McClellan located in two separate housing areas situated around the base. Transient billeting and guest housing are available to both officers and enlisted personnel for short-term occupancy.

Dependent school-age children attend classes in one of the 17 school districts operated in Sacramento County. The base offers a child-care center with the capacity for 140 children. The education services office offers on-base college courses from such institutions as Embry-Riddle Aeronautical University and the University of Idaho.

Personal Services. The USAF clinic at McClellan offers outpatient services to active-duty personnel, retirees, and dependents, with referrals to the David Grant USAF Medical Center at Travis Air Force Base. Other facilities include a base exchange, a commissary, and a package store. Excellent officers and NCO clubs are also available.

Recreation. Recreational facilities include a nine-hole golf course, three swimming pools, a gymnasium, a 20-lane bowling center, hobby shops, numerous clubs and associations, and a two-story recreational center.

The Local Area. McClellan AFB is situated at the intersection of Interstate 80 and Business 80, in the northeast section of Sacramento. The climate in this part of California is temperate, with low humidity most of the year. Annual rainfall averages less than eighteen inches, with most of it falling from December through February. About 1.5 million people live in the Sacramento area, 320,000 in the city of Sacramento itself. San Francisco is 90 miles to the west; Lake Tahoe, Reno, and the Sierras are approximately 120 miles east of the base; and Napa and Sonoma Counties are within easy driving distance.

For more information, write to Public Affairs Office, 3237 Peacekeeper Way, Suite 5, McClellan AFB, CA 95652-1089, or call (916) 643-2111. Home page: *www.mcclellan.af.mil.*

ONIZUKA AIR STATION

(Note: At press time, the functions at Onizuka AS were scheduled to move to Schriever AFB in Colorado by the end of 2001.)

Onizuka Air Station occupies 23 acres at Sunnyvale, 37 miles south of San Francisco. At Onizuka, the Air Force monitors and controls on-orbit military spacecraft from sites all over the world.

History. Onizuka, named for Lt. Col. Ellison S. Onizuka, who died aboard the Challenger space shuttle in 1986, has been in the space business since 1960, when it was the Satellite Test Annex. In 1971, it was renamed Sunnyvale Air Force Station. It became Onizuka Air Force Base in August 1987.

Onizuka is home to the 750th Space Group and Detachments 2 and 6 of the Air Force Space Missile Systems Center. The 750th Space Group controls all Defense Department space shuttle missions from launch through landing. There are about 780 military personnel, 1,200 family members, and approximately 2,200 contractor personnel at Onizuka.

Housing and Schools. Onizuka has control of 711 units of family housing. Children attend schools in the Bay Area. There is a child-care center for 126 children at Onizuka.

Personal and Recreational Services. Onizuka has a small convenience store and a consolidated open mess. A small weight room is available for use by personnel stationed at Onizuka. Beaches, mountain resorts, and Yosemite National Park, as well as the city of San Francisco, are within comfortable driving distance of the base.

For more information, write to Public Affairs, 750SGP, 1080 Lockheed Way, Box 53, Sunnyvale, CA 94089-1235, or call (408) 752-3000. Home page: *www.oafb.af.mil.*

TRAVIS AIR FORCE BASE

Travis Air Force Base has earned its name as "America's First Choice." Until fairly recently, most troops deploying to the Far East and returning home from there processed through Travis. In 1973, Travis welcomed 143 American POWs from North Vietnamese prison camps, and in 1975, the base hosted thousands of South Vietnamese refugees fleeing their country after the Communist conquest.

History. Named in honor of Brig. Gen. Robert F. Travis, who was killed in a B-29 crash at the end of the local runway in August 1950, Travis AFB was activated as Fairfield-Suisun Army Air Field in 1942 and renamed in 1951. Today it occupies over 6,000 acres 50 miles northeast of San Francisco and is home to the men and women of the 60th Air Mobility Wing and the 349th Air Mobility Wing (Reserve). The 60th AMW is responsible for four squadrons that fly the KC-10 Extender and C-5 Galaxy aircraft. Travis is home to 7,300 active-duty personnel, 9,100 family members, 5,200 reserve components personnel, and more than 2,000 civilian employees.

Housing and Schools. There are over 2,400 units of family housing available at Travis, as well as fifty spaces in the on-base mobile home park. Temporary living quarters are available to families traveling on permanent-change-of-station orders.

Travis operates three child-care centers and three elementary schools (kindergarten through fifth grade). A junior high and a high school are located just off base. The base education center provides assistance in enrolling in several undergraduate and graduate-level courses offered on base through Golden Gate University, Southern Illinois University, Chapman University, and Embry-Riddle Aeronautical University.

Personal Services. Medical care is provided by the 300-bed David Grant USAF Medical Center. The commissary at Travis stocks more than 12,000 line items and serves 70,000 patrons each month. The base exchange complex offers a wide variety of concessions. Food concessions available include a Baskin Robbins ice cream shop, a Burger King, Popeye's Chicken, Robin Hood, Taco Bell, Anthony's Pizza, and snack bars. The base club system includes officers and all-ranks enlisted clubs.

Recreation. Athletic and recreational facilities include two swimming pools, an 18-hole golf course, a 32-lane bowling alley, two gyms, an equestrian center, an arts and crafts center, and several jogging courses. Four parks are located on the base: North Gate, Eucalyptus, Travisville, and Airman. Three offer picnicking and playgrounds. The base family camp is open year-round and has 24 camper spaces with hookups and 12 without, restrooms, a playground, and two pavilions with barbecue pits. Camping, volleyball, hiking, and softball, as well as camping- and fishing-gear rentals, are also available.

The Local Area. Travis is immediately adjacent to the twin cities of Fairfield and Suisun. Fairfield has a population of over 80,000, while Suisun City is home to more than 19,000 people. Nearby Vacaville, seven miles north of Travis, has a population of more than 66,000. Sacramento is about 45 miles to the east, and San Francisco is about 50 miles to the west.

For more information, write to Public Affairs Office, 400 Brennan Circle, Travis AFB, CA 94535-2127, or call (707) 424-2011. Home page: *www.travis.af.mil.*

VANDENBERG AIR FORCE BASE

Vandenberg Air Force Base is one of the few places where you can sit in the ice cream parlor in the main exchange complex and savor a dish of chocolate chip while intercontinental ballistic missiles roar overhead to targets 4,200 miles downrange in the Pacific Ocean. Since 1958, Vandenberg has conducted over 1,700 launches. Rocketry is the central feature of all activity on the base.

History. Named after Gen. Hoyt S. Vandenberg, the second Air Force chief of staff, the base was chosen as the Air Force's first missile installation in 1956. Today it is the third-largest base in the Air Force, covering more than 98,000 acres (that's 154 square miles!). The host organization at Vandenberg is the 30th Space Wing.

Housing and Schools. There are 2,068 sets of family quarters at Vandenberg. Transient families traveling on official orders may obtain temporary quarters on a reserved basis. Off-base apartment rentals run from $550 to $800 per month. It runs from $850 to $1,200 per month to rent a three-bedroom house off-base.

The base offers a child-care center, two elementary schools, and a middle school; high school students attend classes off base. The education center is the focal point for college course enrollments.

Personal Services. The 45-bed clinic at Vandenberg provides a basic level of medical care for all active-duty and retired personnel and their families but has no emergency room core services. Among the other service facilities are the $3 million main exchange complex, a commissary, and complete banking facilities.

Recreation. Recreational facilities include a swimming pool, an 18-hole golf course, and a 20-lane bowling center. Also available are officers and NCO clubs, an arts and crafts complex, a rod and gun club, and a gymnasium. Vandenberg also offers an excellent tour program to such places as Las Vegas, Reno, San Francisco, and Los Angeles.

The Local Area. Nearby communities include Vandenberg Village, Mission Hills, and Lompoc. These three towns have a total combined population of 140,000 people, and all are located within ten miles of the base. Santa Maria, the largest local community, has 65,000 residents. Santa Barbara, an hour's drive southeast of Vandenberg, is a city of 89,000 inhabitants.

For most of the year, Vandenberg's average high temperature stays between 60° F and 65° F, with lows ranging between 40° F and 50° F. With its proximity to the ocean, the base experiences considerable periods of heavy fog, especially in the summer months.

Just a few miles west of the base lie the Sierra Madre and Los Padres National Forest. Los Padres covers over 1.7 million acres and offers more than 300 campsites and picnic areas and two major ski areas. Deer, boar, and wildfowl may be hunted in its reserves.

For more information, write to Public Affairs, 30th Space Wing, 747 Nebraska Avenue, Suite A103, Vandenberg AFB, CA 93437-6267, or call (805) 606-3595. Home page: *www.vafb.af.mil.*

Army

FORT IRWIN NATIONAL TRAINING CENTER

When you leave Barstow
To go to Fort Irwin,
There is nothing to show
That the post is there,
The closer you get
The more you wonder
Is there really a post,
WHERE?

—Barbara Parker, Fort Irwin ACS volunteer

Fort Irwin is there, all right, 37 miles northeast of Barstow, California, midway between Las Vegas and Los Angeles—1,000 square miles of some of the most rugged terrain in the United States. As the poet will testify, however, isolated and harsh as the post is, the Army community there has a big heart and offers everyone a warm welcome. As the second-largest employer in San Bernardino County, supporters of the post are quick to quote a former Army chief of staff, "Fort Irwin will close sometime after the Pentagon closes."

History. The land that now constitutes Fort Irwin was first set aside for military training in August 1940. Originally a subpost of Camp Haan, which was adjacent to what is now March Air Reserve Base in Riverside, Fort Irwin was named after Maj. Gen. George Leroy Irwin, commander of the 57th Field Artillery Brigade in World War I. The installation has had a checkered history of deactivations and activations, the most recent in October 1980, when it was activated as the National Training Center (NTC). Today, 10 times each year, 4,000 to 5,500 soldiers deploy to NTC to engage in a strenuous, 28-day training event called "a rotation." There is nothing like it anywhere else in the world. No other training anywhere approaches the battlefield realism, scope, and intensity achieved at the NTC. Soldiers and their leaders come from all over the United States to train in the desert here and improve their fighting skills for future engagements in similar environments, to include urban warfare settings, in a safe, closely controlled environment.

Housing and Schools. There are 2,103 units of government housing available at Fort Irwin, including 75 mobile-home pads. Dependent schooling is provided by the Silver Valley Unified School District: On-post schooling consists of an elementary and middle school; high school students attend Silver Valley High in Daggett, 34 miles south of Fort Irwin. Child care is available through several centers on post. Adult education is provided through the post education office and consists of college courses offered by Barstow College and California Baptist College.

Personal Services. Weed Army Community Hospital, a 22-bed facility, is the primary health-care provider for personnel at Fort Irwin; dental care is available for dependents on a space-available basis. A post exchange and commissary, the Leaders Club, an arts and crafts center, the soldiers club, a Burger King, a laundry and dry-cleaning service, a pizza parlor and delivery service, a flower shop, a barber shop, a beauty salon, a package beverage store, a Baskin Robbins ice cream parlor, and a shoppette are all located on base.

Recreation. Fort Irwin offers beaucoup benefits for those living there. The NTC offers a 20-lane bowling center, a recreation rental center, and riding stables. Soldiers Park, located near the family swimming pool, offers barbecue facilities, picnic tables, and plenty of shade trees. A modern fitness center offers all types of indoor sports, and the Ingalls Recreation Center has a big-screen TV, pool tables, video games, and a 640-seat auditorium for special events. The rod and gun club promotes hunting, fishing, archery, and recreational shooting.

There are two swimming pools at Fort Irwin—the family pool and the troop pool—both open year-round. The information, tours, and travel office arranges tours to many California amusement centers, including Disneyland and Universal Studios.

The Local Area. The weather in this area is hot and dry. The average high summer temperature at Fort Irwin is around 100° F, with an average low in the winter of 37° F. The average annual rainfall is only two and a half inches. Remote as it may seem to be, the Barstow–Fort Irwin area is rich in natural wonders and California history and is still a haven for tourists. Barstow itself is the site of the largest silver strike in California's history, and mining still goes on there today. The San Bernardino National Forest is only 60 miles south of Barstow, San Diego is a four-hour drive away, and world-famous attractions such as Death Valley, Palm Springs, and the Colorado River are all within easy driving distance.

For more information, write to Public Affairs Officer, NTC Public Affairs Office, P.O. Box 105067, Fort Irwin, CA 92310-5000, or call (760) 380-4511, or fax (760) 380-3075. Home page: *www.irwin.army.mil.*

PRESIDIO OF MONTEREY

For most of the more than 2,000 years human beings are known to have lived on the site of the Presidio of Monterey, English has not been the primary language. Today, if the shades of any of the Rumsen Indians or Spanish settlers who lived there in former times still linger on the site, the place must seem to them a veritable Babel of languages, with everything from Albanian to Vietnamese spoken there.

History. The Presidio shares in the great natural beauty of the Monterey Peninsula. Originally claimed by the Spanish in 1602, the area was not permanently settled by them until 1770. The original presidio, or fort, was built in 1792. It was taken over by the United States in 1846. In 1946, the Army established a language school there that became the Defense Language Institute in 1963. Today the Presidio is home to about 315 active-duty permanent-party personnel, 2,600 students, 700 family members, and 970 civilian employees.

Housing and Schools. Because the Presidio's basic mission is to support a school population, housing for married personnel assigned there permanently is limited, with only 43 sets of officer family units and 50 enlisted units actually located on post. Another 440 officer enlisted units are available at the Presidio Annex (formerly Fort Ord). Rooms for 2,500 students are available on the post. Dependent schooling is available off post, and the Presidio operates a child-care center capable of handling up to 145 children.

As of fall 1995, the average monthly rental for a one-bedroom, unfurnished apartment off post was $550; furnished two-bedroom houses were renting for around $1,500 a month; and utility rates ranged from $75 to $200 a month.

Servicemembers assigned to the Defense Language Institute as students or permanent-party personnel may pursue off-duty education. Currently, twenty-four different language courses are taught there to about 2,900 resident and 100,000 nonresident Department of Defense personnel each year. These courses are taught by a military and civilian faculty of 780. The Institute uses 400 classrooms with the latest audiovisual training aids, a library of over 100,000 foreign-language texts and periodicals, and an electronic media center complete with computer-assisted learning aids. The Institute has been accredited by the Accrediting Commission for Community and Junior Colleges of the Western Association of Schools and Colleges. The courses taught vary in length from 25 to 67 weeks, depending on the difficulty of the language being taught.

The Education Center regularly provides counselors who visit the Institute to assist personnel who wish to attend colleges and universities in the immediate area.

Personal Services. The installation offers the basic facilities found on any military post, including a bank, a credit union, clubs, and an exchange store. Commissary and main exchange facilities are available at the Annex, and personnel stationed at the Presidio are eligible to take advantage of all the other facilities offered there.

The Local Area. The climate at the Presidio is one of the most attractive features there because it has no extremes. The lows average 56° F and the highs 75° F year-round. Most rain falls between the months of November and February and averages about 17 inches per year.

For more information, write to Public Affairs Office, Attention: DLIFC, Presidio of Monterey, CA 93944-5006, or call (408) 242-5104. Home page: *www.pom.army.mil.*

Coast Guard

ALAMEDA COAST GUARD SUPPORT CENTER

Located in the Oakland Estuary between Oakland and Alameda, the Coast Guard Support Center is situated on a 67-acre artificial island formed in 1913. Built originally by the federal government to contain office buildings, it has been a Coast Guard station since 1926.

Today the island is home to the Pacific Area Command of the Coast Guard. Other commands sharing the island include the Maintenance and Logistics Command Pacific; Support Center Alameda; Marine Safety Office, San Francisco; Joint Task Force (JTF) 5; and four 378-foot high-endurance cutters—the *Sherman,* the *Morganthau,* the *Munro,* and the *Boutwell.* JTF 5 is a Department of Defense Command, headed by a Coast Guard admiral but representing each military service, with the mission of supporting the war on drugs. Approximately 1,600 active-duty and reserve personnel work on the island.

Family housing and schools for the children of active-duty personnel assigned to the island are available in the surrounding community and at a number of other military installations in the Bay Area. Bachelor quarters for officers and enlisted personnel are available on the station. Medical care is provided on an appointment basis by an outpatient clinic.

Other facilities include a small Coast Guard exchange with a gas station, a fully equipped gym, a swimming pool, and a galley.

For more information, write to Commander (DPA-NR), 11th Coast Guard District, Coast Guard Island, Building 42, Alameda, CA 94501-5100, or call (510) 437-3325. Home page: *www.wenet.net~uscg.*

PETALUMA COAST GUARD TRAINING CENTER

Situated 40 miles north of San Francisco and only ten miles from the Pacific Ocean, the Petaluma Coast Guard Training Center occupies an 800-acre tract of land in northern California's rolling pastoral countryside on the Sonoma-Marin County line. It consists of 219 buildings, including 129 family units, a fully staffed clinic, a chapel, a small police and fire department, and over 200,000 square feet of training facilities.

History. The site of six sheep ranches before it was purchased by the Army in 1942, the land was acquired by the Coast Guard as a training command in 1971. Two of the original ranch houses are still standing: One has the proud distinction of serving as the office of the command's enlisted advisor, and the other is the commanding officer's quarters.

Today the center is the Coast Guard's West Coast resident training facility for petty officers, graduating approximately 7,000 students a year from some 50 courses in subjects such as health services, electronics, leadership and management, and maritime law enforcement. It is also home to the Coast Guard's Chief Petty Officer Academy. The center's resident population averages 500 students plus a faculty and staff of about 330 active-duty personnel, 260 family members, and 55 civilian employees.

Housing and Schools. Petaluma has 127 units of two-, three-, and four-bedroom family quarters available, 120 of them for enlisted personnel. A 50-unit visiting enlisted quarters and an eight-room guest house are available with reservations. A day-care center for 30 children is available on the base, and dependent schooling is provided in Petaluma.

Personal Services and Recreation. Medical care is provided by the Ralph R. Nix, Jr., Clinic that has its own pharmacy, dental care, X-ray, and lab facilities. More definitive care is available at Travis Air Force Base. Although Petaluma has no commissary, it does boast a minimart, a delicatessen, and an exchange. There is also a tailor and dry cleaner, a credit union, a barber shop, a post office, and a gas station. Recreational facilities include an auto hobby shop, a bowling alley, a gym and fitness center, a swimming pool, a movie theater, a library, and a consolidated club facility.

The Local Area. By far one of the most popular attractions at Petaluma is the wonderful rolling countryside that surrounds the center and provides it with the tranquil environment so necessary to the learning process. Petaluma, a small community of about 33,000, is situated 30 miles west of the Napa Valley, a few miles east of the Point Reyes National Seashore, and within easy driving distance of San Francisco.

For more information, write to Public Affairs Office, USCG Training Center, Petaluma, CA 94952-5000, or call (707) 765-7211. Home page: *www.uscg.mil/hq/tcpet/index.htm.*

Marine Corps

BARSTOW MARINE CORPS LOGISTICS BASE

Barstow Marine Corps Logistics Base (MCLB) is situated a few miles east of Barstow, in the Mojave Desert. To the north are Fort Irwin and the China Lake Naval Weapons Center; Edwards Air Force Base lies immediately to the west along Interstate 15; and Twentynine Palms Marine Corps Base is to the east. The gateway to Death Valley National Monument lies about 100 miles from the base. The area is warm and dry.

History. The first Marines landed at Barstow in December 1942. The base actually consists of two sites—the headquarters at Nebo, near Interstate 40, two miles east of Barstow; and Yermo, an annex eleven miles from Barstow (eight miles northeast of Nebo). Both sites are 2,100 feet above sea level and in the heart of the Mojave Desert. Today the base's mission is to procure, maintain, repair, store, and issue all classes of supplies and equipment needed by Marines stationed west of the Mississippi, including those stationed in the Far East as well. MCLB Barstow has the largest rail operation in the Department of Defense and has the only container consolidation point for the Marine Corps. There are approximately 350 Marines and 1,750 civilian workers at the base to do the job.

Housing and Schools. There are 364 sets of family quarters at Barstow, 127 bachelor enlisted, and 8 for bachelor officers. A transient facility, known as the Oasis, is available to incoming personnel on a limited-stay (seven-day) basis. As of the fall of 1995, the median price for housing in the Barstow area was $77,500; an apartment with one or two bedrooms was renting for $450 to $475 per month; and larger units were available for $450 to $650 per month. Mobile home park rentals averaged $175 to $230 per month.

A child-care center is operated on the base with a capacity for 115 children, ranging in age from six weeks to 12 years, and there is a certified home day-care program for 25 children. Nearby Barstow, population 23,000, has a good public school system and is used by the military dependents living on the base. On base, Marines and their dependents may pursue college courses offered through Park College of Missouri and California Baptist College. They may also attend courses at Barstow Community College.

Personal Services. Medical care is provided to active-duty and retired personnel and their families by the base clinic. Dental care is available to active-duty personnel; retired personnel are seen on a time-available basis only. Two branches of Marine Corps West Federal Credit Union are available on base. A commissary, a seven-day store, a Marine Corps exchange, and other activities are offered at Barstow.

Recreation. Barstow is an isolated station. Therefore, recreation services and facilities and morale and support programs are very important. Recreation opportunities include a club system, two swimming pools, a nine-hole golf course, three tennis courts, a gym, a bowling alley, a skeet and trap range, stables (boarding only), two indoor racquetball courts, two lighted outdoor handball courts, one lighted football field, two lighted baseball fields, an auto and crafts hobby shop, and a 50,000-volume library open seven days a week.

The Local Area. The city of Barstow lies on the banks of the Mojave River and has many recreational attractions, including 10 parks, swimming, and municipal golf. Nearby places of interest include Calico Ghost Town, 10 miles north of Barstow, and the San Bernardino Mountains, an hour's drive away, which afford skiing, fishing, hunting, and boating. Las Vegas is only three hours north of Barstow. The Afton and Rainbow Basin and Owl Canyons are also interesting places to visit. The Calico Dig, 15 miles north of Barstow and six miles east of Calico Ghost Town, is an unusual park site arranged around an archaeological excavation developed by the National Geographic Society and the San Bernardino County Museum.

For more information, write to Public Affairs Office, USMC Logistics Base, Barstow, CA 92311-5001, or call (619) 577-6430 or (800) THE-USMC. Home page: *www.bam.usmc.mil.*

CAMP PENDLETON

Within its 125,000-acre area, Camp Pendleton has two mountain ranges and seventeen miles of coastline along the Pacific Ocean. All of this is within an hour's drive of the San Diego city limits.

History. First commissioned in September 1942, Camp Pendleton is now a vast military complex where the daytime population exceeds 90,000. Camp Pendleton, named after Maj. Gen. Joseph H. Pendleton, is now home to the 1st Marine Expeditionary Force, 1st Marine Division ("The Old Breed"), 1st Force Service Support Group, and Marine Aircraft Group 39, 1st Surveillance, Reconnaissance and Intelligence Group.

Housing and Schools. More than 5,600 units of family housing are available at Camp Pendleton. Sixty-four temporary accommodations (35 with kitchens) are also available at Ward Lodge, the hostess house. Priority is given to Marines and Navy personnel permanently stationed at Camp Pendleton. An on-base mobile home park has 248 spaces that are rented by the base housing office. The base offers bachelor accommodations for over 27,000 enlisted and officer personnel.

On-base dependent schooling, from prekindergarten through sixth grade, is available. While there is one junior high school on base, most junior high and high school students attend classes off base. A number of colleges offer courses on base for personnel interested in obtaining academic credits or completing degrees. These institutions include Park, Miracosta, Central Texas, and Palomar Colleges, as well as Southern Illinois University.

Personal Services. As befits a community the size of Camp Pendleton, a variety of services and support facilities are available there, including a Marine Corps exchange with a central exchange complex and satellite facilities located at other places on the base. A main commissary and a commissary annex are also handy. The 156-bed hospital treats an average of 21,000 outpatients monthly. The hospital is located on Lake O'Neill, about 10 miles inland from Camp Pendleton's main gate. There is also an outpatient clinic located in Vista.

Recreation. Recreation facilities at Camp Pendleton are excellent. Chief among them is the Lake O'Neill Recreation Center, with facilities for fishing, boating, and picnicking. Many other facilities are also available, including an archery range; swimming pools; an on-base lake; tennis, basketball, racquetball, and volleyball courts; weight-training facilities; and a skeet and trap range. Because of Camp Pendleton's proximity to the sea, it is ideal for the surfer or beach-goer. Beach parking for RVs is also available.

The Local Area. The surrounding communities offer military personnel much in the way of recreation and the best in gracious living. Oceanside, which lies just to the southeast of the main gate, is in reality a second home for many of the military personnel in the area. Camp Pendleton is bordered on the northwest by San Clemente. The town of Vista, about three miles to the south and seven miles inland from the ocean, is believed to have the most uniformly balanced climate of any spot in the whole country. Generally, the area abounds in state parks and recreational areas, and the mild climate permits year-round enjoyment of the outdoors.

For more information, write to Community Relations Office, Box 555010, Camp Pendleton, CA 92055-5010, or call (619) 725-5569. Home page: *www.cpp.usmc.mil.*

MIRAMAR MARINE CORPS AIR STATION

Miramar MCAS is a 23,400-acre installation located in the northern suburbs of San Diego and is one of the largest military bases in the area. It is home to Fighter Wing Pacific, Marine Air Groups 11 and 46, the 3rd Marine Air Wing, and Carrier Air Wings 2, 9, 11, 14 and other units. Miramar's daytime population consists of over 11,000 active-duty personnel, their 4,500 dependents, and more than 2,000 civilian employees.

History. Known as Camp Kearney before World War II, the station became an auxiliary airfield to the North Island Naval Air Station after the war began. Today it is an all-weather master jet station. Before the recent round of base realignments, Miramar was a naval air station, but today it is a Marine Corps Air Station. Recently, the Navy F-14 squadrons that called Miramar home have redeployed to Oceana Naval Air Station, Virginia.

Housing and Schools. There are 527 housing units and a 108-space mobile home park onboard the station, so the availability of family quarters could be described as tight. The station does have a 90-unit Navy Lodge for the use of all personnel. Average rents for a two-bedroom apartment in the San Diego area range from $600 to as high as $1,000 per month, depending on location.

A child-care center is located on the station. Older children attend school off base. Adults may pursue educational programs during their off-duty time through the Navy Campus.

Personal Services and Recreation. A Navy exchange and commissary store are onboard the station, as is a complete club system. A bowling center, an 18-hole golf course, and a five-acre stocked pond with picnic facilities, as well as a swimming pool, a stable and riding area, and the Mills Park picnic area round out the outdoor recreational facilities offered at Miramar.

For more information, write to Public Affairs Office, MCAS Miramar, 45429 Miramar Way, San Diego, CA 92145-5000, or call (619) 537-1011.

Marine Recruit Training at San Diego Marine Corps Recruit Depot, California USMC PHOTO

SAN DIEGO MARINE CORPS RECRUIT DEPOT

The San Diego Marine Corps Recruit Depot (MCRD) consists of 388 acres located in metropolitan San Diego, adjacent to the international airport (Lindbergh Field) and two major interstate highways serving southern California.

History. The Marine Corps' association with San Diego goes back to July 1846, when a landing party of Marines and sailors from the *USS Cyanne* seized the town from Mexico. The MCRD was acquired from the city of San Diego in 1919. Its recruit training mission dates to 1923. During World War II, more than 223,000 men were trained there. Currently, more than 20,000 young men complete the rigorous 12-week training cycle annually. Approximately 2,000 Marines are permanently assigned to the depot to receive, process, and train male enlisted personnel and supervise the 1,200 recruiters operating out of 450 offices west of the Mississippi River.

Housing and Schools. Other than for senior officers, there are neither government quarters nor guest housing at the depot. Approximately 7,900 units of Navy family housing and 108 mobile home sites spread out over 33 locations in the San Diego area are available to depot personnel. As of May 1993, waiting lists varied from four months in the Cabrillo, Bay View, and Ramona housing areas to 42 months at the Strand. Navy Lodges are available in two locations: San Diego Naval Station and North Island. Permanent change-of-station personnel have priority at these facilities.

There is no dependent schooling at any Navy or Marine Corps installation in the San Diego area. The state of California administers a free school system, which military families utilize. The depot education office offers many services to active-duty personnel and their dependents, including counseling for high school, vocational, college, and university educational programs. The San Diego area has six accredited four-year universities. There are also three regular community college campuses within the city and four others in the county, all of them offering associate of science and associate of arts degrees.

Personal Services. The depot medical clinic sees dependents and retired personnel on an emergency basis only. There is no commissary at the depot, but commissary stores are available at San Diego Naval Station, North Island, San Diego Naval Training Center, and Imperial Beach Outlying Landing Field, all of which are convenient to one or more of the housing areas. A self-service store at the depot, operated by the Marine Corps exchange, offers basic items, such as milk and eggs.

Recreation. There is unlimited recreation both on and off the base: skiing, fishing, sailing, power boating, skin diving, surfing, camping, picnicking, and swimming, just for starters. At the depot are many facilities for sports, including a bowling alley and tennis and racquetball courts. The special services office offers many recreational trips to such places as Disneyland, Las Vegas, and Big Bear Ski Resort.

The Local Area. The city of San Diego (population 1,171,200) offers one of the most equable climates in the world, with an average yearly temperature of 63° F. To the west is the Pacific Ocean, and to the east the land rises gradually to mountains that stand over 6,500 feet high; beyond the mountains is desert. The area is rich in parks and forests and is ideal for camping, fishing, hunting, and backpacking.

For more information, write to Public Affairs Office, Marine Corps Recruit Depot, 1600 Henderson Avenue, Suite 120, San Diego, CA 92140-5093, or call (619) 524-1268, ext. 1365. Home page: *www.sdo.usmc.mil.*

TWENTYNINE PALMS MARINE CORPS AIR-GROUND COMBAT CENTER

Twentynine Palms Marine Corps Air-Ground Combat Center (MCAGCC or "mick-AG-see") is situated six miles north of the community of Twentynine Palms. The town was supposedly named after the 29 palm trees that once grew at the oasis there, but a survey conducted in 1885 was able to locate only 26 of the 29. Nevertheless, the name stuck.

History. The Marine Corps came to Twentynine Palms in 1953, when a Marine Corps base was established there. In 1979, the installation was redesignated the Air-Ground Combat Center. Today it occupies more than 900 square miles of land (three-quarters the size of Rhode Island) in the southern reaches of the Mojave Desert. The vast area is used to evaluate the Marine Corps combined-arms training program. The base is home for the 7th Marines (Reinforced) and the Marine Corps Communications-Electronics School. The center also hosts combined-arms (infantry, artillery, and armor) exercises in brigade- and battalion-sized combat operations designed to evaluate the units' capabilities to fight.

Today the base is home to some 10,500 military personnel and 8,500 family members and employs a civilian workforce of about 1,600.

Housing and Schools. More than 2,400 public quarters are available at the MCAGCC, situated in seven housing areas, and there are 75 mobile home parks. A 24-room temporary lodging facility is also available.

Dependent children attend schools in Twentynine Palms. Day-care facilities are available that can accommodate more than 180 children. Adult education is provided through the education office from the base via Copper Mountain College through Chapman University, and National University.

Personal Services. Medical care is provided by Naval Hospital Twentynine Palms. This is a 40-bed facility; specialty care is available at Camp Pendleton and in San Diego. The center has an excellent Marine Corps exchange facility that offers a wide variety of concessions, including an ice cream shop, a snack shop, an auto rental service, and four snack bars. A commissary store, a package store, a credit union, and officers and NCO clubs are also available.

Recreation. Recreational facilities include three swimming pools, an 18-hole golf course, a 20-lane bowling center, a theater, a riding stable, a gym, a skeet range, and hobby and crafts centers.

The Local Area. The climate at the MCAGCC is arid, with the relative humidity ranging between 29 and 69 percent. The average temperature there is 67° F, but it has been known to drop as low as 15° F and soar as high as 130° F.

About 14,800 people live in the city of Twentynine Palms. Less than an hour's drive to the southwest is Palm Springs, with about 42,000 people. The town of Joshua Tree (population 6,500) is only 15 miles southwest of the base. Both Joshua Tree and Twentynine Palms are gateways to the 500,000-acre Joshua Tree National Monument.

For more information, write to Public Affairs Office, MCAGCC, Box 78801, Twentynine Palms, CA 92278-8101, or call (760) 830-6213. Home page: *www.29palms.usmc.mil.*

Navy

CHINA LAKE NAVAL AIR WARFARE CENTER

The China Lake site of the Naval Air Warfare Center Weapons Division and the Naval Air Weapons Station China Lake are located adjacent to the city of Ridgecrest, about 150 miles north of Los Angeles in southern California's Mojave Desert. The station covers more than a million acres of land and is situated under restricted military airspace of nearly 17,000 square miles, making it the Navy's largest land activity. China Lake is home to about 400 military personnel and 3,000 civilian employees.

History. The Navy came to China Lake in November 1943, when the Naval Ordnance Test Station (NOTS) was established there. In 1967, NOTS became the Naval Weapons Center. The NAWCWPNS and NAWS China Lake were established in January 1992. Today the NAWCWPNS is the Navy's full-spectrum research, development, test, evaluation, and in-service engineering center for air warfare weapon systems. China Lake takes its name from a huge, dry lakebed in the area, which is said to have been named for the Chinese laborers who worked the mines in the area during the 1880s.

Housing and Schools. The China Lake military community has 192 units of family housing at its disposal and supports 2,200 residents. There are also three elementary schools and one junior high school on the station.

Personal Services and Recreation. Personal support facilities include the NWC Federal Credit Union, a branch medical clinic, officers and enlisted clubs, a commissary, and a small exchange. Recreational facilities include an 18-hole golf course with a snack bar, a gym and indoor swimming pool, a bowling alley, and tennis courts. Escorted tours to the Little Petroglyph Canyon are available on weekends.

The Local Area. Ridgecrest, with a population of 30,000, supports a variety of schools, churches, shopping areas, and restaurants. Hiking, fishing, and camping opportunities are abundant in the nearby Sierra Nevada; winter recreational sports can be enjoyed at Mammoth Mountain and June Lake. Historic Randsburg, site of the Yellow Astor gold mine, is located approximately 25 miles south of Ridgecrest. Ninety miles to the northeast is Death Valley National Monument.

For more information, write to Public Affairs Office, Naval Air Warfare Center, China Lake, CA 93555-6001, or call (760) 939-3511. Home page: *www.nawcwpns.navy.mil.*

CORONADO NAVAL AMPHIBIOUS BASE

Coronado Naval Amphibious Base is located on San Diego Bay, adjacent to State Highway 75, about one mile south of the business center of the city of Coronado. The base occupies more than 1,000 acres and is host to more than two dozen commands, among them Commander Naval Surface Force, U.S. Pacific Fleet; Naval Beach Group 1; Naval Special Warfare Command; Tactical Air Control Group 1; and the Expeditionary Warfare Command.

History. Established in June 1943, the base today has the mission of training thousands of regular and reserve personnel of the U.S. Navy, as well as allied forces, in the highly specialized art of amphibious warfare. Approximately 3,900 active-duty and 650 civilian personnel are assigned to the base.

Housing and Schools. There are a number of family housing projects for Navy and Marine Corps personnel in the San Diego area, but housing is still in short supply throughout the area. Housing for personnel assigned to Coronado is handled through the naval base housing office in San Diego. Navy Lodge accommodations for transient personnel are available at North Island NAS and the San Diego Naval Station. The base provides more than 400 bachelor officer units and more than 2,800 dormitory spaces for enlisted personnel. There are 43 family units on the base for officers only.

Dependent children of sponsors assigned to the Naval Amphibious Base attend schools in the California public school system. The base has a child-development center that can accommodate 135 children, from six weeks to five years old. Adults assigned to the base may attend college courses through the Navy Campus Office from Southwestern College, Chapman College, Southern Illinois University, and National University. Off-base programs are offered at San Diego State University, University of California, Point Loma College, Grossmont College, LaVerne University, and San Diego Community College.

Personal Services. Dental and medical care are available on base. Cases that cannot be handled at the Naval Medical Branch Clinic are referred to the San Diego Naval Hospital. There is a Navy exchange at the base and commissary stores at San Diego Naval Station, North Island NAS, San Diego Naval Training Center, and Imperial Beach. Officers and enlisted mess facilities are available at Coronado.

Recreation. Recreational facilities at the base include a bowling alley, a gym, outdoor tennis and basketball courts, a recreational gear locker, and a theater. A marina and RV park are located one mile south of the base on Highway 75. The Gator Beach Recreation Area beside the ocean offers cabanas, a snack bar, showers and changing facilities, barbecue pits, and fire rings and is open year-round for private parties.

For more information, write to Public Affairs Officer, Naval Amphibious Base, Coronado, San Diego, CA 92155-5000, or call (619) 437-2011.

EL CENTRO NAVAL AIR FACILITY

Once home to the Navy's precision flying team, the Blue Angels, El Centro's mission today is much more prosaic but no less important as home to the Strike Fighter Maintenance Unit.

History. Commissioned in May 1946 as the El Centro Air Facility, the installation today occupies over 2,000 acres seven miles west of El Centro, California, and is home to approximately 350 active-duty personnel, 200 family members, and 400 civilian employees.

Housing and Schools. El Centro boasts 30 officer and over 140 sets of enlisted family quarters. Twenty-five officer and over 200 enlisted accommodations are available on the base for unaccompanied personnel. Transient quarters consist of 5 for VIPs, 70 for officers, and more than 360 for enlisted personnel. There is also a campground with spaces for 42 recreational vehicles.

Schools for children are available in nearby Seeley and El Centro. Imperial College and San Diego State University offer courses for adults. A child-care center that can accommodate up to 80 children is available on the base.

Personal Services. El Centro has a medium-size commissary, a small exchange, and a minimart. Medical care on base is available by appointment only. Definitive medical care is provided by San Diego Naval Hospital.

Recreation. Recreational facilities offered at El Centro include a library, a movie theater, swimming pools, a bowling alley, an enlisted club, tennis and basketball courts, baseball fields, a track, and a driving range.

The Local Area. The Imperial Valley of California offers hot summers from June through September and mild winters. Life at El Centro is shirt-sleeve all year round. Rainfall averages less than three inches per year. The Mexican border at Mexicali is only a few miles south of the facility. To the west, along U.S. Highway 8, lie the Anza-Borrego Desert State Park, the Petrified Forest, and the Cleveland National Forest.

For more information, write to Public Affairs, Naval Air Facility, El Centro, CA 92243-5000, or call (760) 339-2699.

LEMOORE NAVAL AIR STATION

Located just to the southwest of Fresno in the beautiful San Joaquin Valley, Lemoore Naval Air Station is at just about the center of the state of California. It is also at the heart of training readiness for the pilots who fly carrier-based aircraft from the Pacific Fleet. As such, the station plays a very important role in national defense.

History. Lemoore is one of the newer Navy facilities in California, having been commissioned in July 1961. Its 18,000 acres contain two 13,500-foot runways officially known as Reeves Field, after Adm. Joseph M. Reeves. The station is headquarters for Commander, Strike Fighter Wing, U.S. Pacific Fleet; ten strike-fighter squadrons; two training squadrons; and four carrier air wings. Today the station is home to 5,100 active-duty personnel and 7,000 family members and employs 1,250 civilian workers.

Housing and Schools. There are 1,590 family dwellings onboard Lemoore, and a 72-unit Navy Lodge for transient personnel and guests. Apartments off base rent for between $350 and $795 a month, and houses are up to $1,500 a month. Two grammar schools and a child-care center are onboard the station, and West Hills College, Chapman University, and Embry-Riddle Aeronautical University offer on-base college-level courses. The Navy Campus for Achievement assists in making arrangements for eligible personnel to attend these courses. Lemoore Adult School helps adults to achieve their high school diplomas.

Personal Services. Medical care is provided by the Lemoore Naval Hospital, a 19-bed facility. A commissary store, a Navy exchange, a theater, a cafeteria, a bowling alley, a service station, a post office, a credit union, and personalized services are all contained in a well-laid-out, beautifully landscaped mall within easy distance of bachelor and family housing and the station administration area.

Recreation. On-base recreational facilities are abundant and include a gym; tennis courts; swimming pools; RV park, pistol, skeet, and trap ranges; and electronics and hobby shops.

The Local Area. The San Joaquin Valley region offers much in the way of outdoor recreation and sightseeing. For boaters and water sports enthusiasts, the Pacific Ocean lies only two hours from Lemoore, and the "high lakes" of the Sierras are easily accessible.

Birds and small game can be hunted in the vicinity of the station, deer and wild boar in the hills around nearby Avenal and Coalinga, and bear in the Sierras. Winter sport facilities are available at resorts such as Sierra Summit, Badger Pass, Dodge Ridge, and Wolverton, all of which are accessible from Lemoore. Yosemite, Kings Canyon, and Sequoia National Parks, as well as other scenic wonders, are in the surrounding area.

Lemoore itself is a small town of about 17,100 and boasts a healthy, arid climate. Fresno, about forty miles to the north, is the largest city in the vicinity.

For more information, write to Public Affairs Office, 730 Enterprise Avenue, Room 15, NAS, Lemoore, CA 93246-5035, or call (559) 998-3394. Home page: *www.lemoore.navy.mil.*

NAVAL MEDICAL CENTER SAN DIEGO

Originally established as a field hospital in 1914, the Naval Medical Center San Diego (NMCSD) is today one of the largest and most modern medical treatment facilities of the Department of Defense. NMCSD includes branch medical clinics at San Diego Naval Station, Coronado Naval Amphibious Base, North Island Naval Air Station, San Diego Naval Training Center, San Diego Marine Corps Recruit Depot.

NMCSD performs its vital mission with a staff of 3,400 active-duty personnel, supplemented by 1,200 civilian employees, who maintain a 500-bed acute-care and a 200-bed light-care facility tending to the needs of nearly 500,000 military eligible beneficiaries in the region.

Housing, Schools, and Personal Services. Under Navy Regionalization efforts, all housing and child-development centers fall under the cognizance of Commander, Navy Region Southwest. Aboard NMCSD, Fischer house is available as temporary accommodation for family members of critically ill patients. There are two small Navy exchanges that run a barbershop, a dry-cleaning facility, an optical shop, and a uniform shop aboard the Medical Center. Meals are available at the award-winning galley, McDonald's, Subway, and Rice King.

The morale, welfare, and recreation department runs fitness facilities, a pool, and the ticket office.

A small Navy exchange operates a retail sales store, barber and beauty shops, a gift shop, a laundry and dry-cleaning facility, an optical shop, a mini-mart, and a pizza parlor. Although there is no commissary at the hospital, commissary facilities are available at other military bases throughout the San Diego area.

Recreation. A base swimming pool and gym and fitness facilities are available at the hospital complex, as are movies, various games, and the Liberty Port Cafe, which offers fast food. A leisure travel service, as well as an information, ticket, and tours office, is operated by the morale, welfare, and recreation office.

For more information, write to the Commander, Naval Medical Center San Diego, Public Affairs, 34800 Bob Wilson Drive, San Diego, CA 92134-5000, or call (619) 532-6400. Home page: *nmcsd.med.navy.mil.*

NAVAL POSTGRADUATE SCHOOL

In June 1880, the "Big Four"—Leland Stanford, Charles Crocker, Collis Huntington, and Mark Hopkins—founded the Hotel Del Monte, overlooking Monterey Bay, billing it as the "most elegant seaside resort in the world." During the sixty-three years between its founding and the property's acquisition by the Navy as a preflight school, the Hotel Del Monte hosted some of the richest and most flamboyant characters of the day. The Barbara McNitt Ballroom of the old hotel is still used today by the postgraduate school.

History. The school was originally established at Annapolis, Maryland, in June 1909 and moved to Monterey in 1951. It is now a 615-acre campus offering thirty-some different curricula, and since 1945, the school has awarded over 18,000 academic degrees to Navy personnel in science, engineering, management, and other fields. The school has a complement of 2,300 military personnel and 1,500 civilian employees assigned as staff and faculty serving 1,800 students from all services.

Housing and Schools. There are 1,470 units of family quarters for officer personnel located at Mesa Village, about two miles from the campus. An additional 130 sets for enlisted personnel are located at Fort Ord, five miles from the school. Although there is no Navy Lodge at Monterey, guest housing is sometimes available at the Presidio of Monterey.

Civilian educational opportunities are accessible to all military personnel stationed in the Monterey area. The Monterey Institute of International Studies, located in downtown Monterey, warmly welcomes military students, and Chapman University operates a resident education center at Fort Ord with on-post evening school programs leading to bachelor's and advanced degrees in the liberal arts.

Personal Services. A Navy exchange at the school offers a wide variety of personal services, including snack bars, a service station, and many others. A commissary store is also available at Fort Ord. Health care is available at the Presidio of Monterey.

With an ideal climate in a state where ideal climate is the rule, the Monterey Peninsula offers recreational activities of all sorts year-round. The school owns three Shields-class sailing sloops, which may be used by personnel stationed there. Also on the campus are an 18-hole golf course, picnic grounds that can accommodate 200 people, and a gym. In addition, tennis and swimming are available, and bottom-fishing trips can be arranged through the recreation department for weekends and holidays.

The Local Area. Monterey's chief industries are fishing, tourism, and the military. In nearby Pacific Grove, the fine for disturbing the butterflies that migrate there each year is $1,000, and the flowers never stop blooming in Carmel-by-the-Sea, only a ten-minute drive from the school.

For more information, write to Public Affairs Officer, 1 University Circle, NPS, Monterey, CA 93943-5000, or call (831) 656-2441. Home page: *www.nps.navy.mil.*

NORTH ISLAND NAVAL AIR STATION

North Island Naval Air Station has been the site of many aviation firsts. The first parachute jump at San Diego was made there in 1914, and in 1923, the first nonstop cross-country flight ended there. Also in 1923, Col. Charles A. Lindbergh took off from North Island for St. Louis on the first leg of his flight from New York to Paris.

History. Commissioned in November 1917, North Island's 2,500 acres today comprise one of the most important naval air and sea bases in California. Its primary mission is to provide support to the Pacific Fleet, and in this role it serves as the home base for over 10,000 personnel assigned to fifty commands and activities, as well as aircraft carriers, cruisers, and supply ships.

Housing and Schools. Housing is very tight at North Island, with only about fifty units, and personnel reporting there are encouraged to check with the housing office in San Diego for quarters elsewhere in the area. There is a 90-room Navy Lodge on the beach at North Island.

The California public school system supplies dependent schooling; child-care centers are operated at both North Island and nearby Imperial Beach. Programs for adults are offered through the Navy campus onboard the station. These range from high school studies to doctorates offered by a number of institutions of higher learning.

Personal Services. Medical care at North Island is provided by an outpatient branch medical clinic; comprehensive care facilities are at San Diego. A commissary and Navy exchange with a convenience store, cafeterias, snack bars, and other facilities are also offered.

Recreation. Recreational opportunities abound at North Island. There are an 18-hole golf course; handball, racquetball, tennis, and squash courts; and a twenty-four-lane bowling center. The gym has a complete physical fitness center, including a seven-mile jogging course that winds its way through the station. Skeet, trap, and pistol ranges are situated in the area just north of the beaches. Fishing is permitted from Piers Foxtrot, Juliet, and Kilo, as well as from the seawall between piers Juliet and Kilo. The beach and picnic areas are open year-round.

The Local Area. North Island forms the south side of San Diego Bay, opposite the Marine Corps Recruit Depot and San Diego International Airport. The island today is actually a peninsula. To the south of the station is Coronado Naval Amphibious Base, which is connected to Imperial Beach by a narrow isthmus known appropriately as Silver Strand Beach. To the west is the Pacific Ocean. The ideal moderation of the climate in the San Diego area makes for year-round comfort.

For more information, write to Commanding Officer, Attention: Public Affairs Office, P.O. Box 357033, San Diego, CA 92135-7033, or call (619) 545-8167. Home page: *www.nasni.navy.mil.*

POINT MUGU NAVAL AIR WEAPONS STATION

The Point Mugu Naval Air Weapons Station Weapons Division comprises four separate locations: the Point Mugu site, primarily responsible for test and evaluation; the China Lake site; the Naval Weapons Evaluation Facility at Albuquerque, New Mexico, handling nuclear weapons training; and the Naval Ordnance Missile Test Station, White Sands, New Mexico, testing surface missile systems. The Point Mugu site is home to approximately 1,900 active-duty personnel, 3,400 family members, and 6,600 civilian employees.

History. From its beginning in 1946 as Naval Air Missile Test Center to its 1992 consolidation with the China Lake installation and the two New Mexico facilities, Point Mugu remains the Navy's full-spectrum research, development, test, evaluation, and in-service engineering center for air warfare weapons. It also maintains and operates the air, land, and sea Naval Western Test Range Complex, including 35,000 square miles of sea test range area along the southern California coast.

Housing and Schools. There are two family housing areas at Point Mugu, with more than 680 sets of quarters. One is at the center, and the other is in Camarillo, eight miles away. The Mugu Lagoon Beach Motel offers a 24-unit modern temporary lodging facility. Although there is no dependent schooling on station at Point Mugu, children are bused to local schools in the Oceanview and Oxnard Unified School Districts. Children residing in family housing in Camarillo attend schools in the Pleasant Valley School District. The Navy Campus for Achievement Office offers advanced schooling through Oxnard and Ventura Colleges and extension courses.

Personal Services. Medical and dental care are provided by branch clinics for active-duty personnel only; dependents and retired personnel and personnel with problems of a specialized nature are referred to the Naval Regional Medical Clinic at Port Hueneme. There are a Navy exchange and a commissary store at Point Mugu, but the larger facilities at Port Hueneme are also used by Point Mugu shoppers.

Recreation. Point Mugu has an eight-lane, ABC-sanctioned bowling alley, a gym and adjacent fitness center, a nine-hole golf course, indoor squash and handball courts, and an outdoor tennis court. The base also features several lighted playing fields for softball, baseball, T-ball, and other sports. A large outdoor swimming pool is adjoined by a shaded picnic area.

For more information, write to Public Affairs Office, Code 75000E, NAWS, 521 Ninth Street, Point Mugu, CA 93042-5001, or call (805) 989-8094.

PORT HUENEME NAVAL CONSTRUCTION BATTALION CENTER

People have been dropping in on the Port Hueneme area since 1542 and liking it. "Endless summer" is the way one early Spaniard described the climate of Ventura County. Hueneme (pronounced "y-nee-mee") is from a Chumash Indian word meaning "resting place" or "halfway."

History. First opened in May 1942, the center is only a few weeks younger than the Seabees it was built to support. Today it is home to four U.S. Naval Mobile Construction Battalions: 3, 4, 5, and 40. Its 1,600 acres are a bustling complex that supports the activities of 3,800 active-duty personnel, 2,400 family members, and 4,400 civilian employees. The center has more than forty miles of roads and streets and twenty-five miles of railroad track.

Housing and Schools. About 800 family quarters are available for eligible personnel in two-, three-, and four-bedroom units both at the center itself and at Camarillo, eight miles from the center. Guest quarters are in the form of a 47-unit Navy Lodge; the maximum length of stay is 30 days, depending on availability of space. Although there is no dependent schooling on the center, there is a prekindergarten program, as well as a child-care center that can accommodate more than 160 children. The Navy Campus for Achievement Office provides assistance in planning educational programs that enable service personnel to advance according to their individual backgrounds and interests.

Personal Services and Recreation. A Navy exchange and commissary store offer a full range of patron services for military personnel and their families. Recreational activities include a bowling center, a golf course, a gym, a swimming pool, tennis courts, and other facilities.

The Local Area. Ventura County is a region rich in the lore of early California, with a wealth of natural beauty and resources that has made it famous. About the size of the state of Delaware, Ventura County includes mountains, farms, cities, seacoast, villages, and ranches. Average year-round temperatures are between 50 and 80° F. Metropolitan Los Angeles is only an hour's drive away, close enough for convenience but far enough away to avoid the congestion and inconvenience of urban living.

For more information, write to Public Affairs Office, CBC, Port Hueneme, CA 93043-4301, or call (805) 982-4711. Home page: *www.cbcph.navy.mil.*

SAN DIEGO NAVAL STATION

The San Diego Naval Station is one of more than a dozen naval installations in the San Diego area. It occupies approximately 1,100 land and sea acres between San Diego and National City along the eastern shore of San Diego Bay, opposite Silver Strand Bay.

History. The station was commissioned in 1922 as the U.S. Destroyer Base, San Diego. It became the San Diego Naval Station in 1946. Today it is home to over 7,000 military personnel and supports a civilian workforce of about 5,300. More than 35,000 officers and enlisted personnel are attached to the station's permanent strength from the 75 surface warfare ships berthed there. The station is the Navy's major West Coast logistics base for surface operations, dependent activities, and tenant activities, of which there are fifty-one, including elements of Commander, Surface Force, U.S. Pacific Fleet, and Fleet Training Center.

Housing and Schools. Thirteen military family housing areas are located throughout the San Diego area, housing about 15 percent of the active-duty personnel and families assigned there. There are only 38 sets of family quarters on the station, plus 108 trailer spaces. Temporary lodging is available at the station's Navy Lodge.

Although there is no dependent schooling onboard the station itself, the San Diego area has a variety of private and public schools for children. The area also has a good selection of community colleges and universities for adult education.

Personal Services and Recreation. The station has a large variety of recreational services, as well as a commissary store, the main Navy exchange, and a smaller fleet store. The facilities include swimming pools, tennis and racquetball courts, and one nine-hole and two 18-hole golf courses at an off-station site called the Admiral Baker Recreation Center. The station also operates three child-care centers.

The Local Area. The station is only seven miles from downtown San Diego, and residential communities are within five blocks of the main gate, although the area is industrially and commercially zoned. The station is 15 miles from the United States–Mexico border.

Shipbuilders National Steel and Shipbuilding and Southwest Marine are on the north and south borders of the station, respectively.

For more information, write to Public Affairs Office, 3455 Senn Road, San Diego, CA 92136-5084, or call (619) 556-7356.

SAN DIEGO NAVAL SUBMARINE BASE

Located on the tip of Ballast Point in the Point Loma area, San Diego Naval Submarine Base is home to Submarine Squadron 11, Submarine Development Squadron 5, the *USS McKee,* the *USS Coronado,* and other activities.

History. The first European to visit this site—named Ballast Point because the stones found there were once used as ballast in sailing ships—was Juan Rodríguez Cabrillo in September 1542. About 160 years later, the first Roman Catholic mass celebrated in what is today the state of California took place at Ballast Point, and a monument commemorating that event stands today at the entrance to the base chapel. The U.S. military came here in 1852, and for many years the installation that is now the submarine base was known as Fort Rosecrans, after Union Army Maj. Gen. William Rosecrans. In 1959, Fort Rosecrans was turned over to the Navy, and in 1981, the installation was designated a naval submarine base.

Today the base's 330 acres are home to 3,800 active-duty personnel, their 4,000 family members, about 300 Naval reservists, and 200 civilian employees.

Housing and Schools. Aside from eight family officer units on base, family housing for married personnel is available at other installations in the San Diego area. There are 50 units for unaccompanied enlisted personnel, 140 for VIPs and visiting officers, and 50 for visiting enlisted personnel.

Schools for dependent children are available in the local community through the Point Loma School District. A child-care center that can accommodate over 250 children is available on base.

Personal Services and Recreation. Definitive medical care is offered from the San Diego Medical Center or local hospitals. Commissary services are available at the San Diego Naval Station, but the base does operate a small exchange and a minimart. A full range of recreational facilities is provided on base, including a gym, a recreation center, a pool and spa, softball fields, basketball, tennis, volleyball, and racquetball courts, and an auto hobby shop.

For more information, write to: Public Affairs, Naval Submarine Base, 140 Sylvester Road, San Diego, CA 92106-3521, or call (619) 553-1011. Home page: *www.subasesd.navy.mil.*

COLORADO

Air Force

PETERSON AIR FORCE BASE

Pikes Peak, at over 14,000 feet high, dominates the skyline of Colorado Springs to the west. With 300 to 350 days of sunshine a year, it's a wonder the military personnel stationed at Colorado Springs can stand by their posts. And there are a lot of military people around town: The U.S. Air Force Academy is on the northwest side of town, the Army's Fort Carson is situated on the southwest border of the city, Cheyenne Mountain Air Station is just southwest of the city, and Schriever AFB is just to the east.

History. The base opened in 1941 and was later named in honor of 1st Lt. Edward J. Peterson, a Colorado native who died in the crash of an F-4 Lockheed aircraft in 1942. Today its 1,176 acres are home to the 21st Space Wing. The wing supports the North American Defense Command, the U.S. Space Command, the Army and Air Force Space Commands, Cheyenne Mountain Air Station, and many other Air Force activities throughout the world. Approximately 4,300 military personnel, 6,000 dependents, 1,200 guardsmen, and 4,500 civilian employees live and work at Peterson and Cheyenne Mountain Air Station.

Housing and Schools. There are 490 units of family housing at Peterson; temporary lodging is also available. Personnel and their families traveling on permanent-change-of-station orders may reserve accommodations.

A child-care center is maintained at the base, but school-age children attend classes in Colorado Springs, for which busing is provided. Adults may pursue college courses at the base education center. Degree programs are offered by a number of colleges, including the University of Colorado, Regis and Webster Colleges, the University of Southern Colorado, and the University of Denver.

Personal Services. A base exchange, a commissary, a shoppette, and many other personal service facilities are available on the base. Medical services are provided by a USAF clinic, with referrals to the Air Force Academy Hospital, Evans U.S. Army Community Hospital, Fort Carson.

Recreation. Recreational facilities include an 18-hole golf course, a 20-lane bowling center, craft and hobby shops, a swimming pool, a skeet and trap range, and a ski shop that also rents equipment. Peterson also has a complete athletic program, but newcomers should acclimate themselves to the elevation (over 6,000 feet) before engaging in any strenuous exercise. For hunters and fishermen, Colorado has a hunting season that runs from late September to late November and has more than 11,000 miles of streams and over 2,400 lakes, most of which are open to public fishing. There is also a fishing program at Peterson, with two stocked ponds. A Colorado fishing license and a Peterson pond permit are required.

For more information, write to 21SW Public Affairs, Peterson AFB, CO 80914-1294, or call (719) 556-7321. Home page: *www.spacecom.af.mil.*

SCHRIEVER AIR FORCE BASE

Groundbreaking for the facilities at Schriever, located ten miles east of Peterson AFB, took place in May 1983, and operations began there on 1 October 1985. The major unit at Falcon is the 50th Space Wing, which has the mission of controlling the Department of Defense satellite system and operating the Air Force Satellite Control Network. To accomplish this mission, the 50th Space Wing operates satellite centers at Schriever and tracking stations around the globe. Schriever's tenant units include the 310th Space Group, the Space Warfare Center, and the Joint National Test Facility. Currently, there are 2,300 military personnel and 1,800 Department of Defense civilians assigned duty at Schriever.

Personal Services and Recreation. Housing, schooling, exchange services, and medical care are available to Schriever personnel at Peterson AFB. Schriever does have a small aid station and dental clinic, as well as an Army–Air Force Exchange Service shoppette, a country store, and an a la carte dining facility that is open to all personnel. Recreational facilities include a weight room, racquetball courts, a par course, outdoor basketball and volleyball courts, and a softball field.

For more information, write to Office of Public Affairs, 50th Space Wing, Schriever AFB, CO 80912-3024, or call (719) 567-5040. Home page: *www.schriever.af.mil.*

U.S. AIR FORCE ACADEMY

History. Established in 1954, the U.S. Air Force Academy is the newest of the three service academies and one of the newest and most beautiful of all Air Force installations. The academy grounds cover approximately 18,000 acres in a beautiful natural setting just eight miles north of Colorado Springs. The site is at the foot of the Rampart Range of the Rockies, and Pikes Peak towers in the distance. The altitude at the academy varies from 6,340 to 8,040 feet above sea level; the area where the cadets live averages 7,300 feet.

Commencement Celebration at the U.S. Air Force Academy, Colorado
USAF PHOTO

The academy has a population of about 2,200 active-duty personnel, 2,400 civilian employees, and 4,100 dependents. The cadets number 4,200. With 800,000 visitors per year, it can get downright crowded. The academy grounds are divided into four areas to separate the cadets, support functions, families of active-duty personnel, and flying areas.

Housing and Schools. There are 1,200 sets of family quarters at the academy. About 28 units are available for transient families, and those traveling on official orders may reserve space in them; visitors are accommodated on a space-available basis only. There are three child-care centers, two elementary schools, and one high school on base, and other schools are adjacent to the academy.

Personal Services. The academy hospital is an ultramodern, 126-bed, fully staffed medical facility that serves the cadets, assigned military personnel, and their dependents, as well as other active-duty and retired people and their families. Located in the housing area is a community center that includes recreational and shopping facilities for assigned military personnel and their families.

Recreation. Among the academy's more notable recreational facilities are the 36-hole Eisenhower Golf Course and the 52,150-seat Falcon Stadium. The academy is a national wildlife preserve and has as many as 1,500 deer on its grounds during the winter. Bear and elk are occasionally seen there, as well as wildcats, antelope, mountain lions, and other types of wildlife. The Peregrine Pines Family Camp offers 53 wooded campsites, 40 with electrical and sewer hookups.

One of the most attractive places on the grounds is the Cadet Chapel, with its 17 spires rising 150 feet into the air, considered one of the leading attractions in Colorado. All regular services held there are open to the general public.

For more information, write to Directorate of Public Affairs, 2304 Cadet Drive, Suite 318, USAF Academy, CO 80840, or call (719) 333-2990. Home page: *www.usafa.af.mil.*

Army

FORT CARSON

Known as the "Mountain Post," Fort Carson is located five miles south of Colorado Springs in the "state closest to heaven" in more ways than one. "The air is fraught with health and vigor. Life is poetry, an idyll of blue sky, clear atmosphere and distant view of the kind that gives wing to the imagination," wrote Gen. William J. Paler, founder of Colorado Springs. Those who visit Fort Carson should be forewarned: They may want to remain there.

History. Named after the famous frontiersman Kit Carson, Fort Carson opened in May 1942 as an infantry training center. Today its 137,000 acres are home for the 3rd Armored Cavalry Regiment, the 43rd Support Group, the 3rd Brigade, 4th Infantry Division (Mechanized), and the 10th Special Forces Group (Airborne). Fort Carson houses 13,000 military personnel, over 29,000 family members, 3,300 civilian employees, and 5,000 reserve components personnel.

Housing and Schools. There are over 1,800 sets of family housing available at Fort Carson. Transient enlisted accommodations are also available at the Colorado Inn's 135 units, which may accept personnel with families, but on a space-available basis only. There are on-post schools for children in kindergarten through eighth grade. High school students are bused to nearby Fountain. A day-care center that can accommodate 380 children is also available on post.

The Army Education Center offers many forms of self-improvement through education, including on-post college courses sponsored by such institutions as the University of Colorado and the University of Southern California.

Personal Services. Fort Carson's medical needs are served by the ultra-modern, 195-bed Evans U.S. Army Community Hospital. A large commissary is located on post, and the post exchange offers a large main store and five troop stores. The main post shopping mall has an Anthony's Pizza shop, a Baskin Robbins ice cream parlor, a Dunkin' Donuts, a Frank's Franks stand, a Burger King, and a Popeye's chicken restaurant.

Recreation. Fort Carson is a gold mine of recreational activities of all kinds. The morale support activities office offers many facilities, including a sauna bath, racquetball-handball and squash courts, tennis courts, and an 18-hole golf course. The outdoor recreation branch offers classes in fishing, gold panning, and rock climbing, as well as an indoor sport climbing wall. Fishing trips are conducted throughout the year, with hunting, white-water rafting, and cross-country skiing in season. Fort Carson is a downhill skier's paradise, with some of the best skiing in the world a short drive away. Five lakes on post are stocked with trout and other kinds of game fish. Guns, ammunition, and recreation equipment may be purchased on post. Fort Carson operates Turkey Creek Ranch, a 1,235-acre recreational area located on the reservation only eleven miles south of the main gate. Picnic areas and other activities are available on the site.

The Local Area. The surrounding area abounds with some of the grand scenic wonders of the United States. Colorado Springs, with 300 days of sunshine a year, is called the Sunshine Capital of the Rockies. The city maintains 3,400 acres of mountain trails, canyons, swimming pools, tennis courts, and golfing facilities. Pikes Peak, a few miles west of Colorado Springs, rises almost three miles above sea level, and it was there that Katharine Lee Bates was inspired to write the words of "America the Beautiful." Just to the north of Colorado Springs is the U.S. Air Force Academy, a spot that draws more tourists than any other place in the state. Denver, a modern metropolis of over one million people, is only 60 miles to the north, and Pueblo, with 120,000 inhabitants, is about 40 miles south of the post.

For more information, write to Public Affairs Office, Fort Carson and 4th Infantry Division (Mechanized), Building 1544, Fort Carson, CO 80913-5000, or call (719) 526-5811. Home page: *www.carson.army.mil.*

CONNECTICUT

Coast Guard

U.S. COAST GUARD ACADEMY

An answer on the TV game show "Jeopardy!" pertaining to the Coast Guard Academy might be "A U.S. square-rigger named originally after a Nazi party hero." The question is "What is the *Eagle?*" Built in 1936 in Hamburg, Germany, and originally commissioned the *Horst Wessel,* the *Eagle* was renamed after being taken as a prize following World War II. Today the *Eagle* is a training bark for Coast Guard cadets and sails the seven seas representing the U.S. Coast Guard's proud traditions.

History. The U.S. Coast Guard Academy was created in 1876 as the Revenue Cutter School of Instruction. Originally based in New Bedford, Massachusetts, the academy came to New London in 1932, when the city gave the Coast Guard ground along the Thames River. Today the academy commissions 160 to 170 ensigns annually. At any given time, the corps of cadets averages 900 members. The academy offers six technical academic majors (civil, electrical, and marine engineering and marine, mathematical, and computer sciences) and two nontechnical academic majors (government and management).

Besides cadets, the workday population at the academy includes approximately 500 active-duty personnel, 900 family members, and 160 civilian employees.

Housing and Schools. Except for the superintendent, the assistant superintendent, the commandant of cadets, the commanding officer of the *Eagle,* and students, all personnel live in the local community. The children of Coast Guard families stationed at the academy attend schools in the local area, although a child-development center with a capacity of more than 80 children is available on the grounds.

Personal Services and Recreation. The academy has a small exchange and minimart but no commissary. An outpatient medical clinic is available for

U.S. Coast Guard Academy, New London, Connecticut USCG PHOTO

cadets and active-duty servicemembers. Commissary services, as well as inpatient medical facilities, are available at the Groton Submarine Base. Recreational facilities and intramural sports programs are offered at the academy.

The Local Area. The academy is located just off Interstate 95, a two-and-a-half-hour drive from New York City (south) and Boston (north). Points of interest in the local area include Ocean Beach Park, the Thames Science Center, and Lyman Allyn Art Museum in New London. The Nautilus Memorial Submarine Museum in Groton and the Mystic Marinelife Aquarium and Seaport located in Mystic are just five and twelve minutes, respectively, from the academy grounds by car.

For more information, write to Commandant, U.S. Coast Guard Academy, Attention: Public Affairs, 15 Mohegan Avenue, New London, CT 06320-4195, or call (860) 444-8270. Home page: *www.cga.edu.*

Navy

NEW LONDON NAVAL SUBMARINE BASE

New London's association with the "silent service" commenced one day in 1915 when the monitor Ozark escorted four subs—the whole U.S. submarine service at that time—into the yard. Today the 500 acres and 400 buildings that constitute the base support a population of 30,000 military and civilian personnel (9,000 active-duty personnel, 20,000 family members, and 1,000 civilian employees) and are home for the vessels and crews of Submarine Group 2, one of the most powerful naval flotillas in the world.

Housing and Schools. There are over 2,600 sets of family quarters available at New London. The waiting list varies from immediate occupancy to as long as a year, depending on the grade of the sponsor and the size of the quarters needed. A Navy Lodge located two miles from the base offers 68 efficiency units, with priority for reservations going to transient personnel on permanent-change-of-station orders. The rental market off base is aggressive. An unfurnished one-bedroom apartment without utilities runs from $400 to $600 a month; a two-bedroom home, from $500 to $750 a month. Older single-family homes with basements may be bought starting around $120,000; newer homes in good locations begin at around $160,000.

Dependent schooling is conducted off base in the nearby area. A child-care center with a capacity for 78 children, ages six weeks to six years, is available. The educational services office assists military personnel in various career-enhancement programs, and the Navy Campus program offers a full range of educational services designed to improve off-duty educational opportunities for Navy personnel. College courses are available from the University of Connecticut, Southern Illinois University, the University of New Haven, Mitchell College, and Three Rivers Community College.

Personal Services and Recreation. Medical care is provided by a 25-bed hospital facility. A commissary store and Navy exchange offering many service facilities are available on the base, as well as a 24-lane bowling alley and a movie theater. There are also a nine-hole golf course; a marina operated by the Navy Yacht Club, Groton; ice skating in the winter at North Lake; and a pool hall and game room. The base also has an indoor 25-meter swimming pool and a gymnasium.

The Local Area. New London Naval Submarine Base is located along the east bank of the Thames River, five miles north of Groton. Winters are moderately cold with occasional storms, and summers are cool along the coast and hot inland; gentle winds prevail most of the time. The local area is rich in history. Most of the towns in the vicinity have been there for more than 300 years: New London was laid out in 1646; Groton was settled around 1650; Waterford in 1663; Ledyard about 1635; Montville in 1670; Stonington in 1649; and East Lyme about 1660.

Many parks, beaches, and hunting and fishing areas can be found throughout the region and are open year-round. Boating is also a very popular pastime in this part of New England.

For more information, write to Public Affairs Office, Box 44, Naval Submarine Base New London, Groton, CT 06349-5044, or call (860) 694-4636. Home page: *www.nssfnl.navy.mil.*

DELAWARE

Air Force

DOVER AIR FORCE BASE

Dover Air Force Base has the only combat-ready C-5 unit capable of employing airdrop and special operations tactics in support of tactical forces and national objectives. Additionally, the wing operates the largest and busiest aerial port in the Department of Defense and the only joint-services mortuary on the East Coast.

History. Dover Air Force Base was opened in 1941 and, since it is situated only three miles east of Dover, took its name from the state capital. Its 3,908 acres are home for the 436th Airlift Wing and the 512th Airlift Wing (Reserve) and its 36 C-5 Galaxies, the largest cargo aircraft in the U.S. Air Force inventory. More than 4,000 active-duty personnel, 6,000 family members, 1,700 reservists, and 1,700 civilian employees call Dover home.

Housing and Schools. More than 1,500 sets of family quarters are located on the base and in nearby Lebanon, about four miles southwest of the installation. Transient family accommodations are available on the base, but reservations are accepted only for families traveling on permanent-change-of-station orders.

A child-care center and two on-base elementary schools are operated at Dover. The base education office offers a number of college courses for adults at institutions, including Southern Illinois University, the University of Delaware, Delaware State College, Wilmington College, and Wesley College.

Personal Services. Outpatient medical care for military personnel and their families is provided by the 436th Medical Group, with referrals to the Malcolm Grow U.S. Air Force Medical Center at Andrews Air Force Base, Maryland. The base exchange offers a wide variety of shopping in the main store and at the many concessions it operates on base. The commissary provides a complete line of food items for a population of approximately 20,000 eligible personnel.

Recreation. Recreational facilities offered at Dover include an eighteen-hole golf course, three swimming pools, a base picnic area, and a twenty-lane bowling alley. Also available are officers and NCO clubs and a gymnasium.

The Local Area. The weather at Dover can be disagreeable at times. Ice and snow are common in the winter, and the summers are hot and humid. The fall and spring are the most pleasant times of the year for this area. But weather permitting, there is much to do and see in the Dover area. Dover has been Delaware's capital since 1777, and the old state house, built originally in 1722, is still standing. Since Delaware was the first state to ratify the Constitution on 7 December 1787, it has the nickname of the "First Star State." The Atlantic beaches along the Delaware coast are famous. Rehoboth Beach is only about 50 miles south of the base, and Ocean City, Maryland, one of the East Coast's more well-known resort areas, is about 75 miles south of Dover.

For more information, write to Public Affairs Office, 201 Eagle Way, Dover AFB, DE 19902-7219, or call (302) 677-3372. Home page: *www.dover.af.mil.*

DISTRICT OF COLUMBIA

THE PENTAGON BUILDING

There is hardly an American who does not know at least something about the Pentagon Building. In fact, so prominent is the defense establishment in this country's news that often the Defense Department and even the military services themselves are referred to simply as "the Pentagon." But one thing many people do not know is that the Pentagon Building is the only defense headquarters in the world that regularly conducts free guided tours, open to the public, or that since 1976, when the tour program started, over two million tourists of all nationalities have taken tours. Now, even if you can't make it to Arlington, Virginia (the Pentagon is actually there and not across the Potomac River in Washington, D.C., as indicated on correspondence), you can still take a tour of the Pentagon—a virtual tour. Just head to the web at *www.defenselink.mil/pubs/pentagon* and take the full 24-minute tour.

These Pentagon tours are something of which we Americans can be justly proud, because their very existence is a concrete expression of the openness that characterizes most of our government's operations and proof that the U.S. government, created to serve its people, really belongs to those people.

Construction began on the Pentagon Building on 11 August 1941, the first occupants moved in on 29 April 1942, and the building was completed on 15 January 1943, at a total cost of $83 million. Built on the site of an old swamp along the Virginia side of the Potomac River, just to the east of Arlington National Cemetery, the original building site required more than five million cubic yards of earth fill and 41,492 concrete piles in the construction of its foundation. The engineers processed 680,000 tons of sand and gravel, dredged from the nearby river, into 435,000 cubic yards of concrete, which was then used to mold the Pentagon's unique form.

The five-sided building stands five floors (more than 77 feet) high and occupies 29 of the 583 acres that comprise the Pentagon Building and its grounds. Each of the building's five sides (hence its name) is 921 feet long, and within those walls are 6.6 million square feet of floor space containing 17.5

miles of corridors, 131 stairways, 284 rest rooms, 691 drinking fountains, and 7,754 windows filled with 309,276 square feet of glass.

To visualize what the Pentagon looks like and how it is organized, think of five five-sided wheels, one set within the other. These wheels are the rings, and they are labeled A through E, the E-ring being the outer and biggest wheel and the A-ring the innermost and smallest in circumference of the five. Now picture 10 spokes radiating from the hub of the concentric five-wheel arrangement. These spokes are corridors, and they are numbered 1 through 10. If a given room number in the building is, say, 2A286, then it is on the second floor, A ring (the inside ring), second corridor, bay 86. Once a person masters this simple floor plan, it is possible to walk between any two points inside the building in seven minutes or less.

Approximately 23,000 military personnel and civilian employees work within the gray, unadorned walls of the Pentagon Building. Each day they consume more than 4,500 cups of coffee, 1,700 pints of milk, and 6,800 soft drinks prepared or served by a restaurant staff of 230 persons dispensed in one dining room, two cafeterias, six snack bars, and, during spring and summer, an outdoor snack bar in the center courtyard of the building (known jokingly as "ground zero"). Those thousands of people log over 200,000 telephone calls each day via 100,000 miles of telephone cable strung throughout the building.

When the Pentagon workers end their day, they wind their way home over more than 30 miles of access highways, including express bus lanes and a subway system that links the Pentagon with the outlying areas of Virginia and Maryland and the District of Columbia. Those who carpool try to locate their automobiles among the 8,770 chariots crammed into the Pentagon's 16 parking lots spread over a total of 77 acres surrounding the building.

Visitors to the Pentagon these days will see a lot of construction. In 1990, a concept plan for the complete renovation of the building was approved. The plan calls for a full-scale renovation of the building and its supporting systems (mechanical, electrical, plumbing). The work is scheduled to be completed by 2011 at a total cost of $1.2 billion for design and construction. The renovation will proceed by "wedges," or building segments (five of them), and this will require the removal of up to 5,000 persons to other accommodations either elsewhere in the Pentagon ("swing space") or to rented office space in the nearby communities. It is estimated that the renovation of just one wedge will require the removal of four million pounds of asbestos and fifteen million pounds of construction debris. More information on this project can be obtained at *http://www.dtic.mil/ref/Renovation/renovatn.htm.*

Guided tours of the Pentagon for individuals and groups of fewer than nine persons are conducted Monday through Friday, except federal holidays, beginning at 9 A.M. and every half hour thereafter until 3:30 P.M. Visitors must present a valid picture ID to go on the tour.

Persons in wheelchairs must have their own pusher. Translations are not permitted for foreign visitors, and if any attempt is made to translate while the tour is under way, the walk will be terminated and the visitors will be escorted out of the building. Persons 16 and older must show valid identification: a driver's license, student ID, Department of Defense building pass, military ID, or any other identification that shows a picture of the bearer, his signature, and date of birth. Children under sixteen must be accompanied by an adult. The tour consists of a short film and a walk through the hallways of the building. The tour covers approximately a mile and lasts one hour and fifteen minutes. Included along the walk are various historical and artistic exhibits that are regularly featured along the building corridors: the Commander-in-Chief's Corridor; Army, Air Force, and Navy Executive Corridors; the Air Force Art Collection; the Time-Life Art Collection; the Hall of Heroes; the Military Women's Corridor; the Flag Corridor; and several corridors dedicated to famous generals. The tour guides are specially selected young men and women of the armed forces—superbly trained and qualified in their military specialties—who volunteer for temporary tour guide duty. Tours depart from the foyer at the top of the escalator stairs just outside the Pentagon Concourse area.

The tour area may be reached via public transportation to the Pentagon Metro Station on the Blue and Yellow Metrorail lines and Metrobus. Parking in lot E-1 near North Parking (just off Interstate 395 South) is available for a minimum fee. Parking is also available at Macy's, just across Army Navy Drive from lot E-1. A shuttle bus leaves lot E-1 every fifteen minutes between 9:15 A.M. and 4:45 P.M. In good weather, visitors can walk, using the pedestrian tunnel under I395. Signs direct visitors to the tour windows. Special arrangements are necessary for the handicapped and require 10 days' notice. Groups of 20 or more must make reservations 10 days in advance.

Group tours of nine or more persons must be arranged in advance by writing to Director, Pentagon Tours, Room 1E776, Pentagon, Washington, DC 20301-1400. Include the name of the group, number of persons, date and time of tour (with alternates), and telephone number of the requester. The e-mail address for the service is *tourschd@pagate.pa.osd.mil;* requests may be faxed to (703) 614-1642. For a recorded message giving tour particulars and directions, call (703) 695-1776.

Access to the Pentagon Building is strictly controlled. Persons holding valid Department of Defense building passes or military identification cards are authorized entry upon display of those documents; all others must pass through a metal detector and be escorted while they are inside the building.

U.S. SOLDIERS' AND AIRMEN'S HOME

The U.S. Soldiers' and Airmen's Home (USSAH) and the U.S. Naval Home (USNH; see the appropriate entry under Mississippi) make up the Armed Forces Retirement Home (AFRH). Although members of all services (including the Coast Guard, when those personnel serve under Navy command) are eligible for admission to either home each maintains the character and traditions of its parent service and gives priority in admission to former members of the Army and Air Force at USSAH and Navy and Marine Corps at USNH.

Neither home requires any support from U.S. taxpayers. Both rely solely on income provided by law from the men and women who are eligible for admission. These contributions take the form of a monthly donation of fifty cents deducted from the pay of all active-duty enlisted personnel, warrant officers, and limited-duty officers, and fines and forfeitures imposed by courts-martial and nonjudicial punishment. Other funds come from the interest paid by the U.S. treasury on the home's trust fund, a monthly user fee paid by each resident, and money donated or bequeathed by estates.

To be eligible for admission, a person must be at least 60 years of age and have been discharged or released from service in the armed forces under honorable conditions after 20 or more years of active service. He or she cannot have been convicted of a felony and must be free of drug, alcohol, or psychiatric problems.

Each facility of the home is managed by a director appointed by the secretary of defense in coordination with the Armed Forces Retirement Home Board. In addition, each home is overseen by a local board of trustees.

U.S. Soldiers' and Airmen's Home. Located two and a half miles north of the U.S. Capitol building, the Soldiers' and Airmen's Home has overlooked the nation's capital since it was founded in 1851. Four presidents, including Abraham Lincoln, have had the summer White House on the grounds of the home. Today its 300 acres boast four structures designated as national historic landmarks.

The home's park-like grounds, with trees and plants of many varieties, spreading lawns, and well-tended, quiet roadways and paths, are more like a college campus than the "old soldiers' home." These grounds include a nine-hole golf course, garden plots for the residents, two fishing lakes with cookout equipment, and four hotel-size dormitories that house 1,600 men and women.

The home offers a spacious guest house, its own laundry facility, a variety of arts and crafts shops, a bank, a post office, a large gym, and a bowling alley. There is a 300-bed long-term medical care facility available on the grounds for the exclusive care of the residents. A new 200-bed facility was completed in April 1992 and is one of the most modern facilities of its kind on the East Coast.

The home's director summarizes its mission like this: "Providing the best possible care and service to our Distinguished Veterans, for they deserve nothing less." Inquiries about admission may be made by writing to Admissions Office, USSAH, 3700 N. Capitol Street, NW, Washington, DC 20317, or by calling (800) 422-9988.

Air Force

BOLLING AIR FORCE BASE

The primary focus of life at Bolling Air Force Base is the city of Washington, D.C., which lies just to the north, within jogging distance, of the base.

History. Named in honor of Col. Raynal C. Bolling, who was killed in World War I, the base was established as Bolling Field in 1918. Today it occupies 604 acres along the east shore of the Potomac River, opposite Washington National Airport. Its 11th Wing provides administrative support to more than 8,000 Air Force members in the Pentagon, the secretary of the Air Force, the chief of staff of the Air Force, all of the Air Force's senior leadership in the D.C. area, and more than 40,000 personnel stationed in eighty different countries, assigned to more than 250 different operating locations. Bolling hosts an additional 7,000 personnel and more than 5,000 family members locally. The wing also plans, directs, and executes United States Air Force Band and USAF Honor Guard support to the secretary of the Air Force, the chief of staff of the Air Force, the White House, and other joint ceremonies and activities.

Housing and Schools. Government family quarters available on the base consist of 1,000 units for enlisted personnel (405 for the Navy and the Marines), plus 285 reserved for officers. In addition, there are another 414 units of leased housing available for junior enlisted and company-grade officers at Landover, Maryland. Off-base housing is very expensive: An unfurnished one-bedroom apartment costs from $600 to $900 a month. A three-bedroom house rents from $1,200 to $1,800 a month. Security deposits of one month's rent in advance are normally required. Guest housing is available for transient personnel on a reserved basis if they are traveling on permanent-change-of-station orders.

A 240-child capacity development center is operated on the base, but schooling for dependent children is available only in the surrounding community. On-base college courses are offered by the University of Maryland, Central Texas College, and Webster University.

Personal Services. The Bolling Clinic is maintained by the 11th Medical Group and offers excellent medical and dental care. Although excellent commissary and base exchange facilities are available at Bolling, nearby Fort McNair, Fort Myer, and Andrews AFB also offer similar outlets.

Recreation. Recreational facilities include a base marina with its own dry dock and berthing for 130 boats. A 30-lane bowling center, an arts and crafts center, a hobby shop for auto enthusiasts, softball and soccer fields, a miniature golf course, a golf driving range, and batting cages are also available.

For more information, write to Public Affairs Office, Headquarters, 11th Wing, Bolling AFB, Washington, DC 20332-5100, or call (202) 767-4781. Home page: *www.bolling.af.mil.*

Army

FORT LESLEY J. MCNAIR

Located where the Anacostia River empties into the Potomac, Fort McNair is rich in U.S. history, and its proximity to the seat of the federal government guarantees it a ringside seat on the future.

History. When Maj. Pierre C. L'Enfant drew up the plans for the federal city of Washington, he intended the land on which Fort McNair now stands to be used for a military garrison. Fort McNair, combined with Fort Myer, Virginia, make up the Fort Myer Military Community, with headquarters at Fort Myer. Established in 1791, Fort McNair is one of the oldest military installations in the country. It was blown up to prevent the British from occupying it in the War of 1812, and the conspirators in President Abraham Lincoln's assassination were executed there in 1865. Maj. Walter Reed conducted much of his research into the causes of yellow fever at the post, where he died in 1902.

Named in honor of Lt. Gen. Lesley J. McNair, Army Ground Forces commander who was killed in Normandy in 1944, Fort McNair today is headquarters for the Military District of Washington, the National Defense University, the Industrial College of the Armed Forces, and the Inter-American Defense College. Approximately 800 military personnel, 50 family members, and 800 civilian employees work within the post's ninety-eight acres.

Housing and Schools. Housing is very limited at Fort McNair, with most of the units reserved for general officers. There are 22 units for officers and a dozen for enlisted personnel. Most married soldiers assigned to duty at Fort McNair live either at Forts Myer and Belvoir in Virginia or elsewhere in the National Capital Region. There are 90 units for single enlisted personnel at the post. Temporary lodging can be reserved by calling (800) 462-7691.

There are no dependent schools at Fort McNair and no day-care program on post. A small education center is located in Building 41, and adult education is provided through programs at Fort Myer and the Pentagon.

Personal Services. Medical care for personnel stationed at Fort McNair is provided by a small health clinic, which provides normal sick-call support. A shopette, a service station, a barber shop, a beauty shop, and a dry cleaner are located on post.

Recreation on post consists of a small nine-hole golf course, a small gym with weight-room facilities, a swimming pool, four tennis courts, an outdoor basketball court, a small picnic area, two softball fields, an arts and crafts center, and two outdoor volleyball courts.

The Local Area. Fort McNair is located in the southwestern portion of the District of Columbia, very convenient to the National Airport and the Pentagon, and is regularly serviced by Department of Defense shuttle buses and local commercial buses. The Bureau of Printing and Engraving, Jefferson Memorial, the Tidal Basin, the Mall, the Lincoln Memorial, the Washington Monument, and the Smithsonian's museums are all a short Metro ride from the post; other local attractions are accessible by public transportation, which services Fort McNair on a regular basis.

For more information, write to Public Affairs Office, Headquarters, U.S. Army Garrison, 204 Lee Avenue, Fort Myer, VA 22211-5050, or call (703) 696-3944. Home page: *www.fmmc.army.mil.*

WALTER REED ARMY MEDICAL CENTER

"The spread of yellow fever can be most effectively controlled by measures directed to the destruction of the mosquitoes and the protection of the sick against these insects," wrote Maj. Walter Reed in 1901. With that simple statement, which seems so obvious to us today, he passed sentence on the scourge of yellow fever and made medical history. In 1902, at the age of fifty-one, he died in the post hospital at Fort McNair, Washington, D.C., from complications following a routine appendectomy.

History. Walter Reed General Hospital opened 1 May 1909 and was named in honor of Maj. Walter Reed. It is founded on principles that integrate patient care, teaching, and research so that patients may no longer die from insect-borne diseases like yellow fever or from surgical complications. Today the main hospital, an ultramodern medical facility, rises 125 feet high in the northeast corner of the main post area, providing accommodations for 22,000 inpatients a year; its outpatient facilities service thousands of people daily. The Walter Reed Army Medical Center is also home for the Walter Reed Army Institute of Research, the Armed Forces Institute of Pathology, and the Army Institute of Dental Research. Approximately 2,100 military personnel and 2,200 civilian employees are assigned to these facilities.

Housing and Schools. On-post housing is severely limited. A few officers quarters are available in the main post area and the Forest Glen facility, but most families live off post. Some 211 enlisted families are housed at the nearby Glen Haven facility. There are no bachelor officer quarters on post or mobile home facilities in the vicinity. The Walter Reed Inn, located across from the Georgia Avenue gate, is a visiting officers quarters. The guest house is available to accommodate incoming families, but priority for reservations goes to families of seriously ill patients. A modern enlisted troop billet provides spaces for over 700 personnel.

Dependent children attend schools throughout the Washington metropolitan area. There is limited day care on post. The Army education center at Walter Reed offers a complete program of counseling and educational planning and testing, as well as both on- and off-duty college courses from a number of institutions.

Personal Services. Officers club facilities are available at the Walter Reed Inn, and an NCO club is located on the main post. There are a commissary and post exchange at nearby Forest Glen (ample parking is available there with bus service to the main post approximately every 30 minutes during normal duty hours), and there are two small exchanges at Walter Reed itself.

Recreation. There are a bowling alley, a movie theater, auto and craft shops, tennis courts, and a picnic area for personnel stationed at Walter Reed.

The Local Area. Walter Reed is very near a number of large military installations in the Washington metropolitan area, such as Fort Myer, Bolling Air Force Base, and Andrews Air Force Base. Facilities not available at Walter Reed are therefore accessible within easy commuting distances.

Walter Reed is located in the northern reaches of the District of Columbia and conveniently close to Maryland and Virginia; downtown Washington, with all the attractions of the nation's capital, is only a few minutes away via a well-developed public transportation network. The center is adjacent to scenic Rock Creek Park, an entrance to which is located opposite the 16th Street gate. The park offers hiking, picnicking, and riding areas.

For more information, write to Walter Reed Army Medical Center, Attention: Public Affairs Office, Washington, DC 20307-5050, or call (202) 782-7177. Home page: *www.wramc.amedd.army.mil.*

Marine Corps

MARINE BARRACKS, WASHINGTON, D.C.

History. Established in 1801, the Marine Barracks, Washington, D.C., is the oldest post of the Corps and has been the residence of every commandant of the Marine Corps since 1806. The barracks occupies one square block in southeast Washington at the corner of 8th and I Streets, only nine blocks from the Capitol. In 1976, the home of the commandants and the barracks were placed on the National Register of Historic Landmarks.

The primary mission of the barracks is to provide a light infantry battalion for ceremonial duties in and around the Washington area. These include Friday evening parades at the barracks and sunset parades at the Marine Corps War Memorial in nearby Arlington, Virginia. The command consists of two infantry companies, a guard detachment, a headquarters and service company, and the Marine Corps Institute. Special units include the Silent Drill Platoon ("The Commandant's Own"), the U.S. Marine Drum and Bugle Corps, the U.S. Marine Band ("The President's Own"), and the U.S. Marine Color Guard. The barracks has a complement of about 1,100 active-duty personnel and 40 civilian employees.

Housing, Schools, and Personal Services. There are five officer family quarters at the barracks. All others are accommodated in several government-owned housing complexes located nearby. Dependent children attend the local public schools.

Off-duty education is available from a variety of local institutions, such as George Washington, Georgetown, Catholic, and American Universities in the

District of Columbia; George Mason University in Fairfax County, Virginia; and the University of Maryland in nearby College Park.

Comprehensive medical, commissary, exchange, and other services are available throughout the local area. At the barracks are a barber shop, a small exchange, a mess hall, and a gym and fitness center.

For more information, write to Public Affairs Office, Marine Barracks, 8th and I Streets, SE, Washington, DC 20390-5000, or call (202) 433-4173.

Navy

WASHINGTON NAVY YARD

The Washington Navy Yard is the headquarters site for several Navy commands, including Naval District Washington (NDW), Military Sealift Command, Naval Criminal Investigative Service, Naval Historical Center, and the U.S. Navy Band. Currently, there are about 1,200 active-duty personnel and 4,000 civilian employees onboard the Navy Yard. Opened in 1799 as a shipbuilding yard on land set aside by George Washington, the Navy Yard is now the longest continuously operated federal facility in the United States and serves as the Navy's ceremonial "quarterdeck" in Washington, D.C., as well as an administrative center.

Housing and Schools. NDW oversees approximately 275 officer and 740 enlisted family housing units in the suburban Washington communities of Woodbridge, Virginia, and Landover, Maryland. At press time, a new housing complex of 188 enlisted family units was scheduled to open south of Bolling Air Force Base in Washington, D.C. Temporary housing is available at the 50-unit Navy Lodge in southwest D.C., also adjacent to Bolling AFB. Billeting for bachelor and transient Navy personnel of all ranks is limited in the Washington area; however, several hotels offer military discount rates, and apartment referral services are available.

Personal Services. In addition to the medical clinics at the Navy Yard and nearby Bolling AFB, there are also several excellent facilities in the immediate area: the National Naval Medical Center in Bethesda, Maryland, Walter Reed Army Medical Center in northwest D.C., and Malcolm Grow Air Force Hospital at Andrews AFB, Maryland. The Navy Yard has a small Navy exchange and uniform shop, a gas station, a credit union, a barber shop, and a catering center. A full-service military exchange and commissary are located at nearby Bolling AFB. Child-care services are provided in a new 300-child center at nearby Naval Station Anacostia. The Navy Family Service Center at the naval station offers a wide range of services for uniformed, family, and retired personnel.

Recreation. The recreational facilities situated at installations throughout the metropolitan area are also available to naval personnel. The Navy Yard itself has an outdoor swimming pool, a gym, five tennis courts, a recreational services lending center, a picnic grounds, and trailer and recreational vehicle parking.

The Local Area. The Navy Yard is host to several tourist attractions, including the U.S. Navy Museum, Navy Art Gallery, Marine Corps Museum, and the permanent display ship, *USS Barry.* All are open year-round for tours. There are also numerous outdoor artifacts on display onboard the Navy Yard, including naval weapons and a Vietnam-era swift patrol boat. During the summer months, the Navy Yard hosts the Navy Summer Pageant, a weekly concert by the U.S. Navy Band highlighted with a live video performance.

For more information, write to Public Affairs Office, NDW, 901 M Street, SE, Washington, DC 20374-5007, or call (703) 545-6700. Home page: *www.ndw.navy.mil.*

FLORIDA

Air Force

EGLIN AIR FORCE BASE

Eglin Air Force Base is located on Choctawhatchee Bay, just a few miles from the open waters of the Gulf of Mexico. The summertime temperatures can sometimes dip to minus 65° F, and snow can accumulate up to 15 inches; at other times the weather here can change from junglelike heat and humidity to a desert aridity with temperatures as high as 165° F and winds over 100 miles per hour. This is not on the Gulf beaches, however, but in the McKinley Climatic Laboratory, where weather conditions are simulated in order to test the capabilities of military equipment. Eglin normally has long, hot summers and short, mild winters.

History. Named in honor of Lt. Col. Frederick Eglin, who was killed in 1937 in an air crash near Anniston, Alabama, Eglin AFB became an autonomous installation in 1940. Today it is home for the Air Armament Test Center of the Air Force Materiel Command. It comprises an area of some 720 square miles, two-thirds the size of Rhode Island. The Eglin Gulf Test Range covers over 97,000 square miles of Gulf water. With a population of nearly 30,000 (7,700 military members, 10,000 civilian personnel, and their 21,000 dependents), the base is in reality a small, self-contained city.

Housing and Schools. Eglin has more than 2,700 family quarters. The base also has two elementary schools for dependent children, a day-care center for 300 children, and an in-home day-care program. College-level courses are offered through the base education center by several universities, including Okaloosa-Walton Community College, the University of West Florida, Troy State University, Saint Leo College, and the University of Florida.

Personal Services. Medical care is provided at the 105-bed Eglin USAF Regional Hospital, which treats an average of 1,000 outpatients every day. The base also has a large commissary and base exchange, each of which operates satellite outlets (shopettes) for the convenience of Eglin shoppers.

Recreation. Recreational facilities at Eglin include a bowling alley, beaches, swimming pools, a gym, two golf courses, boat rentals, beach clubs, and a well-rounded athletics and sports program. The Eglin Family Camp, which is open year-round, has 17 camper spaces with electricity; camping sites; picnic areas; and facilities for picnicking, fishing, and waterskiing.

Some 380,000 acres are available for camping, canoeing, fishing, and hunting. Some of the best hunting in the Southeast is available on the installation, with game animals including deer, quail, turkey, and squirrel.

The Local Area. The area of the Gulf Coast where Eglin is located is known as the Emerald Coast; the natural beauty and bounty of the area centered on Fort Walton Beach and Destin, with Okaloosa Island to the south and Choctawhatchee Bay to the east, make it one of the nation's finest playgrounds. Temperatures range from 70 to 95° F in the summer and from 50 to 75° F in the winter, making outdoor activities possible an average of 340 days a year. During the summer, the Gulf waters reach temperatures in the 80s, and all types of water sports can be enjoyed there.

Eglin is located about 40 miles east of Pensacola, six miles northeast of Fort Walton Beach, and just a bit west of the twin communities of Niceville and Valparaiso.

For more information, write to Air Armament Center, Public Affairs Office, Eglin AFB, FL 32542-5000, or call (850) 882-1110. Home page: *www.eglin.af.mil.*

HURLBURT FIELD

"Any time, any place" is the motto of the 16th Special Operations Wing (SOW), the host unit at Hurlburt Field. And as key players in such military contingencies as the capture of Manuel Noriega in Panama in 1989, Operation Desert Storm in 1991, and Somalia, the airmen of the 16th SOW have lived up to their motto.

History. Named in honor of 1st Lt. Donald W. Hurlburt, who was killed in a crash at nearby Eglin Air Force Base in 1943, the present-day home of the Air Commandos began its life in 1948 as a gunnery and training field, part of the Eglin complex. More than 7,000 active-duty people, 11,000 family members, and nearly 800 civilian employees are assigned to Hurlburt Field. The wing flies the AC-130U Spooky gunship, AC-130H Specter gunship, MC-130E Combat Talon, MC-130H Combat Talon II, MC-130P Combat Shadow, MH-53 Pave Low helicopter, MH-60 Pave Hawk helicopter, UH-1N Huey helicopter, and CASA 212 transport aircraft.

Housing and Schools. There are 380 sets of family quarters at Hurlburt, plus 300 more off base. The waiting list is from one to two years for most families. Rent for off-base housing ranges from $300 a month for a one-bedroom apartment to as much as $700 a month for a three-bedroom house. Preschool and child-care programs are available at Hurlburt. The base education office provides the full range of adult educational programs, including on-base college courses from leading universities.

Personal Services. Personal support services include a USAF medical and dental clinic, a base exchange, a commissary offering over 12,000 line items, a child-care center, and banking facilities. The medical clinic is a satellite facility of the Eglin USAF Regional Hospital, the seventh largest of its kind in the Air Force.

Recreation. Recreational facilities available at Hurlburt Field include a base marina, a swimming pool, an arts and crafts center, an 18-hole golf course, a 12-lane bowling alley, a theater, a library, and officers and NCO clubs.

The Local Area. Hurlburt is located near Fort Walton Beach on Florida's Emerald Coast, which sparkles in the heart of northern Florida's Panhandle region. Fort Walton is about 40 miles east of Pensacola and about 70 miles west of Panama City. This is an area where fishing, tennis, golf, the beaches, and the dining are without question superb.

For more information on Hurlburt Field and environs, see the entry on Eglin Air Force Base or write to Public Affairs Office, 16th SOW, 131 Bartley Street, Suite 326, Hurlburt Field, FL, 32544-5271, or call (850) 884-1110. Home page: *www.hurlburt.af.mil.*

MACDILL AIR FORCE BASE

MacDill Air Force Base is located at the tip of a peninsula that juts into Tampa Bay. Tampa is to the north of the base, and Clearwater and Pinellas Park are to the west, across Old Tampa Bay. The climate is warm, and Tampa remains green year-round.

History. Opened in 1941 and named in honor of Col. Leslie MacDill, today the base is home for the 6th Air Base Wing, which operates MacDill to provide operational, administrative, medical, and logistical support for its tenant units and the MacDill community, including 200,000 retirees and their families. The base is also home to the headquarters of the U.S. Central Command, which has the mission of responding to crises in an area of responsibility covering 19 countries within Southwest Asia, Northeast Africa, the Red Sea, the Gulf of Oman, and the Arabian Gulf. MacDill is also host for the U.S. Special Operations Command, which is responsible for all operations involving U.S. special forces units. In all, MacDill is home to 5,000 active-duty personnel, 8,000 family members, and 1,300 civilian employees.

In addition, MacDill is responsible for the Avon Park Air Force Range, a 106,000-acre bombing range 95 miles east of Tampa. It is one of the largest ranges of its kind in the United States.

Housing and Schools. About 800 units of family housing and temporary lodging are available at MacDill. There are also about 1,300 accommodations for single personnel. A child-care center and an elementary school are maintained on base. The base education center offers college courses for adults through St. Leo College, Troy State University, and Hillsborough Community College.

Personal Services. On-base personal service facilities include a hospital, a base exchange mall, and a commissary.

Recreation. Recreational facilities include two eighteen-hole golf courses, a sixteen-lane bowling center, two outdoor swimming pools, a gym, hobby shops, a beach, and a marina. A base family camp, located at the south end of the installation near the beach, offers 24 trailer pads with electric and water hookups, a snack bar, a playground, and swimming, boating, and fishing. Avon Park also offers much in the way of outdoor recreation, including hunting, fishing, and camping. The annual mean temperature in the Avon Park region is 73° F, as one might expect in a place situated between the town of Frostproof to the north and Lake June in Winter Haven to the south.

The Local Area. Tampa is a handsome metropolis set among beautiful natural surroundings, with a pleasant subtropical climate all year. It offers about everything a modern American could wish for, except snow. Tampa is home to the NFL's Tampa Bay Buccaneers, the NHL's Tampa Bay Lightning, and the Arena Football League's Tampa Bay Storm.

Orlando—and Disney World—is only a 90-minute drive from Tampa, and the Florida Keys and the whole expanse of the Atlantic coast are easily accessible in the course of a weekend trip.

For more information, write to 6th Air Base Wing Public Affairs, 8208 Hangar Loop Drive, MacDill AFB, FL 33621-5502, or call (813) 828-1110.

PATRICK AIR FORCE BASE

Patrick Air Force Base is not only situated on Florida's Space Coast but is also an integral part of the aerospace programs that have made this part of the United States world famous. Cape Canaveral and the Kennedy Space Center are only a few miles north of the base. Patrick itself is the headquarters of the USAF 45th Space Wing, which is responsible for the Eastern Range, extending more than 10,000 miles downrange from Cape Canaveral.

History. The base was opened in 1940 as the Banana River Naval Air Station. It was acquired by the Air Force in 1948 and renamed in honor of Maj. Gen. Mason M. Patrick, chief of the Army Air Service from 1921 to 1927. Tenant units at the base include Headquarters, Air Force Technical Applications Center; the Defense Equal Opportunity Management Institute; and the 1st Rescue Group. About 1,400 military personnel and 5,000 dependents call Patrick AFB home.

Housing and Schools. There are 1,605 units of family housing at Patrick, some of which are located right beside the ocean, just a short walk from the beaches. Good public schools are available for dependent children in the local area, and the Air Force operates a child-care center on base for preschoolers.

College courses are offered on base in both day and evening formats from Brevard Community College, Rollins College, the University of Central Florida, Florida Institute of Technology, and Embry-Riddle Aeronautical University.

Personal Services. Patrick has an excellent medical facility in the 15-bed 45th Medical Group hospital. The commissary at the base was renovated and expanded in 1993 and offers over 86,000 square feet of sales and warehouse space. The base exchange offers over 25,000 items and many concessions, besides its normal retail sales outlets.

Recreation. With Florida's year-round subtropical climate, recreational facilities are plentiful and heavily utilized at Patrick. On-base facilities include two swimming pools, an 18-hole golf course, a marina, boat charters, and a yacht club.

The Local Area. Patrick is located right on Florida's Atlantic coast, just a short distance south of Cocoa Beach. Orlando and Disney World are within an easy drive inland, and Daytona Beach is not far north of Patrick. Hunting, fishing, camping, hiking, swimming, and golf—just about every outdoor recreational activity except mountain climbing and winter sports—are available to the people fortunate enough to live at Patrick AFB.

But by far, the most interesting and thrilling outdoor activity at Patrick is "bird watching." The Atlas, Delta, Trident, Titan, and space shuttle launches are familiar sights along the Space Coast, not to mention the spectacular launches from the Kennedy Space Center that speed astronauts into space. It is a familiar sight to all Americans, but one that never fails to awe even the most jaded space watcher.

For more information, write to Public Affairs Office, 45th Space Wing, 1201 Edward H. White II Street, Building 423, Room C-129, Patrick AFB, FL 32925-3922, or call (407) 494-1110. Home page: *www.pafb.af.mil.*

TYNDALL AIR FORCE BASE

Training F-15 Eagle pilots and maintenance personnel for worldwide combat operations, managing the southeastern air combat maneuvering instrumentation range, and providing mission-ready F-15 air superiority forces in support of Commander in Chief North American Aerospace Defense Command/1st Air Force contingency plans is what Tyndallites do best.

Tyndall is one of the largest bases in the Air Education and Training Command, with the 325th Fighter Wing serving as installation host. Other units include the Air Force Civil Engineering Support Agency, 1st Air Force HQ, Southeast Air Defense Sector and Southeast Sector Operations Control Center, and 53rd Weapons Evaluation Group. Tyndall is home to about 4,400 active-duty personnel, their 5,300 family members, and 1,900 civilian employees.

History. Named in honor of Lt. Frank B. Tyndall, who was killed in a crash near Mooresville, North Carolina, in July 1930, the base was activated in 1941. Tyndall is an air integration and training command asset. Tyndall covers

29,000 acres between the Gulf of Mexico to the south and Saint Andrew Bay to the north and west. It boasts many miles of white, sandy beaches.

Housing and Schools. There are 1,100 family housing units at Tyndall. The Sand Dollar Inn for transient families consists of 40 suites and is available through the base billeting office. A Bay County elementary school is operated on the base for children in kindergarten through sixth grade. Students in seventh through twelfth grades attend other Bay County schools in the vicinity. A child-care center is also located on the base. On-base college courses are offered by Gulf Coast Community College, Troy State University–Florida Region, Embry-Riddle Aeronautical University, and the Florida Engineering Education Delivery System.

Personal Services. Medical facilities at Tyndall are provided by the 325th Medical Group, which operates a 15-bed complex consisting of an 18-chair dental clinic, as well as a family practice and other clinics. The community mall includes a commissary, a main base exchange, a snack bar, barber and beauty shops, a flower shop, an optical shop, and a watch repair facility. Also available are four shopettes, a TCBY yogurt shop, a Burger King, a service station, a theater, a beverage store, an auto repair shop, and a marina club.

Recreation. Recreational facilities at Tyndall are excellent. The family camp there offers three fully furnished cottages, 17 RV sites with full hookups, 14 RV sites with electric and water hookups, and eight primitive tent sites. The camp also offers a bathhouse, a playground, mail service, horseshoes, shuffleboard, miniature golf, and RV accessory and TV rentals.

Indoor recreational facilities consist of an arts and crafts complex, a sixteen-lane bowling center, youth and community activity centers, and a fitness center with complete exercise and weight-lifting equipment. Swimming pools and an excellent beach area (with bathhouse facilities and a snack bar) are also available at Tyndall. Golfers will be delighted with the Tyndall 18-hole, championship golf course, which is open year-round.

The Local Area. The weather in the Panama City–Tyndall area is generally very comfortable. During January and February, the temperatures sometimes drop to freezing, but a raincoat with a removable liner is usually all the Tyndall resident needs.

The Bay County area of the Florida Panhandle offers miles and miles of sugar-white beaches, scores of freshwater lakes, and acres and acres of forest that make the location a paradise for hunters, fishermen, and water-sports enthusiasts. The area boasts a population of around 140,000, with the largest cities being Panama City and Panama City Beach. Pensacola is about 100 miles to the west, and Tallahassee is 100 miles to the east; Disney World at Orlando is about 350 miles south of Tyndall.

For more information, write to Public Affairs Office, 325th Fighter Wing, 445 Suwannee Road, Suite 129, Tyndall AFB, FL 32403-5541, or call (850) 283-1110. Home page: *www.tyndall.af.mil.*

Coast Guard

CLEARWATER COAST GUARD AIR STATION

Located on the St. Petersburg–Clearwater International Airport, Clearwater Air Station is twenty-two miles north of St. Petersburg, on the west side of Old Tampa Bay. The station moved from downtown St. Petersburg's Albert Whitted Airport in 1976, when C-130 aircraft were added to its inventory.

The station's motto, "Anytime, anywhere," accurately reflects its mission, with over 450 search-and-rescue cases flown annually in the southeastern United States, Bahamas, and the Caribbean. Clearwater became the largest Coast Guard air station in 1987, when its law enforcement mission expanded to include Operation Bahamas, Caicos, and Turks. The "War on Drugs" received redoubled attention in 1997 with operations "Frontier Shield," "Gulf Shield," and "Frontier Lance." It is home to 500 active-duty personnel and civilian employees. Air Station crews have pulled tens of thousands of storm and rough sea victims from the Caribbean waters. In 1999 alone, over 480 persons were saved or assisted when their vessels were found in distress.

History. In 1934, the air station known today as the U.S. Coast Guard Air Station Clearwater was commissioned on the west coast of Florida under the name Albert Whited Airport in downtown St. Petersburg. Coast Guard amphibious aircraft and helicopters were in residence, and in 1976, C-130s appeared, prompting the move to St. Petersburg/Clearwater International Airport. Thereafter the new name applied.

Housing and Schools. There are no on-base housing or schools at Clearwater. The Pinellas County school system has over 120 schools serving 90,000 students. All senior high and postsecondary schools are accredited by the Southern Association of Colleges and Schools. Typical rents for three-bedroom homes in the Tampa area range from $850 to $1,100 per month.

Personal Services. There are an exchange-package store and a barber shop on the station. MacDill AFB offers the closest commissary, and there is a full-service exchange at Coast Guard Group, St. Petersburg. Health needs for active-duty personnel are met by a medical clinic that includes a pharmacy and dental branch. There are limited services available for dependents. MacDill AFB, a thirty-minute drive away, has a full-service hospital and provides transient accommodations for Clearwater.

Recreation. The station provides outdoor basketball and tennis courts, a pool, a softball field, and a weight room.

The Local Area. Pinellas County consists of 265 square miles and has a population of over 800,000. It is easily accessible by car via Interstates 4, 75, and 275, U.S. Highway 19, and State Road 60. There are three bridges connecting Tampa with St. Petersburg and Clearwater. The area is served by two major airports: Tampa International and St. Petersburg–Clearwater International.

For more information, write to Public Affairs Office, USCG Air Station, Clearwater, FL 34622-2990, or call (727) 535-1437. Home page: *www.uscg.mil/d7/units/as-clearwater.*

MIAMI COAST GUARD AIR STATION

Originally commissioned at Dinner Key on Biscayne Bay in June 1932, Miami Coast Guard Air Station (CGAS; also known as "Airsta Miami") was moved to its present location at Opa Locka Airport, just a few miles north of Hialeah, in 1965.

The station's missions include search and rescue, maritime law enforcement, environmental protection, and logistics. To carry out these missions, the station operates eight HU-25C "Falcon" jets and one VC-4A Gulfstream jet. From fiscal years 1990 to 1998, Airsta Miami has conducted an average of 678 search-and-rescue missions each year. This station launches hundreds of search-and-rescue missions each year, saving thousands of lives and millions in property. The mission continues and saves lives and property that would otherwise be lost without prompt action. Law-enforcement efforts by station personnel have resulted in the confiscation of hundreds of tons of marijuana and cocaine.

CGAS Miami has a complement of 350 military personnel, their 400 family members, and 40 civilian employees.

Housing, Schools, and Personal Services. CGAS Miami controls about 100 units of family quarters. Schools are available in the local area. Health care is provided by a small medical and dental clinic. There are a small commissary and an exchange at the station.

For more information, write to Public Affairs Office, CGAS Miami, Opa Locka Airport, Opa Locka, FL 33054-2397, or call (305) 953-2100.

Navy

CORRY STATION NAVAL TECHNICAL TRAINING CENTER

Corry Station Naval Technical Training Center lies three miles north of Pensacola Naval Air Station in West Pensacola, its southern border formed by Interstate 98.

History. The training center was named in honor of Medal of Honor winner William M. Corry, Jr., and the Navy first came to this location in 1928. Originally called Corry Field, the installation was used to train fighter pilots. In 1973, the station was redesignated a naval technical training center. Today it trains Navy personnel in cryptology, electronic warfare, aviation electronic warfare, and optical instrumentation (repair and calibration of optical instruments, such as compasses, binoculars, and sextants). The center graduates about 6,000 students a year. The average daily complement at the center is 3,400 active-duty personnel.

Housing and Schools. Family housing at Corry Station consists of about 200 enlisted units situated in the family housing area in the southeast section of the installation. Officer housing is available at Pensacola Naval Air Station. Unaccompanied enlisted personnel live in barracks (bachelor enlisted facilities) that accommodate about 2,800 personnel.

A small child-care facility is available on the station, but dependent children attend local public schools. Adult education courses can be arranged through the Navy Campus located in Building 506 at the center.

Personal Services. A medical clinic and a dental clinic are at Corry Station, and definitive medical care is available from the Naval Aerospace Regional Medical Center, just west of the station, off Interstate 98. A very large Navy exchange commissary complex is situated next to the family housing area.

Recreation. Corry Station has an officer and enlisted club for those who prefer to relax indoors. There are also a bowling center, an amusement center, craft and hobby shops, a library, and a gymnasium. Outdoor recreation facilities include a running track, a swimming pool, and tennis and handball courts.

For more information, write to Commanding Officer, Attention: Public Affairs, Code PAO, Naval Technical Training Center, 640 Roberts Avenue, Room 24, Pensacola, FL 32511-5138, or call (850) 452-2000.

JACKSONVILLE NAVAL AIR STATION

Jacksonville Naval Air Station is situated on the banks of the Saint Johns River, just 13 miles to the south of the heart of Jacksonville. Jacksonville NAS is home to Commander, Naval Base Jacksonville and other tenant units, with an on-base active-duty population of 8,700 active-duty personnel, their 123,000 family members, over 4,600 reservists, and more than 10,000 civilian employees, qualifying it as one of the largest industrial employers in northeast Florida.

Housing and Schools. More than 371 units of family quarters are located at Jacksonville NAS. The waiting period for occupancy is from one to 18 months, depending on the sponsor's rank and bedroom entitlement. There are also 36 mobile-home spaces at the station. The Navy Lodge consists of 50 two-bedroom units. With the closure of NAS Cecil Field, NAS Jacksonville has taken over 199 units in the Yellow Water Navy Family Housing area. Costs for off-base rentals range from $410 to $575 (one bedroom), $500 to $700 (two bedrooms), and $650 to $800 (three bedrooms) per month.

Dependent schooling is conducted off base in the various public and private schools located about Duval and Clay Counties. There is a day-care facility on the station. Higher education is available through a variety of institutions in the Jacksonville area, including the University of North Florida, Jacksonville University, and Florida Community College at Jacksonville.

Personal Services. Jacksonville has a commissary and Navy exchange complex. The exchange at Jacksonville offers services ranging from clothing to home and garden supplies to an ice cream shop, several cafeterias and snack bars, and video rental.

Medical care for military personnel and their dependents is provided by the Naval Hospital Jacksonville, a 176-bed facility for inpatient care, as well as clinics for outpatient services. Assistance is available to help military families with their healthcare options for TRICARE Prime, TRICARE Extra, and TRICARE Standard, when seeking civilian medical services.

Recreation. Recreational facilities abound at Jacksonville: an 18-hole golf course, outdoor and indoor swimming pools, tennis courts, fishing in lakes on the base or the Saint Johns River, a full-service marina, picnic grounds with playgrounds and barbecue grills, ball fields, a full-service gymnasium, a fitness center, and officer and enlisted clubs.

For more information, write to Public Affairs Office, Box 2, NAS, Jacksonville, FL 32212-0102, or call (904) 542-4032.

Home page: *www.nasjax.navy.mil.*

KEY WEST NAVAL AIR STATION

The southernmost city in the continental United States, the two-by-four-mile island city of Key West derives its name from the corruption of the Spanish Cayo Hueso (pronounced ky-o wes-o), which means "island of bones." This grim name is supposed to have originated when an early Spanish visitor discovered a pile of bones there, remains from an Indian battleground. A place that has never known frost, Key West draws thousands of Americans every year who go there to warm their bones in its semitropical climate.

History. Naval air came to Key West in July 1917 when ground was broken for construction of a small coastal air patrol station at Trumbo Island. Key West's strategic importance to our defense in the Caribbean has increased steadily ever since. In 1943, planes from Boca Field virtually eliminated the German U-boat threat off the Keys. Today Key West NAS is home for 1,600 military personnel, 2,500 family members, and 1,300 civilian employees. It well deserves its nickname, "Gibraltar of the Gulf."

Housing and Schools. There are 1,390 sets of family quarters at Key West, including a 26-space mobile home park. As a general rule, the waiting period for Navy family housing in Key West is from six to nine months. Rental housing in the city of Key West is expensive and scarce. Rates range from $900 a month for a small two-bedroom apartment to $1,500 a month or more for a three-bedroom unit. The Navy Lodge, completed in 1993, offers 26 rooms at $40 per night. There is no guest house at Key West.

A child day-care center is located on base, with a maximum occupancy of ninety children between the ages of two months and seven years; family home day care is also available. School-age children attend schools in the city of Key West. In addition, the Florida Keys Community College is open to military personnel from the station, and courses are offered by Troy State University and St. Leo College.

Personal Services and Recreation. A commissary store, Navy exchange, and other service facilities onboard the station enhance the quality of life there. Anyone on a normal tour of duty at the station would have a hard time not being served by the special services office, which offers boating, swimming pools and beaches, tennis, fishing, and a wide variety of indoor programs, such as bowling, movies, hobby shops, and gymnasiums.

The Local Area. With an annual mean temperature of 77.7° F, outdoor activities are the rule year-round in the Keys. And of course, fishing and water sports are the area's recreational mainstays. Key West itself is one of the fishing capitals of the world, with 600 varieties of fish to be caught in the warm, clear waters that surround the island city. Special military rates are offered for some deep-sea fishing excursions. No license is required for saltwater fishing. Skin diving in the crystal-clear waters offshore is a popular pastime.

The Key West nightlife is another unique feature of the area, since most of the clubs and restaurants are open-air due to the year-round mild climate. The nearest shopping available is in the Miami area, approximately 160 miles from the station.

For more information, write to Public Affairs Office, NAS, Key West, FL 33040-6300, or call (305) 293-2627.

MAYPORT NAVAL STATION

Mayport Naval Station provides logistical support for the operating forces of the Navy and other commands. Twenty-three ships are currently home-ported at Mayport. Ships can put to sea from Mayport more quickly than from any other naval complex in the United States. A two-mile channel permits vessels to be in deep water in less than 45 minutes under emergency conditions.

History. Commissioned in December 1942, Mayport today occupies 3,400 acres at the mouth of the St. Johns River, east of Jacksonville, is homeport to more than twenty-two vessels, and boasts a population of 13,000 active-duty personnel, 26,000 family members, and 1,600 civilian employees.

Housing and Schools. Mayport has over 1,700 units of family housing, both on and off base. A new oceanfront Navy Lodge was opened in the summer 1996 season, replacing the nineteen two-bedroom trailers previously operated there as a Navy Lodge.

Although there is no dependent schooling onboard the station, elementary and junior high schools are located in the immediate vicinity, and high school students are bused into Jacksonville. The Navy campus at Mayport sponsors a full range of programs designed to assist Navy personnel in advancing their professional and academic education. Several colleges offer courses on the base, and both Florida Community College and the University of North Florida are within easy driving distance.

Personal Services. Mayport has a full range of support services and facilities, including Navy exchange and commissary store facilities. The branch medical clinic provides care for active-duty personnel. Dependents and retirees are eligible to use the NAVCARE clinic just one mile outside the station's main gate, along Mayport Road.

Recreation. Recreational facilities of all kinds abound for Navy personnel at Mayport. The base features an eighteen-hole golf course, oceanfront beaches, and several lighted ball fields and tennis courts. There is also a gymnasium complex with a full range of indoor sports and exercise facilities. The base also offers a club system and an auto hobby shop.

The Local Area. Interesting things to see and do are offered within easy traveling distance of Mayport. The city of Jacksonville is a modern metropolis of over 700,000 inhabitants, and today it is the largest city in land area in the United States, with over 841 square miles within its boundaries.

St. Augustine, North America's oldest city, is only 35 miles south, along the Atlantic coast from Mayport, and Daytona Beach is only an hour-and-a-half drive away. A weekend outing is sufficient to take in Disney World at Orlando or the Cocoa Beach resort area.

For more information, write to Public Affairs Office, P.O. Box 280032, Naval Station, Mayport, FL 32228-0032, or call (904) 270-5226. Home page: *www.nsmayport.com.*

PANAMA CITY COASTAL SYSTEMS STATION

Established originally in 1942 as a naval section base, the Panama City Coastal Systems Station (CSS) has been involved with surface warfare research and development since it became a mine countermeasures station in 1945. Today it is a major activity under the Naval Surface Warfare Center with an active-duty complement of 750 military personnel and a civilian workforce of over 1,100 persons.

Housing, Schools, and Personal Services. There are only sixty-five units of family housing at the CSS. Dependent children attend schools in the local community. On-base medical care is provided by a dispensary; referral and inpatient care are available at nearby Tyndall Air Force Base. Likewise, commissary facilities are available at Tyndall, but CSS does have a small Navy exchange complex consisting of a retail store with personalized services.

Recreation. CSS has a ten-lane bowling center, a fitness center, a swimming pool, hobby shops, a library that boasts 6,000 volumes, and an outdoor recreation center with a marina, campsites, and other facilities.

For more information, write to Commander, Coastal Systems Station, Attention: Public Affairs, Code CP20, Panama City, FL 32407-7001, or call (850) 235-5107. Home page: *www.nswc.navy.mil.*

PENSACOLA NAVAL AIR STATION

Pensacola is quite literally the "Cradle of Naval Aviation." In 1913, it was selected as the site for the first naval aeronautic station, and in 1914, nine pilots

Aircraft Carrier *USS Lexington* off Pensacola Naval Air Station, Florida
U.S. NAVY PHOTO

and 23 mechanics arrived to fulfill its mission; by 1944, the installation was training 12,000 aviators a year.

History. The Navy first came to Pensacola in November 1825, when several officers wrote to President John Quincy Adams recommending a spot on Pensacola Bay for a Navy yard. Today the base occupies over 16,500 acres and has a population of over 12,000 military personnel and 4,000 civilians. Pensacola Naval Air Station is home to the Chief of Naval Education and Training and a number of other commands, including the Blue Angels Flight Demonstration Squadron.

Housing and Schools. There are over 800 units of family housing at Pensacola, situated on 125 acres throughout the area. The Navy Lodge offers thirty-eight guest units for active-duty personnel and their dependents.

Dependent children of Navy families at Pensacola attend school in Escambia and Santa Rosa Counties, where there are a total of 60 elementary, 15 middle, and 13 senior high schools. There is a child-care center on base as well. The Navy Campus offers assistance in taking courses from Pensacola Junior College, George Stone Vocational Technical School, Troy State University, Embry-Riddle Aeronautical University, and the University of West Florida, whose campus is only ten miles northeast of downtown Pensacola.

Personal Services. Medical care is provided by the 342-bed, eight-story Naval Hospital Pensacola. Other services include a commissary store and a Navy exchange with a full range of concessions, from an ice cream shop to a flower shop.

Recreation. Recreational facilities at Pensacola NAS are excellent. There are a 27-hole and an 18-hole golf course; a 21-lane bowling center; outdoor and indoor swimming pools; clubs (officers and consolidated); and an active athletic program that includes a well-equipped gym. Oak Grove Park, a recreation area located on the station and open year-round, offers a magnificent opportunity to relax on the Gulf of Mexico. Facilities available there include 12 beach condos, 42 RV lots, fifteen tent sites, and three group picnic areas. The park stretches one and a half miles along the beach. Sherman Cove, near the west gate of the station, offers boats and motors and other equipment for rent, as well as storage facilities for privately owned boats. Pier fuel, bait, and tackle are also available there.

Pensacola NAS is located on Pensacola Bay, opposite Fort Pickens and the Gulf Islands National Seashore. The city of Pensacola (population 60,000) is just to the north of the station. Opposite Pensacola, on East Bay, is Eglin Air Force Base. Pensacola is 50 miles east of Mobile, Alabama, and 200 miles west of Tallahassee, Florida.

For more information, write to Public Affairs Office, NAS, Pensacola, FL 32508-5000, or call (850) 452-2311. Home page: *www.cnet.navy.mil/nasp-cola.htm.*

WHITING FIELD NAVAL AIR STATION

Welcome to "Scratch Ankle," a nickname the town of Milton, Florida, acquired during the days when smugglers used to experience some difficulty climbing the brier-covered steps of the local trading post. Today Milton is eight miles south of Whiting Field and the only time anyone scratches his or her ankle anymore is at the city's springtime Scratch Ankle Festival.

History. Whiting Field Naval Air Station was commissioned in July 1943 and named in honor of Capt. Kenneth Whiting, a pioneer military aviator who was taught to fly by Orville Wright himself. Today Whiting Field is home to Training Air Wing 5, which includes 1,600 active-duty personnel, their 4,000 family members, and the 1,200 civilian employees of Training Squadrons 2, 3, and 6 and Helicopter Training Squadrons 8 and 18. Property holdings of the station total 3,973 acres at the main complex and 13 outlying landing fields in a five-county region.

Housing and Schools. Whiting Field has over 400 units of family housing available in two housing areas—329 units at Whiting Pines and 82 units in Magda Village. Bachelor officers and enlisted personnel live in two-room suites with a shared lounge area. There are 72 transient rooms for officers and enlisted personnel, and reservations for these accommodations can be made up to ninety days in advance.

Although no dependent schooling is conducted at Whiting, the local schools are rated very highly. One facet of the adult education program available at Whiting Field is Pensacola Junior College, which offers service personnel a college prep program and a variety of practical and academic credit courses at the station. Troy State University and the University of West Florida also offer courses on base.

Personal Services and Recreation. Whiting Field offers a complete spectrum of Navy exchange and commissary services, as well as clubs, messes, and medical and dental care. The special services facilities include a 12-lane bowling center, two swimming pools, tennis courts, an 18-hole golf course, skeet and archery ranges, and the newly constructed Whiting Field Sports Complex, which includes two softball fields, a football field, a running track, a concession stand, three tennis courts, and a playground. For outdoor recreation, Whiting offers the Whiting Park recreation area, located on the Blackwater River in Milton. The outdoor recreation area includes rental johnboats, party boats, fishing, waterskiing, and tubing equipment; facilities for refueling boats; a picnic area with covered pavilions; and a riverside beach swimming area.

The Local Area. The Florida Panhandle is noted for its pleasant overall quality of life and relaxed atmosphere; the climate there is ideal, with sunshine more than 340 days of the year.

There are national parks, national seashore areas, beautiful beaches, and historic sites within just a few miles of the station. Whiting Field is 35 miles northeast of Pensacola and only a few miles to the northwest of Eglin Air Force Base. The Gulf of Mexico lies directly to the south, as does the Gulf Islands National Seashore.

For more information, write to Public Affairs Office, NAS, Whiting Field, 7550 USS Essex Street, Suite 206, Milton, FL 32570-6155, or call (850) 623-7651. Home page: *www.navy.mil/naswf.*

Armed Forces Recreation Center

SHADES OF GREEN

Here is the stateside vacation of a lifetime!

For as little as $66 a night, you can enjoy a championship golf course, two heated swimming pools, one of 287 oversized rooms with a private balcony, and a full-service restaurant, lounge, and sports bar—all in a wooded setting only minutes from Walt Disney Magic Kingdom. It ain't heaven, but it is the Shades of Green Armed Forces Recreation Center located at the Walt Disney World Resort near Orlando, Florida.

The accommodations at Shades of Green are available to all active-duty and retired military personnel, Department of Defense civilians, and their families. Rates are based on grade and range from $66 a night for personnel in the grades E-1 through E-5 up to $99 a night for flag officers and retired civilians. Shades of Green also offers package deals for stays from four to nine nights. (Note: Prices are not guaranteed, and these offers are subject to change without notice.)

The rooms at Shades of Green can accommodate up to five persons and include ironing boards, an in-room safe, hair dryers, and coffee makers. There is also a laundry facility, an exercise room, gift shops, travel services, and transportation to Walt Disney World.

Other features available at Shades of Green include length-of-stay passes to the Magic Kingdom, Epcot, Disney-MGM Studios, Animal Kingdom theme park, and Disney water parks and general admission to Disney's Wide World of Sports Complex, as well as DisneyQuest. Or you can visit any of the dozens of other attractions available in central Florida that include swimming, boating, dining, and night life.

For more information, write to Shades of Green on Walt Disney World Resort, 1950 W. Magnolia Palm Drive, Lake Buena Vista, FL 32830-2789, or call (888) 593-2242. For reservations, call (407) 824-3600. Home page: *www.shadesofgreen.org.*

GEORGIA

Air Force

MOODY AIR FORCE BASE

History. The idea for an air base in the Lowndes County, Georgia, area began when a group of public-spirited citizens interested the War Department in a 9,300-acre tract called the Lakeland Flatwoods Project northeast of Valdosta. In May 1941, the Agriculture Department granted the War Department exclusive use of the land, and on 19 February 1942, the Moody Field Advanced Pilot Training School opened its doors there. Today Moody is responsible for over 11,000 acres of land, including two 8,000-foot runways, and during fiscal year 1998, the base had a total estimated economic impact of $198 million on the local economy.

Named after Maj. George Putnam Moody, who was killed in an aircraft accident in Wichita, Kansas, in April 1941, the base today is home to the 347th Wing's 68th and 69th squadrons flying the F-16C/D Fighting Falcon, the 70th Fighter Squadron flying A/OA-10s, and the 41st and 71st Rescue Squadrons flying the HC-130P and the HH-60 Pave Hawk. Approximately 4,000 military personnel and 5,600 dependents call Moody home these days. The base employs over 600 civilian personnel, and more than 15,000 military retirees and their families use its facilities.

Housing and Schools. There are 303 units of family housing available at Moody, 270 for enlisted personnel and 33 for officers. Off-base rentals are reasonable and range from as little as $350 a month for some apartments to as much as $900 a month for duplexes and town houses. Moody operates a thirty-nine-space mobile-home park and has over fifty units for visiting officers and enlisted personnel. The Moody Inn offers 32 family units.

There are no on-base schools for dependent children at Moody, although a child-development center is operated on base. Adult education is conducted through the Education Services Office and consists of both graduate and undergraduate programs through Georgia Military College and Valdosta State Colleges, Park College, and Embry-Riddle Aeronautical University.

Personal Services. Medical care at Moody AFB is supplied in an outpatient clinic setting by appointment only. Priority for care is given to active-duty and TRICARE Prime enrollees with limited availability of space-available care. The commissary at Moody is large and well stocked. The base exchange, besides operating a "tank and tote" (convenience store and service station), also offers barber and beauty shops, a garden shop, an optical center, florist shops, a laundry facility, and a dining area that includes Burger King, Anthony's Pizza, and Robin Hood Sandwiches.

Recreation. Besides the Moody Field co-located club, Moody offers the full range of outdoor recreational activities. Picnicking and fishing are available at Mission Lake on base and at Grassy Pond, about 22 miles south of the base. Grassy Pond is a 500-acre site with two ponds covering a total of 275 acres. Back on base, there are a nine-hole golf course, two swimming pools, a physical fitness center, arts and crafts programs, a base library with 30,000 volumes and a computer lab with Internet access and data resources, all free of charge, a movie theater, and a fourteen-lane bowling center.

The Local Area. Moody Air Force Base is located ten miles northeast of Valdosta, a city of 48,000. Valdosta was named for Georgia ex-governor George M. Troupe's estate, Val D'Aosta, which means "the vale of beauty." Valdosta is the county seat of Lowndes County and is situated only 20 miles from the Florida–Georgia border. Today the area is an important producer of naval stores, such as turpentine and resin, which come from area pine forests. The proximity of both the Atlantic Ocean and the Gulf of Mexico gives the Valdosta area a mild, almost subtropical climate with an average annual rainfall of forty-seven inches. May through September are the hottest months in this part of Georgia, with temperatures averaging 90° F in the afternoons with 80 percent humidity. The winters are mild, with lows in the 40s, and wet, with three to four inches of rain per month, November through March. Snow is rare in this area.

For more information, write to 347th Wing Public Affairs Office, 5113 Austin Ellipse, Suite 6, Moody AFB, GA 31699-1599, or call (912) 257-3395. Home page: *www.moody.af.mil.*

ROBINS AIR FORCE BASE

Robins Air Force Base, specifically the Air Logistics Center there, is the largest single industrial complex in the state of Georgia. It employs more than 18,000 military and civilian personnel and extends over nearly 8,800 acres, within which there are 92 miles of paved roads and thirteen miles of railroad. The base has an economic impact in the surrounding communities of more than $2 billion.

History. Robins AFB is named after Brig. Gen. Augustine Warner Robins, ex-chief of the Air Corps Materiel Division. The adjacent city of Warner

Robins, population 50,000, also takes its name from the general. The base was opened in March 1942 as Wellston Depot, after the original name of the hamlet that later became the town of Warner Robins. In September 1942, the depot was renamed Warner Robins Air Depot, and the base was redesignated Warner Robins Army Air Field. Robins is home to 4,900 military personnel and their families, plus more than 12,000 civilians.

Housing and Schools. There are 1,396 units of family housing on the base. Completely furnished temporary housing is available for families near Luna Lake. These units—40 of them, sleeping five persons each—are assigned on a space-available basis only for periods of seven to 30 days.

A child-care center and two elementary schools, Robins and Linwood, are operated on the base. High schools are available in the town of Warner Robins. The Robins Resident Center offers undergraduate and graduate-level college courses for adults. These courses are conducted by the University of Georgia, Macon Junior College, and Georgia College; Georgia College offers advanced-degree programs through the Robins Graduate Center. Mercer University also offers undergraduate and postgraduate courses on the base.

Personal Services. Medical care is provided by a 20-bed USAF hospital staffed by approximately 390 personnel. A commissary and base exchange complex are also available.

Recreation. Recreational facilities include an officers and enlisted club system, hobby shops, a recreation center, picnic areas, five swimming pools, a riding stable, a skeet range, a 6,100-yard golf course, a 16-lane bowling facility, and a completely equipped gym. Robins Park, a 200-acre recreational area located in the southern sector of the base, offers a family camp, lakes, and family garden plots. The family camp has trailer pads and tent sites and is open year-round. Three lakes—Duck, Luna, and Scout—are available for fishing and boating.

Adjacent to Robins AFB is the Museum of Aviation, which more than 200,000 people visit each year to see the aircraft and missile exhibits, static displays, and films on aviation history shown daily in the theater.

The Local Area. Warner Robins is located in approximately the geographical center of the state of Georgia, about 16 miles south of Macon. Macon, a city of 106,000, offers much in the way of cultural activities and recreation, with 600 acres of parkland and playgrounds within the city limits. Lake Tobesofkee, two miles from the city, offers boating and fishing, and Lake Sinclair, 35 miles north of town, offers fishing, picnicking, and camping. The state of Georgia has more than 300,000 acres of man-made lakes and hundreds of miles of coastline along the Atlantic Ocean. The mild climate permits outdoor recreation year-round.

For more information, write to WR-ALC/PA, 215 Page Road, Suite 106, Robins AFB, GA 31098-1662, or call (912) 926-1113.

Home page: *www.robins.af.mil.*

Army

FORT BENNING

> "For two centuries I have kept your Nation safe, purchasing freedom with my blood. To tyrants, I am the day of reckoning; to the suppressed, the hope for the future. Where the fighting is thick, there am I . . . I am the Infantry! FOLLOW ME!"

Thus proclaim the opening lines of the poem "I Am the Infantry." And those are the most apropos of words for the "Home of the Infantry," Fort Benning, Georgia.

History. Named in honor of Maj. Gen. Henry Lewis Benning, a distinguished Confederate soldier, Fort Benning came to life in October 1918, when the first troops arrived there to begin training for the battlefields of France in World War I. That same month the Infantry School of Arms was established at Fort Benning. Today the post's 182,000 acres provide training and maneuver areas for soldiers preparing to become infantrymen through twenty-three different courses, including Infantry Officer Basic and Advanced Courses, the Airborne and Ranger courses, and others. In addition, basic infantry training is conducted there, and Fort Benning is also home for the 3rd Brigade, 3rd Infantry Division, and the 36th Engineer Group. Fort Benning's population consists of more than 21,000 active-duty personnel, 11,000 reservists, and 7,000 civilian employees.

Housing and Schools. Fort Benning has over 4,000 units of family housing. The Fort Benning Guest House offers accommodations for military personnel, their guests, and dependents.

Dependent schools are operated on post for students in kindergarten through grade eight, as well as prekindergarten. The post education center offers opportunities ranging from basic-skills review through job-skills education and postsecondary and graduate degrees. Participating institutions include Chattahoochee Valley State Community College, Vincennse University and Georgia Military College, Columbus State University, and Troy State University. Professional educational counseling services are offered, as well as military and civilian academic testing.

Personal Services. Martin Army Hospital is a completely renovated, nine-story building with a 250-bed capacity that provides medical care to an eligible patient population of more than 100,000.

Fort Benning has a large main exchange with various specialty shops and 27 branch exchanges. The commissary offers all the conveniences of a modern urban grocery store complex.

Recreation. Fort Benning also has a complete range of recreational services and activities, including two bowling alleys, five swimming pools, two

18-hole golf courses, a 10-screen movie multiplex, arts and crafts centers, tennis courts, gymnasiums, and two camping and fishing areas.

The Local Area. Fort Benning is located on the south side of Columbus (population 175,000). Phoenix City, Alabama, is just across the Chattahoochee River from Columbus. The Columbus area's mean annual temperature is 65° F, making outdoor activities a year-round possibility. A wealth of recreational opportunities exists in and around the cities, including 2,000 acres of parks, as well as hunting and fishing and water sports. The Destin Recreation Center, on Florida's Gulf Coast, between Pensacola and Panama City, is operated by Fort Benning. During heavy usage (Memorial Day through Labor Day), personnel stationed at Fort Benning have priority for cabins; in other seasons, other active-duty and retired personnel may reserve these facilities. Trailer pads and camper spaces are available all the time on a first-come, first-served basis.

For more information, write to Army Community Services Officer, U.S. Army Infantry Center, Fort Benning, GA 31905-5065, or call (706) 545-2211. Home page: *www.benning.army.mil.*

FORT GORDON

Located on 55,000 acres of farmland and woodlands nine miles southwest of Augusta, Fort Gordon covers portions of four Georgia counties. During its more than 40-year history, Fort Gordon has hosted infantry, armor, and military police training. Today it is the home of the Signal Corps and is dedicated to training soldier-technicians in the installation, operation, and maintenance of the Army's modern communications-electronics equipment. Fort Gordon's population consists of 11,000 military personnel, 2,100 family members, and 4,800 civilian employees. In the area, the total civilian/military dependent and retiree population is a whopping 44,000!

History. Named in honor of Confederate Lt. Gen. John Brown Gordon, Fort Gordon was activated in December 1941 and trained the men of two infantry divisions and an armored division for combat on the battlefields of World War II. The Signal Corps Training Center was established there in September 1948, and Fort Gordon's history has been associated with the communicators ever since.

Housing and Schools. More than 800 sets of family quarters are situated on the post, as well as modern guest-house facilities. Although no dependent schools are operated on the post, many fine schools are nearby. The post offers four child-care facilities. The Fort Gordon Education Center offers a program that includes courses leading to a high school diploma, and college-level courses for both undergraduate and postgraduate degrees are offered by Southern Illinois University, Georgia Southern University, Ohio University, Central Michigan University, and other institutions of higher learning.

Personal Services. Every convenience for graceful living is available at Fort Gordon. The fourteen-story, 310-bed Dwight David Eisenhower Army Medical Center provides up-to-date patient care to a population of some 60,000 active and retired military personnel and to their families.

Recreation. The mild climate that prevails in the area permits outdoor activities year-round. Outdoor recreation facilities include the Fort Gordon recreation area, an 865-acre lake reservoir located 26 miles from the post and featuring camping, water skiing, a beach, and picnic areas. Mirror Lake and Wilkerson Pond, on post, also provide recreation facilities. The post boasts an eighteen-hole and a nine-hole golf course, a stable, five gyms, two swimming pools, two bowling alleys, auto and craft hobby shops, officers and enlisted club systems, and an FM radio station.

The Local Area. Augusta is a rapidly growing community on the banks of the Savannah River on the Georgia–South Carolina border, 125 miles northwest of Savannah. The Augusta metropolitan area boasts a population of over 396,000. Augusta offers Fort Gordon residents and visitors many cultural advantages and a number of large and attractive parks and playgrounds. Sumter National Forest is just to the north, over the South Carolina border, and numerous state parks in the area offer swimming, boating, hunting, and fishing.

The cost of living in the greater Augusta area is very close to the national average and just a little over for utility costs.

For more information, write to Public Affairs Office, ATTN: ATZH-PAO, Fort Gordon, Georgia 30905-5283, or call (706) 791-0110. Home page: *www.gordon.army.mil.*

FORT MCPHERSON

Known affectionately as "Fort Mac" to Atlantans and post personnel, Fort McPherson occupies 487 acres of well-landscaped grounds four miles southwest of downtown Atlanta. Fort McPherson also operates a subpost at Fort Gillem, a 1,500-acre site located in Forest Park, ten miles from Atlanta.

History. Named after Maj. Gen. James Birdseye McPherson, a Union Army general killed during the battle for Atlanta in 1864, Fort McPherson came into existence in the summer of 1885 and received its first garrison, nine batteries of the 4th Artillery Regiment, in 1889. Today it is home for Headquarters, Forces Command, which has the mission of maintaining the readiness of active Army and reserve units throughout the United States and its territories. It also serves as headquarters for the 3rd U.S. Army and Army Reserve Command. Fort Gillem is home for the 1st U.S. Army, the U.S. Army Southeast Region Recruiting Command, the Army/Air Force Exchange Distribution Center, the military processing station, and other activities. Fort McPherson is home to more than 3,000 active-duty personnel, 13,000 family members, 2,500 reservists, and 5,000 civilian employees.

Housing and Schools. Fort McPherson is a very small post, with only 110 sets of family quarters, so most military personnel live off the installation. There are, however, guest accommodations available for all ranks. Temporary-duty and permanent-change-of-station personnel have priority; all others may be accommodated on a space-available basis only.

Although there are no on-post schools for dependents at Fort McPherson, there is a small day-care center for children. The post education center provides counseling and testing services, as well as college-level courses at both undergraduate and graduate levels.

Personal Services and Recreation. Fort McPherson provides welfare and morale services for assigned active-duty personnel, plus an estimated 35,000 retired personnel and their families in the Atlanta area. These include a U.S. Army Health and Dental Clinic, an eighteen-hole golf course, a swimming pool, a gymnasium, bowling lanes, picnic areas, an automotive shop, a community club, and sports facilities.

There are commissary and post exchange services at both Fort McPherson and Fort Gillem. Fort McPherson operates an excellent recreation area at Lake Allatoona, one hour north of Atlanta, with motel, cabin, boating, beach, and picnicking facilities.

The Local Area. Fort McPherson is practically in Atlanta and surrounded by suburbia. The climate is mild to hot almost the whole year, permitting outdoor activities most of the time. The Atlanta area is rich in Civil War history, as well as state parks and recreation areas. Fort McClellan, Alabama, and Fort Benning, Georgia, are within easy driving distance. Fort Gordon, near Augusta, and Fort Stewart, near Savannah, are a bit farther removed but still accessible to military personnel desiring to use the many facilities at these places.

For more information, write to Headquarters, Fort McPherson, Attention: AFZK-PO, 1386 Troey Row, SW, Fort McPherson, GA 30330-1069, or call (404) 464-2980. Home page: *www.mcpherson.army.mil.*

FORT STEWART/HUNTER ARMY AIRFIELD

In 1975, Fort Stewart was a stagnant backwater community comprising mostly World War II facilities with a dim and uncertain future. Then, with the announcement of plans for the reactivation of the 24th Infantry Division at Fort Stewart, a tremendous construction program began to upgrade the post's facilities. Fort Stewart is the largest installation east of the Mississippi River, covering an area of more than 279,000 acres and measuring thirty-nine miles east to west and nineteen miles north to south. Hunter Army Airfield, on the southwest side of Savannah, covers 5,400 acres.

History. Named in honor of Brig. Gen. Daniel Stewart, Revolutionary War hero, great-grandfather of Theodore Roosevelt, and great-great-grandfather of Eleanor Roosevelt, Fort Stewart was activated in June 1940 as an Antiaircraft

Artillery Center. The post reached its peak strength of 55,000 men in August 1943, and then declined steadily until 1 July 1974, when the 1st Battalion (Ranger), 75th Infantry, parachuted into the area to mark a new beginning for the post as a home for infantry units. The 24th Division was activated there in September 1975. On 25 April 1996, the 24th Infantry Division was deactivated and the division was designated the 3rd Infantry Division (Mechanized), which had been stationed in Germany. Troop strength was unchanged during the transition—only the shoulder patches changed. Today Fort Stewart's units are an important element of this nation's Rapid Deployment Force. It is home to 16,000 active-duty personnel, 32,000 family members, and 3,300 civilian employees.

Housing and Schools. Fort Stewart has over 2,800 family housing units and 106 mobile-home spaces. Guest facilities are limited at Fort Stewart, with personnel being accommodated at the seventy-room guest house on a space-available basis only.

Two elementary schools provide educational facilities on post from kindergarten through sixth grade; children in grades seven through twelve attend schools in nearby Hinesville. The Army education center offers a full array of educational services, including innovative master's degree programs enabling personnel to obtain degrees in 11 to 15 months.

Personal Services. Complete post-exchange and commissary facilities are available at Fort Stewart and Hunter Army Airfield. Winn Army Community Hospital provides medical care for active-duty and retired military personnel and their eligible family members.

Recreation. The morale support activities office provides a wide range of programs and facilities, from modern air-conditioned multipurpose craft shops to outdoor recreation; the Stewart-Hunter Sports Program is one of the most comprehensive in the Army Forces Command. The installation also provides shooting, hunting, fishing, and picnic areas, and sporting equipment rentals for nominal fees.

The Local Area. Fort Stewart is located about 41 miles southwest of Savannah, "the Hostess City of the South," a bustling modern city with a population of about 150,000, and it is located in one of the most spectacular recreational and sporting areas along the whole Atlantic coast. The winters are mild and the summers are semitropical—hot and humid—providing opportunity for outdoor activities almost the whole year. Savannah Beach, about thirty minutes from Hunter Army Airfield, is a summer resort offering swimming, fishing, boating, and other outdoor activities. Hilton Head, South Carolina, a forty-five-minute drive across the Talmadge Memorial Bridge, is another major tourist center.

For more information, write to Headquarters, 3rd Infantry Division and Fort Stewart, Attention: AFZP-PO, Fort Stewart, GA 31314-4941, or call (912) 767-5457/5458. Home page: *www.stewart.army.mil.*

Marine Corps

ALBANY MARINE CORPS LOGISTICS BASE

Although the Marine Corps Logistics Base Drum and Bugle Corps is renowned for blatting out such traditional military airs as "No Slum Today," it's the job of the people at the logistics base, through the stores distribution system, to see that Marines do have their "slum"—an old word for meat stew, not garbage, although Marines who have to subsist on the field rations proffered by today's logisticians might prefer yesteryear's "slum" instead.

History. The Marine Corps Logistics Base was commissioned in March 1952. Today it has the overall mission of acquiring, repairing, storing, issuing, rebuilding, and distributing supplies and equipment and providing a central quality assurance program for the Marine Corps. The base is home to 370 active-duty personnel and their 675 family members and has a civilian workforce of more than 2,000.

Housing and Schools. There are more than 660 sets of government family quarters at the MCLB. Waiting times for these units range from five to 30 days. There are no temporary or guest quarters at the base, but there are twenty trailer spaces for privately owned house trailers. Off-base housing is also available.

Dependent children of personnel assigned duty at the base attend the local public schools. Three child-development centers and one preschool are available on base. The base education center offers college courses through Darton College, Albany State College, and Albany Technical Institute.

Personal Services. Medical care is provided by a branch clinic of the Naval Regional Medical Center, Jacksonville, Florida. The dental clinic is operated under the auspices of the Naval Dental Clinic, Jacksonville. Retired military personnel and dependents not covered under the Delta Dental Plan are seen there on a space-available basis.

An excellent commissary store and a Marine Corps exchange are available at the base. The exchange operates a service station, a beauty shop, a barber shop, a snack bar, a laundry and dry cleaner, and a seven-day store.

Recreation. Recreational facilities at MCLB include a nine-hole golf course, four swimming pools, a base theater, a six-lane bowling alley, a skeet range, a gymnasium, an auto hobby shop, and a base library. Officers and enlisted clubs are also located at the MCLB.

The base rod and gun club (which also operates the skeet range) offers members assistance in obtaining Georgia state hunting and fishing licenses. Both hunting and fishing are permitted on the base; permits are obtained through the natural resources and environmental affairs office.

The Local Area. Albany lies on the banks of the Flint River, approximately 175 miles south of Atlanta, in the southwestern corner of Georgia. Fort Benning and Columbus are about 80 miles to the northwest of Albany. Robins

Air Force Base is about eighty miles due north of the MCLB, with Macon 20 miles beyond. Tallahassee, Florida, is about 100 miles south of Albany.

For more information, write to Public Affairs Office, MCLB, Albany, GA 31704-1128, or call (912) 439-5000. Home page: *www.mtcom.usmc.mil.*

Navy

ATLANTA NAVAL AIR STATION

Atlanta Naval Air Station and Dobbins Air Force Base are like love and marriage: You can't have one without the other. Situated in northwestern Georgia at Marietta, the two bases are only 15 miles northwest of Atlanta, and they share the same runways. Dobbins, however, is strictly an Air Force Reserve installation with a very small active-duty complement.

History. Atlanta NAS consists of 181 acres just outside the town of Marietta. The facility began operations there in 1959, after moving from its original location at Fort Gordon. Today, among other tenants, NAS Atlanta is home for Fleet Logistics Squadron 46, flying the McDonnell Douglas C-9 "Skytrain," and Marine Aircraft Group 42, flying the OV-10D Bronco and the AH-1J Cobra helicopter. The station is home to approximately 1,100 active-duty personnel, their 10,000 family members, and 200 civilian employees. Its primary mission is the training of reserve personnel, about 1,800 of whom train there on a regular basis.

Housing and Schools. Housing is very tight at Atlanta NAS, with about nine sets of government quarters available on the station. The housing referral office assists newcomers in finding accommodations in Marietta or Atlanta. There are no dependent schools at Atlanta NAS either, but the station does operate a day-care facility that can accommodate 178 children.

Personal Services. Medical care is provided by a small dispensary, and there is no commissary at Atlanta NAS. The station does have a small exchange and a package store; Dobbins has a small exchange and a shopette. Commissary facilities are available at Fort McPherson in Atlanta.

Recreation. Recreational facilities at the station include a consolidated mess, an outdoor swimming pool, a racquetball/handball court, and a six-lane bowling alley. A new fitness center and auto hobby shop are also available. Camping and athletic equipment can be obtained from the special services office. At Dobbins, there are a consolidated open mess, a gymnasium, and sixteen slots for recreational vehicles. The Lake Allatoona Recreational Area, about twenty miles from Marietta, has a wide variety of outdoor recreational facilities, including nine cabins, three trailers, and twelve campsites. Camping, fishing, swimming, hiking, and boating are available, as are equipment rentals.

The Local Area. The climate in the Atlanta area is generally mild, with average temperatures of 43° F and about 50 inches of rainfall per year. Civil War history buffs will find this a fascinating area. The symbol of Atlanta, the phoenix, represents the city's rise from its ashes after it was burned by Union troops.

The surrounding countryside offers a large and diversified selection of recreational activities available year-round, from county and state parks to Kennesaw Mountain National Battlefield Park. The city of Atlanta itself offers all the conveniences and advantages of a large metropolitan area.

For more information, write to Public Affairs Office, NAS, Atlanta, GA 30060-5099, or call (770) 919-6392.

KINGS BAY NAVAL SUBMARINE BASE

History. Kings Bay Naval Submarine Base was constructed beginning in 1978 on the site of a former U.S. Army Ocean Terminal. Today it covers an area of approximately 16,000 acres. The base provides support to the submarine-launched ballistic missile system (SLBM) and operates facilities providing that support. Currently, Kings Bay supports two squadrons of five Ohio-class fleet ballistic missile submarines, which include the *USS Tennessee,* the *USS Pennsylvania,* the *USS West Virginia,* the *USS Kentucky,* the *USS Maryland,* the *USS Nebraska,* the *USS Rhode Island,* and the *USS Maine,* of Submarine Squadron 20.

The base population consists of approximately 5,600 active-duty personnel, 15,000 family members, and over 2,500 civilian employees.

Housing and Schools. A total of 665 government family housing units are available on the base: one- to four-bedroom units for enlisted personnel and two- to four-bedroom dwellings for officers. There are 1,675 enlisted and 154 officers quarters for single and unaccompanied personnel. Temporary lodging is available in the 26-room Navy Lodge. The lodge permits guests to stay up to 14 days.

Schools in the area include the Crooked River Elementary School (one mile from the family housing area) and other elementary, middle, and high schools. The base has a day-care center that can accommodate 185 children, ages four weeks to 12 years. Adult education is available from the Navy Campus through Valdosta State College and other institutions.

Personal Services. Kings Bay has an outpatient medical clinic and a dental clinic. The nearest naval hospital is at Jacksonville Naval Air Station, sixty miles south of Kings Bay. Both commissary and Navy exchange facilities are available on the base. Also available are the base personalized services center, a beauty shop, a barber shop, the Navy Federal Credit Union, a cafeteria, a pizzeria, a package store, a coin laundry, a convenience store, and a service station.

Recreation. Recreational facilities include a gymnasium with racquetball courts, lighted outdoor basketball courts, lighted softball fields, lighted tennis courts, a lighted football/soccer field, an eighteen-hole golf course, an outdoor swimming pool, a sixteen-lane bowling center, an auto hobby shop, fishing lakes, and an outdoor recreation checkout facility with campers, boats, and other equipment.

The Local Area. This part of Georgia enjoys a temperate climate with mild, short winters and long, comparatively warm summers. The year-round temperature averages 67° F, with winter averages of 54° F and summer averages of 80° F. Normal rainfall in the Kings Bay area amounts to fifty-one inches, most of it occurring during the afternoon hours in the summer months.

Kings Bay is located in Camden County, the southeasternmost county in Georgia. The base is about five miles east of Interstate 95 from exit 1, 2, or 2A. The closest major cities are Jacksonville, Florida, and Brunswick, Georgia, about 40 miles south and north of the base, respectively.

For more information, write to Public Affairs Officer, 1063 USS Tennessee Avenue, Naval Submarine Base Kings Bay, GA 31547-2606, or call (912) 673-2001. Home page: *www.subasekb.navy.mil.*

HAWAII

Air Force

HICKAM AIR FORCE BASE

Hickam Air Force Base lies about nine miles west of downtown Honolulu, between Pearl Harbor and Honolulu International Airport. It is home for Headquarters, Pacific Air Forces, the Air Force component of the Pacific Command; the host unit at the base is the 15th Air Base Wing. The base is located in some of the most beautiful country in the United States.

History. Named in honor of Lt. Col. Horace M. Hickam, who died in an air crash in 1934, the base was completed in 1938. Today it is a 2,700-acre worksite for nearly 6,000 military personnel and 1,200 civilian employees. The 15th Air Base Wing provides support for Air Force units stationed in Hawaii and other places in the Pacific area.

Housing and Schools. There are over 2,600 units of family housing at Hickam. Two elementary schools are operated on base. Excellent public and private schools are available for dependent children throughout Hawaii, and a child-care center for 144 children is operated at Hickam. The Hickam Education Center provides undergraduate and evening classes on base under the auspices of Chaminade University, Embry-Riddle Aeronautical University, Wayland Baptist University, Troy State University, the University of Oklahoma, and Hawaii Pacific University.

Personal Services. A USAF clinic at Hickam provides routine medical care for active-duty and retired personnel and their families. Nearby Tripler Army Medical Center, a 358-bed complex, offers definitive inpatient care for all eligible personnel. Hickam also offers a commissary, a base exchange, a credit union, and a bank.

Recreation. Recreational facilities for personnel stationed at Hickam are excellent. The base has two golf courses, one 18-holer by the ocean and a par-three course in the Ohana Nui Housing Area. Hickam Harbor offers swimming, boating, sailing, fishing, and picnicking. Small boats may be rented. In addition,

Freedom Tower Landmark on Hickham Air Force Base, Hawaii USAF PHOTO

an excellent recreation center and a fully equipped arts and crafts center are available, as well as two freshwater swimming pools and a thirty-lane bowling center.

There are excellent recreational areas for military personnel and their families assigned to Hickam. One is the Bellows Air Force Station, twenty-five miles from the base. The station sits on about 1,500 acres of land and has a 12,000-foot beachfront with 102 furnished beach cottages available year-round. Approximately 220,000 personnel take advantage of the site each year. Kilauea Military Camp, located on the big island of Hawaii, is situated 4,000 feet up the side of Kilauea Volcano and is operated as a joint-service recreational facility. It is open year-round and offers cabins, apartments, dormitories, an exchange, a dining hall, bowling, hiking, tennis, golf, and guided tours of Volcano National Park and other local points of interest.

For more information, write to Headquarters, Pacific Air Forces, Attention: Public Affairs, Hickam AFB, HI 96853-5328, or call (808) 471-7110. Home page: *www.hickam.af.mil.*

Army

FORT SHAFTER

Named after Maj. Gen. William R. Shafter, who led troops in Cuba during the Spanish-American War in 1898, Fort Shafter was the first permanent U.S. military installation established in the Hawaiian Islands when it was built in 1907.

The major activity at Fort Shafter today is Headquarters, U.S. Army, Pacific (USARPAC), the Army component of U.S. Commander in Chief, Pacific (USCINCPAC). USARPAC is responsible for providing Army ground combat forces throughout the Pacific region (except Korea), support for those forces administratively and logistically, and reserves and contingency plans to meet any ground threat to U.S. interests in the Pacific. USARPAC's area of responsibility embraces over 100 million square miles in fifty countries, which have a total population of 2.5 billion. The USARPAC general staff is situated in Richardson Hall, named in honor of Lt. Gen. Robert C. Richardson, Jr., a veteran of both world wars. Built in 1944, Richardson Hall is known as the "Pineapple Pentagon."

Located next door to Tripler Army Medical Center, Fort Shafter has a population consisting of 1,200 active-duty personnel, 1,000 family members, and 700 civilian employees.

Housing and Schools. In general, personnel assigned duty at Fort Shafter who are eligible to occupy family housing will be assigned to one of the 4,000 sets of family quarters the Army administers in Hawaii. At Fort Shafter itself are bachelor officer and senior enlisted quarters, as well as guest-house units. The Hawaiian public school system operates an elementary school on post; older children attend school in Honolulu. College courses available through the Army Education Service include on-post courses from the University of Honolulu, Central Michigan University, Chaminade University, and Hawaii Pacific University.

Personal Services. There is a dental clinic on post; full medical services are provided by Tripler Army Medical Center next door. Fort Shafter has both a commissary and a post exchange. Also available are barber and beauty shops, a gas station, snack bars, a tailor shop, a watch repair shop, a car-care center, a shoe repair shop, and other retail outlets.

Recreation. In addition to the unlimited variety of recreational opportunities available everywhere in the Hawaiian Islands, Fort Shafter has a par-sixty-eight, 5,661-yard, nine-hole golf course; a 22-lane bowling alley; a swimming pool; a gym; volleyball, tennis, and basketball courts; and a baseball field. For the more sedentary, there are officers and NCO clubs, a craft shop, a theater, and a community center.

For more information, write to Public Affairs Office, U.S. Army, Pacific, Fort Shafter, HI 96858-5100, or call (808) 471-7110. Home page: *www.usarpac.army.mil.*

SCHOFIELD BARRACKS/WHEELER ARMY AIRFIELD

Anyone who has seen the movie classic *From Here to Eternity* has seen Schofield Barracks, because the picture was filmed there. Bullet holes from the Japanese attack on the morning of 7 December 1941 can still be seen in some of the buildings.

History. Named in 1909 in honor of Lt. Gen. John M. Schofield, a Civil War veteran, Schofield Barracks's 14,000 acres today are home to the 25th Infantry Division (Light), "Tropic Lightning." After distinguished service in three wars—World War II, Korea, and Vietnam—the division is back at Schofield, which has been its permanent home since it was established there in October 1941. Schofield's population today includes about 12,000 military personnel, 11,000 dependents, and 2,600 civilian employees. About 4,000 Guard and reserve personnel also train there.

As of 1 November 1991, Wheeler Army Airfield (formerly Wheeler Air Force Base) came under the control of Schofield Barracks. The landing strip at Wheeler was first cleared in 1922 and that same year was named Wheeler Field in honor of Maj. Gen. Sheldon H. Wheeler. Today its 1,300 acres are home to the men and women of the 25th Infantry Division's aviation brigade and other units. Fort Shafter is also under the control of Schofield Barracks, as are many other activities throughout the Pacific area.

Housing and Schools. There are over 5,000 units of family housing (667 officer, 4,600 enlisted) available to personnel stationed at Schofield and Wheeler, and 192 units of guest housing are available. Housing is rather expensive. A typical two-bedroom apartment in the area ranges between $650 and $850 per month. Renting a home can also cut into locality pay, with a two-bedroom home with one bathroom ranging from $900 to $1,200 per month.

Two elementary schools are available on post for Schofield/Wheeler's children. Another elementary school is located at Fort Shafter. Child-care facilities with a capacity for 250 children are also available. The post education center offers courses from Chaminade University, Hawaii Pacific University, University of Hawaii, Central Michigan University, and Honolulu Community College.

Personal Services. Medical care at Schofield is provided by a U.S. Army health clinic. Extensive care is available at Tripler Army Medical Center, about fifteen miles south of the post. A commissary is located on the post, and commissaries are also located at Hickam Air Force Base and Pearl Harbor Naval Complex. The post exchange at Schofield offers a wide variety of concessions, including four snack bars, a service station and garage, an optical shop, banking facilities, a car rental service, barber and beauty shops, and a Baskin Robbins ice cream parlor.

Recreation. Recreational services at Schofield Barracks are excellent and include an arts and crafts shop, an auto repair shop, a movie theater, two bowling centers, two 18-hole golf courses, and a gym. Officers and enlisted clubs are also on post. Recreational equipment rentals are available, including camping, fishing, and diving equipment. Bicycles may be rented at very reasonable fees.

The Local Area. Schofield Barracks is 25 miles north of Honolulu on the island of Oahu, the most heavily populated island in the chain (three-quarters of the state's population of about one million people). In size, Oahu is the third-largest of the Hawaiian Islands. In addition to being the cultural and social center of the state, Oahu is the site of famous Waikiki Beach and the *USS Arizona* Monument at Pearl Harbor. The main campus of the University of Hawaii is in Honolulu, in Manoa Valley.

For more information, write to Public Affairs Office, 25th Infantry Division (Light), Attention: APV's-PAO, Schofield Barracks, HI 96857, or call (808) 471-7110. Home page: *www.usarpac.army.mil.*

(Note: More information is available on the web concerning the Inn at Schofield: *www.innatschofield.com.*)

TRIPLER ARMY MEDICAL CENTER

Located eight miles from Waikiki, Tripler Army Medical Center is the largest military treatment facility in the Pacific and is the only Army medical center not located on the U.S. mainland.

True to its motto, "Partners in the Journey to Wellness," Tripler routinely provides out- and inpatient care to 62,000 active-duty personnel of all services, 93,000 dependents and retirees, 152,000 Pacific Islands beneficiaries, and 110,000 veterans, which includes the beds provided at Tripler under the auspices of the Department of Veterans Affairs. Tripler is also a major teaching center. The hospital staff consists of 1,700 active-duty personnel and 1,150 civilian employees.

History. Named in 1920 in honor of Brevet Brig. Gen. Charles Stuart Tripler, the first medical director of the Army of the Potomac during the Civil War, Tripler originally opened in 1907 as a post hospital at Fort Shafter. The center was moved to its present location on Monalua Ridge in 1948.

Wings A through E, completed in 1948, are 1.6 million square feet and have 537 beds (with room to expand to 1,100 in an emergency). Three new wings, F, G, and H, were begun in 1982 and opened in 1985 at a cost of $106 million. These wings comprise 433,000 square feet and house the emergency room, pathology unit, lab, surgical units, and specialty inpatient care units.

Housing. Approximately 200 units of family housing are available at the center itself; additional housing is located at Fort Shafter. Guest housing consisting of forty-one units is also available. The center also administers thirty-five units of bachelor officer and twenty-eight units of bachelor enlisted housing.

Personal Services and Recreation. There is no commissary and only a small post exchange at Tripler. Schools and day-care facilities for dependents are also unavailable there; these services are offered at various nearby military installations. The center does have a bowling alley, a swimming pool, a gymnasium, a library, a driving range, and racquetball and tennis courts. Tripler Army Medical Center is located only eight miles from Honolulu and offers an excellent view of the city from its elevation. Waikiki is a twenty-five-minute drive from Tripler.

For more information, write to Headquarters, Tripler Army Medical Center, Attention: HSHK-IO, Tripler AMC, HI 96859-5000, or call (808) 433-2778. Home page: *www.tamc.amedd.army.mil.*

Marine Corps

CAMP H. M. SMITH

Named after Lt. Gen. Holland M. "Howlin' Mad" Smith—who ironically is best known for the incident in World War II when he got howling mad at Army Gen. Robert C. Richardson, after whom Richardson Hall at Fort Shafter is named—Camp Smith began as the site of a Navy hospital in 1942 and was acquired by the Marine Corps in 1955. Today Camp Smith is headquarters for Commander in Chief, Pacific; Marine Forces, Pacific; and other commands. The installation is home to 1,300 active-duty personnel and more than 500 civilian employees.

Housing and Schools. Camp Smith has a few family housing units for officers and quarters for about 144 single enlisted personnel. Children of sponsors assigned duty at Camp Smith attend local schools. There are no child-care facilities at Camp Smith.

Personal Services. There is a medical clinic at Camp Smith for active-duty personnel, but definitive medical care is provided by Tripler Army Medical Center. No commissary is available, but there is a small Marine Corps exchange, as well as a gas station, a laundry and dry-cleaning facility, a beverage store, a tailor shop, and a snack bar.

Recreation. Camp Smith offers a spectrum of recreational facilities, including a library, a campground, an auto hobby shop, racquetball and handball courts, horseback riding, a swimming pool, tennis and volleyball courts, and a weight room. Officers, staff NCO, and enlisted clubs are also available.

For more information, write to Commanding General, Fleet Marine Force Pacific, Attention: Force PAO, Box 64124, Camp H. M. Smith, HI 96861-4124, or call (808) 477-6331. Home page: *www.mfp.usmc.mil.*

MARINE CORPS BASE HAWAII (KANEOHE)

The Marine Corps has reorganized all of its installations in Hawaii into a single entity: Marine Corps Base Hawaii (MCBH). In addition to the former

Marine Corps Air Station at Kaneohe Bay, the base includes Camp Smith in Aiea, Puuloa Rifle Range near Ewa Beach, and a small training facility on the island of Molokai. The Kaneohe base is home to the 3rd Marine Regiment (Reinforced), Combat Service and Support Group 3, the aviation support element of the 1st Marine Aircraft Wing, the Marine Forces Pacific Band, and a number of separate battalions and other units. About 7,000 military personnel are assigned to Kaneohe Bay; there are also 4,400 family members and 1,700 civilian employees.

History. The first military occupants of Kaneohe Bay were members of the U.S. Army Coast Artillery, who remained there until after World War II. The Navy began construction of an air station there in 1939. The station closed in 1949, only to be recommissioned as a Marine air station in 1951. Kaneohe Bay lies on the north side (the windward side) of the island of Oahu, opposite Honolulu and across the Koolau Mountains, which rise to a height of 4,000 feet. Kaneohe Bay is situated on the Mokapu Peninsula, which forms the eastern shore of the bay and is the site of the University of Hawaii's marine laboratory and the Kaneohe Bay Park.

Housing and Schools. There are over 1,800 sets of family quarters at Kaneohe Bay. There is also a temporary lodging facility available. Mokapu Elementary School, which is part of the Hawaii state school system, operates at Kaneohe, and there are also a child-care center and a preschool on base. Intermediate and high school students are bused off base. A wide range of educational programs is offered by the base education office.

Personal Services. Medical and dental services are available at clinics at Kaneohe Bay and Camp Smith; definitive medical care is provided by Tripler Army Medical Center. Other services include an exchange and a commissary, banking facilities, and a complete club system for all ranks.

Recreation. A wide range of recreational activities is available, including golf, a riding stable, a marina, hobby shops, a gym, excellent beaches, parks, and cultural centers.

For more information, write to Director, Consolidated Public Affairs Office, MCBH, Kaneohe Bay, HI 96863-3002, or call (808) 471-7110. Home page: *www.mcbh.usmc.mil.*

Navy

PEARL HARBOR NAVAL COMPLEX

Pearl Harbor takes its name from the Polynesian *wai momi,* which means "water of pearl," the name the ancient Hawaiians bestowed on the location after the pearl oysters that once plentifully populated those waters.

History. At 7:55 A.M. on 7 December 1941, Pearl Harbor earned an unsought place in history, and today the sunken hulk of the *USS Arizona,* the tomb of more than 1,100 sailors and Marines who died when Japanese bombs sunk her, lies under thirty-eight feet of water at the bottom of the harbor.

Established first as a coaling station in 1901, today the naval complex in Hawaii has become the most important base in the Pacific. Major commands include Commander-in-Chief, U.S. Pacific Fleet; Commander, Submarine Force, U.S. Pacific Fleet; Commander, Patrol and Reconnaissance Force, U.S. Pacific Fleet; Commander, Navy Region Hawaii; Commander, Naval Surface Group, Middle Pacific; Commander, Naval Facilities Engineering Command, Pacific Division; and Commander, Third Naval Construction Brigade. Pearl is homeport for more than 17,000 sailors, 10,000 family members, and nearly 9,000 civilian employees working in seventy commands located on Oahu and Kauaii. The base occupies more than 12,500 acres of prime real estate just to the west of downtown Honolulu.

Housing and Schools. Aside from a few sets of quarters reserved for senior officers, family housing is not available on base. However, the Navy operates 7,300 family housing units in the Hawaii area, most of them off base in scattered areas on the island of Oahu. Waiting periods vary according to the season with a greater turnover in the summer months than at other times of the year.

Preschool and child-care centers are located at Pearl Harbor, but schooling for dependents of personnel stationed there is available off base in the Hawaii public school system. Opportunities for adult education are excellent everywhere in Hawaii. Personnel who desire to finish high school or obtain advanced academic degrees use the University of Hawaii, Chaminade University, Hawaii Pacific College, and other institutions.

Personnel Services. The Navy exchange at Pearl Harbor offers eighty-seven facilities and 66 sales outlets. There are also a Navy exchange, chapel, health and dental services, and a child-development center at the former Naval Air Station, Barbers Point. Medical care is provided by various outpatient clinics, with major treatment available at nearby Tripler Army Medical Center.

Recreation. Recreational facilities abound at Pearl Harbor, with two bowling centers, six swimming pools, 12 tennis courts, five indoor and three outdoor squash and racquetball courts, deep-sea fishing, trips, an 18-hole golf course, a marina, and a sports arena. The Navy retained 1,100 acres at the former Barbers Point Naval Air Station, which contains the White Plains and Nimitz beaches, both of which are open to military personnel and their families, as well as the general public.

The Local Area. The Hawaiian Islands are the proverbial tropical paradise, and off-base outdoor recreational activities are available throughout the year. While very mild temperatures prevail at sea level, temperatures can become quite cool at higher elevations inland. Rainfall varies from very wet in some areas to very dry in others, so the islands offer contrasts of tropical rain forests and desertesque areas within just a few miles of each other.

It should be remembered that Hawaii is really a chain of eight principal islands, and when a mainlander refers to Hawaii, he is usually thinking of Oahu, the site of Honolulu. The island of Hawaii lies farther to the east and is several times larger and much less densely populated than Oahu. All the Hawaiian

Islands offer many attractions, including the 13,000-foot peak of Mauna Loa Volcano on Hawaii.

For more information, write to Public Affairs Office, Commander, Navy Region Hawaii, 517 Russell Avenue, Pearl Harbor, HI 96860-5020, or call (808) 471-7110. Home page: *www.hawaii.navy.mil.*

Armed Forces Recreation Center–Hawaii

HALE KOA HOTEL

The words *hale koa* in Hawaiian mean "house of the warrior," and for armed forces personnel, their dependents, and guests looking for first-class accommodations on Honolulu's world-famous Waikiki Beach at Fort DeRussy, that means the Hale Koa Hotel.

The Hale Koa was built with nonappropriated funds generated by profits from military clubs and exchanges around the world. Reserved exclusively for the use of armed forces personnel, it enjoys a well-earned reputation as the military's most attractive and most popular recreation facility. It is estimated that over one million military personnel and their dependents use the Hale Koa's facilities each year. Active-duty and retired military personnel of all services, including National Guard and reserve members, cadets and midshipmen from the service academies, personnel on active duty for training, and individuals classified by the Department of Veterans Affairs as 100 percent disabled are eligible to use Hale Koa. Department of Defense civilian employees are also eligible.

The Hale Koa has 814 guest rooms, each offering a private bath, a refrigerator, air-conditioning, color TV, and a balcony with a panoramic view of the Pacific Ocean or the verdant Koolau Mountains. Room rates vary, depending on rank, as well as room location and the amount of ocean view afforded. The 2000 room rates based on double occupancy ranged from $61 to $163 per night. Reservations can be made up to a year in advance by calling (800) 367-6027.

The Hale Koa occupies 66 acres right on Waikiki Beach. Guests may enjoy one-third of a mile of white-sand beach for sunbathing, swimming, snorkeling, and surfing. Three freshwater swimming pools, tennis courts, and sand volleyball courts are located on the grounds. Indoors is a complete range of conveniences, including an activities desk, a fitness center, self-service laundry facilities, a post exchange, a car rental desk, a barber and beauty shop, a discount tour and travel office, and a jewelry shop.

The superb dining and entertainment facilities offered by the Hale Koa are available not only to hotel guests but to all military personnel and their guests. Weekly dinner shows include Tuesday Night Magic, Tama's Polynesian Revue, and even a Hale Koa Hawaiian Luau on the beach, all at affordable prices. Live entertainment is featured nightly in the Warriors Lounge. For quick snacks and meals, there are two outdoor snack bars with ready-to-go items like hamburgers, fried chicken, and local-style favorites. The modestly priced Koko Cafe serves breakfast, lunch, and dinner every day of the week. The pride of the hotel is its signature restaurant, the Hale Koa Room, renowned for its distinctive menu, beverages, and service. On Sundays, the Hale Koa features a champagne brunch buffet.

For more information, write to Hale Koa Hotel, 2055 Kalia Road, Honolulu, HI 96815-1998, or call (808) 955-0555. For reservations, call toll free from the continental United States, (800) 367-6027, or fax toll free to (800) HALE-FAX. Home page: *www.halekoa.com.*

IDAHO

Air Force

MOUNTAIN HOME AIR FORCE BASE

Although its name sounds like the title of a folk ballad, Mountain Home Air Force Base is appropriately named. It sits on a plateau nearly 3,000 feet above sea level and is surrounded by the Sawtooth Mountains to the northeast and the Owyhee Mountains to the southwest. Some of the peaks to the north rise as high as 9,500 feet. The Snake River, which flows by about three miles south of the base, has carved a 600-foot-deep canyon.

History. Opened in 1943, the base today is home for the Air Force's 366th Wing, which flies the F-15C Eagle air-superiority fighter, F-15E Strike Eagle air-to-ground/air-superiority fighter, F-16C Fighting Falcon multirole fighter, B-1B Lancer bomber, and KC-135-R Stratotanker air refueler. About 4,200 active-duty personnel, 6,000 family members, 2,600 Guardsmen, and 400 civilians call Mountain Home home.

Housing and Schools. More than 1,500 units of family housing are on base, situated in six housing areas. They range from row-type houses to duplex and town-house dwellings. Temporary lodging is available at the Sagebrush Hotel, and guests may be accommodated there when space is available. Elementary and junior high school students attend on-base schools; there is a senior high school in the city of Mountain Home. A child-care center is operated on base. Adult education can be obtained on base from Boise State University, Park College, Embry-Riddle Aeronautical University, and the University of Oklahoma.

Personal Services. Medical and dental care are provided by a new thirty-one-bed USAF hospital. A commissary, a base exchange, a service station, a shopette/Class VI store, and an open mess system are available.

Recreation. Recreational facilities include a 16-lane bowling center, arts and crafts and auto hobby shops, an 18-hole golf course, a rod and gun club, an indoor 25-meter swimming pool, and a riding stable with twenty acres of fenced pasture. The base Outdoor Adventure Program sponsors organized skiing, white-water rafting, hiking tours, and other outdoor events, while the recreation center sponsors a variety of trips to nearby cultural areas. The base also operates its own private marina facility at the nearby Strike Dam Recreation Area.

The Local Area. The climate in southern Idaho is dry, with hot summers and cold winters. The average annual snowfall in the Mountain Home area is only eleven inches. This means, of course, that some kind of outdoor activity is possible all year.

The base is located ten miles southwest of the friendly little town of Mountain Home (population 10,000) and 50 miles southeast of Boise, the capital city of Idaho and home to about 135,000 people. Hunting, fishing, many outdoor attractions, and lots of sightseeing are Idaho's special features. The state operates 21 parks, and there are over two dozen ski resorts there, as well as more than 3,000 miles of snowmobile trails. Deer, elk, moose, antelope, bighorn sheep, mountain goat, and black bear are hunted in the state, and many varieties of freshwater fish can be caught in its many lakes, rivers, streams, and ponds.

For more information, write to Public Affairs Office, 366th Wing Public Affairs Office, Mountain Home Air Force Base, Idaho, 366 Gunfighter Avenue, Suite 153, Mountain Home AFB, ID 83648-5392, or call (208) 828-2111. Home page: *www.mountainhome.af.mil.*

ILLINOIS

Air Force

SCOTT AIR FORCE BASE

History. Unlike all other U.S. Air Force installations, Scott AFB is named after an enlisted man, Army Cpl. Frank S. Scott, who was killed in the crash of his Wright biplane at College Park, Maryland, on 28 September 1912.

Scott AFB opened in 1917 as a training field for World War I pilots. Today the base extends over 3,000 acres and supports a population of 6,800 active-duty military personnel, their 10,000 dependents, 1,100 Reservists, 4,200 civilian employees, and 13,000 military retirees. Scott is home to the U.S. Transportation Command Headquarters, Air Mobility Command Headquarters, Air Force Communications Agency Headquarters, the 375th Airlift Wing, the 932nd Airlift Wing (Reserve), the 126th Air Refueling Wing (Air National Guard), and more than 40 other units.

Housing and Schools. Scott has more than 1,700 family quarters, as well as spaces for 104 private mobile homes. Thirty-six units of temporary housing are available for military families in transit. The cost of living in southern Illinois is moderate compared with other parts of the country.

There is an on-base school, Scott Elementary School, for younger children. Middle school and high school students attend classes at nearby community schools. There is a child-development center on base. The base educational service office offers many educational opportunities for military personnel, civilians, and their dependents at Scott. A full range of counseling and testing is available, plus college courses from such institutions as Belleville Area College, McKendree College, Park College, Webster University, and Southern Illinois University at Carbondale and Edwardsville.

Personal Services. Medical care is provided at the seventy-bed USAF medical center. Other services at Scott include a commissary with 31,375 square feet of sales space, a main exchange with many concessions, a banking facility, and a credit union. The family support center offers a variety of programs and assistance.

Recreation. Recreational facilities at Scott include an 18-hole golf course, two gymnasiums, a 24-lane bowling alley, swimming pools, an arts and crafts center, and an aero club. A rod and gun club offers three skeet and two trap ranges and a small-bore rifle and pistol range. Officers and enlisted clubs are colocated. A recreation area at Scott Lake is used for picnicking, hiking, biking, and other activities. The base also sports three outdoor swimming pools and a movie theater.

The Local Area. Scott AFB is seven miles northeast of the community of Belleville, which has a population of over 44,000. The biggest attraction in the area is St. Louis, Gateway to the West, which is 20 miles to the west of the base. St. Louis has a population of 2.5 million and is a thriving cultural and economic center on the Missouri side of the Mississippi River.

For more information, write to Public Affairs Office, Scott AFB, IL 62225-5004, or call (618) 256-4241. Home page: *http://public.scott.af.mil.*

Army

CHARLES MELVIN PRICE SUPPORT CENTER

Located in Granite City just across the Mississippi River from St. Louis, the 686 acres of the Charles Melvin Price Support Center (CMPSC) are home to the U.S. Army Reserve Personnel Center, Army Recruiting Command, 2nd Battalion, 334th Regiment, and 226th Transportation Company (Railway Engineer).

CMPSC's mission is to provide administrative, logistical, and quality-of-life support to Department of Defense and other federal agencies in the St. Louis area. There are 600 active-duty personnel assigned to the center, along with their 1,800 family members, 4,000 Guard and reserve personnel, and 250 civilian employees.

Housing and Schools. There are more than 160 units of family housing at the center. Children attend local schools, but a day-care center is available on post.

Personal Services. Health care is provided by Scott Air Force Base, about twenty-five miles southeast of Granite City, or by local institutions. A commissary and post exchange are located at the center.

Recreation. Recreational facilities include tennis courts, softball and soccer fields, a swimming pool, a bowling alley, auto and arts and crafts shops, a golf course, a library, and a gym. For those who prefer to relax with a potent beverage or delectable comestibles, there is also the Depot Junction Club.

For more information, write to U.S. Army Charles Melvin Price Support Center, Attention: AMSAM-RA-PC, Bldg. 100, Granite City, IL 62040-1801, or call (618) 452-4214. Home page: *www.cmpsc.army.mil.*

ROCK ISLAND ARSENAL

Rock Island Arsenal is a 946-acre island situated in the Mississippi River and bordered on the south by Rock Island and Moline, Illinois, and on the north by Davenport and Bettendorf, Iowa. The island is about three miles long and three-quarters of a mile wide at its widest point.

History. The island was acquired by the U.S. government through a treaty with the Indians in 1804, and Fort Armstrong was built there in 1816. The arsenal was first established in 1862, and in 1863, a prison was built there to accommodate 12,000 Confederate prisoners of war.

The total island population today is 7,000 military and civilian personnel. The arsenal is responsible for the production of carriages, recoil mechanisms for towed and self-propelled artillery, and tank armament. It is also home to HQ, U.S. Army Industrial Operations Command.

Housing and Schools. Fifty-eight sets of government family quarters are located at Rock Island. One guest transient facility is also available. Dependent children attend local public schools. A child-development center on post can accommodate 160 children, and certified child-care homes are also available.

Personal Services. Medical care is provided by the U.S. Army Health Clinic. Dependents and retired personnel are seen there by appointment. A post exchange and a commissary are also available, as are a club, a cafeteria, and a barber shop.

Recreation. The Quad Cities offer recreational opportunities and facilities for every member of the family. The area boasts more than eighty parks and playgrounds, a forest preserve, and ten public and seven private country clubs. Other facilities include archery ranges, baseball and softball diamonds, bowling alleys, bridle paths, driving ranges, horseshoe courts, movie theaters, swimming pools, trap shooting ranges, and a zoo. Arsenal Island itself contains many interesting attractions, including pre-Columbian Indian mounds and the Rock Island National Cemetery. The cemetery was established in 1865 and contains the remains of about 10,000 veterans and some of their dependents from all the services. The Confederate Cemetery contains the bodies of about 2,000 prisoners who died at Rock Island while interned there during the Civil War. On the western tip of the island is the Fort Armstrong Blockhouse replica, which was erected in 1916 on the centennial of the fort's founding. Not far from there is Pioneer Cemetery, where soldiers and early settlers of the area lie. Fort Armstrong was a focal point in the Black Hawk War of 1832, and such American greats as Zachary Taylor, Jefferson Davis, and Abraham Lincoln gathered there with the expedition that fought the Indians.

The Local Area. About 306,000 people live in the vicinity of the arsenal. Davenport has about 100,000 inhabitants, followed by Rock Island with about 50,000 and Moline with 47,000, while Bettendorf follows up with around 30,000 and East Moline with 22,000.

For more information write to Public Affairs Office, Rock Island Arsenal, Rock Island, IL 61299-5000, or call (309) 782-4786. Home page: *www.ria.army.mil.*

Navy

GREAT LAKES NAVAL TRAINING CENTER

From the day in 1911 when Great Lakes Naval Training Center received its first trainee, Seaman Recruit Joseph W. Gregg, the Naval Training Center's Recruit Command has been turning landsmen into sailors—approximately three million to date. Each year, the Recruit Training Command graduates more than 50,000 new recruits.

The total average population at Great Lakes, including the Naval Training Center, tenant commands, active-duty and civilian personnel, and their dependents, is about 30,000. This includes approximately 22,000 military personnel, their 4,500 family members, and 4,000 civilian employees. Great Lakes is a small city, and as such, it has all the facilities and services required to keep a metropolis going.

Housing and Schools. More than 2,880 sets of government quarters are available in various locations for married personnel at Great Lakes. There are also accommodations for 1,200 unmarried enlisted personnel, 7,000 students, and 13,000 recruits.

Children of Great Lakes personnel attend off-base schools in the North Chicago public school system, although a large child-care facility that can accommodate 358 children and 44 infants is operated on the base. The Navy campus offers college-level programs through local institutions, as well as night classes on base and in local schools for those who wish to complete high school graduation requirements.

Personal Services. Medical care is provided to the community at the 15-floor, 136-bed naval hospital, which has 16 clinics and 11 operating rooms. A commissary store and a Navy exchange with several branches and numerous services are available, including two automotive service stations, cafeterias, three beverage convenience stores, and a flower shop.

Recreation. Located on the shores of Lake Michigan, Great Lakes Naval Training Center offers diverse recreational opportunities year-round. Winter sports include skiing, sledding, and ice skating. During the summer, swimming is available at two beaches on base or at the outdoor pool, and there is a marina on base. A comprehensive recreation program offers something for everyone, including tennis and racquetball courts, a physical fitness center, an 18-hole golf course, and fishing areas. The recreational services department runs an excellent intramural sports program.

The Local Area. By far the biggest attractions in the area are the cities of Chicago and Milwaukee. Chicago offers a wide variety of sightseeing and recreational opportunities, from museums to the architectural wonders of the world's tallest office building. There are also Six Flags Great America amusement park and shopping in some of America's largest malls. But if the big city is not to your liking, you can always try your lungs calling hogs at the Illinois State Fair, show your prize petunias in Dixon, or just relax and visit one of the state's 62 parks.

The area averages 36 inches of snow in winter and 32 inches of rain annually. The coldest month is January, with an average temperature of 24° F; July is the warmest month, with an average temperature of 72° F.

For more information, write to Public Affairs Office, Naval Training Center, Great Lakes, IL 60088-2845, or call (847) 688-3500. Home page: *www.ntcgl.navy.mil.*

KANSAS

Air Force

MCCONNELL AIR FORCE BASE

McConnell Air Force Base lies in the southeastern quadrant of Wichita, which in the 1920s was the home of many of aviation's pioneers, such as Clyde V. Cessna, Walter H. Beech, and J. H. Engstrom. The base was established at Wichita primarily so that training in the B-47 jet bomber could take place near the aircraft factory where it was being produced. Since that time, the city has expanded out to the vicinity of the base.

History. Established in June 1951 as Wichita Air Force Base, the facility was renamed McConnell Air Force Base in 1952 in honor of two of the three "Flying McConnell Brothers" from Wichita, who enlisted in the Army Air Corps during World War II. Today the base is home to the 22nd Air Refueling Wing and several tenant units and boasts a permanent population of over 2,900 military personnel, 6,000 dependents, 1,500 Guard and reserve personnel, and 380 civilian employees.

Housing and Schools. There are 580 units of family housing at McConnell. Limited guest-house facilities are available with reservations taken only for temporary-duty personnel.

A child-care center and an elementary school for dependent children are located on base. Older children attend junior and senior high schools off base. Off-duty educational opportunities for adults are excellent. College-level courses are offered on base by Butler County Community College, Kansas Newman College, Embry-Riddle Aeronautical University, and Webster College.

Personal Services and Recreation. A commissary, base exchange facilities, a service station, officers and NCO open mess systems, banking facilities, and other personal services are available on base. Recreational facilities include a wood craft shop, an automotive center, an arts and crafts center, an outdoor swimming pool, a gymnasium, and a nine-hole golf course. A base park with an all-weather pavilion and an outdoor multipurpose recreation court are also provided.

The Local Area. Wichita is a bustling metropolis of more than 270,000 people. The city operates over 2,000 acres of parks and playgrounds and a 210-acre zoo. There are also a symphony orchestra, a ballet, and eighty private and three municipal golf courses.

For more information, write to Public Affairs Office, McConnell Air Force Base, KS 67221-5000, or call (316) 652-6100.

Home page: *www.mcconnell.af.mil.*

Army

FORT LEAVENWORTH

Fort Leavenworth is a post of many firsts. It was the first fort established west of the Missouri River, the first continuously occupied settlement in Kansas, and the site of the oldest continuously occupied house in Kansas (the Rookery, built in 1832 as a post headquarters).

History. Named after Col. Henry Leavenworth, who founded the post in 1827, Fort Leavenworth has been witness to much of the history of the American West. The Oregon and Sante Fe Trails crossed the Missouri River, and ox teams pulled loaded wagons through Fort Leavenworth on their way west. The post was an important Army headquarters in the West during the Mexican War of 1846, the Civil War, and the Indian Wars. Since 1881, it has been the home of the Army's Command and General Staff College, the oldest in the Army's advanced educational system. Since 1873, it has also been the site of the U.S. Disciplinary Barracks (the "Fort Leavenworth Long Course"). Today Fort Leavenworth is home to the U.S. Army Combined Arms Center. More than 3,100 active-duty personnel, their 4,300 dependents, and 2,200 civilian employees call Fort Leavenworth home.

Housing and Schools. Fort Leavenworth is a completely self-contained military post. It has 1,586 units of family housing and 12 guest-house units available to personnel of all ranks. Reservations are required and can be made at (913) 684-4091. The post has three elementary schools and a junior high school, as well as day-care and preschool programs; complete educational services are also available for military personnel on the post.

Personal Services and Recreation. Fort Leavenworth hosts a post exchange and commissary and the ten-bed Munson Army Health Center. The full range of support and morale services available on post includes a bowling alley; an 18-hole golf course; squash, handball, and tennis courts; a movie theater; swimming pools; gymnasiums; craft shops; and a riding stable.

The Local Area. Fort Leavenworth is adjacent to the city of Leavenworth (population 43,000), about 35 miles northwest of Kansas City, Missouri, on the Missouri River. The average temperatures range from a low of 21° F in January to a high of 92° F in July. Normal annual rainfall is 30 inches.

U.S. Cavalry Museum at Fort Riley, Kansas U.S. ARMY PHOTO

For more information, write to Headquarters, Combined Arms Center and Fort Leavenworth, Attention: Public Affairs Office, 600 Thomas Avenue, Fort Leavenworth, KS 66027-1399, or call (913) 684-5604. Home page: *www.leav.army.mil.*

FORT RILEY

Fort Riley may well be the only post in the history of the U.S. Army to have been commanded by an enlisted man. When the senior officer at the post, Maj. E. A. Ogden, died in a cholera epidemic on 3 August 1855, the installation was left temporarily without a commander. Into the gap strode ex-sergeant of dragoons Percival Lowe, Ogden's supervisor of transportation. He put down an attempted mutiny and restored order to the garrison. Approximately 200 people died during the epidemic, and their unmarked graves occupy a corner of the Fort Riley Cemetery.

History. Fort Riley was named after Maj. Gen. Bennett Riley, a Mexican War hero. Construction began on Fort Riley in May 1853. Fort Riley served as a training ground for several leaders destined for fame during the Civil War: J. E. B. Stuart, the Confederate cavalryman; Lewis Armisted, who died leading his brigade in Pickett's Charge at Gettysburg; and John Sedgwick, famed leader of the Army of the Potomac's VI Corps. During the Indian Wars, the post played an important role. The famed 7th Cavalry Regiment formed there in 1866; in 1890, the 7th was back at Riley, and it moved out from there to participate in the last campaign of the Indian Wars, which culminated at the Battle of Wounded Knee on 29 December 1890. Today Fort Riley's 101,000 acres are home for the 1st Infantry Division ("Big Red One"). It is home to more than 10,000 active-duty personnel, their 9,500 family members, 25,000 Guardsmen and reservists, and 3,500 civilian employees.

Housing and Schools. More than 3,000 sets of family quarters are available at Fort Riley, and the waiting list ranges from only a few months to over two years based on eligibility date and bedroom requirements within grade catagories. Guest-house accommodations are available in the order confirmed reservations are received, and their rates range from $18 to $30 per day. Bachelor officer and NCO housing are also available.

Fort Riley has five elementary schools and one junior high school in addition to a preschool, and a child-care center is operated to accommodate children between the ages of six weeks and twelve years. The Fort Riley Army Education Center provides a full range of educational services, from a high school completion program to graduate studies. Because these courses are offered on the post, they may be started and completed during a soldier's tour there. Classes are also available from Kansas State University, Central Michigan University, Upper Iowa University, Central Texas College, and Barton Community College.

Personal Services. Irwin Army Medical Community Hospital, a multistory, forty-eight-bed facility, offers complete patient-care services to the military personnel and their families stationed at Fort Riley. Six dental clinics are operated on post. A post exchange, a commissary (located on Camp Forsyth), and other facilities are also available.

Recreation. A full range of athletic and recreation programs is available at Fort Riley. The Outdoor Recreation Center has fishing boats and water skis for the 16,000-acre Milford Reservoir Area. There are four picnic parks on post, as well as the Camp Moon Lake picnic and playground area, and there are hunting opportunities on the 108,000 acres of nearby public land.

The Local Area. Fort Riley is located about two miles east of Junction City and 14 miles west of Manhattan, home of Kansas State University. From the post to Abilene is 25 miles; Kansas City, 130; Lawrence, 91; Topeka, 64; and Wichita, 114. Because of its location, the weather at Fort Riley is subject to frequent and often sharp changes. The winters are generally dry and cold, and the summers are hot, windy, and sometimes very humid. Just to the west of the post is Milford Lake, and immediately to the northeast is Tuttle Creek Lake and Tuttle Creek Pottawatomie State Fishing Lake, both ideal for fishing and water sports.

For more information, write to Community Relations Officer, Fort Riley, KS 66442-5016, or call (785) 239-2672. Home page: *www.riley.army.mil.*

KENTUCKY

Army

FORT CAMPBELL

Fort Campbell is situated between Hopkinsville, Kentucky, to the north and Clarksville, Tennessee, to the south, astride the Kentucky–Tennessee border with most of its acreage in Tennessee. It not only is beautiful country but also is country rich in history.

History. Named after Gen. William Bowen Campbell, a hero of the Mexican War and former governor of Tennessee, Fort Campbell came into being in February 1942 as an armor and infantry training center. In 1956, the famous 101st Airborne Division ("Screaming Eagles") was reactivated at Fort Campbell under the command of Maj. Gen. Thomas Sherburne, Jr. Known today as the 101st Airborne Division (Air Assault), the Screaming Eagles still call Fort Campbell home. Today Fort Campbell is home to 22,000 active-duty personnel, 39,000 family members, and 3,800 civilian employees. Approximately 16,000 reservists also train there.

Housing and Schools. There are more than 4,100 units of family quarters at Fort Campbell, situated in nine separate family housing areas. Transient family quarters are also available, as well as a 74-room guest house, with first priority going to incoming personnel on permanent-change-of-station orders.

Fort Campbell operates its own school system consisting of four elementary schools, two junior high schools, and a high school; prekindergarten and nursery services are also available. The Army education center offers a full range of educational services and benefits available for military personnel, including on-post college courses provided by City College of Chicago, Embry-Riddle Aeronautical University, Austin Peay State University, Murray State University, and Hopkinsville Community College.

Personal Services. Fort Campbell boasts a modern, 241-bed hospital, one of the finest facilities of its kind in the Kentucky–Tennessee area. The post exchange and commissary complex at Fort Campbell afford residents and eligible visitors the convenience of modern shopping. The post exchange mall and liquor store are open seven days a week. A large number of post exchange concessions, such as a Burger King, a Baskin Robbins, a barbecue and pizza shop, a cafeteria, an optical shop, a radio-TV repair shop, and beauty shops, are located within the modern mall.

Recreation. Entertainment and recreational activities, both indoor and outdoor, are also available on post. These range from a cabaret dinner theater to parks and picnic areas. With moderately hot summers and long and mild autumns, outdoor activities of all kinds are possible in the Fort Campbell area year-round.

The Local Area. Hopkinsville, a town of about 30,000, lies about 15 miles to the north of Fort Campbell; Louisville is 161 miles northeast. Clarksville, Tennessee (population 55,000), is five miles to the south; Nashville is 70 miles south. The area is rich in Civil War history. The Henry and Donelson Campaign took place in the area in February 1862, and Fort Donelson National Military Park and Cemetery may be seen just across Lake Barkley from Fort Campbell. North of Fort Donelson and about an hour's drive from the post is the Land Between the Lakes—170,000 acres of public land developed for outdoor recreation. Lake Barkley on the east and Kentucky Lake on the west were formed when Kentucky and Barkley Dams were constructed as part of a Tennessee Valley Authority program. They offer 220,000 surface acres of water and more than 3,500 miles of shoreline.

For more information, write to Headquarters, 101st Airborne Division (Air Assault) and Fort Campbell, Attention: AFZB-PO, Fort Campbell, KY 42223-5125, or call (502) 798-2151. Home page: *www.campbell.army.mil.*

FORT KNOX

Most people think of Fort Knox only as the site of the U.S. Bullion Depository, the structure that houses most of the gold stocks of the United States; sorry, no visitors are permitted! Less well known, yet just as important in many ways, is Fort Knox, home of the U.S. Army Armor Center; visitors are always welcome here. One can, by way of consolation, visit the "Gold Vault" in this neck of the woods.

History. Named after Maj. Gen. Henry Knox, George Washington's chief of artillery, Fort Knox was established in June 1918 as an artillery training center. In July 1940, a small armor school was created there, and since that time the installation's role has been inextricably associated with tanks. The mission of the Armor Center today is to train officers and enlisted soldiers for mounted combat and to develop weapons and tactics for their use. The Armor Center also conducts basic training and is the home of the U.S. Army Recruiting Command.

Today Fort Knox, a "Kentucky Certified City," is a post of 110,000 acres with a daytime population of over 7,800 active-duty personnel, 7,300 family members, and 5,200 civilian employees. More than 4,700 reservists also train there, while the post serves over 164,000 retired personnel and their families in the area.

Housing and Schools. Approximately 4,000 family housing units and 400 bachelor transient housing units are available. The Wickam Guest House offers hotel accommodations at considerable savings to the military traveler on a first-come, first-served basis. By way of comparion, homes near the post are about $100,000 to $115,000 for two-car garage, 2,100 to 2,500 square foot, three- to four-bedroom models. The Pritchard Housing Area, completed in summer 1999, offers 140 units to junior enlisted personnel.

Duty at Fort Knox offers soldiers and their families the advantages of gracious living to be found at all major military installations and a few that are not found at other places. The post operates nine schools for children in kindergarten through high school. Preschool and child-care centers are also available. The continuing education branch offers college courses from such institutions as the University of Kentucky, the University of Louisville, and Western Kentucky University.

Personal Services. Military personnel and their dependents are provided with the best possible medical care at the 170-bed Ireland Army Community Hospital, which has approximately two dozen general medical, surgical, and specialty clinics; in addition, five dental clinics are located on post. A large commissary and a large post exchange offering a furniture store and several annexes are located at Fort Knox.

Recreation. The morale support division operates a complete range of arts and crafts and automotive craft shops, six swimming pools, two golf courses, 25 tennis courts, six gyms and fitness centers, and other attractions. The Houston Bowling Center and Kelley Cosmic Bowling & Family Fun Center offer not just bowling but games and a wide variety of food to attract all members of the military family. The Camp Carlson Outdoor Recreation Area at Fort Knox features an Army Travel Camp with a lodge and family cabins for rent. Hunting and fishing licenses, firearms instruction, and shooting ranges are all available on post.

The private organizations at Fort Knox catering to the morale and welfare of its military families are too numerous to mention, but they range in scope and activity from Alcoholics Anonymous to the Tank Town Twirlers Round and Square Dance Club.

The Local Area. Fort Knox is located on the Indiana-Kentucky border, approximately 35 miles south of Louisville, on U.S. Route 31W. The Fort Knox area is a scenic and historical locale that offers a wide variety of outdoor activities from parks and picnic areas to hunting and fishing.

For more information, write to Public Affairs Office, U.S. Army Armor Center and Fort Knox, Attention: P.O. Box 995, ATZK-PAO, Fort Knox, KY 40121-5000, or call (502) 624-4788. Home page: *http://knox-www.army.mil.*

LOUISIANA

Air Force

BARKSDALE AIR FORCE BASE

Barksdale Air Force Base occupies over 22,000 acres near Shreveport and Bossier City and is an integral part of those communities. With a population numbering almost 6,500 active-duty military and their 10,000 dependents, 1,600 reservists, and 1,000 civilian employees, the economic impact of the base on the local area exceeds $400 million annually.

History. Dedicated in February 1933, the base is named after Lt. Eugene Hoy Barksdale, a World War I airman who died while flight testing an observation airplane in 1926. Today Barksdale is home for Headquarters, 8th Air Force, and the 2nd Bomb Wing. The wing operates the B-52 Stratofortress bomber. Barksdale is also home for the 917th Wing, which flies the A-10 Thunderbolt II and B-52H.

Housing and Schools. There are nearly 700 units of family housing at the base and 24 units of guest housing. Guest housing is reserved only for military families traveling on official orders; all others are accommodated on a space-available basis only. Although no dependent schools are operated on the base, the base education center provides a wealth of professional, academic, and vocational opportunities for adults. Louisiana Tech University, Georgia Military College, Southern Illinois University, and many others offer undergraduate and graduate programs there.

Personal Services and Recreation. Personal services and facilities include the 2nd Medical Group's acute care clinic, a base exchange, a commissary, an 18-hole golf course, a bowling alley, a gymnasium, two pools, a movie theater, a riding club, two picnic areas, hunting and fishing, and auto, wood, and arts and crafts shops, as well as a hiking trail, a canoe trail, and a skeet and archery range.

The Barksdale Family Camp, located on the installation, offers twelve camper spaces with water and electricity hookups, a softball field, and a playground, as well as areas for picnicking and camping. Equipment for rent includes tents, stoves, lanterns, and other camping supplies. The camp is situated in both open and wooded areas and has many shade trees.

The Local Area. Barksdale AFB is situated four miles east of Shreveport, within the city limits of Bossier City in the northwestern portion of Louisiana. Summer months there are consistently warm, with maximum temperatures exceeding 100° F about ten days of the year and 95° F about 45 days of the year. The humidity is high in all seasons. Spring and fall are the most pleasant times of the year, and autumn is generally the best time for outdoor activities.

Toledo Bend, Caddo, Cross, Bodcau L'Erling, and Bistineau Reservoir Lakes are nearby and offer a wide variety of water recreation from fishing to skiing, boating, and swimming.

For more information, write to Public Affairs Division, 841 Fairchild Avenue, Suite 103, Barksdale AFB, LA 71110-2270, or call (318) 456-2252. Home page: *www.barksdale.af.mil.*

Army

FORT POLK

Fort Polk has suffered from a "Camp Swampy" image through the years. As troops passed through there for training, the word got out that if you loved swamps, mosquitoes, and boredom, Polk was the place. But this image changed forever in 1974 when the 5th Infantry Division (Mechanized) moved there. Redesignated the 2nd Armored Division in 1992, the division moved to Fort Hood, Texas, to be replaced by the 2nd Armored Cavalry Regiment, Warrior Brigade and also is home to the 519th Military Police Battalion and the Joint Readiness Training Center. Today Fort Polk is home to over 7,000 active-duty personnel, nearly 9,000 family members, over 30,000 reservists, and 2,000 civilian employees.

History. Named after Confederate Gen. Leonidas Polk, Fort Polk was built in 1941 to support the famous Louisiana Maneuvers. Fort Polk has always been one of the Army's best training facilities. The reservation covers some 198,000 acres of varying terrain from dense, jungle-type environment to broad, rolling plains.

Housing and Schools. Fort Polk has nearly 5,000 sets of family quarters. The seventy-unit Magnolia House, built in 1988, offers sixty-five units for transient personnel. Bachelor officers may be assigned quarters in a new 150-suite high-rise, and senior enlisted personnel have a modern 36-suite billet. There are over 3,000 rooms available for single enlisted personnel. There are also accommodations for 119 mobile homes on the post; spaces are available on a first-come, first-served basis. Ultramodern barracks complexes resembling college dorms have replaced the old wooden facilities. Each complex includes a post exchange branch store, a snack bar, a gymnasium, a chapel, and a dining facility.

On-post schooling is conducted through the local school system for dependent children in kindergarten through fourth grade. Other children attend schools in Pickering and Leesville. The Army education center offers college programs from Central Michigan, Louisiana State, and Upper Iowa Universities and Central Texas College. Language training and testing programs of various kinds are also available. The Fort Polk campus of Northwestern University offers a four-year curriculum.

Personal Services. In 1977, a $2.5 million commissary offering 51,000 square feet of shopping space was opened, and in 1978, a large, solar-powered shopping mall was completed. The commissary was enlarged and renovated in 1989. Medical care is provided by the 169-bed Bayne-Jones Army Community Hospital (appointments can be made by calling (318) 531-3000). TRICARE is available.

Recreation. On-post recreational facilities include a bowling alley, three swimming pools, an 18-hole golf course, an auto hobby shop, a skeet and trap range, over a dozen tennis courts, a lake, a dinner theater, a new athletic complex, a theater program and dinner theater, and a youth activities center.

The Local Area. The rolling hills of western Louisiana are a sportsman's paradise. The year-round mild climate permits constant outdoor activity. Fort Polk maintains the Toledo Bend Recreation Facility, with mobile homes for rent, located to the northwest of the post on the Toledo Bend Reservoir on the Texas–Louisiana border. The Lake Charles area, noted as a water sports center for the entire Gulf Coast region, is located 60 miles south of Fort Polk; the country south of Lake Charles is composed of deep marshes providing the finest duck and goose hunting in the country. The Gulf of Mexico lies a little less than 100 miles south of the reservation.

Fort Polk is adjacent to the small communities of DeRidder (population 10,300), eight miles south of Leesville (population 7,600), New Llano (population 2,600), and Rosepine (population 1,500). The city of Alexandria to the northeast of the post has excellent shopping centers, recreational activities, and historical attractions. Just a few miles south of the Alexandria-Pineville area begins the Cajun country, with its French heritage. Baton Rouge is about 100 miles to the southeast of Alexandria, New Orleans is 150 miles southeast, and Houston is 195 miles southwest.

For more information, write to Joint Readiness Training Center and Fort Polk, Fort Polk, LA 71459-5000, or call (318) 531-2911. Home page: *www.jrtc-polk.army.mil.*

Navy

NEW ORLEANS NAVAL AIR STATION

Nestled among 3,200 acres along the west bank of the Mississippi River, 12 miles southeast of New Orleans, New Orleans Naval Air Station is home to

1,200 full-time active-duty personnel, 865 family members, almost 900 civilian employees, and 3,400 reservists. It is the first military installation in the nation to be designed, built, and commissioned as a joint-use facility (Navy, Air Force, Marines, and Coast Guard).

History. The station was commissioned in December 1957, and in January 1958, the first aircraft were flown from the new runways. In April 1958, the installation was dedicated to Alvin Andrew Callender, a native of New Orleans who lost his life in World War II. Therefore, the station is sometimes referred to as Callender Field. Today the station is home to Fleet Logistics Support Squadron 54, Marine Air Group 46, and Air Force Reserve and Louisiana Air National Guard units, as well as other tenant commands, including a Coast Guard.

Housing and Schools. There are 216 units of family housing available at New Orleans NAS, as well as a 22-unit Navy Lodge at the Naval Support Activity, just off General de Gaulle Avenue, not far from the Superdome.

Schools for dependent children are available in the surrounding area, but a day-care center is operated on the station. The Navy Campus offers classes toward bachelor's and master's degrees on the air station and at the Naval Support Activity. In addition, the city of New Orleans offers many educational opportunities for military personnel in their off-duty time.

Personal Services and Recreation. There is a branch of the Navy exchange at the station, but commissary and main exchange facilities are located at the Naval Support Activity nearby. A dispensary provides medical care for personnel onboard the station. The special services department operates recreational equipment rental, a swimming pool, picnic grounds, athletic courts and fields, boat and camper rentals, an auto hobby shop, a bowling center, and a gym. Also available is an 18-hole golf course and an ongoing intramural sports program.

For more information, write to Commanding Officer, Attention: Code 005, NAS, New Orleans, LA 70143-5012, or call (504) 678-3253.

NEW ORLEANS NAVAL SUPPORT ACTIVITY

Situated on both banks of the Mississippi River, the New Orleans Naval Support Activity (NSA) has a complement of over 3,800 active-duty personnel, 700 family members, and more than 2,400 civilian employees.

History. The west bank portion of the NSA has been of interest to the Navy since 1849, when the site was originally purchased for a Navy yard, which was never developed. Today the west bank facility is home to the NSA and other activities, such as the Medical Clinic New Orleans, Special Boat Unit 22, and HQ 8th Marine Corps District.

The east bank facility was acquired in 1919 and today houses the operations of a number of active-duty and reserve component commands, including Commander Naval Reserve Force, Commander Marine Forces Reserve,

Enlisted Personnel Management Center, Fast Sealift Squadron 1, Military Sealift Command Unit New Orleans, and Navy Recruiting District New Orleans.

Housing and Schools. The NSA manages over 200 units of family housing situated on or near the base. Bachelor officer and enlisted accommodations are available in a twenty-two-unit Navy Lodge. Children attend the Orleans Parish public schools. A child-care facility for 42 children is available at the west bank facility. College courses available through the Navy Campus are provided by Northwood Institute and Troy State University.

Personal Services. Outpatient medical care is provided by the Naval Medical Clinic New Orleans. A clinic is also available at the naval air station in Belle Chasse. Definitive medical care is available from local hospitals or at Keesler Air Force Base, Mississippi. A commissary store and Navy exchange are available, as well as a minimart and package store, a service station, an optical shop, barber and beauty shops, a cafeteria, and other retail outlets.

Recreation. For those who enjoy relaxing over food and drink, the NSA offers the Fairwinds officers/chief petty officers' club, the Port-O-Call all-hands dining facility, and the Big Easy West enlisted club. There is also a McDonald's in the Navy exchange.

More strenuous recreational activities are available at the swimming pool; an eight-lane bowling center; fitness centers on both banks of the Mississippi; tennis, racquetball, and basketball courts; and softball and football/soccer fields. A picnic grounds and a recreational trailer park with sixteen hookups are also available. And for those who wish to read about life on the Mississippi, there is a 13,000-volume library open to all.

Shuttle boat service across the Mississippi is available on a scheduled basis throughout the day during the week.

For more information, write to Public Affairs Office, Naval Support Activity, 2300 General Meyer Avenue, New Orleans, LA 70142-5007, or call (504) 678-5011. Home page: *www.navy.mil/navresfor/nsa.*

MAINE

Navy

BRUNSWICK NAVAL AIR STATION

History. Brunswick was first settled in 1628 by Thomas Purchase, who fled to Boston in 1675 after his settlement was attacked by Indians during King Philip's War. Built on land that for two centuries had been used for growing blueberries, Brunswick NAS was commissioned in April 1943 to train Royal Canadian Air Force pilots in formation flying, gunnery, and carrier landings. Today the station is home to the 2,700 military personnel, 6,900 family members, 600 civilian employees, and 945 reservists of four maritime patrol squadrons and other tenant commands.

Housing and Schools. There are 756 sets of family quarters on the station: 118 officer and 638 enlisted. The on-base housing shortage is critical. Local monthly rentals vary from $400 to $700 for one-bedroom apartments to $750 to $1,200 for four-bedroom houses. Utilities are often extra and, because of the severity of the winters in Maine, can add up to $200 per month to those costs. There are 40 rental mobile home spaces available. The station also has a 16-unit Navy Lodge motel. Personnel not on permanent-change-of-station orders are accommodated on a space-available basis.

School-age children attend schools off base, but a nursery and a preschool are operated on the station. The Navy Campus offers programs from high school completion to undergraduate and postgraduate college courses, as well as vocational courses and educational testing. College degree programs are offered by New Hampshire College.

Personal Services and Recreation. Medical service at Brunswick is provided by a branch clinic. There is no inpatient medical care, and outpatients are seen by appointment only, except for emergencies. Martin's Point Medical Facilities also provide a range of medical services to uniformed personnel and dependents.

A commissary and a Navy exchange with many customer services are available at Brunswick. The morale, welfare, and recreational services office operates a well-equipped fitness center, a nine-hole golf course, a hobby complex, picnic grounds, a twelve-lane bowling alley, tennis courts, an indoor swimming pool, and other recreational facilities and programs.

The Local Area. Hunting, fishing, hiking, and skiing are among the outdoor attractions either on the station or nearby. In 1978, over five kilometers of cross-country ski trails were completed on the base. Good hunting and fishing can be enjoyed within a short drive of the base. Outdoor recreational equipment, from skis to motorized canoes, can be rented through the station recreational services office. Outdoorsmen especially should remember that the weather in Maine is unpredictable, with warm and humid summers and lots of snow and cold in the winter. The average snowfall is about 77 inches annually. With 3,500 miles of coastline, 6,000 lakes, and 5,100 rivers, Maine is one of the most beautiful states in the Union.

The town of Brunswick has about 20,000 people, and Topsham, across the Androscoggin River, has 7,000 more. Bath, a few miles east of the station on the Kennebec River, is a thriving little community of 10,000, best known for its marine museum and the Bath Iron Works, a prime contractor for the Navy. Brunswick lies about halfway between Portland to the south and Augusta, the state capital, to the north, and is accessible by Interstate 95.

For more information, write to Public Affairs Officer, NAS, Brunswick, ME 04011-5000, or call (207) 921-1110.

WINTER HARBOR NAVAL SECURITY GROUP ACTIVITY

History. The Navy first came to this area in August 1917, when a radio station was commissioned at Otter Cliffs, about five miles across Frenchman Bay from the current main base on the tip of the Schoodic Peninsula. The main site was opened in 1935 as the U.S. Navy Radio and Direction Finding Station, Winter Harbor. (The town of Winter Harbor lies five miles north of the main base, on the other side of the eastern extension of Acadia National Park.) In 1958, the station's name was changed to Naval Security Group Activity (NSGA), Winter Harbor.

Today the NSGA plays a vital role in the Navy's Tactical Ocean Surveillance System, training people who maintain and operate it worldwide. The NSGA has a complement of 370 active-duty personnel and 114 civilian employees. About 200 family members also call Winter Harbor home.

Housing and Schools. The NSGA operates five housing areas consisting of a total of 124 family housing units. The waiting time for these quarters is from one to three months. There are accommodations at the main site for about 195 unaccompanied personnel. Local rental housing is in short supply and short-term to accommodate the tourist season (May through September). Utilities during the winter can run as much as $200 per month.

Dependent children attend schools in Winter Harbor and East Sullivan. There is a child-development center at the main site that can accommodate 26 children, ages six weeks to six years.

Personal Services. Medical and dental care are provided by branch clinics at the main site. Definitive medical care is available in Bandgor and Ellsworth, Maine. There is a Navy exchange at Winter Harbor, as well as a gas station and a galley/mess hall. At the main site is also a small but well-stocked commissary store.

Recreation. The NSGA operates five house trailers and six recreation cabins, fully furnished and open year-round. Reservations are recommended, especially during the summer months. There is also a campground with seven camper sites and three tent sites that is open 15 April through 15 October. For those who enjoy outdoor sports, there are two miles of hiking trails on base through wooded and shorefront areas, tennis and racquetball/handball courts, and a multiuse recreation area that includes a ball field, a playground, and barbecue pits. Indoor recreation facilities include a community center, a gym and fitness room, a four-lane bowling alley, an auto hobby shop, and a skating rink.

The Local Area. Maine has four distinct seasons with variable weather. Summers are mild with temperatures averaging in the 70s. Fog is common along the coast. Winter sees subfreezing temperatures, snow, wind, and frequent storms. Winter driving can be very hazardous. Overall, however, Maine is one of the most beautiful states in the nation, with more than 17 million acres of forestland, 3,500 miles of coastline, 6,000 lakes, and 5,100 rivers.

For more information, write to Commanding Officer, Naval Security Group Activity, 10 Fabbri Green, Suite 10, Winter Harbor, ME 04693-7001, or call (207) 963-5534. Home page: *www.navy.mil/homepage/nsgawh/home.html.*

MARYLAND

Air Force

ANDREWS AIR FORCE BASE

Almost everybody who is anybody has landed at Andrews Air Force Base at one time or another since it was opened in 1942; the base serves as the aerial port of entry for visiting foreign heads of state and other official U.S. government visitors. It is also the home base for the president's plane, Air Force One. But there are many other activities at the base—none quite so glamorous as receiving kings and presidents, but important nonetheless.

History. The installation was known as Camp Springs Army Airfield when it first opened in 1942. Its name was changed in 1945 to honor Lt. Frank M. Andrews, who was killed in an air crash in 1943. Today the base covers over 4,300 acres ten miles southeast of Washington, D.C., and is both home and workplace for 7,600 active-duty personnel, their 15,000 dependents, and 1,700 civilian employees. The major unit is the 89th Airlift Wing.

Housing and Schools. There are over 2,000 units of family housing at Andrews, plus 1,200 additional units at nearby Summerfield, 400 of which are for Air Force personnel. Andrews has over 2,200 dormitory spaces for single enlisted personnel.

Schooling is available in Prince George's County. Adult education programs at the base are excellent. Undergraduate courses are offered by Prince George's Community College, the University of Maryland, and others. Embry-Riddle Aeronautical University, Florida Institute of Technology, and Central Michigan University offer graduate programs on the base. Sixty colleges and universities are located within commuting distance of the base, making it one of the finest spots in the Air Force for higher education.

Personal Services. Other services are also excellent. Malcolm Grow USAF Medical Center, a 185-bed multispecialty hospital and dental facility, offers definitive medical care. A complete commissary and base exchange complex are also available.

Recreation. The base has two eighteen-hole golf courses, a skeet range, a 24-lane bowling center, tennis courts, three outdoor swimming pools, auto and wood hobby shops, a ski and camping shop, a frame shop, a 1,000-seat base theater, officers and NCO clubs, and a family camping area that offers tent sites and 12 spaces for campers with hookups. The 234-acre Summerfield housing area includes a 34-acre park with tennis, basketball, softball, and soccer.

The Local Area. The recreational activities available to Air Force personnel stationed in the Washington, D.C., area are too numerous to mention here. The nation's capital offers almost unlimited attractions, from touring government buildings to visiting museums and attending concerts. A great variety of restaurants and nightclubs abound in the District of Columbia, and major points of interest in both Virginia and Maryland are within easy driving distance of the base. A family cannot see all the things there are to see or do all the things there are to do in this remarkable part of the United States on just one tour at the base.

For more information, write to 89 AW/PAA, Building 1535 Command Drive, Suite A207, Andrews AFB, MD 20762-7002, or call (301) 981-1110. Home page: *www.andrews.mil.*

Army

ABERDEEN PROVING GROUND

Aberdeen Proving Ground (APG), the Army's oldest active proving ground, was established on 14 December 1917. Located on a 72,500-acre tract extending along and into the Chesapeake Bay, APG provides installation support services to more than 55 tenant activities. Aberdeen includes two distinct areas separated by the Bush River: the Aberdeen Area and the Edgewood Area (formerly Edgewood Arsenal). Today APG is home to the U.S. Army Test and Evaluation Command, the U.S. Army Ordnance Center, and the Army Research Laboratory, with a daytime population of 4,500 military personnel, 7,600 civilian employees, and nearly 2,900 family members.

Housing and Schools. More than 1,100 sets of family quarters are located at Aberdeen, including 70 trailer spaces. Unaccompanied enlisted personnel are accommodated in over 4,000 barracks spaces. Transient accommodations include a 45-room guest house. Children attend schools in Harford County. The two child-development centers available on post have a capacity of over 150 children.

Personal Services. Health care at Aberdeen is provided by the Kirk Army health clinic that provides optometry, pediatric care, internal medicine, gynecology, physical therapy, general medicine, surgery, and dental treatment. Inpatient care is available at Fort Meade and Walter Reed Army Medical Center. A large commissary and a large exchange are located at Aberdeen, with small exchange and commissary annexes at nearby Edgewood.

Recreation. Two physical fitness centers, three gyms, two recreation centers, six arts and crafts centers, two golf courses, a theater, two libraries, and fishing, hunting, camping, and picnicking can all be enjoyed at Aberdeen. APG is also home to the U.S. Army Ordnance Museum, displaying a collection of U.S. and foreign tanks from WWI onward that literally stretches for one mile. It also boasts a twenty-five-acre tank/artillery park exhibiting 225 items. The museum is open every day during daylight hours.

For more information, write to Public Affairs Office, USA Garrison, Attention: STEAP-IM-PA, Aberdeen Proving Ground, MD 21005-5055, or call (410) 278-1153. Home page: *www.apg.army.mil.*

FORT DETRICK

Medical research is the major activity at Fort Detrick. Its 1,200-acre site is home to the U.S. Army Medical Research and Materiel Command, including the U.S. Army Medical Research Institute of Infectious Diseases and the National Cancer Institute. Fort Detrick's population consists of more than 1,300 active-duty military personnel, their 1,700 family members, and more than 2,000 civilian scientists and technicians.

Housing and Schools. Housing is tight at Fort Detrick, with only 155 units—30 for officers and 125 for enlisted personnel. There is usually a waiting period of six to nine months before on-post housing becomes available. Adequate housing can be obtained in Frederick, and new arrivals normally locate off-post housing within two weeks; the housing referral office assists newcomers in the home-hunting process.

Dependent children of military personnel stationed at Fort Detrick attend local schools in Frederick County, but a child-care and development center is located on post for children from six weeks to 12 years of age. Also available is an in-home family child-care program provided by adults living in government quarters who are certified by Fort Detrick's child-development services office. Adult educational services are provided by the post education center, which arranges tuition assistance for eligible personnel to attend college courses at local campuses, such as Hood College or Frederick Community College, in Frederick, or Mount Saint Mary's College, located nearby.

Personal Services. A new commissary opened at Fort Detrick in the spring of 1992. The commissary at Fort Meade, 35 miles away, is also available. The post exchange complex at Fort Detrick is a modern self-service store. Near the post exchange are laundry and dry-cleaning services and a hair-care facility. A military clothing sales store opened in January 1993. A three-pump gas station is also operated by the exchange service.

Routine health care is provided by a health clinic and a dental clinic. The latter offers care to retired personnel and family members on a space-available basis. Referral hospitals for specialized or emergency inpatient care are located in Frederick or the Washington, D.C., area.

Recreation. A variety of recreational activities are available on post, including the post field house, which provides basketball, racquetball, squash, handball, weight training, and a sauna. The post also has six surfaced tennis courts, a four-lane bowling center, family garden plots, an outdoor swimming pool, a well-stocked library, and picnicking and fishing at the Nallin Farm Recreational Area. The information, ticketing, and registration office offers discount tickets to amusement parks in Maryland, Virginia, and Pennsylvania, and tickets and transportation to various sporting and cultural events throughout the area.

The Local Area. Frederick is a community of 50,000 that was laid out in 1745. It was in the Frederick County Courthouse that on 23 November 1765 twelve judges proclaimed the first repudiation of the British Stamp Act, an act of defiance that led eventually to the American Revolution. Hessian prisoners from various Revolutionary War battles were once quartered in the stone barracks, which is still standing on the grounds of the Maryland School for the Deaf. Frederick is also famous as the last resting place of Francis Scott Key, composer of the "Star-Spangled Banner."

Despite its proximity to Washington and Baltimore and its own gradual expansion over the years, Frederick remains essentially an agricultural community with a quiet charm characteristic of small-town America. Nevertheless, many high-tech research firms have moved into the area so that Frederick today is considered a part of the Washington–Baltimore metropolitan area, with a corresponding rise in housing costs. But the city abounds with parks and playgrounds, and the downtown area, complete with shops and restaurants of every kind, has been dubbed "Georgetown North," after the exclusive Georgetown area of the District of Columbia.

For more information, write to Public Affairs Office, Fort Detrick, MD 21702-5000, or call (301) 619-8000.

Home page: *www.armymedicine.army.mil/detrick.*

FORT MEADE

History. Established in May 1917 and named in honor of Maj. Gen. George G. Meade, who commanded the Union Army at the Battle of Gettysburg, today Fort Meade comprises over 6,000 acres between Baltimore and Washington, D.C., just a few miles south of the Baltimore–Washington International Airport. It is home for the 9,000 active-duty personnel, 5,900 family members, and more than 30,000 civilian employees of the National Security Agency and many other units and activities.

Housing and Schools. There are more than 2,800 sets of family quarters on the post, allocated into several different housing areas. A guest house with 54 units is also available there.

Fort Meade has four elementary schools, a middle school, and a high school. There is also a child-care center capable of handling up to 570 children.

Adult education is available through the Army education center. College courses are offered from the University of Maryland, Bowie State University, George Washington University, American University, and Central Michigan University.

Personal Services. Medical care at Fort Meade is provided by the Kimbrough Ambulatory Care Center. A commissary and main post exchange shopping complex are also available. Post exchange concessions range from a beauty shop to a tailor service, and several branch exchanges operate throughout the post.

Recreation. Excellent recreational facilities are offered at Fort Meade. For the person who enjoys indoor activities, the McGill Recreation Center has a ballroom, a stage and dressing rooms, a lounge, and classroom and game areas. The Gaffney Sports Arena offers basketball, squash, and handball courts; a sauna; weight rooms; and a twenty-five-meter Olympic swimming pool. And the club system on post allows sportsters to relax over a cup of decaf after a hard session of toning up the muscles. Also on post are a 36-lane bowling center, a large post theater, and an arts and crafts center.

Outdoor recreation facilities at Fort Meade include Burba Park, a recreation area with a lake, four picnic pavilions, and a cottage. In addition, there are two 18-hole golf courses, a rod and gun club, a riding stable, 17 tennis courts, two outdoor swimming pools, and an equipment issue facility.

The Local Area. Fort Meade is centrally located for the serious sightseer. Baltimore, suburban Maryland, Washington, D.C., and northern Virginia are all accessible by bus or subway. Historic Annapolis, the majestic Chesapeake Bay, and the Eastern Shore of Maryland are all less than a 30-minute drive from Fort Meade.

For more information, write to Garrison Public Affairs Office, ANME-PA, Fort George G. Meade, MD 20755-5025, or call (301) 677-6261. Home page: *www.ftmeade.army.mil.*

Navy

ANNAPOLIS NAVAL STATION

Situated just across the Severn River from the U.S. Naval Academy, the Annapolis Naval Station's existence has been inextricably entwined with that of the naval academy for nearly 150 years.

History. The U.S. Navy first came to this part of Maryland in 1851, six years after the founding of the naval academy, when the first midshipman training ship, *USS Preble,* arrived at what was then Fort Severn. The academy was officially commissioned 15 May 1947. Today the 850 active-duty personnel, 230 family members, and 300 civilian employees at the station provide service support for the professional development of the midshipmen through small-craft operations, the Robert Crown Sailing Center, the Naval Construction Battalion Unit 403, and the Marine barracks.

Housing and Schools. There are 422 units of family housing and sixteen mobile-home pads available to personnel assigned to the station, but they are shared by naval academy faculty and staff. Unaccompanied enlisted personnel are billeted at the station; about 200 beds are available. The station also has a Navy Lodge with 50 rooms available. Reservations may be made by calling (800) NAVYINN.

The Naval Academy Primary School, located on the station golf course, accommodates children from prekindergarten through the fifth grade. A child-care center with a capacity of 105 children is also on base.

Personal Services. A commissary-Navy exchange complex is located just outside the naval station's main gate. This includes barber and beauty shops, a car rental place, a flower shop, a gift wrap and package delivery service, a garden shop, laundry and dry-cleaning services, an optical shop, and a tailor shop. There are also a gas station, a minimart, a beverage store, and a McDonald's.

Primary medical care is available at the naval medical clinic at the academy complex. There is a branch dental clinic onboard the station. Emergency and specialized medical care are available at the National Naval Medical Center in Bethesda, outside Washington, D.C., or at Anne Arundel General Hospital and Medical Center in Annapolis.

Recreation. In addition to the Naval Academy Golf Course, which borders the north side of the naval station, onboard are a marina, auto and wood hobby shops, a swimming pool, a tennis court, picnic grounds, and Little League, hardball, and softball fields. Adjacent to the picnic grounds is the Retelle Recreation Area, with a fishing pier, 14 RV campsites, tenting, and a party room. The marina can accommodate boats up to thirty feet. Two sailboats, one 27 feet and the other 28 feet long, are available for rental, as are smaller boats and windsurfing boards.

The Clipper Club, an all-hands facility featuring family dinners, special events, and other activities, is located just inside the main gate. The officers club is located at the Naval Academy.

For more information, write to Commanding Officer, Naval Station, 58 Bennion Road, Annapolis, MD 21402-5054, or call (410) 293-1000. Home page: *www.usna.edu/naval/station.*

BETHESDA NATIONAL NAVAL MEDICAL CENTER

Located just across Wisconsin Avenue from the National Institutes of Health and one mile inside the Capital Beltway (Interstate 495), the National Naval Medical Center (NNMC) in Bethesda is certainly one of the most important, well-known, and attractive military installations in the entire Washington-Baltimore metropolitan area.

History. The site for the NNMC was personally selected by President Franklin D. Roosevelt in 1938. The year before, using a piece of White House stationery, he sketched the design for the center's main hospital building.

Groundbreaking took place on 29 June 1939, and the center was officially commissioned on 5 February 1942.

Today, the center is staffed by 2,200 military and 1,200 civilians. As the referral medical facility for cases worldwide, NNMC admits over 17,000 patients each year and, with an operating capacity of more than 210 beds, is one of the largest medical facilities in the United States. The center itself comprises ten adjoining buildings. Building 1, which rises more than 18 stories above the center grounds, is the original hospital building. Today it houses the NNMC headquarters, outpatient clinics, and offices. Other activities onboard the center include the Uniformed Services University of the Health Sciences, a fully accredited medical school operated by the Assistant Secretary of Defense for Health Affairs, the Armed Forces Radiobiology Research Institute, the Naval School of Health Sciences, the Naval Medical Research Institute, and others.

Housing and Schools. At the center itself are only eight sets of family quarters, all for officers. Enlisted housing is available nearby in the form of fifty rental units for personnel in pay grades E-4 and above. Eligible military personnel are authorized housing at nearby installations operated by the Naval District Washington and other services. Bachelor officer and enlisted accommodations are available at the center. The Navy Lodge at the center has 22 units available at the rate of $35 per day for families on permanent-change-of-station orders and the relatives of inpatients at the NNMC. The Zachary and Elizabeth Fisher House offers accommodations for military families undergoing life-threatening medical crises. It can accommodate up to 16 people in its seven units.

The children of personnel assigned to the NNMC attend local public schools. A child-care center at the NNMC has a capacity of 300 children. Adult education is available from colleges and schools throughout the area.

Personal Services. Although the NNMC has no commissary, a small Navy exchange is available, as well as a minimart, a package store, a restaurant, a Baskin Robbins ice cream shop, and a service station. Commissary facilities are available at nearby military installations, such as Fort Myer and Fort Meade.

Recreation. Both officers and enlisted clubs are available at the center, as well as a gym with an indoor swimming pool, a spa, a sauna, and a weight and Nautilus room; five tennis courts; a 20-lane bowling center; and an intramural sports program.

For more information, write to Public Affairs, National Naval Medical Center, Bethesda, MD 20889-5600, or call (301) 295-4611. Home page: *www.nnmc.med.navy.mil.*

PATUXENT RIVER NAVAL AIR STATION

History. The present quarters of the Naval Air Warfare Center Aircraft Division commander—part of the Mattapany Estate—are built upon the site of a Jesuit mission that was established there shortly after 1634. This was the same year local Indians saw property values skyrocket when the first white settlers landed at Saint Mary's, about seven miles from the station's main gate. The mission property was confiscated by Lord Baltimore, and some of the original structure of a brick home built on the site in 1666 was incorporated into the existing structure, which may date from as early as 1722. Quarters "W," the official residence of the Naval Air Station commander, the Somerville House, was built by Dr. George Somerville between 1780 and 1790.

Today the major activity at Patuxent River NAS is the Naval Air Systems Command and the Naval Air Warfare Center Aircraft Division, which has as its mission the full spectrum of research, development, test and evaluation, engineering, and fleet support for air platforms. Station population includes over 3,000 active-duty personnel, over 2,000 dependents, and nearly 8,000 civilian employees.

Housing and Schools. Although there are 796 housing units at the station, there is a 90-day to two-year waiting period for them. A new temporary Navy lodging facility opened in 1991.

Public and private schools are available in Saint Mary's County for dependent children, but there are a day school and child-care center onboard the station. Active-duty personnel and dependents may take courses from a number of colleges, including Embry-Riddle Aeronautical University, the University of Maryland, the University of Tennessee Space Institute, and Florida Tech School of Extended Graduate Studies. Other educational opportunities are available through the Southern Maryland Higher Education Center.

Personal Services. Personal services available at the station include a naval clinic with a full range of outpatient services. The commissary and the Navy exchange provide a complete line of merchandise, along with dry-cleaning services, Western Union, UPS, engraving, film developing, and a flower shop.

Recreation. Recreational facilities include an officers and enlisted club system, a community center, a bowling center, and indoor and outdoor swimming pools. Outdoor facilities include the West Basin Marina, an 18-hole golf course, a three-barn stable, and numerous campgrounds. Several of these have water and electrical hookups, while others are primitive tent or self-contained trailer sites; a large number of 15- and 23-foot camper trailers may be rented through the auto hobby shop at the station.

The Local Area. Saint Mary's County, located at the southernmost tip of the state of Maryland, is surrounded by water, the Potomac River to the west and the Patuxent River to the east. The southernmost portion of the land juts into the Chesapeake Bay. Washington, D.C., is 65 miles to the northwest of Lexington Park, a small community situated just outside the station's main gate; Baltimore is seventy-nine miles to the north.

For more information, write to Public Affairs, Commanding Officer, Attention: NAS PAO Building 409, 22268 Cedar Point Road, Unit NASAD, NAS, Patuxent River, MD 20670-1154, or call (301) 342-3000. Home page: *www.nawcad.navy.mil/pax.*

U.S. Naval Academy at Annapolis, Maryland U.S. NAVY PHOTO

U.S. NAVAL ACADEMY

The U.S. Naval Academy's mission, quite simply stated, is to develop midshipmen morally, mentally, and physically and to imbue them with the highest ideals of duty, honor, and loyalty in order to provide graduates who are dedicated to a career of naval service and have potential for future development in mind and character to assume the highest responsibilities of command, citizenship, and government.

History. The naval academy was originally founded as the Naval School in October 1845. The Naval School was redesignated the U.S. Naval Academy in 1850.

The academy accomplishes its mission on a beautiful 338-acre site located on the south shore of the Severn River at Annapolis, the capital of Maryland and one of the oldest communities in the East. The commandant of midshipmen commands a 4,000-member brigade of midshipmen, whose education is directed toward a bachelor of science degree and a commission in the Navy or Marine Corps.

The academy is supported by the personnel of Annapolis Naval Station, a subordinate command of the academy, located across the river.

The academy's population consists of 4,000 midshipmen, 1,400 active-duty personnel, and their 1,000 family members and 1,500 civilian employees.

Housing and Schools. There are over 400 units of family housing at the station for officers and enlisted personnel assigned there. Guest or temporary housing is limited, but a Navy Lodge opened in early 1999 to help relieve the housing demand. A dependent school for children through the fifth grade is operated at the station, and a child-care center is operated by the morale, welfare, and recreation office. Dependent children may attend advanced schools, public and private, in the Annapolis area.

Personal Services. A commissary and Navy exchange are located on the naval station. The latter provides a number of outlets, including a gas station, a garden shop, and a minimart.

Recreation. The MWR office at the naval station offers recreational programs and facilities ranging from golf tournaments to intramural sports. Sailing facilities and qualified instructors are also available, as is a marina for the use of all personnel who own boats. There are also a swimming pool, an ice rink, a movie theater, and a gymnasium onboard the naval station.

The Local Area. Founded originally in 1649 as Providence, Annapolis today is a picturesque community of 35,000 inhabitants. It is situated about midway between Washington, D.C., and Baltimore in what is primarily farming country. Many original eighteenth-century buildings are preserved within the city's boundaries. The waterfront section of the city is a registered national historic landmark. Annapolis is a two-hour drive from the Civil War battlefield at Antietam. Baltimore, one of the most important seaports on the Atlantic Coast, is thirty miles north of Annapolis and contains many historic and cultural attractions, including the Fort McHenry National Shrine and Museum. Across the Chesapeake Bay from Annapolis is the famed Maryland Eastern Shore, and beyond is the Delaware–Maryland–Virginia Atlantic coastline.

For more information, write to Public Affairs Officer, U.S. Naval Academy, 121 Blake Road, Annapolis, MD 21402-5000, or call (410) 293-1000. Home page: *www.usna.edu;* Web address (other information): *www.visit-annapolis.org.*

MASSACHUSETTS

Air Force

HANSCOM AIR FORCE BASE

Hanscom Air Force Base owns neither runways nor aircraft. No military aircraft have been stationed there since 1973. Neither does Hanscom handle weapons systems or munitions. Hanscom Air Force Base handles information, and as all military personnel know, information is power.

History. Named in honor of Laurence G. Hanscom, who died in an aircraft crash in 1941, the base opened in May 1941 as a training installation. Today it is home for the Electronic System Center (ESC) of the U.S. Air Force. ESC develops electronic systems that enable Air Force commanders to make the most effective use of their forces. Were it an industrial corporation, it would rank in the upper half of Fortune's listing of the 500 largest American corporations. Over 2,000 civilian professionals—engineers, computer specialists, business managers, logisticians, and contracting specialists—assist in the ESC mission in company with 2,400 active-duty personnel and 3,500 dependents.

Housing and Schools. Hanscom has 800 units of family housing plus 42 temporary lodging units for transient families. The Hartwell Mobile Home Park has 98 trailer sites as well. A child-care center and a preschool are operated on the base, as is an elementary school for children in kindergarten through eighth grade. Educational opportunities for adults are available on the base from such institutions as Western New England College.

Personal Services. A USAF clinic provides outpatient medical care for active-duty personnel and their dependents at Hanscom. The U.S. Public Health Service Hospital at Brighton is used for referrals. A base exchange and commissary are available on the installation, as well as officers and NCO open messes.

Recreation. Recreational facilities and programs include a 12-lane bowling center, an Olympic-size swimming pool, a fitness center, tennis courts, and an auto shop. The base shares a nine-hole golf course about four miles from the base with the Veterans Hospital in Bedford, five miles away. Base personnel also have access to the Fourth Cliff Recreational Area, located on the tip of a small peninsula south of Boston. The site offers 16 chalets, 11 camper spaces, and 20 tent sites. Swimming, fishing, and picnicking are permitted there.

The Local Area. Hanscom is located about 18 miles northwest of Boston, within the boundaries of four of the most historic towns in the United States—Lexington, Concord, Bedford, and Lincoln—placing it in the center of American Revolution country. Bedford produced the only flag carried in the initial combat against the British, and south of the base lies Walden Pond, made famous by Henry David Thoreau. Nearby are also the homes of Ralph Waldo Emerson, Louisa May Alcott, and Nathaniel Hawthorne.

Massachusetts offers a great variety of cultural and recreational opportunities. The state has 1,500 miles of Atlantic coastline, 270 golf courses, 29 state forests, and 40 skiing areas.

For more information, write to Public Affairs Office, 9 Eglin Street, Hanscom AFB, MA 01731-5000, or call (718) 377-4466. Home page: *www.hanscom.af.mil.*

Coast Guard

CAPE COD COAST GUARD AIR STATION

The Cape Cod Air Station is located in one of the most famous tourist areas of the country, and the thousands of people who visit Cape Cod each season give the men and women of the air station plenty of business—more than 400 search-and-rescue missions per year.

History. Established in 1970 as a tenant command at Otis Air Force Base when Air Station Salem, Massachusetts, and Air Detachment Quonset Point, Rhode Island, were consolidated, Cape Cod Air Station became the largest active-duty military command in the area when the Air Force departed in 1973. Today it is home to more than 300 military personnel, 2,000 family members, and 230 civilian personnel. Air station crews fly both helicopters and fixed-wing aircraft in the performance of a variety of Coast Guard missions in the offshore areas from the Canadian border to central New Jersey.

Housing and Schools. There are 631 sets of family quarters on base, consisting of single ranch-type units, single flat-top units, and multiplex units. The waiting list for these homes varies, depending on time of year. Off-base rentals vary with the season, but weekly summer rentals may cost as much as monthly rates during the winter. The average year-round rates range from $400 to $650 a month for a one-bedroom apartment to $600 to $1,000 a month for a three-bedroom house.

Children of personnel assigned to the station attend three elementary schools on base that are operated under the Bourne Public School Department.

A day-care center on base can accommodate up to 100 children. The station education office is a full-service center offering courses from Cape Cod Community and Western New England Colleges.

Personal Services and Recreation. Medical service is provided at a Coast Guard combined medical and dental outpatient clinic. A commissary and Coast Guard exchange offer a wide variety of customer services. The MWR department provides a large selection of recreational and other equipment, including boats, camping gear, lawn mowers, and sporting equipment. Discount tickets to theater productions, concerts, museums, and sporting events are available. MWR also operates a nine-hole golf course, an auto hobby shop, a bowling alley, a library and an activity center.

The Local Area. Cape Cod, curling seventy miles out into the Atlantic, is one of the most scenic and historic regions of New England, best known for its beaches, quaint towns, and outdoor attractions. To the south are such famous attractions as Nantucket, Martha's Vineyard, and the Elizabethan Islands. The cape has 15 townships constituting Barnstable County. Many of the townships, established two or three centuries ago, are divided into villages that offer a lifestyle and atmosphere uniquely their own.

Cape Cod National Seashore occupies almost the entire shore of the Lower and Outer Cape and offers ideal access to dunes, woods, marshlands, and beaches. Fishing, boating, and hunting opportunities abound on Cape Cod. Fishermen can choose from game, bottom, freshwater, and surf fishing. There are several harbors where boats can be moored, but most people use one of the many town or public ramps on both sides of the Cape's shores. An abundance of migratory birds and wildfowl can be shot in season. Deer can also be hunted, including during a short season on Otis in the more remote parts of the base.

For more information, write to Public Affairs Officer, USCG Air Station Cape Cod, Otis ANGB, MA 02542-5024, or call (508) 968-1000. Home page: *www.uscg.mil.*

MICHIGAN

Air Force

SELFRIDGE AIR NATIONAL GUARD BASE

Located 21miles north of Detroit on the shores of Lake Saint Clair, Selfridge Air National Guard Base (ANGB) is one of the most active and diverse military installations in the country, supporting the needs of the Army, Navy, Marine Corps, Air Force, and Coast Guard.

History. Selfridge was officially activated as a military installation on 1 July 1917 as Selfridge Field, named in honor of 1st Lt. Thomas E. Selfridge, the first person to die in an aircraft accident. It was designated Selfridge Air Force Base in 1947 and Selfridge ANGB on 1 July 1971. Today, Selfridge hosts units of the Michigan Air National Guard, the Army's Tank Automotive Command, Navy Reserve units, a Marine wing support group, and Coast Guard Air Station, Detroit. The base has an active-duty population of 300 active-duty personnel from all services, 1,300 civilian workers, and 4,200 family members. In addition, approximately 4,000 reservists and guardsmen train at Selfridge.

Housing and Schools. Between Main Base and Sebille Manor, three miles from the base, Selfridge has almost 1,000 sets of family quarters. Off-base housing is expensive. A one-bedroom unfurnished apartment rents for about $600 per month without utilities, depending on the season.

Selfridge also has a 27-room facility for transient personnel that costs $22.50 a night, and $33 a night for VIPs. The base guest house offers 16 units for $16 to $19 per night. Bachelor quarters consist of 17 rooms for officers at $5.40 to $6.00 per day, and 21 rooms for NCOs at $4.50 per day. Unaccompanied enlisted personnel are accommodated in a barracks that has facilities for 52 Army personnel and another that has 95 rooms for Navy personnel.

Children attend schools in the local area. An on-base child-care facility can accommodate 123 children, ages six weeks to 12 years. Adult off-duty college courses are available at the base education center through Northwood Institute.

Personal Services. Outpatient medical care is provided by a U.S. Army health clinic and a dental clinic. Emergency and specialized care are available at local community hospitals. The Selfridge base exchange system consists of a main store and three branches. The main store includes barber and beauty shops, a dry cleaner and laundry, a snack bar, and an Anthony's Pizza. Banking facilities and a beverage store are also available. Selfridge has a large, well-stocked commissary, and there is a gas and service station on the base.

Recreation. Selfridge ANGB has an officers club offering dining, cocktail lounges, and special events. Indoor recreation includes auto and wood hobby shops, a multicraft center, a photo lab, a bowling center, a fitness center, a library, and a large pool. For outdoor recreation, there are five tennis courts, two baseball fields, three softball fields, a soccer field, and an 18-hole golf course. There are also a rod and gun club, with skeet and trap ranges, and an archery club. The outdoor recreation center schedules camping, hiking, and fishing trips and offers equipment rental, boat slip rental reservations, and recreational vehicle storage.

The Local Area. Selfridge sits on Anchor Bay, the northern extension of Lake Saint Clair, which is fed by the Saint Clair River from Lake Huron to the north and flows by the Detroit River into Lake Erie to the south. Ontario, Canada, is just across the bay from Selfridge. The average temperature in this region is 80° F in the summer and down to -5° F in the winter. Camping, hiking, fishing, skiing, and hunting opportunities, as well as resorts and historic sites, abound throughout the state.

For more information, write to Commander, USA TACOMSA-Selfridge, Attention: AMSTA-CYAF, Building 780, Selfridge ANGB, MI 48045-5016, or call (810) 307-4011. Home page: *www.miself.ang.af.mil.*

MISSISSIPPI

Air Force

COLUMBUS AIR FORCE BASE

Columbus Air Force Base opened in 1941 as Kaye Field, an advanced twin-engine flying school that trained 8,000 pilots for the Army Air Corps during World War II. It was closed in 1946 and then reactivated in 1951. Today it is home for the 14th Flying Training Wing and 1,300 military personnel, about 1,400 military dependents, and 1,350 civilian employees.

Housing and Schools. There are over 600 units of family housing at Columbus, mostly duplexes. The area has an affordable cost of living. Off-base housing and rentals are reasonable.

There is a child-development center on the base. Dependent children are bused to Columbus City schools; several parochial and private schools can also be found in the city. Educational opportunities for adults consist of college courses offered by East Mississippi Community College, Mississippi University for Women, Mississippi State University, the East Mississippi Community College's Vocational-Technical Center, and Embry-Riddle Aeronautical University.

Personal Services and Recreation. Services available include a medical clinic, a commissary and base exchange, banking facilities, a club system for enlisted personnel and officers, and snack bars. Recreation facilities include two swimming pools; a gymnasium; a nine-hole golf course; a bowling center; a youth activities center; a community center; auto, wood framing, and engraving hobby shops; several playground areas; picnic facilities; horse stables; a skeet range; and fishing and seasonal hunting areas.

The Local Area. As northeastern Mississippi's largest city, Columbus offers entertainment, shopping, and cultural attractions. Also nearby are two premier schools of the Southeastern Conference: Mississippi State University, a pacesetter in college baseball and basketball; and the University of Alabama and its football tradition of the Crimson Tide. Only hours away are the Atlanta Braves, Falcons, and Hawks and the New Orleans Saints. Memphis, Nashville,

Birmingham, New Orleans, and the Florida Panhandle are all popular weekend getaways. Bass fishing, boating, and waterskiing are popular on the Tennessee-Tombigbee Waterway. Hunting is among the best in the country. A state park and several U.S. Army Corps of Engineers–managed campgrounds are nearby.

For more information, write to Public Affairs Office, 14th Flying Training Wing, 555 Seventh Street, Suite 203, Columbus AFB, MS 39710-1009, or call (662) 434-7068. Home page: *www.columbus.af.mil.*

KEESLER AIR FORCE BASE

History. During the more than forty-five years Keesler Air Force Base has existed, its mission has been training. During World War II, more than 336,000 men went through the Army Air Forces Technical School and Basic Training Center located there, at the rate of about 35,000 per year. During the Korean War, more than 30,000 technicians were graduated from Keesler's courses every year, and today around 25,000 men and women attend its 250 different courses in such fields as computers, avionics, communications, personnel, and administration.

Named in honor of 2nd Lt. Samuel Reeves Keesler, Jr., a native Mississippian who gave his life in France during World War I, Keesler's 3,600-acre tract, which is fully inside the city limits of Biloxi, houses the Air Education and Training Command, the 81st Training Wing, and other units. The home of the "Hurricane Hunters" is also home to over 6,000 active-duty military personnel, 6,000 dependents, and a civilian workforce of over 2,500. Approximately 1,400 reservists train at the base as well.

Housing and Schools. Keesler has over 1,900 family housing units. In addition, the base offers over 1,500 billets for unaccompanied personnel, 1,300 transient units, and a 51-space mobile home park. A child-care center and kindergarten are available at Keesler, and there are parochial and public schools in Biloxi. In addition, a summer day camp is held on base each year for children ages six to thirteen. Biloxi offers adult education courses at Jefferson Davis Junior College, the University of Southern Mississippi, and Embry-Riddle Aeronautical University.

Personal Services. The 81st Medical Group's 100-bed inpatient hospital is staffed by more than 2,000 medical personnel, making it one of the largest medical facilities in the U.S. Air Force. The base also has a complete commissary and exchange system, a club system, and banking facilities.

Recreation. Recreational facilities include two gymnasiums; two recreation centers; two bowling centers, one with 24 lanes and the other with twelve; four swimming pools; an 18-hole golf course; hobby shops; a marina and picnic park; and two playgrounds for children.

The Local Area. Keesler AFB is located in the city of Biloxi, a historic community on the Gulf of Mexico that has seen many flags in its day: French, English, Spanish, the Republic of West Florida, the United States, Magnolia

State, and the state of Mississippi. Jefferson Davis, president of the short-lived Confederacy, lived at Biloxi in his Beauvoir estate for a dozen years, and today the property has been restored to its original condition.

Recreational activities abound in the Biloxi area, from fishing in the Gulf and surrounding bays, bayous, and rivers to hunting. Small game and wildfowl are available in the surrounding woodlands. For sightseeing, New Orleans is not far to the west, and Mobile, Alabama, is close to the east. North of Biloxi is the DeSoto National Forest, which offers much in the way of camping, hiking, and fishing. To the south is the Gulf Islands National Seashore Park.

For more information, write to Public Affairs Office, 720 Chappie James, Room 106, Keesler AFB, MS 39534-2603, or call (228) 377-1110. Home page: *www.keesler.af.mil.*

Navy

GULFPORT NAVAL CONSTRUCTION BATTALION CENTER

Gulfport Naval Construction Battalion Center plays an important role in the Seabees' global mission. The Naval Construction Training Center, one of the Seabee Center's major tenant commands, trains over 6,000 students per year in a total of 20 formal courses and 159 special training courses. Naval mobile construction battalions deploy throughout the world; individual Seabees may be called upon anytime to undertake specialized assignments anywhere in the world.

History. The Navy first occupied the Gulfport site in June 1942 as an advanced base depot. The Naval Construction Battalion Center was established there in 1952. Today the center is home for the 20th Naval Construction Regiment (Naval Mobile Construction Battalions 1, 7, 74, and 133), the Marine and Naval Reserve Centers, and the Training Center. The base is home for over 4,000 active-duty personnel, 2,500 family members, and 1,300 civilian employees.

Housing and Schools. Over 200 sets of enlisted family quarters are available at Gulfport. These quarters consist of five- and four-bedroom units. There are also seven sets of officers quarters consisting of single houses and duplexes. In addition, the center provides spaces for 25 mobile homes and accommodations for 1,200 single personnel. The typical three-bedroom home on the local economy rents for $600 to $1,000 per month.

Although there is no dependent schooling at the center, a child-care facility is provided. The Navy campus offers advice and assistance to active-duty personnel and their dependents who desire to pursue college courses during their off-duty hours.

Personal Services. Medical care is provided by the Naval Aerospace and Naval Regional Medical Center (NRMC) branch clinic located at the center. Personnel who require care beyond the scope of that provided at the branch clinic are referred to the USAF medical center at Keesler AFB, a 255-bed facility, or to the NRMC itself, at Pensacola, Florida. The Navy exchange provides a retail store with 16,000 feet of display space, and a commissary store carries more than 3,500 line items.

Recreation. An enlisted sports club is available, as are an 18-hole golf course, a 12-lane bowling center, a gymnasium, automotive and hobby shops, two swimming pools, and a recreation park and fishing lake.

The Local Area. The city of Gulfport lies about ten miles west of Biloxi and some sixty miles east of New Orleans, along the Gulf of Mexico. The entire Gulf coast area is famous for its fishing and its easy, gracious lifestyle. Due to the generally mild climate, residents enjoy outdoor activities year-round. The nearby communities of Long Beach, Bay Saint Louis, Pass Christian, and Ocean Springs provide many opportunities for recreation and sightseeing.

For more information, write to Public Affairs Office, 5200 CBC Second Street, Gulfport, MS 39501-5001, or call (601) 871-2555.

MERIDIAN NAVAL AIR STATION

Meridian Naval Air Station is situated 15 miles northeast of downtown Meridian, a community that considers itself a part of the Navy "family" and whose citizens freely admit that their town is a better place to live because of the men and women of the U.S. Navy.

History. Meridian NAS was commissioned as a naval auxiliary air station on 14 July 1961 and later redesignated as a naval air station in July 1968. The main base occupies more than 8,000 acres, with an additional 5,000 under its control at the outlying field, Joe Williams, and the Sea Ray target facility. Meridian is home for Commander, Training Air Wing One; the Naval Technical Training Center; three training squadrons; various tenant commands; and over 1,900 military personnel, 800 family members, 1,300 reservists, and 1,500 civilian employees.

Housing and Schools. There are over 500 military family housing units onboard Meridian. Assignments are made according to the applicant's rank, family composition, and category of quarters needed. While the station does not offer a Navy Lodge, the billeting office complex is capable of housing 2,000 male and female personnel.

Dependent schooling is conducted off base in the various public and private schools situated in Lauderdale County. Higher education is available at the Meridian Community College campus, which offers both day and night courses. In addition, a degree-granting campus of Mississippi State University, located on the Meridian campus, enables military personnel to obtain college credits leading to master's degrees. College courses are also offered on station.

Personal Services. Medical care is provided by a modern, well-equipped branch medical clinic. Specialty care and hospitalization are available at Pensacola, Florida, or through civilian sources locally. The Navy exchange and commissary provide all the conveniences and are centrally located. Also available are a bank, a bowling alley, a beauty shop, a laundry and dry cleaner, a tailor, a uniform shop, a McDonald's, a Subway, a country store, and a service station.

Recreation. Mississippi is famous as an outdoor state, because of its mild climate year-round. At Meridian there are an 18-hole golf course; two swimming pools; tennis and racquetball/handball courts; a riding stable with many backwoods trails; boating, hunting, and fishing in season; and the boisterous camaraderie of the Sportsmen's Association. For those who enjoy indoor activities, the station offers a library stocked with 12,000 books and subscriptions to over sixty newspapers and magazines, a new gymnasium, an all-hands club, an auto hobby shop, and a wood shop.

The Local Area. The city of Meridian is home to about 45,000 people and boasts a fine public school system, a 65-piece symphony orchestra and symphony chorus, and 104 churches representing twenty-five different denominations. The Meridian area Navy League supports the military community in many ways, two of which are the Military Citizen of the Year award and Flight Instructor of the Year award.

Meridian is 155 miles southwest of Birmingham, Alabama; 90 miles east of Jackson, Mississippi; 247 miles north of New Orleans; and 180 miles north of Pensacola, Florida. Vicksburg, about 120 miles west of the station, is the site of one of the most important sieges and battles of the Civil War, and nearer by is the Lake Okatibbee Reservoir, 4,000 acres licensed to the Mississippi Game and Fish Commission for public hunting.

For more information, write to Public Affairs Officer, 1155 Rosenbaum Avenue, Suite 13, Naval Air Station Meridian, MS 39309-5003, or call (601) 679-2211. Home page: *www.cnet.nav.mil/meridian.*

PASCAGOULA NAVAL STATION

One of our newest naval installations, Pascagoula Naval Station is located on Singing River Island, ten miles from the Gulf of Mexico, 35 miles east of Gulfport, Mississippi, and 35 miles west of Mobile, Alabama. Groundbreaking ceremonies for construction of the installation took place on 28 May 1988. Personnel moved onto the installation in January 1991, and it was officially opened 4 July 1992.

History. The Pascagoula Indians welcomed the French in 1699, and less than twenty years later, the lands on Pascagoula Bay were ceded to them. From 1763 to 1781, the English owned the territory. Then came the Spanish in 1781 to 1798—thereafter it was part of the United States to the current day. General Zachary Taylor built Pascagoula's first housing project. Another American noteable, Admiral David Farragut captured Pascagoula, his home town, as a Union naval officer in 1861. Today Pascagoula is home port for the *USS Ticonderoga, Yorktown, John L. Hale, Stephen W. Groves,* and *Thomas S.Gates.* The station has a total population of about 2,000 active-duty personnel, 1,000 family members, and 500 civilian employees.

Housing, Schools, and Personal Services. There are no family quarters at Pascagoula Naval Station. Navy families live in Pascagoula, a town of about 29,000, and in the surrounding communities, and their children attend local public schools. On the station itself are accommodations for 154 unaccompanied sailors. Medical care is provided by branch medical and dental clinics, with inpatient care available at nearby Keesler Air Force Base or local community hospitals. There is a small exchange but no commissary at Pascagoula. Recreation is offered in the form of a sports and fitness center, and all the facilities of Keesler Air Force Base and Gulfport Naval Construction Battalion Center, about 30 miles west of Pascagoula, are open to Pascagoula personnel.

The Local Area. Pascagoula Naval Station is a model for environmental quality. It was constructed with no asbestos or lead and has modern in-ground tanks and an ongoing recycling program. The pier, connected by a 2.8-mile causeway to the mainland, is a state-of-the-art double-deck structure, one of only six such facilities in the Navy today.

For more information, write to Commanding Officer, Naval Station Pascagoula, Attention: Public Affairs, Pascagoula, MS 39567-5000, or call (228) 761-2444. Home page: *www.cnsl.spear.navy.mil/simapasc/welcome.html.*

U.S. NAVAL HOME, ARMED FORCES RETIREMENT HOME

The U.S. Naval Home facility of the Armed Forces Retirement Home, located on the Mississippi beach in Gulfport, has a long and distinguished history as "a comfortable harbor" for sailors, Marines, and Coast Guard members. (For details on the overall policies pertaining to the operation of the Armed Forces Retirement Home, see the entry for the U.S. Soldiers' and Airmen's Home, Washington, D.C.)

Sanctioned on 10 July 1832 by Congress "to provide an honorable and comfortable home for old and disabled personnel of the Navy and Marine Corps, and the Coast Guard while operating as a part of the Navy, who are entitled to benefits of the institution," the original home was established in 1833 on land once owned by the William Penn family in Philadelphia, where it remained until August 1976.

The present-day home stands on the grounds that were once those of the Gulf Coast Military Academy, a military preparatory school for boys founded in the early years of this century.

The home is ideally situated about 75 miles east of New Orleans NAS and 100 miles west of Pensacola NAS, which offer many attractions and services. Locally there is ample shopping and entertainment. Both Gulfport and nearby Biloxi are resort-oriented communities offering a wide variety of outdoor activities. The weather is generally mild, almost tropical.

The home now welcomes retired soldiers and airmen, although most of the members are from the sea services. In addition to medical care, the home provides residents with private rooms, complete dining and food services, a barber and beauty shop, a movie theater, an exercise room, a swimming pool, chapel services, a greenhouse, a post office, banking services, a bowling alley, and an overpass to the beach.

The single rooms each have a bed, a built-in desk, a nightstand, a lamp, a chair, and a half bath with lavatory and toilet. Communal showers and baths are located on each floor. The home provides an ideal setting in a thriving resort community. Members can participate in home volunteer activities, community activities, recreation, entertainment, arts, and pure relaxation. A user fee is charged each resident equal to 25 percent of any federal payments he or she receives each month.

All in all, the U.S. Naval Home is today what it always was intended to be: "A home . . . for the faithful tar who has been either worn out or maimed in fighting the battles of his country. A comfortable harbor . . . where he may safely moor and ride out the ebb of life, free from the cares and storms by which he has been previously surrounded."

For more information, write to Director, U.S. Naval Home, 1800 Beach Drive, Gulfport, MS 39507-1597, or call (800) 332-3527.

MISSOURI

Air Force

WHITEMAN AIR FORCE BASE

Whiteman Air Force Base is located two miles south of Knob Noster, a community of 2,300 souls. One might well ask how the town and the base derived their names. Early settlers named the town after the Latin *noster,* which means "our," and two knobs or hills that overlook the original townsite. The base got its name in honor of 2nd Lt. George A. Whiteman, the first aviator to die in combat in World War II. Lt. Whiteman was a native of Sedalia, a town 19 miles to the east of the base.

History. Whiteman AFB opened in 1942 as the Sedalia Army Airfield and was renamed in 1951. Today it is home to the 509th Bomb Wing. The wing was once responsible for 150 Minuteman II intercontinental ballistic missiles (ICBMs) based within a 10,000-square-mile area of Missouri countryside—now all the missiles are gone. The 509th Bomb Wing, home of the B-2 bomber, was activated there in 1993. Approximately 2,900 active-duty personnel, their 6,500 dependents, and 700 civilians live and work at Whiteman.

Housing and Schools. There are more than 900 units of government housing available at Whiteman. The Whiteman Elementary School provides educational services for children in kindergarten through fourth grade; older children attend schools off base in the communities of Knob Noster, Warrensburg, and Sedalia. A child-care center for 150 children is operated on base. On-base college courses are available from Park College, Webster University, and State Fair Community College.

Personal Services. Personal services available at Whiteman include a USAF hospital, an $8 million complex that provides outpatient services. Banking facilities, a commissary with over 17,000 square feet of space, a base exchange, a community center, and a colocated club are also part of the scene at Whiteman.

Recreation. Recreational facilities include an 18-hole, 6,525-yard golf course; a recreation center; a 16-lane bowling center; a gymnasium; a large outdoor swimming pool; and Peace Park, where static aircraft displays are set up. There are also an outdoor picnic area, two base lakes for fishing, a library, and a 350-seat base theater that offers a Cinemascope screen.

The Local Area. Whiteman is located about 65 miles east of Kansas City and Independence. Jefferson City, the state capital, is approximately eighty miles to the east of the base. About 50 miles southeast of the base is the Lake of the Ozarks Recreation Area, Grand Arm. The facility is operated by the Army at Fort Leonard Wood and contains 40 trailers, eight camper spaces, and 20 tent sites and provides camping, fishing, boating, hiking, and waterskiing, as well as sporting equipment rentals.

Not quite so far away is Knob Noster State Park, a wooded recreational area covering 3,400 acres where fishing, camping, picnicking, and swimming are available. The state of Missouri affords a wide variety of outdoor activities and points of interest. There are, for instance, more than 4,000 caves in the state, 23 of them commercially operated with guided tours.

For more information, write to Public Affairs Division, 509th Bomb Wing, 509 Spirit Boulevard, Suite 111, Whiteman AFB, MO 65305-5097, or call (660) 687-1110. Home page: *www.whiteman.af.mil.*

Army

FORT LEONARD WOOD

Spread over 63,000 acres in the south-central Missouri Ozarks, Fort Leonard Wood (called Fort Wood locally) is one of the larger Army training centers in the United States. Surrounded on three sides by the Mark Twain National Forest, Fort Leonard Wood is a clean, fresh, and unspoiled location where the military has managed to blend its activities with nature.

History. Named after Maj. Gen. Leonard Wood, Medal of Honor winner in the Geronimo Campaign of 1886, the post was established as a basic-training center in 1940. Since then, Fort Wood has introduced more than one million men and women to the Army. With the transfer of the U.S. Army Engineer Center and School from Fort Belvoir, Virginia, to Fort Leonard Wood in May 1988, Fort Wood became the home of the Army Engineers, and its name was officially changed to the U.S. Army Engineer Center and Fort Leonard Wood. The post also recently acquired the U.S. Army Military Police School and Chemical Corps School, transferred from Fort McClellan. Today Fort Leonard Wood is home to over 3,900 active-duty personnel, 7,500 family members, and 4,000 civilian employees.

Housing and Schools. Fort Wood is a completely self-contained installation providing every service and facility required by a community of well over

30,000. There are two main housing areas for military families consisting of more than 2,500 sets of quarters that range in size from two- to four-bedroom units. Waiting lists are established by a date of eligibility based on the date of departure from the previous duty station. Seventy guest-house units are also available for the use of authorized personnel and their families and guests. These facilities cannot be reserved. In addition, there are 340 units of bachelor officer and NCO housing on post.

On-post schools provide dependent children with educational facilities from kindergarten through the eighth grade. The Army education center provides educational opportunities ranging from the basic skills education program to graduate-level courses offered by Drury and Webster Colleges and the University of Missouri. In addition, Columbia and Central Texas Colleges offer on-post undergraduate courses.

Personal Services. General Leonard Wood Army Community Hospital is an extremely modern, 500-bed facility that provides the military community with excellent medical care. The post has a main exchange and five branch exchanges, a garden shop, and a toy store. There is also a very large main commissary plus two convenience stores.

Recreation. Fort Leonard Wood has a vigorous recreation services program ranging from libraries to golfing, swimming, bowling, and intramural sports. Outdoor recreational facilities and activities are also available on post. A twenty-five-mount riding academy is maintained by the morale support activities division on the post, and the Big Piney hiking and riding trail is located only six miles south of the post. The trail winds seventeen miles through a variety of Ozark terrain.

The Fort Leonard Wood Lake of the Ozarks Recreation Area, a 360-acre tract bounded on one side by the Lake of the Ozarks, is located 15 miles northeast of Camdenton, a 60-minute drive from the post. In addition to a post exchange snack bar and a warm-weather pavilion with a dance floor, the site offers 40 air-conditioned trailers, a swimming area, picnic grounds, campsites, and a marina.

The Local Area. Fort Leonard Wood's central location provides convenient access to major cities and tourist attractions of the Midwest. St. Louis is 135 miles northeast; Springfield is 85 miles southwest; and Rolla is 28 miles northeast. St. Robert (population 1,400) is immediately outside Fort Leonard Wood's main gate, and Waynesville (population 3,500) is seven miles northwest.

For more information, write to Headquarters, U.S. Army Engineer Center and Fort Leonard Wood, Attention: Public Affairs, Hoge Hall, Building 3200, Fort Leonard Wood, MO 65473-5000, or call (573) 596-0131. Home page: *www.wood.army.mil.*

MONTANA

Air Force

MALMSTROM AIR FORCE BASE

Malmstrom Air Force Base is located two miles east of Great Falls in "Big Sky country," prairie land 3,300 feet above sea level. The area was visited by the Lewis and Clark expedition in 1805, which duly noted the "great falls" of the Missouri River located there.

History. Known as Great Falls Army Air Force Base when it opened in 1945, the installation was renamed in 1955 in honor of Col. Einar Axel Malmstrom, who was killed nearby in the crash of a T-33 jet. Today its host unit is the 341st Missile Wing, which is responsible for 200 Minuteman III missiles spread out over 23,000 square miles of Montana countryside. The base population consists of 3,500 active-duty personnel, 5,000 family members, and 500 civilian employees.

Housing and Schools. Malmstrom has over 1,400 units of government housing. There are no dependent schools on base, but there is a child-care center, and public and parochial schools are available off base in Great Falls. The base education center offers on-base courses from the University of Great Falls, Embry-Riddle Aeronautical University, and Park College.

Personal Services and Recreation. Services available at Malmstrom include an Air Force clinic, a commissary, a base exchange, banking facilities, and officers and NCO clubs. Recreational facilities include a swimming pool (summer only), a 16-lane bowling center, an arts and crafts center, and auto, welding, and wood crafts shops. A sports arena provides various facilities for sports and physical fitness. The base also operates a family camp open from 1 May to 31 October that offers ten camper spaces with all hookups. Some of the many recreational attractions offered by Malmstrom include Giant Springs Park, one of the world's largest freshwater springs, which includes a picnic area, fishing hatcheries, and a park visitor center. Also to be enjoyed are museums, music festivals, hunting and fishing, and even ghost towns for the adventurous! Glacier and Yellowstone National Parks, Lewis and Clark Caverns, and much more are located near the base.

The Local Area. More than 1,500 lakes are to be found in the state of Montana, many of them excellent fishing spots. Game that can be hunted includes moose, elk, deer, antelope, grizzly and black bear, fur-bearing animals, varmints, and game birds.

Two major national parks, Yellowstone and Glacier, are located in the state, and the area around Great Falls is dotted with thousands of acres of woodland comprising the Lewis and Clark and Helena National Forests. Helena, the capital of Montana, is about 70 miles south of Great Falls. The Canadian border is about 120 miles north of the base. Modern travelers to Montana are as impressed by the state's vast natural beauty as were the men of the Lewis and Clark expedition of 1805.

For more information, write to 341 Space Wing Public Affairs Office, 7015 Goddard Drive, Malmstrom AFB, MT 59402-6863, or call (406) 731-1110. Home page: *www.malmstrom.af.mil.*

NEBRASKA

Air Force

OFFUTT AIR FORCE BASE

The earth has turned many times since the men of the 22nd U.S. Infantry established Fort Crook in 1896. Today what used to be called Fort Crook, a post that was home to the foot-slogging infantry, is the control center for one of the most awesome fleets of modern weapons ever assembled.

The first landing strip was built at Offutt in 1921, and in 1924, it was named Offutt Field in honor of 1st Lt. Jarvis Jennes Offutt, a native of Omaha who was killed in an air crash during World War I. Offutt is the home of the 55th Wing, which has the mission of conducting global electronic and scientific reconnaissance missions. In addition, the wing supports three major associate units: U.S. Strategic Command, a unified command combining Air Force and Navy strategic forces; Headquarters, Air Force Weather Agency, the largest computerized weather production facility in the world; and the 1st Airborne Command and Control Squadron. It is home to more than 9,000 active-duty personnel, 14,000 family members, and 3,000 civilian employees.

Housing and Schools. There are over 500 officer and 2,200 enlisted housing units at Offutt. Over 260 units of temporary housing and visiting and bachelor officer quarters are also available; single enlisted personnel live in dormitory housing providing about 1,500 spaces. Apartment rental prices in the area vary greatly. A two-bedroom apartment ranges from $500 to $600 per month. New homes in Plattsmouth start at around $70,000; in Papillion, the range is from $90,000 to $120,000.

Three elementary schools, a preschool, and a child-care center are operated on the base. Junior and senior high school students attend local schools. For adults wishing to extend their education, the base education office offers on-base programs leading to bachelor's degrees from such institutions as the University of Nebraska–Omaha, Southern Illinois University, and Embry-Riddle Aeronautical University. Graduate programs are offered from the University of Nebraska, the University of Oklahoma, Creighton University, and Embry-Riddle.

Personal Services. The Ehrling Bergquist USAF Regional Hospital at Offutt offers excellent medical care to military personnel and their families. A base exchange and three miniexchanges provide military shoppers with numerous retail bargains, and the base commissary is a completely modern facility offering over 10,000 items stocked in 32,000 square feet of sales space.

Recreation. Recreational facilities at Offutt extend from hobby and arts and crafts shops to a 9-hole golf course, a 20-lane bowling center, and a complete gymnasium. There are also four swimming pools, a movie theater, a recreation center, and officers and NCO clubs. The base family camp, located on the shores of a well-landscaped, man-made lake, offers ten camper spaces with electricity and other facilities. Picnicking and fishing can be enjoyed there, and camping and fishing equipment may be rented on the site.

The Local Area. Offutt is located about ten miles south of Omaha on the outskirts of the city of Bellevue, a community of over 32,000 people situated on the banks of the Missouri River. Omaha, a city of over 600,000, dominates the immediate vicinity and offers many recreational opportunities, from live theater and excellent dining to ballet and football, to the personnel stationed at Offutt.

The weather in the Omaha area is diverse. Summer temperatures usually average below 90° F. In winter, the average temperature is 33° F. Depending on whether you're an optimist or a pessimist, the sun shines about half the time or it's overcast half the time.

For more information, write to Public Affairs Division, 906 SAC Boulevard, Suite 1, Offutt AFB, NE 68113-3206, or call (402) 294-1110. Home page: *www.offutt.af.mil.*

NEVADA

Air Force

NELLIS AIR FORCE BASE

If a military installation can be said to have a personality, that of Nellis Air Force Base is clearly split between the sparkle and glitter of Las Vegas, eight miles to the southwest, and the Department of Energy's Nuclear Testing Site, located in the 1,350-square-mile Nellis Range that begins some 65 miles northwest of the city. The Las Vegas Valley is one of the fastest growing communities in the nation. Frenchman Flat and Yucca Flat are the primary weapons testing sites, although only Yucca and Pahute Mesa are used for atomic-weapons testing these days, and the "bangers" are all set off underground anyway. Its high-profile missions make it both a show base and a linkpin in the nation's security.

History. Named in honor of Lt. William Nellis, a Nevadan who was killed in combat over Luxembourg, 27 December 1944, while flying a P-47 Thunderbolt I, Nellis was established as an Army Air Corps gunnery school in 1941. At the end of World War II, the field went briefly dormant—after 1947, it reopened and continues to be one of America's premier bases. Today Nellis AFB and the Air Warfare Center partake of the most important missions in the Air Force. Not only the home of the demonstration team known as the Thunderbirds, this busy air base counts training, reconnaissance, surveillance, and targeting as among its daily duties. The base population consists of 7,000 active-duty personnel, 14,000 family members and veterans, and 1,300 civilian employees.

Housing and Schools. There are approximately 1,200 sets of family quarters available at Nellis, as well as 100 mobile-home sites. The base also has 1,100 spaces for unaccompanied personnel, as well as accommodations for about 760 transient airmen.

The one elementary school located on base is run by the Clark County School District. Off-duty adult educational opportunities are numerous with undergraduate and graduate classes taught on base by institutions such as

Embry-Riddle Aeronautical University and the University of Phoenix and off-base at both Community College of Southern Nevada and University of Nevada–Las Vegas.

Personal Services. Nellis has a base exchange, a commissary and home and garden center, a shoppette, and several concessionaires all within walking distance of each other. The Mike O'Callaghan Federal Hospital has over 100 beds and is a joint operation with the Department of Veteran Affairs.

Recreation. Recreational facilities include a recreation center, a gymnasium, swimming pools, bowling lanes, a golf course, hobby and craft shops, an open mess system, and two youth centers. The Nellis rod and gun club provides information concerning local hunting and fishing sites and licensing procedures. Trout and bass are plentiful in local streams and lakes, and dove, pheasant, quail, and other game birds (as well as big game) may be hunted in the surrounding countryside. There are 48 RV spaces available on the base campground.

The Local Area. Las Vegas, with a population of more than 310,000, deserves its title of "Entertainment Capital of the World." Not only do its world-famous casinos and hotels cater to the millions of tourists who come here each year to gamble, but they also offer shows that regularly feature some of the world's greatest stars.

If you fancy the priceless treasures of the outdoors, Hoover Dam and the Lake Mead Recreation Area are only a few miles from the base. A dry climate makes for comfortable living year-round. Three national parks, Bryce, Zion, and Grand Canyon North Rim, are situated within easy driving distance of the base, and the Nellis Community Center offers special rates to service personnel and their families at nearby ski resorts.

For more information, write to Public Affairs Office, 4370 N. Washington Boulevard, Suite 223, Nellis AFB, NV 89191-7078, or call (702) 652-1110. Home page: *www.nellis.af.mil.*

Navy

FALLON NAVAL AIR STATION

If your children grow up to become swaggering, carousing old salts, they won't have learned their bad habits at Fallon Naval Air Station. A state famous for its legalized gambling, Nevada frowns upon minors participating, and anyone under the age of 21 caught gambling is subject to the full power and majesty of Nevada's legal system.

History. The station was commissioned in 1944 as an auxiliary station under the control of Alameda Naval Air Station (now closed), California, and redesignated a naval air station in January 1972. Today it is home to approximately the 1,800 naval personnel, their 1,900 family members, and the 1,300 civilian employees of the Naval Strike and Air Warfare Center and other tenant units.

Housing and Schools. There are 360 sets of family quarters available at Fallon. A Navy Lodge offers five three-bedroom units and one two-bedroom unit for transients and visitors, with permanent-change-of-station personnel getting priority. Billets are available for over 300 single personnel and 1,900 visiting personnel.

Dependent schooling is available for grades one through 12 in the nearby Churchill County School System. Child care is also available. High school completion programs are available at Fallon, and Western Nevada Community College at Fallon offers various associate's degree programs.

Personal Services. A commissary store, a Navy exchange, an enlisted and officers club system, and a dispensary are located at Fallon. Specialty and inpatient care required by dependents is handled under the TRICARE program with local physicians.

Recreation. Because the sun shines over Fallon an average of ten months out of the year, outdoor recreation of all kinds can be enjoyed there. The station offers a go-cart speedway, two lighted tennis courts, horseshoe pits, three picnic areas, a basketball court, three softball fields, and a fitness trail. Indoor recreation in the form of a gymnasium, a hobby shop and auto shop complex, and an indoor swimming pool is also offered. Boating can be enjoyed at Lake Lahontan just west of Fallon. Skiing is available at twenty-five resorts located within a 150-mile radius of the station. Charter bus tours to various points of interest are frequently arranged through the special services office. Some casinos in Fallon even provide bus service to and from the base.

The Local Area. The city of Fallon has a population of 7,000 and is the principal city in Churchill County. Reno is approximately 70 miles to the west. The area boasts several ghost towns, including Fairview, Wonder, and Rawhide.

One of the most interesting natural features of the area is Sand Mountain, 24 miles east of Fallon, where strange vibrating moans and roars greet you as you climb the mountain. Scientists believe the noises are caused by heat, friction, and possibly electrical forces. Others think they are the echoes of the poor souls who have lost their money in Reno's casinos.

For more information, write to Public Affairs Office, NAS, Fallon, NV 89406, or call (775) 426-5161. Home page: *www.fallon.navy.mil.*

NEW HAMPSHIRE

Navy

PORTSMOUTH NAVAL SHIPYARD

History. The Portsmouth Naval Shipyard was authorized in 1799. The first vessel built there was the *USS Washington,* a 74-gun ship, but the first ship built along the Piscataqua was *HMS Falkland* in 1690, perhaps the first warship ever built in North America. During the Revolution, several ships were constructed in this area for the Continental Navy, including John Paul Jones's flagship, *USS Ranger.* As the only naval shipyard solely responsible for the repair and overhaul of nuclear submarines, Portsmouth is not open to visits by the general public, but active-duty or retired personnel and their dependents are authorized the use of all personnel support, morale, and welfare facilities located on the base. The base population consists of 400 active-duty personnel, 1,000 family members, 4,100 civilian employees, and an average of about 1,000 active-duty sailors in port at any given time.

Housing and Schools. There are 260 sets of family quarters at the shipyard, 60 officer and 200 enlisted. Enlisted housing consists of units with two, three, and four bedrooms. Temporary lodging is available for officers and enlisted personnel, but reservations are required. There are also accommodations for 30 single enlisted personnel and 40 visitors/transient personnel.

Dependent schooling is available in the local area, and a child-development center is operated on the base. The University of New Hampshire at Durham, a few miles to the west of Portsmouth, offers programs to active-duty personnel, as do other small colleges in the area.

Personal Services. There are a small Navy exchange and a commissary at Portsmouth. An officers, CPO, and enlisted club system is operated at Portsmouth. Outpatient medical care is available at the Navy Medical Clinic.

Recreation. Recreational facilities and activities offered include bowling, a hobby shop, a library, a gymnasium, billiard tables, and tennis, squash, and handball courts. Outdoor activities include ice skating, a marina and boat launch area, and swimming and picnicking on Jamaica Island at the far end of the base during the summer months. Licensed freshwater fishing is permitted at Meade Pond; saltwater fishing off Pier 15 is authorized in the back channel, with no license required. Hunting and fishing licenses may be purchased at the MWR office, where complete information may also be obtained concerning base activities, as well as events in the surrounding area. This office also assists in purchasing tickets for events as far away as Boston.

The Local Area. Portsmouth Naval Shipyard is located on Seavey's Island, across the mouth of the Piscataqua River from the city of Portsmouth. The town of Kittery, Maine (population 10,000), is just to the north across the back channel, via the causeway. Kittery was the home port for John Paul Jones's *Ranger;* the first U.S. submarine, L-8, was built at Kittery in 1917.

The Portsmouth area has an average annual temperature of 45° F, with minimum temperatures as low as -12° F and highs of 95° F. Snowfall averages about seventy-two inches per year, and rainfall averages forty-two inches annually. Moose and White Mountains lie just to the north of Portsmouth, and the immediate area has many good camping sites and opportunities for outdoor recreational activities for all seasons, including sightseeing.

For more information, write to Public Affairs, Portsmouth Naval Shipyard, Portsmouth, NH 03801-5000, or call (207) 438-1000.

NEW JERSEY

Air Force

MCGUIRE AIR FORCE BASE

As the home for the 305th Air Mobility Wing, the Air Mobility Warfare Center, and the 621st Air Mobility Operations Group, McGuire Air Force Base has earned its title as "America's Eastern Gateway for Global Reach." The terminal at McGuire is a familiar sight to countless numbers of military personnel and their families who have embarked there for flights to Europe and come back into the country again through the same facility.

History. Opened in 1937 as an Army Air Corps facility under the control of nearby Camp Dix (now closed), the base was renamed in honor of Maj. Thomas B. McGuire, Jr., a native of Ridgewood, New Jersey, who won the Medal of Honor in World War II. Today McGuire AFB covers 4,000 acres of land some eighteen miles south of Trenton, the state capital. It is home to 5,000 military personnel and their 8,000 family members, 4,600 reservists, and 1,000 civilian employees. The 305th Air Mobility Wing is the host unit and flies the C-141B Starlifter and KC-10 Extender.

Housing and Schools. More than 1,700 sets of family quarters are available at McGuire, with very limited mobile-home space. Temporary lodging for families consists of 400 units and is restricted to families traveling on permanent-change-of-station orders. There are 1,200 units available for unaccompanied enlisted personnel. Transient housing is available for about 230 personnel. Local housing is both scarce and expensive. A one-bedroom, unfurnished apartment may rent for $350 to $525 per month. Because local landlords require one month's rent in advance and a security deposit equal to one-half the first month's rent, figure on between $1,500 and $2,275 to cover move-in costs.

Two child-development centers with the capacity for 300 children are operated on base, with home care available for another 300 children. School-age children attend public schools in the community of North Burlington, and private and parochial schools are also located in the immediate vicinity. The base education office offers excellent opportunities for service personnel and their families to obtain college credits. Courses are offered by such institutions as Southern Illinois University, Embry-Riddle Aeronautical University, and the University of Southern Colorado.

Personal Services. Outpatient medical care is offered by the 305th Medical Group, through Walson Air Force Facility on neighboring Fort Dix (which still provides some support services for active-duty personnel). The McGuire AFB base exchange/post exchange complex and McGuire commissary offer a full range of convenience shopping, including barber and beauty shops, specialty shops, an optical shop, a photo shop, a car-care center, and a Burger King.

Recreation. Recreational facilities on base include a twenty-four-lane bowling alley; an 18-hole, par-72 golf course; a complete gymnasium; auto shops; tennis courts; three swimming pools; and a base movie theater. In addition, the McGuire Aero Club provides the military community the opportunity to learn to fly and to acquire advanced pilot certificates.

The Local Area. The base is only about 45 miles from Philadelphia, and both Newark and New York City are easily accessible from McGuire. The climate is moderate, with warm summers and winter temperatures averaging from 22° to 36° F in January. The summers are modified somewhat by the state's proximity to the Atlantic Ocean. New Jersey boasts 127 miles of excellent beaches. Recreational activities available in the state range from horse racing at Monmouth Park and other places to fishing, hunting, sailing, and surfing.

For more information, write to Public Affairs Officer, 305th AMW/PA, 2901 Falcon Lane, McGuire AFB, NJ 08641-5002, or call (609) 724-1100. Home page: *www.mcguire.af.mil.*

Army

FORT DIX

From its earliest days, Fort Dix has been dedicated to the development of the "ultimate weapon"—the infantryman. Training is still the major military activity at Fort Dix today, in support of the reserve components now—more than one million man-days per fiscal year.

History. Named after Maj. Gen. John Adams Dix, a nineteenth-century soldier-statesman, Camp Dix was originally established in 1917 as a training post for troops who would fight in Europe during World War I. In 1939, the post was designated a permanent Army installation and renamed Fort Dix. The post was earmarked for semiretirement in 1988, but the 1991 Base Closure and Realignment Commission recommended transition to reserve components training instead, and this was completed in 1993.

Covering more than 30,000 acres of wooded New Jersey countryside including 4,000 for maneuvers and training and 13,000 for ranges and impact areas, Fort Dix's ranges can accommodate all weapons from pistols to tanks and eight-inch howitzers. It shares common boundaries with McGuire Air Force

Base and Lakehurst Naval Air Station. Major tenants today include the Kelly U.S. Army Reserve Center, the National Guard High Technology Training Center, Readiness Group Dix, the Federal Bureau of Prisons, the FBI, the U.S. Coast Guard's Atlantic Strike Team, and the New Jersey Department of Corrections.

Approximately 1,200 active-duty personnel of all services are stationed at Fort Dix, along with a civilian employee population of 6,000. The average reserve component training strength at Fort Dix is 23,000 personnel.

Housing, Services, and Recreation. Fort Dix has retained 1,197 sets of family quarters available in one- to four-bedroom units. Guest-house facilities are also offered. Medical care at Fort Dix is provided by the Walson Air Force (formerly Army) Community Hospital. The post exchange and commissary at Fort Dix are both large and well stocked. Recreational facilities include a bowling alley, an 18-hole golf course, minigolf, batting cages, a sports arena, tennis and handball courts, two swimming pools, a skeet and trap range, and two movie theaters. Picnicking and camping are permitted around the Brindle Lake Recreation Area.

The Local Area. Fort Dix is situated near the center of New Jersey, 17 miles southeast of Trenton, 72 miles south of New York City, and 45 miles east of Philadelphia. Its climate is generally moderate. Snowfall averages 20 inches per year, and the annual average rainfall is 29 inches. Outdoor recreation—hunting, fishing, camping, and tourism—is available year-round to military personnel stationed at Fort Dix. The installation commander annually designates authorized hunting and trapping areas on the reservation, and permits are sold at the Fort Dix Outdoor Recreation Center.

New Jersey is a state with so much to see and do that the visitor is well advised to "expect the unexpected." Attractions from American Revolution sites to luxurious resorts are available throughout the year. A wide variety of winter sports can be enjoyed at many locations throughout the state.

For more information, write to Public Affairs Office, Fort Dix, NJ 08640-5000, or call (609) 562-4034. Home page: *www.dix.army.mil.*

FORT MONMOUTH

Some little-known facts about Fort Monmouth are that it has 79 miles of electric power lines, 50 miles of water lines, 41 miles of sewage lines; did not figure in the Revolutionary War Battle of Monmouth (so Molly Pitcher never slept there); and is right smack dab in the middle of one of the most beautiful resort areas in the northeast.

History. The U.S. Army came to Fort Monmouth on 4 June 1917, and shortly thereafter the site was designated Signal Corps Camp, Little Silver. Later that same year the installation's name was changed to Camp Alfred Vail, in honor of the New Jersey inventor. In 1925, the post was officially designated Fort Monmouth, after the men who died on the Revolutionary War battlefield nearby.

The year 1917 also saw the Signal School established here. Scientists here developed radio communications and aerial photography, alongside communications via carrier pigeon. Today the U.S. Army Communications–Electronics Command engages in the research, development, deployment, and maintenance of command, control, communications, computer, intelligence, and electronic warfare equipment that is part of every weapon system and can be found throughout the world in aircraft, tanks, missiles, and in the hands of individual soldiers.

The post's 1,560 acres are also home to the U.S. Military Academy Preparatory School and to the Joint Interoperability Engineering Organization. Fort Monmouth's population is made up of 800 military personnel, their 1,600 family members, 800 reservists, and about 6,000 civilian employees.

Housing and Schools. There are over 1,100 units of family housing at Fort Monmouth, situated in three housing areas, one on the main post and two located nearby. The post has a 90-room guest house normally available to active-duty and retired personnel and their guests for up to a week at a time. There are also about 150 accommodations available for transient personnel. Off post, a one-bedroom apartment rents for $650 a month during the off-season and up to $1,200 a month during the summer, plus utilities.

The post operates a preschool for dependent children and latchkey and certified child-care home programs. Adult education is available through the education center, which offers college classes from Brookdale Community College, Fairleigh Dickinson University, Kean College, Temple University, and Monmouth University.

Personal Services. Medical care is provided to Fort Monmouth residents by Patterson Army Health Clinic, an acute-care health facility. A ten-chair dental clinic provides comprehensive dental care for assigned military personnel and routine care for dependents on a space-available basis.

The post commissary offers 65,000 square feet of shopping space. The post exchange is located in the same complex as the commissary. This complex offers one-stop shopping and includes a cafeteria, a barber shop, an optical shop, a watch repair shop, a tailor shop, laundry and dry-cleaning facilities, a credit union and bank, a military clothing sales store, and a four-seasons store. The complex has parking for 600 cars.

Recreation. A unique recreational feature at Fort Monmouth is the Army Communications–Electronics Museum, which offers a significant collection of historical equipment and documents that trace the development of Army communications from 1860 to the present day. The post also offers a field house with an Olympic-size swimming pool; a 20-lane bowling center; craft shops; a 1,000-seat movie theater; a library containing 100,000 books, magazines, and newspapers; and an outdoor recreation program that includes an 18-hole golf course, tennis courts, garden plots, a marina on Oceanport Creek, and year-round fishing on Husky Brook Pond. There is also a swimming pool at the Charles Wood Housing Area.

The Local Area. Fort Monmouth is located 50 miles south of New York City and 40 miles south of Newark International Airport. The post is within easy driving distance of such notable sites and recreation spots as the Monmouth Battlefield and Freehold Raceway to the west, the Atlantic coast to the east, Gateway National Recreation Area to the northeast, and the megalopolis of New York City to the north. Monmouth Park Racetrack is only five minutes from the post's east gate.

For more information, write to Public Affairs Office, Attention: AMSEL-IO, HQ, U.S. Army Communications–Electronics Command, Fort Monmouth, Fort Monmouth, NJ 07703-5016, or call (732) 532-9000. Home page: *www.monmouth.army.mil.*

Coast Guard

CAPE MAY TRAINING CENTER

Located on a 450-acre point of land between the Atlantic Ocean and Cape May Harbor, a large portion of Cape May Training Center is preserved in its natural state as protected wetlands. In fact, Cape May is the nesting grounds for two species of endangered birds. The Coast Guard began operations on this property in 1948. The center's mission is to "graduate motivated entry-level enlisted men and women ready and able to serve with a sense of pride and commitment in the nation's finest seagoing service." The training center itself is staffed by 1,100 active-duty men and women and 100 civilian employees. Also onboard are approximately 1,800 family members and 500 other personnel assigned to the Cape May Coast Guard Station, Cape May Group and Air Station, and the cutters *Vigorous, Hornbeam, Mako, Point Batan,* and *Point Highland.*

Housing and Schools. The center maintains 180 family housing units just outside the front gate. The permanent-party barracks consist of 75 rooms. A small transient lodging facility is available for personnel on orders. There are no schools on base, but there is a child-care facility for about 100 children.

Personal Services. There is just a small commissary at Cape May, but the exchange does $5 million worth of business a year. Besides a 10,000-square-foot retail store, there are officers and enlisted clubs, a package store, a laundry and tailor shop, a barber and beauty shop, and a uniform shop. The contractor-operated dining facility onboard the center seats 550 on the recruit side, 80 on the permanent-party side, and another 24 in the CPO dining room.

Medical care at Cape May is provided by a 22-bed dispensary staffed by seven Public Health Service (PHS) medical doctors, seven PHS dentists, and seven civilian nurses. The facility has its own pharmacist and an enlisted staff of 58 hospital men. Contract services include a pediatrician, a gynecologist, an optometrist, a psychiatrist, and a dental hygienist. Military retirees and dependents of active-duty personnel are eligible for care on a space-available basis.

Recreation. The center provides two gyms; an Olympic-size swimming pool; two racquetball courts; indoor and outdoor tennis courts; two softball fields; indoor and outdoor volleyball courts; an aerobic, therapy, and weight room; and a steam room with a hot tub. There are also a picnic pavilion and equipment rental of campers, power- and sailboats, canoes, camping equipment, and a 15-passenger van for excursions.

The Local Area. Located about 90 miles southeast of Philadelphia at the end of the Garden State Parkway, Cape May is situated in one of the most scenic parts of New Jersey. Atlantic City, about 45 miles north of the base, is famed for its nightlife and casinos. The nearby resort towns of Wildwood Crest, Wildwood, and North Wildwood have a population of about 5,000 each.

For more information, write to Public Affairs Office, U.S. Coast Guard Training Center, Cape May, NJ 08204-5000, or call (609) 898-6900. Home page: *www.dot.gov/dotinfo/uscg/hq/capemay.*

Navy

EARLE NAVAL WEAPONS STATION

Earle Naval Weapons Station (NWS) is located in Colts Neck, New Jersey, 54 miles south of New York City and 79 miles north of Philadelphia. Founded 13 December 1943, it is named for Rear Adm. Ralph Earle, chief of the Bureau of Ordnance during World War I.

Earle NWS provides support and home-port services to Atlantic Fleet ammunition ships and is home to Mobile Mine Assembly Unit 3, Shore Intermediate Maintenance Activity, and the ammunition ships *Seattle, Detroit,* and *Arctic.* The station's complement is about 5,000 active-duty personnel, their 2,600 family members, 500 reservists, and 300 civilian employees.

Housing and Schools. Earle NWS operates over 800 units of family housing, 37 quarters for officers and 774 for enlisted personnel. There are also eight mobile-home spaces available and accommodations for 209 unaccompanied enlisted personnel. There is no dependent schooling on the station, but there is a child-development center that can accommodate 104 children from six weeks to five years of age.

Personal Services. Outpatient medical care is provided by the branch medical clinic and its waterfront annex clinic, with referrals to local civilian hospitals or Patterson Army Health Clinic at Fort Monmouth. Among its other services, the clinic offers smoking cessation programs. Although there is no commissary at the station, one is available at Fort Monmouth and McGuire Air Force Base. There are a small Navy exchange and a convenience store at Earle.

Recreation. Earle NWS offers two gyms, three outdoor pools, outdoor tennis courts, ball fields, a fitness center, a youth center, a picnic pavilion, and a bowling center. There are also two all-hands clubs at the station, as well as auto and ceramics hobby shops. Hunting is authorized in certain areas onboard the station, where rabbit, squirrel, quail, and grouse may be taken in season.

For more information, write to Commander, Naval Weapons Station Earle, Attention: Public Affairs Office, 201 Highway 34 South, Colts Neck, NJ 07722-5005, or call (732) 866-2500. Home page: *www.earle.nav.mil.*

LAKEHURST NAVAL AIR ENGINEERING STATION

Lakehurst is remembered chiefly as the site of the *Hindenburg* disaster, which occurred there on 6 May 1937, when the dirigible was destroyed by a fire of undetermined origin during mooring operations. The crash site is just to the front of where the Navy exchange stands today. From 1921 to 1961, Lakehurst was the United States' lighter-than-air airship center, and today Hangar Number One still stands, a reminder of the days when it housed the *Graf Zeppelin,* the *Hindenburg,* and every rigid airship in the U.S. Navy at one time or another. Today it houses the world's largest training aid, a 400-foot aircraft carrier flight deck.

History. Established originally as an ammunition proving ground for the Russian imperial government in 1915, Lakehurst became a U.S. Army ammunition proving ground in 1917 and was named Camp Kendrick. Camp Kendrick was taken over by the Navy as an air station in 1921. Today the station is home to the Naval Air Technical Training Center and the Airborne Engineering Evaluation Support Activity, occupying 7,400 wooded acres approximately 60 miles east of Philadelphia and only ten miles from New Jersey's famed seashore resorts. The military population at Lakehurst is over 600, with an additional 900 family members, 1,500 reservists, and 2,300 civilian employees, most of whom are engineers, scientists, and technicians. These people are dedicated to providing quality products and services to the fleet in support of naval aviation.

Housing and Schools. Approximately 180 units of government housing are available at the center, as well as 45 mobile home sites and rooms for more than 580 unaccompanied personnel. The Navy exchange operates a Navy Lodge for transients and visitors. Permanent change-of-station personnel may obtain spaces on a reserved basis at this facility. Although there are no schools for dependent children at the station, there is a day-care facility there that can accommodate up to 100 children.

Personal Services and Recreation. The station lies just to the east of the Fort Dix Military Reservation, so military families stationed there may enjoy the many facilities available at both Fort Dix and McGuire Air Force Base. The station has both medical and dental facilities, a commissary and exchange, and a consolidated club. The Navy exchange also operates a package store. Recreational facilities include a bowling center, a golf course, tennis and racquetball courts, a swimming pool, a gymnasium, and a conservation area where hunting and fishing are permitted in season.

The Local Area. Philadelphia is one hour to the west of the center, and New York is about an hour's drive to the north. The northern New Jersey and Catskill ski regions are also nearby, and New Jersey's famous shore resorts are only minutes to the east of the center. The station is located in the state's famous Pine Barrens, a national reserve studded with beautiful lakes, rivers, and forests offering camping, hunting, hiking, swimming, boating, and fishing.

For more information, write to Public Affairs Office, Code O1P, Naval Engineering Station, Lakehurst, NJ 08753-5041, or call (732) 323-2011.

NEW MEXICO

Air Force

CANNON AIR FORCE BASE

The lowest point in the state of New Mexico is 3,000 feet above sea level. The highest spot is more than 13,000 feet, and Cannon Air Force Base is four-fifths of a mile high, at 4,295 feet. This puts Cannon squarely in the high plains country of eastern New Mexico and the Texas Panhandle.

History. Named in honor of Gen. John K. Cannon, one of the nation's outstanding leaders in the development of airpower, Cannon AFB traces its existence back to 1942, when the Army Air Corps took control of the civilian airfield at Clovis and named the site Clovis Army Airfield. Today the base is home to the Air Force's 27th Fighter Wing, which operates the swing-wing F/EF-111 aircraft and F-16 Falcons. The base now covers a land area of almost 4,500 acres and boasts a population of 3,300 military personnel, their 3,500 dependents, and 468 civilian employees.

Housing and Schools. There are 1,722 units of family housing at Cannon, as well as 44 temporary living units that may be used by families traveling on official orders. Cannon AFB operates two day-care centers and a preschool for dependent children. Clovis has several elementary and junior high schools and one high school to which military children living at Cannon are sent. Adult education available at the base includes courses offered by Clovis Community College, Eastern New Mexico University, Chapman College, and other institutions.

Personal Services. Base facilities include a modern and well-equipped ambulatory clinic and a commissary that stocks more than 10,000 line items in its 25,000-square-foot sales area. The base exchange and its concessions, as well as a base shopette and several food facilities, offer much to the quality of life at Cannon AFB.

Recreation. Recreational facilities include a 16-lane bowling alley, an 18-hole golf course, a movie theater, a youth center, softball and football fields, a rock-climbing wall, a completely equipped gymnasium, two swimming pools, a skeet and trap range, officers and enlisted clubs, and a recreation center. The outdoor recreation program offers trips and tours throughout the year.

The Local Area. Cannon AFB is situated 7 miles west of Clovis, a town of about 34,500, and is 105 miles west of Lubbock, Texas. Albuquerque, population 285,000, is about 260 miles west of Clovis. The climate in this part of the state is dry, with little rainfall or snowfall during an average year. Although winter temperatures are sometimes low and summers are hot, the low humidity makes them bearable.

Clovis, established in 1906 by the Santa Fe Railway, takes its name from Clovis I, king of the Franks from 461 to 511 A.D. There are eight public parks in Clovis, totaling 240 acres and offering recreational activities from bowling to a zoo. Portales, fifteen miles south of Cannon, is a city of museums: The Roosevelt County Museum, the Paleo-Indian Institute, the Miles Museum, and the National History Museum are all on the main campus of Eastern New Mexico University; the Blackwater Draw Early Man Museum is just a few miles north of town on U.S. Highway 70. All these museums are fitting for a place that has been populated for at least 12,000 years, although the town has been there only since the 1880s.

For more information, write to 27 FW Public Affairs, 100 S DL Ingram Boulevard, Suite 102, Cannon AFB, NM 88103-5216, or call (505) 784-4131. Home page: *www.cannon.af.mil.*

HOLLOMAN AIR FORCE BASE

Six miles southwest of Alamogordo is Holloman Air Force Base. Nestled between the Sacramento and the San Andreas Mountains, the base is home to the 49th Fighter Wing. Holloman's aircraft include the AT-38B, F-4EF, and F-117A stealth fighter.

History. The history of Holloman began in February 1942, when Alamogordo Army Airfield was established on the site. On 16 July 1945, the atomic age was ushered in with the explosion of the first atomic bomb in the northwest corner of the airfield's bombing range, now known as Trinity Site. In February 1948, the base was renamed after Col. George V. Holloman, a pioneer in the guided-missile-research field.

The 3,900 military and 900 civilian personnel at Holloman are responsible for the base's 55,000 acres, which are spread throughout south-central New Mexico. More than 6,600 family members call Holloman home.

Housing and Schools. More than 1,500 units of family housing are available at Holloman, and there are 50 temporary quarters for newcomers, as well as more than 280 units for visitors and a campground that can be used by both incoming personnel and transients.

Holloman operates a child-care center, as well as a school complex that includes kindergarten through grade eight. Middle and senior high schools are available in nearby Alamogordo. The education center offers adults college courses from a variety of institutions, including New Mexico State University–Alamogordo, Park College, Troy State, and Central Texas College.

Personal Services. Excellent medical facilities are offered at Holloman in the form of a twenty-bed USAF hospital. William Beaumont Army Medical Center is available in El Paso, Texas, about 90 miles south of the base. Holloman has a commissary stocked with 10,000 line items and a base exchange that features numerous concessions.

Recreation. Recreation facilities at Holloman are also outstanding. The base offers a 24-lane bowling center, a nine-hole golf course, two swimming pools, a physical fitness center, a consolidated hobby shop, a skeet and trap club, a boarding stable, and a community center. The Holloman Family Camp, open year-round, has 12 camper spaces with all hookups, picnicking, fishing, and camping equipment rentals.

The Local Area. Holloman AFB is located ten minutes from the White Sands National Monument, which is open year-round. Alamogordo has a population of about 31,000, just large enough to offer the advantages of a modern metropolis and none of the disadvantages, such as crowding and pollution.

The climate in this part of New Mexico is dry and hot. Summer temperatures average from the mid-80s to the mid-90s, but low humidity, about 35 percent year-round, makes the heat bearable. The winters are fairly mild, with little or no snowfall.

For more information, write to Public Affairs Office, 490 First Street, Suite 2800, Holloman AFB, NM 88330-8287, or call (505) 475-6511. Home page: *www.holloman.af.mil.*

KIRTLAND AIR FORCE BASE

The fiscal year 1998 economic impact that Kirtland Air Force Base provided to both its local community and the Air Force was over $2 billion. But the operational impact of this particular base was as inestimable as it was indispensable. Kirtland is located on the southeast side of Albuquerque, beside the Albuquerque International Airport. The elevation of the airport is 5,312 feet above sea level. The sun shines there 76 percent of the time, and the humidity averages 30 percent in summer and only 44 percent in the winter.

History. Kirtland AFB was named in honor of Col. Roy C. Kirtland, an early military aviator. Military aviation first came to Albuquerque in 1939. Today the base is home to the Air Force Operations Test and Evaluation Center, Sandia National Laboratories, and other tenant units hosted by the 377th Air Base Wing. More than 3,900 military personnel, their 4,400 family members, and over 2,600 civilian employees call Kirtland home these days. The largest organization at Kirtland is Sandia National Laboratories, which employs the majority of the civilian personnel on the base.

Housing and Schools. There are more than 1,800 sets of family quarters at Kirtland. The base also offers 58 units in its temporary-living facility, which may be obtained by families traveling on official orders; visitors may be accommodated on a space-available basis only.

A child-care center is operated on the base, and there are three Albuquerque elementary schools located there as well. Junior and senior high school students attend schools in Albuquerque. On-base college programs are offered by Chapman College, Embry-Riddle Aeronautical University, Southern Illinois University, the College of Santa Fe, New Mexico Highlands University, Webster College, and the University of New Mexico.

Personal Services. The Air Force hospital provides both inpatient and outpatient medical services. The commissary at Kirtland is one of the largest in the Air Force. The base exchange service operates a wide variety of retail stores and concessions; the main exchange building was extended and renovated in 1989.

Recreation. Recreation facilities at the base are quite excellent and include two gymnasiums, four swimming pools, an 18-hole golf course, bowling lanes, and many other facilities and programs designed to permit base personnel to make the most of their leisure time. The National Atomic Museum, open seven days a week, is a major tourist attraction. Its displays chronicle the development of nuclear weapons, as well as the peaceful development of atomic energy. Films and lecture demonstrations are also offered.

The Local Area. Albuquerque, a city of 560,000 people, was founded by the Spanish in 1706 and takes its name from La Villa de San Francisco de Albuquerque, after the king of Spain's patron saint and the duke of Albuquerque. The city offers residents and visitors over 100 parks, and the Albuquerque Zoo is one of the best in the country.

For more information, write to Public Affairs Division, 377th Air Base Wing, 2000 Wyoming SE, Kirtland AFB, NM 87117-5606, or call (505) 846-5991. Home page: *www.kirtland.af.mil.*

Army

WHITE SANDS MISSILE RANGE

White Sands Missile Range is a national test range designed to support research, development, testing, and evaluation for the Army, Navy, Air Force, National Aeronautics and Space Administration, and other approved U.S. government agencies and foreign governments. The range also plans and conducts development testing and evaluation of Army missiles, rockets, and materiel systems.

History. White Sands Missile Range is located in south-central New Mexico in a region known as the Tularosa Basin, between the Sacramento Mountains to the east and the San Andres and Organ Mountains to the west. The range opened on 9 July 1945 as White Sands Proving Ground. One week later the first atomic bomb was exploded on the range at an area now known as Trinity Site. Missile testing began in September 1945 with Tiny Tim firings and "took off" with captured German V-2 rockets in 1946. White Sands served as the landing site for the space shuttle Columbia on 30 March 1982, at the range's Northrup Strip. Today, 430 military personnel, their 1,300 family members, and 2,800 civilian employees call White Sands home.

Housing and Schools. White Sands has over 600 sets of family quarters. Temporary quarters are usually available for new families. Civilian personnel are authorized on-base housing on a space-available basis. More than 80 units are available for unaccompanied military personnel as well.

Dependent children attend school on post from kindergarten through grade eight; high school is available at Onate High in Las Cruces, about a 30-minute bus ride from the base. The education center offers college courses from New Mexico State University, Dona Ana Branch of New Mexico State, Troy State University, and Florida Institute of Technology.

Personal Services and Recreation. Medical care is provided by the McAfee U.S. Army Health Clinic, a modern outpatient medical facility. There is also a dental clinic at White Sands, and as a designated remote facility, the clinic offers comprehensive dental care for military personnel and their families. The post offers a commissary with 10,000 line items and a post exchange with many concessions, such as an optical shop, a flower shop, a cafe, a service station, and a shopette with a full line of convenience foods. Recreational facilities include a swimming pool, a golf course, tennis courts, a gymnasium, hobby and craft shops, a park with RV hookups, and camping and hiking areas.

The Local Area. At an elevation of almost 4,000 feet, with an average rainfall of only ten inches, White Sands is a dry area, with temperatures averaging a high of 92° F in summer and a low of 36° F in winter.

Las Cruces, a few miles from the main post, is a community that reflects the blending of three cultures—Indian, Spanish-Mexican, and American. The "Whole Enchilada Fiesta" brings alive the history of the area, as do other pageants and programs throughout the year; the Indians of Tortugas hold an annual Christmas pageant, as they have for centuries. The town also benefits from a wide variety of cultural activities sponsored by New Mexico State University. El Paso, Texas, just to the south, is called the "Gateway to the West," and along with other attractions in the area, Fort Bliss is located there, with its many splendid facilities. Within a day's driving, one can see a range of natural features, from mountains and Indian ruins to lava beds formed by ancient volcanoes.

For more information, write to Public Affairs Office, Building 122, White Sands Missile Range, NM 88002-5047, or call (505) 678-1134. Home page: *www.wsmr.arm.mil.*

NEW YORK

Army

FORT DRUM

A few miles to the east of Fort Drum begins the Adirondack Park, some 6,000 square miles of lakes, forests, mountains, and streams that form one of the most famous tourist attractions in the northeastern United States. Just to the northeast of the post are the St. Lawrence River's Thousand Islands and Thousand Islands State Park. Across the river is Ontario, Canada, and to the west of Fort Drum and Watertown is Lake Ontario, the easternmost of the Great Lakes. Fort Drum boasts the most modern facility in the Army with a state-of-the-art deployment facility, located at Wheeler Sack Army Airfield, and a 10,000 foot runway.

History. Named after Lt. Gen. Hugh A. Drum, a commander of the 1st U.S. Army during the early years of World War II, Fort Drum is now the home of the 10th Mountain Division (Light Infantry) and also a training facility for more than 30,000 U.S. Army National Guard and Reserve troops each year. The 10th Mountain Division has been the Army's most-deployed division in the 1990s, seeing action in Somalia and the Balkans, during Desert Shield/Storm, and on numerous other headline-grabbing assignments. Training, mobilization, and sustained deployment remain the focus of the 10th Mountain Division. It is comprised of two infantry brigades with three battalions each, a brigade-sized artillery, aviation and division support command units, and additional battalion-sized support units. The post is situated nine miles northeast of Watertown (population 29,000). Fort Drum is currently home to 10,800 active-duty personnel, their 8,800 family members, and over 2,200 civilian workers accommodated by the fort's 107,265 acres. Syracuse is 80 miles to the south via Interstate 81, and Kingston, Ontario, is 70 miles to the north. Lake Placid, site of the 1932 and 1980 Olympics, is 100 miles to the east. Toronto and Montreal are only five hours away by car.

Housing and Schools. There are over 560 units of officer and 3,900 units of enlisted family housing available at Fort Drum. Temporary lodging is provided by a 112-room inn.

No dependent schooling is available on post, but Fort Drum's education office offers a wide range of programs, including college courses up to the graduate level. Most courses are affiliated with Jefferson Community College in Watertown, Syracuse University in Oswego and Potsdam, and Empire State College.

Personal Services and Recreation. Fort Drum has a post exchange, a commissary, and a health clinic. There is a swimming and picnic beach on the installation, as well as an outdoor equipment rental facility. A physical fitness center and soldiers' gym include indoor pools. The post also has a bowling alley, a movie theater, an arts and craft center and hobby shops, tennis and racquetball courts, numerous outdoor sports fields, and similar morale-boosting resources.

New construction includes a consolidated facility, the Commons at Dillenbeck's Corners. This facility replaced both officer and NCO clubs and includes a restaurant sports bar and banquet rooms. The summers at Fort Drum are mild and short, and the winters are long and cold. Snow falls from November to April, with heavy accumulation from December through February. Other tenant units include the U.S. Army Medical Department Activity, U.S. Army Dental Activity, 20th Air Support Operations Squadron, U.S. Army Corps of Engineers, NCO Academy, 725th Ordnance Company, 174th Infantry Brigade, and many smaller units.

For more information, write to Public Affairs Office, Building P10000, Room 121, Fort Drum, NY 13602-5028, or call (315) 772-5461. Home page: *www.drum.army.mil.*

FORT HAMILTON

History. The military presence at Fort Hamilton stretches back to the very birth of the American Republic when, on 4 July 1776, a small American battery on the site of the present-day installation fired into one of the British men-of-war convoying troops to suppress the Revolution. The cornerstone of Fort Hamilton was put into place in June 1825, although at the time it was known as Fort Lewis. The installation was not officially named Fort Hamilton—after our first secretary of the treasury, Alexander Hamilton—until the twentieth century. During its long history, such notables as Robert E. Lee and Thomas "Stonewall" Jackson served there.

Today Fort Hamilton is home for the 1179th Deployment Control Group, 343rd Combat Support Hospital, 423rd Medical Battalion, and other tenant units. It is the only active Army post in the New York metropolitan area. There are more than 470 active-duty personnel, their 1,300 family members, 1,400 reservists, and 540 civilian employees assigned to Fort Hamilton.

Housing and Schools. Fort Hamilton controls over 440 units of family housing. The forty-eight-unit Adams Guest House is available for incoming permanent change-of-station personnel for up to 30 days; others may use the facility on a space-available basis with a seven-day-maximum-stay rule.

Although a child-development center is operated on the post, schooling for dependent children is available only in the local community. Adult educational services are available from the post education center and include a full range of academic testing, as well as tuition assistance for those who wish to attend off-duty college courses.

Personal Services. Personal support facilities include the Ainsworth U.S. Army Health Clinic, an outpatient health-care facility. Referrals are made there to local hospitals or military hospitals at installations elsewhere along the East Coast. The post exchange offers a full range of shopping possibilities, as well as numerous concessions, including a Burger King, a service station, and a package beverage store. There is also a commissary at the post that is open six days a week.

Recreation. Morale and welfare facilities include a community club, a bowling center, a gymnasium, a post theater, and a library containing 28,000 volumes and over 50 magazine and newspaper titles. Located in the best-preserved portion of the original fort is the Harbor Defense Museum, which houses a collection of artifacts that tell the fascinating story of the discovery and fortification of New York Harbor.

The Local Area. The neighborhood around Fort Hamilton offers a tremendous variety of shops and other attractions and conveniences. Adequate public transportation is available for trips to Manhattan (via subway and bus), Governors Island, and the Statue of Liberty.

For more information, write to Public Affairs Office, NYAC, Fort Hamilton, NY 11252-5700, or call (718) 630-4820. Home page: *www.nad.usace.army.mil.*

U.S. MILITARY ACADEMY

The U.S. Military Academy (USMA) is our nation's oldest military academy. Steeped in tradition and history, its purpose is "to educate, train, and inspire the Corps of Cadets so that each graduate is a commissioned leader of character committed to the values of Duty, Honor, Country; professional growth throughout a career as an officer in the United States Army; and a lifetime of selfless service to the Nation." The West Point community includes approximately 5,000 officers and enlisted staff and faculty members whose primary duty is the education and training of the more than 4,000 cadets at the USMA.

History. Located on the Hudson River some sixty miles north of New York City, West Point is situated in some of the most beautiful and historic countryside of the Northeast. It was Benedict Arnold's attempt to deliver the plans of the fortress at West Point to the British in 1780 that revealed him as a traitor. In 1802, the fort at West Point was designated a training school for officers by an act of Congress. Famous generals such as Grant, Lee, Pershing, MacArthur, Eisenhower, Patton, Custer, Westmoreland, and Schwarzkopf are among West Point's graduates.

U.S. Military Academy at West Point, New York U.S. ARMY PHOTO

The academy is supported by more than 1,400 active-duty personnel, their 4,200 family members, and 3,400 civilian employees.

Housing and Schools. About 1,000 units of government quarters are available at West Point. They range in size from two to five bedrooms, while bachelor quarters range from efficiency apartments to two-bedroom units. The oldest quarters were built in 1894 and the newest in the 1970s. Some are located at West Point proper and some at Stewart Army Subpost, approximately 17 miles northwest of the reservation. Guest quarters ranging from single rooms with shared bathrooms to three-bedroom apartments are available only at Stewart and must be reserved thirty days before occupancy. Assignment to family quarters is mandatory; approval must be obtained from the housing office before moving off post.

There are on-post schools for children in kindergarten through grade eight; high school students are bused to schools in nearby Highland Falls. The post education center assists active-duty personnel with a variety of educational programs, from basic skills enhancement through graduate-level college courses.

Personal Services and Recreation. Keller Army Community Hospital is a 65-bed modern health-care facility that provides complete health services to the Corps of Cadets and active-duty and retired military personnel and their dependents. West Point also has a post exchange, a commissary, and other facilities and services for military personnel and their families, including a wide variety of both indoor and outdoor recreation activities, from swimming and bowling to golf and ice skating. Outdoor recreation equipment can be obtained from the Community Recreation Division, including backpacks, sleeping bags, camping equipment, fishing boats with motors, and trailers.

Opened in 1854, the West Point Museum is the oldest military museum within the Department of Defense. It contains what is probably the largest, most diverse collection of military artifacts in the Western Hemisphere. It offers six exhibition galleries that focus on key topics of a military nature, ranging from the history of warfare to a detailing of America's wars, as well as a history of West Point and the history of small and large weapons used by the Army. Admission is free and the museum is open daily from 10:30 A.M. to 4:15 P.M.; it is closed Thanksgiving, Christmas, and New Year's Day.

The Local Area. The West Point military reservation is only a ten-minute drive north of the Palisades Interstate Park, which offers visitors outdoor recreation year-round. The Hudson River Valley is full of beautiful scenic and interesting historic landmarks, including Washington's Revolutionary War headquarters in Newburgh. The famous resort area of the Catskill Mountains is only a little more than one hour north of West Point via good roads, and New Hampshire, Vermont, Massachusetts, Connecticut, and upstate New York are within easy driving distances for longer trips. In addition, the cultural and historic attractions of New York City are only an hour away.

For more information, write to Public Affairs Office, U.S. Military Academy, West Point, NY 10996-1788, or call (914) 938-4011. Home page: *www.usma.edu.*

WATERVLIET ARSENAL

Known as "America's Cannon Factory," this smaller Army-owned and operated manufacturing facility is located just outside of Albany in upstate New York. It is a little facility that packs a lot of wallop.

History. Built in 1813, this arsenal has played a leading role in America's defense throughout its long history of producing large-bore cannon and a wide variety of other military wherewithal. The billion dollar arsenal manufacturing complex is situated on a 42-acre site and spans 72 buildings with 1.2 million square feet of manufacturing space. It is also home to the Army Benet Lab, with the mission of developing arsenal products and technology.

Housing and Schools. The Rotterdam Housing Area is located just outside Schenectady, New York, and has 51 housing units for enlisted families and six officer units. Most of the military personnel are recruiters or ROTC instructors. There are 20 officers' quarters with two to five bedrooms. At nearby Rotterdam housing, there are 45 enlisted units. There are active-duty military officer quarters available, but the waiting list is six to twelve months. Typical monthly apartment rents range from $500 to $700, and house rentals range from $850 to $1,200 per month. There are both Department of Defense Dependents School opportunities and public/private schools in the local area. The Maplewood School has much to offer, and private schools consist of elementary through high school. Colleges and universities include Hudson Valley Community College located in Troy, the College of St. Rose in Albany, and the State University of New York–Albany.

Personal Services. A very small health clinic is available to personnel stationed at Watervliet. Sick call takes place in the mornings and appointments are recommended. Though small, the facility has some conveniences available, including a beauty shop (Great Expectations), a credit union, and a few convenience stores. Life at an arsenal usually translates into living in the surrounding civilian community and looking there for most community resources. While there is an officer's club, an enlisted club is not available.

Recreation. There are some excellent opportunities for relaxation, including Lake George, where a gamut of water sports are available to the public. Call Lake George officials at (518) 761-6366 for more details. There is also a recreational center, a 9-hole golf course, a gym, a tennis court, and a public swimming pool.

The Local Area. Watervliet is eight miles from Albany, New York (population 85,000). Across the Hudson River is Troy with its history of shirtmaking and iron manufacturing. Albany's over four centuries of significant culture-shaping historical events make the area worth exploring, particularly for colonial history buffs.

For more information, write to the Commander, Watervliet Arsenal, Attention: SIOWV-ISA-A, Building 21, Watervliet, NY 12189-4050 or call (518) 266-5103. Home page: *www.wva.army.mil.*

Navy

SCOTIA NAVAL ADMINISTRATIVE UNIT

The Scotia Naval Administrative Unit provides logistical support and services to the Naval Nuclear Power Training Unit (NPTU) in West Milton, New York, and personal property and administrative services in the West Milton, Saratoga, Schenectady, and Scotia areas of New York for approximately 1,700 resident active-duty Navy personnel, their 3,000 dependents, and 63 civilian employees.

Housing, Schools, and Personal Services. Scotia operates 200 units of family housing in Saratoga Springs, about seven miles from NPTU and twenty from Scotia: 100 modern two-bedroom apartments for students and 100 two-bedroom town-house units for resident enlisted personnel grade E-6 and below. Local rentals for families average between $500 and $900 per month; bachelors can expect to pay between $175 and $300 per month, as long as they are willing to share their accommodations. Dependent children attend school in the Saratoga Springs City School District. There are several colleges in the area, public and private, including Skidmore College, Rensselaer Polytechnic Institute, Russell Sage College, and State University of New York–Albany.

Medical care is provided by an outpatient medical clinic located in the Benedict Community Health Center at Ballston Spa. Referral and emergency care are provided by Saratoga Hospital. There are a commissary and a Navy exchange store at Scotia, as well as a minimart at the Saratoga Springs housing complex. Recreational facilities available at Scotia include outdoor sports areas, a playground, and a picnic area; equipment rental is available at both Scotia and Ballston Spa.

The Local Area. Scotia is three miles west of downtown Schenectady; NPTU, Ballston Spa, is about 25 miles north. Nestled among the Adirondacks, Catskills, and Berkshire Mountains, the area offers plenty of outdoor recreational opportunities, including fishing, boating, camping, hiking, and winter sports. The world-famous spa at Saratoga Springs (population 25,000) is a major attraction, as are the horse races held there every August. The Revolutionary War's Saratoga Battlefield is another attraction. Boston, New York City, and Canada are all within only a few hours' drive. The summers in this part of the state are mild, with daytime temperatures in the 80s, dropping into the 50s at night; winters can be harsh, with as much as 100 inches of snow and temperatures that can dip to -20° F.

For more information, write to Administrative Office, Naval Administrative Unit, 26 Quiet Harbor Drive, Saratoga Springs, NY 12866, or call (518) 395-3600. Home page: *www.2.netcom.com\~fsc4.*

NORTH CAROLINA

Air Force

POPE AIR FORCE BASE

The airmen at Pope are fond of pointing out that it is they who put the "air" in "airborne" for the Army paratroopers stationed at nearby Fort Bragg, North Carolina. This is a fact, because the C-130E Hercules aircraft of the 43rd Airlift Wing based at Pope airlift Army paratroopers daily in the performance of their training missions. In addition, Pope's aviators are trained and ready to deliver personnel and equipment to just about any place in the world where they might be needed—with or without parachutes and at a moment's notice. Also assigned to Pope are the Combat Control School, 24th Special Tactics Squadron, and Joint Special Operations Command. Today Pope's population consists of 4,800 airmen, their 2,400 family members, and 500 civilian employees.

History. Pope Air Force Base is one of the oldest Air Force installations. Named after 1st Lt. Harley Halbert Pope, who was killed on 7 January 1919 when his aircraft crashed into the Cape Fear River near Fayetteville, the base was commissioned in March 1919.

Housing and Schools. An important fact of life at Pope is Fort Bragg, where airmen and soldiers enjoy the joint use of the many facilities and programs for military personnel and their families. Pope has over 400 sets of family quarters for Air Force personnel. The waiting list for these quarters varies from two to 20 months, depending on the sponsor's date of arrival at the base and the size of his or her family; the average waiting time is about 20 months. But Pope personnel also share some of the more than 4,000 quarters situated on Fort Bragg. Temporary lodging is available on base for transient personnel, with reservations going only to incoming and outgoing permanently assigned airmen and their families. Many rental properties are available off base. A family can expect to pay about $600 a month or more for a three-bedroom, two-bath home in the Fayetteville area.

A child-care center is operated at Pope. Dependent children go to school in Fayetteville, where there are 19 public schools. The education center on base offers college courses for adults from Embry-Riddle Aeronautical, Golden Gate, and Southern Illinois Universities, as well as Webster, Central Texas, and Methodist Colleges.

Personal Services. A small base exchange and commissary are available at Pope, with larger facilities at Fort Bragg. Officers and NCO club systems and many other personal services are offered at Pope. Medical care is provided at a USAF clinic, with consultation and inpatient care provided at nearby Womack Army Hospital.

Recreation. Recreational services include an 18-hole golf course, a sixteen-lane bowling alley, a swimming pool, a gymnasium, hobby shops, tennis courts, and a picnic area overlooking the base. There is also a wonderful variety of recreational activities at Fort Bragg.

The Local Area. Recreation and sightseeing are available almost everywhere in North Carolina, with over one million acres of national forests and thirteen state parks that are open to residents and visitors. The Atlantic coast to the east and the Blue Ridge and Great Smoky Mountains to the west are near enough to Pope to be accessible for weekend trips.

For more information, write to Public Affairs Office, 43rd Airlift Wing, 259 Maynard Street, Pope AFB, NC 28308-2391, or call (910) 394-1110. Home page: *www.pope.af.mil.*

SEYMOUR JOHNSON AIR FORCE BASE

Seymour Johnson Air Force Base is located within the city limits of Goldsboro, which lies about fifty miles southeast of Raleigh, the state capital.

History. The base was named after Lt. Seymour Johnson, a native of Goldsboro who was killed in an aircraft accident near Norbeck, Maryland, in 1941. The host unit at the base is the 4th Fighter Wing, which flies the F-15E Strike Eagle. The major tenant unit is the 916th Air Refueling Wing, a reserve unit that flies the KC-135 Stratotanker. The base's military population consists of 4,400 active military personnel, their 6,900 family members, 800 reservists, and around 1,000 civilians.

Housing and Schools. There are currently more than 2,000 units of family housing on base, in addition to 45 mobile home spaces. Temporary lodging on base, with or without dependents, may be obtained on a space-available basis. Local rentals range from $350 to $600 monthly for two-bedroom apartments to as much as $600 to $800 a month for a three-bedroom unit. Two- and three-bedroom homes rent for $550 and up. The average cost for a two-bedroom mobile home is $300 per month.

A child-development center and before- and after-school programs operate on the base. Local public and private schools offer a variety of curricula for military family members. The base education center provides assistance and guidance to adults wishing to continue their educational development.

Personal Services and Recreation. Two clinics provide medical and dental services for military personnel and their dependents at the base: The Koritz Clinic provides outpatient care, and the Kiecker Clinic provides dental care. Seymour Johnson AFB also offers commissary and exchange facilities and enlisted and officers club systems. An on-base family camp, open year-round, is available with hookups for seven campsites. Fort Fisher Air Force Recreation Area, located at Kure Beach, North Carolina, near Wilmington, is also available. A fitness center, a golf course, a theater, and many other recreational facilities are also on base.

For more information, write to Family Support Center, 1200 Wright Brothers Avenue, Seymour Johnson AFB, NC 27531-2404, or call (919) 722-5400. Home page: *www.seymourjohnson.af.mil.*

Army

FORT BRAGG

Things are "jumping"at Bragg, "Home of the Airborne." It has earned this reputation over the years as troopers from the XVIII Airborne Corps, the 82nd Airborne Division, the 1st Special Operations Command (Airborne), and the Army Parachute Team (Golden Knights) continually parachute out of "perfectly good" airplanes.

History. Named after Confederate Gen. Braxton Bragg, a former artilleryman and North Carolinian, Camp Bragg emerged as a field artillery post in August 1918. It was redesignated Fort Bragg in September 1922, and the first military parachute jump was made there in 1923 from an artillery observation balloon. The first airborne units trained there in 1942, and during World War II, all five airborne divisions used in the war—the 82nd, the 101st, the 11th, the 13th, and the 17th—trained there. Today the post's 149,000 acres provide homes and maneuver areas for over 49,000 active-duty personnel, their 11,000 dependents, and more than 9,000 civilian employees who also work at Fort Bragg. A subinstallation, Fort Pickett, Virginia, consists of 45,000 acres with an active-duty population of 100 personnel. Fort Pickett is a training site for more than 21,000 reserve component personnel annually.

Housing and Schools. There are more than 4,800 sets of family quarters at Fort Bragg, ranging from two- to four-bedroom multiple apartments to single houses in nine separate housing areas. A 44-room guest house is available for transients, as well as more than 500 units for visitors.

Seven elementary schools, a middle school, and a junior high are operated on post, with a student enrollment of over 4,900, and the Army education center offers programs that include an individual learning center and MOS library, a language school, and college courses offering degrees up to the master's level.

Personal Services. Fort Bragg is an entirely self-contained installation that offers soldiers and their families the complete range of facilities and services available to the modern military community, from commissary and post exchange facilities to complete medical and dental care.

Recreation. Fort Bragg's morale support activities division offers an outstanding leisure-time program with over 70 different facilities, including 19 tennis courts, three 24-lane bowling centers, three movie theaters, a riding stable, an 18-hole golf course, a skeet range, a rod and gun club, an ice-skating rink, and nine physical fitness centers offering everything from weight lifting to swimming. The outdoor program includes Smith Lake, with picnic areas, a beach, and an Army travel camp with twenty-four sites for recreational vehicles.

The Local Area. Fayetteville, a city of more than 75,000, is just off post on Bragg Boulevard. The community offers many cultural opportunities and interesting historic sites. A one-hour drive in any direction will take the traveler to some feature of North Carolina's "Variety Vacationland." Fayetteville is a two-hour drive from the state's famed Atlantic beaches, and within a 200-mile radius are some of the nation's most unspoiled parks and campgrounds and the Blue Ridge Mountains.

For more information, write to Public Affairs Office, 18th Airborne Corps and Fort Bragg, Fort Bragg, NC 28307, or call (910) 396-0011. Home page: *www.bragg.army.mil.*

Coast Guard

ELIZABETH CITY COAST GUARD SUPPORT CENTER

Established in 1940 as a seaplane base, the Elizabeth City Coast Guard Support Center is located about 50 miles south of Norfolk, Virginia. There are presently five units onboard the center: Air Station Elizabeth City, Aircraft Repair and Supply Center, Support Center Elizabeth City, Aviation Technical Training Center, and the National Strike Force Coordination Center. With the exception of the Strike Force, all commands are colocated on the approximately 800 acres of real estate that comprise the center complex. The Strike Force is located approximately five miles east of the complex. The center is home to 600 active-duty personnel, 1,800 family members, and 500 civilian employees.

Housing and Schools. Seventy-two housing units and numerous leased units are maintained by the center. A permanent-party barracks is available for all single personnel in grade E-6 or below. There are also nine temporary lodging rooms in the barracks. Also available are six trailers and four RV spaces. While there are no schools or day-care facilities onboard, the Elizabeth City–Pasquotank School System serves nearly 6,300 students in the area; there are also two four-year universities and a two-year community college for adult education in the immediate vicinity.

Personal Services and Recreation. There are a small country store and an exchange at Elizabeth City. Medical care onboard the center is limited to active-duty outpatient care; definitive medical care is available locally or at Norfolk. The complex has a gym, a pool, hobby shops, an all-hands club, a driving range, a fitness trail, and a beach. The Hangar 7 Community Center is available for lunches and dances.

The Local Area. Elizabeth City is situated along the Pasquotank River, in the northeastern corner of North Carolina, and is the seat of Pasquotank County. The county population numbers 32,000 and is considered the cultural, commercial, medical, and educational center of the Albemarle area. The average temperature in the region is 34° F in winter and 79° F in summer. Elizabeth City boasts two industrial parks with 450 acres of land. Water sports such as boating, skiing, and fishing are available on the Pasquotank River. There are two 18-hole golf courses and a nine-hole par-three course available. The city's recreation department has a wide range of activities, including softball leagues for all ages, soccer, baseball, and aerobics.

For more information, write to Public Affairs Officer, U.S. Coast Guard Air Station, Elizabeth City, NC 27909-5004, or call (252) 335-6229.

Marine Corps

CAMP LEJEUNE

Camp Lejeune occupies 153,439 acres consisting of sandy beaches and swamps along the North Carolina coast between Wilmington to the south and Cherry Point Marine Corps Air Station a few miles to the north. Camp Lejeune has an actual perimeter of some 85 miles, with fourteen miles fronting the ocean paralleled by the famous Intracoastal Waterway. The New River divides the installation roughly in half.

History. Construction began on the installation, named in honor of Gen. John Archer Lejeune, in April 1941. Today it is home to more than 39,000 military personnel, 10,000 dependents, and a civilian workforce of over 4,200. The major commands aboard are the 2nd Marine Expeditionary Forces (MEF), the Marine Forces Atlantic, the 2nd Marine Division, the 2nd Force Service Support Group, and the Marine Corps Base. Marine Aircraft Groups 26 and 29 are based at Marine Corps Air Station (New River), an installation of 2,600 acres, immediately adjacent to Lejeune.

Housing and Schools. Camp Lejeune offers every facility and service available on a major military installation, including about 4,300 units of family housing, ranging in size from one-bedroom dwellings to four-bedroom town houses. Camp Lejeune also has a 90-unit hostess house for personnel in transit, their families, and authorized guests. The Camp Lejeune dependents school system includes all grades, kindergarten through high school. The base education

Marine Corps Training at Camp Lejeune, North Carolina USMC PHOTO

office offers adult education programs that range from mere "fun" classes to college-level courses.

Personal Services. The commissary at Camp Lejeune offers excellent shopping, as does the one at the New River facility—over 4,000 line items at each outlet. The Marine exchange offers over 100 activities at Camp Lejeune and New River; indeed, the Lejeune exchange is one of the largest in the Corps. Medical service is provided by the U.S. Naval Hospital, a 265-bed facility, one of the largest and best-equipped military hospitals in the South.

Recreation. Recreational activities abound at Camp Lejeune, from horseback-riding facilities, swimming pools, and skeet and trap shooting to beach cabanas. The new state-of-the-art French Creek Fitness Center offers the latest in fitness technology. New River has several picnic recreation areas and a marina. The base also operates Onslow Beach, a year-round seashore recreational facility with 74 campsites. Reservations are required thirty days in advance for stays of not more than seven days. Campsites are on the beach and in heavily wooded areas on the inland waterway. The coastal regions of the Carolinas are good places for hunting and fishing. Animals that can be hunted include turkey, bear, deer, and duck; both freshwater and saltwater fishing can also be enjoyed.

Camp Lejeune is 116 miles southeast of Raleigh, the capital of North Carolina and a city of 500,000. Wilmington, North Carolina, is about 40 miles south of Camp Lejeune. The small town of Jacksonville is five miles east.

For more information, write to Public Affairs Office, PSC Box 20004, Camp Lejeune, NC 28542-0004, or call (910) 451-1113.

CHERRY POINT MARINE CORPS AIR STATION

Cherry Point Marine Corps Air Station occupies about 12,000 acres of land at its primary complex, approximately midway between New Bern and Morehead City, adjacent to the town of Havelock, just off U.S. 70 along the Neuse River. Croatan National Forest borders the station, and to the southwest is Camp Lejeune. Not far to the north are Pamlico and Albemarle Sounds and the Cape Hatteras National Seashore area. Altogether, this is fascinating country, rich in history and an outdoorsman's paradise.

The air station was commissioned in May 1942, and today it is home for 66,000 Marines and sailors, their 23,000 family members, and approximately 6,000 civilian employees of the Marine Corps air station and the naval aviation depot. Cherry Point MCAS is one of the best all-weather jet bases anywhere, and it is the largest Marine Corps air station. It is also the largest air station in the Marine Corps. The AV-8B Harrier II with its vertical/short take-off and landing capacity is also one of the supported aircraft at this station.

Housing and Schools. The MCAS controls over 2,900 units of family housing. Depending on the availability of these quarters, waiting periods of a few weeks to a few months are not uncommon. There is also a 76-space mobile home park and guest accommodations for over 250 visiting personnel.

Cherry Point has no on-base schooling, but a child-care center is open from September through May. Hourly care is provided Monday through Friday and Sunday morning for church services. The education-extension school offices offer a testing section, counseling on all subjects related to adult education, and enrollment in a large number of college programs consisting of undergraduate and postgraduate degree work offered by Boston and Southern Illinois Universities, Park College, and Craven Community College, among others.

Personal Services and Recreation. A Marine Corps exchange, a commissary, and a wide range of athletic and recreational facilities and programs are provided at Cherry Point. Medical care at the station is provided by a 23-bed naval hospital, known as the Halyburton Naval Hospital after a fallen World War II corpsman mortally wounded while giving aid to his comrades. On-station recreation includes a bowling alley; three swimming pools; a movie theater; handball, racquetball, and tennis courts; an 18-hole golf course; a riding stable; a gymnasium; and an archery range. Picnic and camping areas on the station may be used year-round. Hunting and fishing are permitted on the station, providing state and local licensing requirements are met.

The Local Area. The region of North Carolina in which Cherry Point MCAS is situated offers a great diversity of recreational opportunities, from the pine forests inland to the Atlantic Ocean seashore just a few miles east of the station. Cape Hatteras is only ninety miles to the northeast.

Just outside the main gate is the town of Havelock. New Bern is situated seventeen miles northwest of the air station. Founded in 1710 by Swiss and

German colonists, it is North Carolina's second-oldest city. Eighteen miles southeast of Cherry Point is Morehead City, home to the largest fleet of charter fishing boats in the central Atlantic Coast area. The generally mild climate permits some form of outdoor activity year-round.

For more information, write to Joint Public Affairs Office, Marine Corps Air Station, Cherry Point, NC 28533-5001, or call (252) 466-2811. Home page: *www.cherrypt.usmc.mil.*

NEW RIVER MARINE CORPS AIR STATION

Originally established in April 1944, the New River Marine Corps Air Station today comprises over 2,600 acres just south of the city of Jacksonville, across the New River from Camp Lejeune. It is home to Marine Aircraft Groups 26 and 29 and more than 7,000 active-duty personnel, almost 300 civilian employees, and 1,700 family members.

Housing, Schools, and Personal Services. The station operates more than 5,000 sets of family quarters for officers and enlisted personnel, as well as a 187-unit mobile home park and a 90-unit inn for guests. There are an elementary school and a child-care center at New River. Routine health care is provided by a branch clinic, with referral and inpatient care available at Camp Lejeune. Both commissary and exchange services are available at New River. A full range of recreational facilities is provided at the station, and station personnel and their families may also take advantage of the Onslow Beach recreation area operated by Camp Lejeune.

For more information, write to Joint Public Affairs Office, H&HS, PSC Box 21002, MCAS New River, Jacksonville, NC 28545-1002, or call (910) 451-1113. Home page: *www.lejeune.usmc.mil/mcasnr.*

NORTH DAKOTA

Air Force

GRAND FORKS AIR FORCE BASE

Dakota comes from an American Indian word meaning "friend." Grand Forks Air Force Base, with the 319th Air Refueling Wing's KC-135R Stratotankers poised to soar into flight in the event of provocation or contingency, is a great reassurance to those who are our friends and an equally great deterrent to those who are not.

Construction began at Grand Forks AFB in 1956, and the first Strategic Air Command weapon system, a KC-135 Stratotanker, arrived there in 1960. Today the base occupies over 5,000 acres 15 miles west of the city of Grand Forks and is home and workplace for 2,000 military personnel, their 4,200 dependents, and 500 civilian employees.

Housing and Schools. There are over 1,500 sets of family dwellings at the base. About forty temporary lodging units are also available, with first priority going to permanent-change-of-station personnel, although personnel on leave and guests of airmen assigned to Grand Forks are also welcome when space permits. The housing scene is rounded out with nearly 850 rooms for single personnel and 60 units for visitors.

Dependent schooling, kindergarten through eighth grade, is provided on base. High schools are available in downtown Grand Forks. A child-care center that can accommodate up to 140 children is also available. Higher education is provided through the base education office and includes on-base courses offered by the University of North Dakota, Park College, Central Michigan University, and Embry-Riddle Aeronautical University.

Personal Services. Medical care at Grand Forks is provided by a 20-bed facility operated by the 319th Medical Group. Dental care for dependents is limited to emergency procedures and preventative dental care. A well-stocked (8,500 line items) commissary and base exchange, banking facilities, NCO and officers clubs, and an on-base taxi service on call 24 hours a day add to the overall convenience of life at Grand Forks.

Recreation. Recreational activities include an indoor swimming pool; a modern, air-conditioned recreation center; a twenty-four-lane bowling center; a nine-hole golf course; hobby shops; and other activities.

The Local Area. Grand Forks is a modern city of over 49,000 people. The surrounding area abounds with things to do. Larimore, fifteen miles west of the base, offers golf, fishing, and swimming. Boating, swimming, and camping are available at Park River, two miles west of Grand Forks. At Mayville, thirty-five miles south of the base, the Golden Lake Game Management Area offers camping, swimming, boating, and fishing. The Canadian border is about 75 miles north of Grand Forks, and the major Canadian city of Winnipeg, with many historic and scenic attractions, is about 65 miles north of the border, which requires no passport to cross.

For more information, write to Public Affairs Office, 319 ARW, Grand Forks AFB, ND 58205-6321, or call (701) 747-3000. Home page: *www.grandforks.af.mil.*

MINOT AIR FORCE BASE

Minot Air Force Base occupies about 5,000 acres thirteen miles north of the city of Minot in land that is flat and treeless, where it gets very cold in the winter and hot in the summer, where agriculture is the main business in the surrounding countryside, and where you can listen to a symphony orchestra or attend art exhibitions among the various shopping malls located in Minot.

History. The Air Force first came to Minot in 1957, and today it is a major Air Combat Command base for the Minuteman III ICBM and the B-52H bomber. The base is headquarters for the 5th Bomb Wing, which is responsible for the 91st Space Group, as well as other units scattered throughout the state. More than 4,000 military personnel, their 6,500 family members, and nearly 500 civilian employees call Minot home.

Housing and Schools. There are over 2,100 sets of family quarters at Minot. Also on base are a hotel for transient officers and enlisted personnel and 40 units of temporary quarters for families awaiting permanent housing. Unaccompanied enlisted personnel may take advantage of more than 1,200 comfortable suites paid for by Uncle Sam. A child-care center is operated on the base, as are elementary and junior high schools. High schools are available in Minot. The base education services center provides high school equivalency programs and continuing-education programs offering degrees from Minot State University, North Dakota School of Science, and Central Michigan University.

Personal Services. Medical care is provided by the 5th Medical Group. Personal services include a commissary, a base exchange with numerous concessions, officers and NCO club facilities, banking, a credit union, and a theater.

Recreation. Recreational activities include a twenty-two-lane bowling center, two full gymnasiums, a nine-hole golf course, snowmobiling, stables, and the base's own theater troupe.

The Local Area. Minot is a thriving little metropolis of 35,000 people that boasts many fine recreational facilities for all seasons: gardens, swimming pools, and tennis in the summer; skiing, hockey, curling, and even ice sculpturing in the winter. The state of North Dakota is well watered and contains many excellent fishing spots. Hunters will also find lots of game there, and the state offers many excellent recreational sites.

For more information, write to Public Affairs Representative, 201 Summit Drive, Unit 4, Minot AFB, ND 58705-5000, or call (701) 723-1110. Home page: *www.minot.af.mil.*

OHIO

Air Force

WRIGHT–PATTERSON AIR FORCE BASE

Wright–Patterson Air Force Base is one of the nation's most important military installations. The base population consists of 6,200 active-duty personnel, their 11,000 family members, 1,900 reservists and 11,800 civilian employees, making it one of the single largest employers of any U.S. military installation in the world. It is the headquarters for a vast worldwide logistics system and is also the foremost research-and-development center in the U.S. Air Force. This is particularly fitting because nearby Dayton, home of the Wright brothers, is the "Birthplace of Aviation."

History. Known as McCook Field when it was established in 1917, renamed Wilbur Wright Field in 1924 and then Patterson Field in 1931 (after Lt. Frank Patterson, who died there in an airplane crash), Wright–Patterson got its present name in 1948. Today the base occupies 8,174 acres a few miles east-northeast of Dayton. The host organization is the Aeronautical Systems Center. Wright-Patterson is home to more than 6,700 military personnel, their 11,000 family members, and 1,900 reservists.

Housing and Schools. There are more than 680 officer and 1,500 enlisted family units at Wright–Patterson and 64 mobile homes in the base trailer park. Forty units of temporary lodging are also available on a reserved basis for incoming or outgoing permanently assigned personnel; temporary housing is on a space-available basis for all others. Single enlisted personnel are accommodated in 300 units, and there are 650 units for visiting personnel.

A preschool and six child-care centers are operated on the base, but dependent schooling is available only off base, in the surrounding communities. The base education office assists adults in furthering their education, from evening high school classes to participation in the Dayton Miami Valley Consortium, an association of local universities and colleges offering various degrees. These include Urbana, Clark Technical, Antioch, Wilmington, Southern State, Sinclair

Community, and Edison State Colleges; Wright State, Wilberforce, and Central State Universities; United Theological Seminary; and the Air Force Institute of Technology.

Personal Services. The Wright–Patterson Medical Center here is the second largest medical facility in the U.S. Air Force. Its staff provides medical services to more than 50,000 beneficiaries in the immediate area and also for the Defense Department's seven-state (Region Five) jurisdiction. The base commissary stocks over 5,000 items and is the fifth largest in the Air Force. The commissary is part of a shopping complex covering four acres, all under one roof.

Recreation. Recreation facilities on base include one nine-hole and two 18-hole golf courses, three gymnasiums, four swimming pools, four indoor and eight outdoor tennis courts, a 24-lane bowling alley, four lakes, a recreation center, an arts and crafts shop, an auto hobby shop, two health clubs, picnic areas, and a family camp with trailer pads and tent sites. The base has 60 acres of man-made lakes with good fishing and about 1,000 more acres where hunting is permitted. Hadden Park Recreation Area consists of 60 acres of woodland.

The Local Area. Over four million people live in the greater Dayton area, within ninety minutes' commuting distance of the city. Cincinnati is due south of Dayton; Springfield and Columbus are a bit to the northeast.

For more information, write to Aeronautical Systems Center, Public Affairs Office, 1865 Forth Street, Room 240, Wright–Patterson AFB, OH 45433-7129, or call (937) 257-1110. Home page: *www.wpafb.af.mil.*

OKLAHOMA

Air Force

ALTUS AIR FORCE BASE

Altus Air Force Base is home for some of the largest and most powerful aircraft in the world. With the best information available, the base had ten C-5 Galaxies, fourteen C-141 Starlifters, and twenty-five KC-135R Stratotankers. In the spring of 1996, Altus received the first of a projected eight C-17 Globemaster III aircraft. The C-5, one of the world's largest aircraft, is so huge that only 17 of them would have been needed to complete the whole Berlin Airlift, an operation that needed 308 conventional aircraft. The C-141s are big airplanes too, but the C-5's cargo floor area is triple that of the C-141A and double that of the C-141B models. With four engines that can develop 38,000 pounds of thrust apiece, the Galaxies' engines roar at Altus.

History. Altus had a modest beginning in 1942, when it was opened as a flight training school during World War II. Today its 4,694 acres are home to the 97th Air Mobility Wing, which provides aircrews with transition training on the C-141s and C-5s and worldwide air-refueling support. Altus is home to 2,000 active-duty personnel, their 2,900 family members, and 2,000 civilian employees. At any given time, there may be as many as 400 military students taking courses at Altus as well.

Housing and Schools. There are over 1,000 units of family housing at Altus. Also available are two three-bedroom units and a 30-family transient lodging facility used as guest housing, primarily for incoming and outgoing airmen permanently assigned to the base; others are permitted on a space-available basis only. Single airmen are housed in over 650 units, while there are about 500 units available for visiting personnel.

A child-care center is offered on the base. The town of Altus has an excellent public-school system consisting of six elementary schools (one on base), one junior high school, and a 70-acre senior high campus. The base education office arranges for off-duty college-level courses at both the undergraduate and graduate levels. Western Oklahoma State College in the Altus community offers a curriculum divided into seven divisions, covering business, communications, math and science, humanities and fine arts, social science, physical education, and military science.

Personal Services and Recreation. A commissary, a base exchange, a family medical clinic, a dental clinic, and banking facilities are only a few of the services offered on the base. Recreational facilities include an eighteen-hole golf course, two swimming pools, officers and NCO clubs, a gymnasium with a variety of fitness machines, a ten-lane bowling alley, hobby and craft shops, and a vigorous intramural sports program.

The Local Area. Altus is a thriving community of 25,000. The weather there is excellent, with approximately 340 flying days out of the year and an average rainfall of 22 inches. The base is only a couple miles from the town, 149 miles from Oklahoma City, and about a dozen miles to the nearest bend of the Red River and the Texas–Oklahoma border.

Outdoor recreational facilities abound in this region of the state. The Quartz Mountain State Park, with fishing, boating, and skiing, is 18 miles north of Altus. Hunting areas are located at the upper end of the Altus Reservoir and on the shores of the Steed Reservoir, 30 miles east of the base, in the Mountain Park Public Hunting Area. Buffalo, elk, deer, and longhorn steer may be observed, but not hunted, in the Wichita Mountain Wildlife Refuge.

For more information, write to 97th AMW Public Affairs Office, 100 Inez Boulevard, Suite 2, Altus AFB, OK 73523-5047, or call (580) 481-8100. Home page: *www.lts.aetc.af.mil.*

TINKER AIR FORCE BASE

Tinker Air Force Base occupies over 5,000 acres of land nine miles southeast of Oklahoma City. Much of that acreage was donated to the government by the community, and Tinker has become so integral a part of the economy of the city that its citizens have acquired control of large acreages in the vicinity to assure the compatibility of their community development with base operations.

History. Established in 1941 as an industrial plant geared for the repair of long-range bombers, the base was named in honor of Maj. Gen. Clarence L. Tinker, a native of Pawhuska, Oklahoma, who was killed leading a bomber attack against Wake Island during World War II. Today approximately 34,000 military and civilian personnel live and work at the base at the Oklahoma City Air Logistics Center, 72nd Air Base Wing, 552nd Air Control Wing, and associate units. The base population breaks down into about 8,600 military personnel and their 11,300 family members, 1,600 reservists, and 12,400 civilian employees.

Housing and Schools. Air Force personnel have 880 family housing units for their use, and 39 temporary lodging units are available on a reserved basis for permanent change-of-station personnel. All others are accepted on a space-available basis only. Visitors are offered 165 lodging units, while unaccompanied airmen are housed in no fewer than ten domitory-style buildings.

An elementary school on base provides education for children in kindergarten through sixth grade. The Air Force operates two on-base child-care centers and one preschool for dependent children. There are several colleges and university campuses in the city. The education services center of the base education office provides assistance to personnel desiring to participate in courses offered by these institutions, as well as a highly developed work-skill and vocational-training program.

Personal Services. The 72nd Medical Group at Tinker provides excellent medical care for active-duty and retired personnel and their families. The base exchange offers excellent shopping opportunities, and through its large number of concessions, it offers a full range of dining and service facilities. Tinker also has a very large main commissary and three shopettes.

Recreation. A wide range of recreational activities are offered at Tinker, including a 22-lane bowling center, tennis courts, a twenty-five-meter swimming pool, enlisted and officers clubs, hobby and craft shops, and an 18-hole, par-72 golf course. Outdoor facilities include a base picnic area and a family camp with 29 camper pads and other facilities.

The Local Area. The climate in the Oklahoma City area is mild, with hot summers and cool winters. Annual average snowfall is less than ten inches, and rainfall averages about thirty-two inches per year. Severe thunderstorms and tornadoes sometimes occur in the area, generally from March through early June.

Oklahoma City itself is home to over 444,000 people, with more than 958,000 people living in the metropolitan area. The city is bordered by two famous rivers: the Cimarron to the north and the Canadian, which forms the southwestern border of the town. The many lakes, reservoirs, and streams in the vicinity afford plenty of opportunities for water sports and fishing. Many spots nearby are rich in the history of the American West, such as the Cowboy Hall of Fame in Oklahoma City, the American Indian Hall of Fame State Memorial at Anadarko, Fort Sill, and the Chisholm Trail Museum near Kingfisher.

For more information, write to Public Affairs, 3001 Staff Drive 1AG78A, Tinker AFB, OK 73145-3010, or call (405) 732-7321. Home page: *www.tinker.af.mil.*

VANCE AIR FORCE BASE

History. The U.S. government bought the land on which Vance Air Force Base is now situated from the city of Enid for $1. That was back in 1941, and the base was used then as a flying school. In July 1949, it was named in honor of Lt. Col. Leon R. Vance, a former resident of Enid who won the Medal of Honor posthumously for action in World War II. Today Vance is home for the

71st Flying Training Wing of the Air Training Command. The 71st graduates about 140 pilots from its undergraduate pilot training program each year. Vance's population consists of about 700 active-duty personnel, their 1,400 family members, and 200 civilian employees.

Housing and Schools. About 230 units of military family housing are available at Vance. There are no dependent schools on base, but an elementary school is located just outside the main gate. Older children attend local schools in Enid and Waukomis. A child-development center is operated on base. Graduate, undergraduate, and vocational classes are available in the local area. Phillips University, Enid Higher Education Program, and O. T. Autry Vocational School are the three main institutions serving base personnel. The Enid Higher Education Program consists of Northern Oklahoma College and Oklahoma State, Northwestern Oklahoma State, and Phillips Universities.

Personal Services. Inpatient medical care for airmen and their families is not available at Vance. Persons requiring care beyond the capabilities of the USAF clinic are sent to the regional hospital at Sheppard Air Force Base, Texas, or to a civilian hospital in Enid. Dependent dental care is limited to X rays and emergency care. A commissary with 32,000 square feet of sales space, a new base exchange, a club system, a clothing store, and a banking facility are among the personal services available at Vance.

Recreation. The Vance morale, welfare, and recreation office provides hobby shops, four tennis courts, an eight-lane bowling alley, two swimming pools, a gymnasium, a golf driving range, and a picnic area with playground equipment, barbecue facilities, and a pavilion that is open year-round.

The Local Area. Vance is located about three miles south of Enid, a city of 45,000. It is considered the retail trade center for northwestern Oklahoma, and a variety of stores (including Oakwood Mall on the west side of town) are stocked with the latest merchandise. Enid is also the major medical center in northwest Oklahoma and serves as the principal referral center for physicians throughout this area of the state. Farming is the primary business in the countryside surrounding the city. With a generally temperate climate, the area around Vance experiences four distinct seasons in the year, with no extremes. Snow does not stay long on the ground when it does fall, and annual rainfall averages less than 30 inches. Oklahoma City, the state capital, lies approximately 80 miles to the southeast. The city is famous for its many museums, including the National Cowboy Hall of Fame and Western Heritage Center, the Air and Space Museum, and the Kirkpatrick Center Science and Arts Museum. Oklahoma City is also home of Tinker AFB and the Oklahoma City Zoo. With many amusement parks, malls, theaters, movies, and fine eating establishments, Oklahoma City can provide an enjoyable weekend.

For more information, write to 71st Flying Training Wing, Public Affairs Office, 246 Brown Parkway, Suite 120, Vance AFB, OK 73702-5028, or call (580) 213-2121. Home page: *www.vnc.aetc.af.mil.*

Army

FORT SILL

Many sites in the old Southwest can claim "Geronimo slept here," because the famous Indian warrior actually stopped in many places en route to his captivity in Florida. Not only did Geronimo once sleep in the Old Post Guardhouse at Fort Sill, he also sleeps nearby, in his grave near Quinette Road and Dodge Hill Road.

History. Named after Brig. Gen. Joshua Sill, a Union officer killed in action during the Civil War, Fort Sill was established in January 1869 as a post for cavalry and infantry units charged with the mission of pacifying the Plains Indians. The first artillery units came to Fort Sill in 1876. Today it is known as the "Home of the Field Artillery," and its more than 94,000 acres provide ranges and training areas for thousands of military personnel attending courses at the U.S. Army Field Artillery School and Field Artillery Center each year. Its population consists of 18,000 permanent-party personnel, their 36,000 family members, and over 5,800 civilian employees.

Housing and Schools. Fort Sill has over 1,400 units of family housing and also has a 75-room guest unit. Visitors may occupy these room no more than seven days at a time, based on space availability; personnel awaiting assignment to family quarters may stay in them up to 30 days.

The Fort Sill Army Education Center provides military personnel with a complete program of educational activities. Courses are available from area colleges and universities, including Cameron University at Lawton, the University of Oklahoma at Norman, Webster University, and Pikes Peak Community College.

Personal Services. Medical care at Fort Sill is provided by the 116-bed Reynolds Army Community Hospital. The post commissary covers more than 33,000 square feet. A main post exchange and various concessions are also available, including a four-seasons store, a toy store, a shopette, and a cafeteria.

Recreation. On-post recreational facilities consist of a 36-lane bowling alley; four seasonal swimming pools, with one open year-round; two 18-hole golf courses; two recreation centers; and 36 intramural sports programs.

The Local Area. With an average annual temperature of 63° F and average yearly precipitation of 38 inches (including seven inches of snow), the Fort Sill area is well suited for all sorts of outdoor activities. Fort Sill's community and family activities office operates camping facilities on the Lake Elmer Thomas Recreation Area located on the post's West Range. Fort Sill also operates a recreational equipment rental facility. The Fish and Wildlife Branch sells Oklahoma and Fort Sill hunting and fishing permits.

Fort Sill and Lawton lie about 60 miles southwest of Oklahoma City. Lawton (named after Maj. Gen. Henry W. Lawton, who served at the post during the Indian Wars) plays an important role in the community life of Fort Sill. A city of 88,700 inhabitants, its schools and commercial and cultural activities are utilized by the military personnel stationed at Fort Sill. The Wichita Mountain Wildlife Refuge, just northwest of Fort Sill, is a 59,000-acre outdoor wonderland that provides the visitor with a spectacular glimpse of unspoiled nature.

For more information, write to Public Affairs Office, Headquarters, U.S. Army Field Artillery Center and Fort Sill, Fort Sill, OK 73503-5100, or call (580) 442-8111. Home page: *http://sill-www.army.mil.*

PENNSYLVANIA

Army

CARLISLE BARRACKS

History. History and scholarship are the most distinguishing features of Carlisle Barracks. Home today for the U.S. Army War College, the Center for Strategic Leadership, and the U.S. Army Military History Institute, the post traces its founding back to May 1757, when the site served as a supply base for British expeditions against the French and their Indian allies in the West. During the Revolution, it was used as an arsenal and also as the first American artillery school for the Continental Army. Known then as Washingtonburg, Carlisle Barracks picked up its present name around 1807. The post was burned by Confederate cavalry in July 1863 during the Gettysburg Campaign. From 1879 to 1918, it served as the famous Carlisle Indian School. The War College moved there in 1951.

Carlisle Barracks is a small post, four-fifths of a mile long and half a mile wide, containing 217 total acres. The resident student body is composed of approximately 320 personnel, all of whom are fairly senior officers. The permanent-party complement consists of approximately 730 active-duty personnel, their 1,800 family members, and about 950 civilian employees.

Housing and Schools. There are 290 units of family housing at or nearby Carlisle Barracks for the use of permanent-party and student officer personnel. Assignments are made upon arrival. Limited guest quarters are available for personnel awaiting assignment to family quarters. A post nursery school provides day care for children six months to ten years of age, and there are a preschool and a child-development center that provides day care to approximately 250 children.

Personal Services and Recreation. Medical and dental care are provided by the Dunham U.S. Army Health Clinic, a modern medical outpatient treatment facility. A commissary and post exchange with a garden shop and a convenience store are also available.

Recreational facilities include an automotive craft shop; an 18-hole golf course; a gymnasium; a 6-lane bowling alley; a community club; a track; a movie theater; an archery range; squash, racquetball, and tennis courts; a swimming pool; stables; soccer and football fields; an outdoor recreation facility; and a variety of arts and crafts shops.

The Local Area. Carlisle Barracks is located in the Cumberland Valley of Pennsylvania, about 18 miles west of Harrisburg, the state capital, on U.S. 11. The city of Carlisle is one mile southwest of the post and 27 miles north of Gettysburg. The driving time from Washington, D.C., to Carlisle is approximately two and a half hours.

Although hunting is prohibited on the post, wild game is plentiful in the surrounding countryside. Military personnel become eligible for resident hunting and fishing licenses after living 60 days in Pennsylvania. The morale support activities office provides military personnel the loan of campers, tents, fishing equipment, ski equipment, and other recreational gear. The Carlisle Barracks Ski Club offers memberships to military personnel and their families and offers special rates on equipment and season ski passes. There are about 95 ski days each winter on the slopes near the post.

For more information, write to U.S. Army War College, Attention: AWCCI, Carlisle Barracks, PA 17013-5050, or call (717) 245-3131. Home page: *www.carlisle.arm.mil.*

FORT INDIANTOWN GAP

Fort Indiantown Gap (FTIG) is a major reserve component installation situated in a scenic and historic part of south-central Pennsylvania. It is 23 miles east of Harrisburg, easily accessible from Interstates 81 and 78 and State Route 72.

History. Fort Indiantown Gap draws its name from the many Indian villages that once flourished in the vicinity during the seventeenth and eighteenth centuries. During the French and Indian War, many forts and blockhouses were constructed in the area. In 1930, the Pennsylvania National Guard conducted horse cavalry maneuvers at Fort Indiantown Gap, and between 1933 and 1940, the commonwealth of Pennsylvania acquired the land there and erected buildings for a National Guard campsite. The federal government leased the site from the state in 1941.

Today FTIG consists of 19,200 acres of land. The major tenant units at FTIG include the Pennsylvania Department of Military Affairs, the National Guard Training Site, the Eastern Army National Guard Aviation Training Site, and the 56th Ordnance Detachment (EOD). The Department of Military Affairs is the headquarters of the Pennsylvania National Guard. These activities are staffed by approximately 200 military personnel and 2,000 civilian employees.

Housing and Schools. Housing at FTIG is very limited. The waiting period for on-post quarters is 18 to 24 months for all ranks. There is one mobile-home park at FTIG; sites are available only to personnel who own their own trailers. Additional government quarters are available at the Defense Distribution Center, New Cumberland, about twenty miles southwest of FTIG. Most accompanied personnel find accommodations in the surrounding communities, where a two-bedroom unfurnished apartment rents for about $400 a month plus utilities from $80 to $140 a month. Dependent children attend various public and parochial schools in the school districts adjacent to FTIG. Daycare and preschool facilities are available at the installation.

Personal Services. Medical care at FTIG is provided by a small health clinic. Dependents of active-duty personnel are supported by the Dunham Clinic at Carlisle Barracks. Billeting can be reached at (717) 861-2512, and post information can be reached at (717) 861-2000. Hours of operation for most other services at FTIG are seasonal, or extended during the training season (May through September) and somewhat shorter during the rest of the year. Personal services available include passports, ID cards, information management, and Army Community Service/Army Emergency Relief. There is no commissary at FTIG, but the commissaries at the Defense Distribution Center, New Cumberland, and Carlisle Barracks are available. The post exchange is a modern, self-service facility open to eligible National Guard, reserve, active-duty, and retired personnel and their dependents. The post exchange offers a snack bar, a barber shop, a shopette and service station, and an alterations shop.

Recreation. Recreational facilities include six ballfields (two lighted), tennis courts, picnic areas with pavilions, and an outdoor swimming pool. A sports arena features one full-size basketball court convertible to two volleyball courts, as well as two racquetball courts and a sauna. Skiing and boating are available at nearby Marquette Lake. Hunting and fishing are permitted on the installation during season.

The Local Area. FTIG is 23 miles east of Harrisburg, the capital of Pennsylvania; 46 miles west of Reading; and 14 miles north of Lebanon. Hershey, the home of Hershey chocolate and Hershey Park, is only 15 miles southwest of the installation. Other attractions include the Tulpehocken Manor Plantation; Cornwall Iron Furnace, which began operation in 1742; Indian Echo Caverns near Harrisburg; the Middle Creek Wildlife Area, a 5,000-acre wildlife management area; and Penn National Race Track, 12 miles east of Harrisburg, offering thoroughbred racing at its finest.

Philadelphia, Baltimore, Washington, D.C., Gettysburg and Sharpsburg (Antietam) Battlefield Parks, Valley Forge, and New York City are all within reasonable driving distance from FTIG.

For more information, write to Public Affairs Office, Headquarters, Fort Indiantown Gap, 1 Garrison Road, Annville, PA 17003-5040, or call (717) 861-2193. Home page: *www.state.pa.us/pa_exec/military_affairs/.*

Navy

NAVAL SUPPORT STATION MECHANICSBURG

The 807-acre Navy facility in Mechanicsburg is home to several important Navy and Defense commands and activities, including the Naval Supply Systems Command (NAVSUP) Headquarters. NAVSUP's main mission is to provide U.S. naval forces with quality supplies and services. Employing a work force of more than 820 servicemembers and over 9,000 civilians, NAVSUP orchestrates logistical programs in supply, ammunition, contracting, resale, fuel, transportation, security assistance, and mobile fleet hospital support. Additionally, NAVSUP is responsible for quality of life issues for our naval forces, including food service, postal services, Navy exchanges, and movement of household goods. Total civilian employment on the base is approximately 5,300 persons, with a military population of approximately 190.

History. The Navy's history in Mechanicsburg dates to World War II, when the land was acquired for an inland supply depot. Initial construction on the facility began in January 1942, and the Naval Supply Depot Mechanicsburg was commissioned on 1 October 1942.

In July 1970, the Naval Supply Depot was decommissioned, and the base was renamed the Navy Ships Parts Control Center (SPCC) for the new host command. On 1 October 1995, SPCC was consolidated with the Aviation Supply Office in Philadelphia, its sister command, into the Naval Inventory Control Point, and the base was renamed accordingly. On 1 October 1998, the base became the Naval Support Station Mechanicsburg.

Housing. NAVSUP Mechanicsburg has 67 married officers' quarters, ranging from apartments and town houses to single-family dwellings. These include 15 four-bedroom units and 52 three-bedroom units. Enlisted housing includes 24 units—six four-bedroom and 14 three-bedroom town houses and 4 three-bedroom apartments. There are no bachelor officer or enlisted quarters on the base.

Children of military personnel who reside on the base attend schools in the surrounding community.

Personal Services. There is a Navy exchange, with a barber shop, on the compound. Commissaries are available at two nearby military bases, U.S. Army Carlisle Barracks in Carlisle, Pennsylvania, and the Defense Distribution Region, East, New Cumberland, Pennsylvania. There is a naval hospital branch clinic on the base that offers routine medical services, Monday through Friday. More specialized medical services are available at nearby Carlisle Barracks.

Recreation. The recreation services office offers a range of athletic facilities, including a well-equipped exercise area, indoor basketball, indoor and outdoor tennis courts, and a nine-hole golf course. Recreation services offers a wide range of sports and recreation equipment for rent by base military and civilian personnel. A mullet-bay automobile hobby shop facility is available for use by base personnel as well.

The Local Area. South-central Pennsylvania offers a wide variety of recreation attractions and opportunities. The world-famous Hershey Park is nearby, as is the Gettysburg National Battlefield Park. There are professional sports teams in the area, including baseball, hockey, and soccer, as well as sports teams at the numerous colleges and universities in the region. Pennsylvania is renowned for its outdoor sporting opportunities, including hunting and fishing; there are also several ski areas within local driving distance.

For more information, write to Commander, Naval Supply Systems Command, Attention: Public Affairs Office, P.O. Box 2050, Mechanicsburg, PA 17055-0791, or call (717) 605-3338.

WILLOW GROVE NAVAL RESERVE AIR STATION

The "Minutemen" (and women) of Willow Grove Naval Reserve Air Station—the naval reservists who train there—come from as far away as California and work hard to master the science of antisubmarine warfare. They are assisted in day-to-day squadron operations by a small cadre of Navy professionals who make up the active-duty complement onboard the station. The station is operated and maintained by the 913th Tactical Air Group, with the mission of delivering combatants and warfare wherewithal via C-130 "Hercules" cargo planes. Members of the 913th train one weekend a month and serve two weeks a year on active duty, training either at the installation or at other bases throughout the world. The 913th plays host to other organizations, including the Pennsylvania Air National Guard.

History. Commissioned in 1943, Willow Grove NAS takes its name from the nearest post office, the traditional method for naming naval air stations. Willow Grove's 1,100 acres are the weekend home to the more than 5,000 reservists who train there each month, as well as a contingent of 1,500 active-duty Navy personnel, 5,000 dependents, 4,700 reservists, and 600 civilian employees.

Housing and Schools. Housing for enlisted personnel assigned to Willow Grove consists of about 200 town houses located at Shenandoah Woods, about eight miles from the station, in Warminster. Eligibility requirements are strict. There are no guest facilities at Willow Grove. Enlisted bachelor housing consists of 250 units. There are also ten family suites for incoming enlisted personnel and another ten suites reserved for visitors.

Although no dependent schooling is offered on the station, adequate public schooling is available nearby, and there is a child-development center at the station. Opportunities for off-duty adult education abound in this area as well. Numerous colleges offering many different programs are located in the suburban area around Willow Grove, and many others in Philadelphia can be utilized by Navy personnel.

Personal Services and Recreation. Medical care is provided by a branch clinic located at Warminster; more comprehensive care is available at the Army hospital at Fort Dix, New Jersey. Willow Grove NAS offers many personal services, including a colocated Navy exchange and a minimart. A commissary store is available at Fort Dix, New Jersey.

The station has an outdoor Olympic-size swimming pool and other physical fitness facilities, including tennis and racquetball courts, a gym, weight-lifting equipment, a bowling center, an auto hobby shop, and a library. The station operates three 24-foot and two 19-foot campers at Cape May, New Jersey, which are available from Memorial Day through September.

The Local Area. Located in suburban Philadelphia, Willow Grove participates in the best of both possible worlds: the exciting life of one of the world's great cities and the natural beauty of eastern Pennsylvania with its wide variety of geographical and historic attractions.

Willow Grove (population 20,000) is located only twenty miles north of downtown Philadelphia. The city itself offers every attraction, from professional sports to historical events and other activities. National and state parks and water-recreation activities are available throughout the area. Both the Pocono Mountains and the South Jersey shore are reasonable drives from Willow Grove and are popular vacation sites.

For more information, write to Public Affairs Office, Naval Air Station, Willow Grove, PA 19090-5203, or call (215) 443-1000. Home page: *www.nasjrbwillowgrove.navy.mil.*

RHODE ISLAND

Navy

NEWPORT NAVAL EDUCATION AND TRAINING CENTER

History. The Newport Naval Education and Training Center (NETC) sits along the eastern shore of Narragansett Bay, just north of Newport and west of Middletown. The Navy first came to the Narragansett Bay area in 1869, when an experimental torpedo station was established on Goat Island. (Goat Island was transferred to the city of Newport in 1951.) In 1881, the Navy acquired Coasters Harbor Island from the city of Newport, and it was there, a few years later, that the U.S. Naval War College and the Navy's first recruit-training station were established. Luce Hall, Pringle Hall, and Mahan Hall—the original buildings—are still in use at the war college complex on the island.

Today, there are 30 separate commands in Newport that are devoted to the mission of officer training and education. The Newport naval complex, including NETC, the Naval War College, and the Naval Undersea Warfare Center, has a permanent population of over 1,500 military personnel, their 3,500 family members, and 4,500 civilian employees. The center has a daily student population of 2,000. The Navy is the single largest employer in Newport.

Housing and Schools. About 1,500 units of government housing in several housing areas throughout Rhode Island (the island where Newport and the NSN are located, not the state in general) are available for personnel assigned to the center. In addition, a 50-unit mobile home park is available, as is a 67-unit Navy Lodge.

Dependent children attend local public and parochial schools. Nursery, child-care, and preschool facilities are also available. The Navy Campus offers associate's degree programs from Roger Williams and Johnson and Wales Colleges on base, and off-base college programs are available from Salve Regina University, the University of Rhode Island, Bryant College, Rhode Island College, and Brown University, in Providence.

Personal Services. Medical and dental care are provided by the naval dental clinic and the outpatient medical clinic. Other support facilities include Navy exchange retail stores, a commissary store, a package beverage store, and a gas station that offers car rentals and repairs. There are also snack bars, a cafeteria, beauty and barber shops, officers and enlisted clubs, and other facilities.

Recreation. Recreational facilities include the Carr Point Recreational Area, with excellent outdoor facilities, as well as the Bishop's Rock Picnic Area on Coddington Point. On base are an indoor swimming pool, tennis courts, a gymnasium, and an auto hobby shop with 15 repair stalls.

The Local Area. Newport is a fine old town, replete with magnificent mansions and museums. It was at Newport that French Gen. Rochambeau landed in 1780, with men and materiel for the American Army that proved so decisive in winning the Revolution. Nearby Portsmouth hasts the site of Rhode Island's only major Revolutionary War land battle, at Butts Hill Fort. Such greats as Lafayette, Hancock, Greene, and Sullivan participated in the fighting on 2 August 1778. This battle also saw the first black regiment to fight for the American flag.

In Newport is the sloop *Providence,* naval hero John Paul Jones's first command, built in 1768 and now fully restored. In Touro Park, at the corner of Bellevue Avenue and Mill Street, is the Old Stone Mill, a mysterious edifice that some people believe was built by the Vikings hundreds of years before Columbus discovered America. There is not a shred of proof for this claim, but it is true that the tower was once owned by a colonist named Benedict Arnold, who used it as a windmill. Another interesting place to visit is Newport's famous Cliff Walk and Ocean Drive, where you can take in the breathtaking scenery along the rocky seacoast and visit some of the stately mansions that grace the neighborhood.

For more information, write to Family Service Center, Building 1260, NETC, Newport, RI 02841, or call (401) 841-2311. Home page: *www.cnet.navy.mil/newport/netc.htm.*

SOUTH CAROLINA

Air Force

CHARLESTON AIR FORCE BASE

If you have ever dreamed of living in a town by the sea that is steeped in history but as up-to-date as the C-17 Globemaster III aircraft and where the climate is mild and pleasant all year, look no farther, because Charleston is the place.

History. Charleston Air Force Base is actually located ten miles north of the city and is part of North Charleston, a community of around 100,000 people. Although an airfield existed on the present site of the base long before World War II, the Army Air Corps did not take full control of the facility until 1941. Today the base contains more than 3,500 acres under the jurisdiction of the 437th Airlift Wing, and it serves as one of three aerial ports on the Atlantic coast. The base is home for about 4,500 active-duty military personnel, 7,500 family members, 1,100 civilian workers, and 2,800 reservists.

Housing and Schools. Charleston offers 1,400 family housing units, all of them built between 1959 and 1961. Waiting periods vary from thirty days to ten months. The longest wait is for two-bedroom homes; six months is the average maximum. Unaccompanied enlisted personnel have over 900 suites available. There are 30 temporary lodging units for transient personnel, as well as 23 campers, and visitors may take advantage of accommodations on a space-available basis at Charleston House, a 116-room guest facility.

Dependent children attend school off base. On-base educational opportunities for adults are offered through the education center and include programs from Trident Technical College, Embry-Riddle Aeronautical University, and Southern Illinois University. Off-base programs are offered by the Citadel, the College of Charleston, and other institutions.

Personal Services. Outpatient medical care is provided by the USAF medical clinic, but inpatient care is available from the Trident Medical Center. The base commissary carries 9,000 items, and base exchange facilities offer several concessions for military shoppers. Other services include a child-development center, a club system for officers and enlisted personnel, and banking facilities.

Recreation. With its subtropical climate and four distinct but mild seasons, recreation is a key aspect of life in the Charleston area. The Air Force provides a wide variety of sport and hobby facilities. There are a swimming pool; an 18-hole golf course; rod and gun, aero, and saddle clubs; a 16-lane bowling alley; a fully equipped gymnasium; and a family campground with sites for all types of recreational vehicles and an adjacent picnic grounds.

The Local Area. Charleston abounds with historic attractions, not the least of which is Fort Sumter, the site of the bombardment that started the Civil War. Parks and camping facilities abound, and the Atlantic coast affords access to public beaches, with swimming, sailing, waterskiing, pleasure boating, and deep-sea fishing.

For more information, write to Public Affairs Office, 437th AW/PA, Charleston AFB, SC 29404-5154, or call (843) 963-6000. Home page: *www.charleston.af.mil.*

SHAW AIR FORCE BASE

The four F-16 Fighting Falcon squadrons of the 20th Fighter Wing are the heart of operations at Shaw Air Force Base. Shaw is also home to the 9th Air Force and Central Command Air Forces Headquarters.

History. Named after 1st Lt. Ervin Davis Shaw, a Sumter County native who was shot down while flying a long-range reconnaissance mission over France during World War I, today the base is a small city of nearly 6,000 military personnel, 850 civilian employees, and over 12,000 military dependents. The base occupies 3,336 acres seven miles west of Sumter and has responsibility for an additional 12,500 leased acres at Poinsett Range, southwest of Sumter.

Housing and Schools. On-base housing consists of 1,700 units. The longest waiting period for two- and three-bedroom on-base housing averages about 30 to 90 days. The wait for other units is from three to six months. Guest housing is also available for transients and guests. The cost of living in the Shaw-Sumter area is reasonable.

Dependent children of service families stationed at Shaw attend primary schools in the immediate vicinity of the base. Educational opportunities for adults wishing to further their education are excellent. The base education center assists personnel in taking courses offered by the University of South Carolina, Saint Leo College, Central Carolina Technical College, Florence-Darlington Technical College, and Troy State University.

Personal Services. Medical care at Shaw is provided by the 20th Medical Group's 25-bed facility. A commissary with over 29,000 square feet of space, with many concessions, is among the many personal services available at Shaw.

Recreation. Shaw is not short on recreational facilities either. The base offers an 18-hole golf course, three swimming pools, an excellent fitness center and annex, a bowling alley, a rod and gun club, a picnic area, tennis courts, and officers and enlisted open messes. Three small lakes on base are stocked with fish. Wateree Lake Recreation Area is located 35 miles from the base, north of Camden. Fishing, sailing, and ski boats may be rented there, as well as cabins.

The Local Area. The city of Sumter has a population of 50,000 and boasts eight playgrounds and parks. The summers last from May through September, and the winters are mild, with some snow, but generally the snow does not remain long on the ground. The state of South Carolina in general is a recreational paradise, with fifty parks comprising 80,000 acres. There are also 400,000 acres of fishing lakes and over 290 species of salt- and freshwater fish. With a 281-mile coastline, water sports are available year-round.

Shaw is 34 miles west of Columbia, 94 miles southeast of Charleston, and 106 miles south of Charlotte, North Carolina.

For more information, write to Commander, 20th Fighter Wing Public Affairs, 517 Lance Avenue, Shaw AFB, SC 29152-5041, or call (803) 895-1110. Home page: *www.shaf.af.mil.*

Army

FORT JACKSON

History. "Victory starts here," proudly proclaims Fort Jackson's motto, and to underscore this fact, the statue of Gen. Andrew Jackson, for whom the post is named, stands at the main entrance. From 2 June 1917, when a new Army training center was established to answer America's call for trained fighting soldiers in the early days of World War I, Fort Jackson has become the largest and most active basic training installation in the world. Fort Jackson is also home to the Soldier Support Institute, Chaplain Center and School, and most recently, the Department of Defense Polygraph Institute.

The installation is located in Columbia, the capital city of South Carolina, and is about 100 miles from Augusta, Georgia, to the west; Charlotte, North Carolina, to the north; and Charleston, South Carolina, to the south. Fort Jackson is a community of 4,300 assigned active-duty soldiers, 11,000 family members, a civilian workforce of 4,000, and 121,000 retirees and their family members. In addition, more than 35,000 soldiers pass through basic and advanced individual training and another 16,000 graduate from the Soldier Support Institute, Chaplain Center and School, and Drill Sergeant School each year.

Housing and Schools. With over 1,200 sets of family quarters, Fort Jackson offers soldiers and their families all the amenities of modern military living. Guest accommodations are also available on the post. Dependent children living on post attend one of two elementary schools at Fort Jackson. There is also a child-development center on post. Youth family members living on post attend one of three elementary schools at Fort Jackson. The Army education center offers college courses at the graduate and undergraduate levels, as well as counseling, testing, basic skills training, high school completion, and computer training services.

Personal Services and Recreation. Moncrief Army Community Hospital, Fort Jackson's main medical facility, is a 12-story acute-care community medical facility that has 91 inpatient beds, 58 infirmary beds, and 30 ambulatory clinics. The post has a large commissary, three convenience stores, and a large post exchange. Recreation facilities include a movie theater, a bowling center, an auto craft shop, swimming pools, a 36-hole golf course, tennis courts, and fitness centers. The largest recreational area on the post is 240-acre Weston Lake Recreation Area, which is set among 1,200 rolling acres of woodland, where soldiers and their families may picnic, camp, and fish.

The Local Area. South Carolina is a state filled with hundreds of years of history preserved in museums, churches, monuments, and plantation houses. Its mild climate encourages visitors and residents to participate in some form of outdoor recreation nearly year-round. This bountiful land with abundant game appeals to hunters, anglers, and nature lovers. Columbia is also noted for its zoo and botanical gardens, sports, arts, and local special events. The city is located in the center of the state and is accessible from three major highways—Interstates 20, 26, and 77. Both Interstates 85 and 95 are a short drive away.

For more information, write to Public Affairs Office, 4394 Strom Thurmond Boulevard, Fort Jackson, SC 29207, or call (803) 751-1742. Home page: *www.jackson.army.mil.*

Marine Corps

BEAUFORT MARINE CORPS AIR STATION

Beaufort Marine Corps Air Station comprises more than 6,700 acres at the airfield complex itself, on the northern side of Port Royal Sound, just off Highway 21, and another 1,100 acres three miles to the west, where the Laurel Bay family housing area is located.

The station was commissioned in June 1943. Today Beaufort is home to the ultrasophisticated F/A-18 Hornet fighter bombers of Marine Aircraft Group 31. MCAS Beaufort is currently home and workplace for approximately 3,500 military personnel, 7,000 dependents, and 650 civilian employees.

Housing and Schools. There are 176 units of family housing at the main airfield complex and another 1,100 quarters at Laurel Bay. There are also 157 spaces available in a mobile home park. The Detreville House offers temporary lodging at a reasonable price for those reporting in for duty or just staying a night or two. This hotel-like facility offers cable TV, a picnic and playground area, kitchenettes, laundry facilities, and other conveniences. More than 1,800 living spaces are available for single marines and sailors.

Two elementary schools are operated at Laurel Bay; high schools are available in nearby Beaufort. The Joint Education Office offers on-base classes that range from high school completion to postgraduate studies. In addition, the University of South Carolina–Beaufort Campus and the Technical College of the Lowcountry are available for off-post attendance.

Personal Services and Recreation. Medical care for personnel and their families at Beaufort MCAS is available from the Beaufort Naval Hospital in nearby Port Royal. There are a small dispensary and a dental clinic located at the station. Although there is no commissary at the station itself, there is a large one at Parris Island Recruit Depot, only eight miles away. An exchange and convenience store are located onboard the station, as are a service station and other concessions.

Recreational facilities include a 12-lane bowling alley, three swimming pools, auto and craft hobby shops, tennis courts, a gymnasium and physical fitness center, a skeet range, five fishing piers, two boat ramps, 15 wildlife management areas, stables, and rentals for boating, camping, and sports equipment at moderate prices. Officers, staff NCO, and enlisted club facilities are also available at the station, and there is a full range of recreational activities at the Parris Island Recruit Depot.

The Local Area. Beaufort MCAS is located about seventy miles south of the city of Charleston, one of the most historic and beautiful places anywhere along the Atlantic coast. The nearest towns to the station are Beaufort, population 25,000, and Port Royal, population 3,000. These are beautiful, rustic towns whose major industry is tourism. Hundreds of thousands of people visit Hunting Island State Park on the Atlantic, about 20 miles due east of Beaufort, each season.

For more information, write to Joint Public Affairs Office, Marine Corps Air Station, Beaufort, SC 29904-5001, or call (843) 522-7100. Home page: *www.beaufort.usmc.mil.*

PARRIS ISLAND MARINE CORPS RECRUIT DEPOT

History. The earliest people to suffer the ordeal of initiation into a new world on Parris Island might have been French Huguenots, who came there in 1562. Since 1915, thousands of young Americans have endured the ordeal of boot camp at the Parris Island Marine Corps Depot, passing initiation into the world of the U.S. Marines. "We MAKE Marines" is the Parris Island motto.

The first Marine Corps post established at Parris Island was commissioned in 1891 and consisted of a very small garrison under the command of a first sergeant. The depot's mission today is to administer recruiting and training for all the states east of the Mississippi (and training for female recruits nationwide). Parris Island itself consists of marsh and land area composed of several islands and extending over about 8,000 acres, 3,200 of which are habitable. Parris Island derives its name from Alexander Parris, who secured the title to the land in 1715. Today Parris Island is home to 2,000 active-duty personnel, 3,500 family members, and 800 civilian employees. About 19,000 recruits are graduated each year, and on any given day, over 4,000 will be in training.

Housing and Schools. There are over 500 family housing units available to Marines stationed at the depot and 125 mobile home spaces in the Argonne Trailer Park. An officers guest house and a hostess house provide inexpensive temporary lodging; the latter may not be used for longer than seven days, however.

Two elementary schools are open to military dependents at the Laurel Bay housing area. There are three high schools, three junior high schools, and 12 elementary schools in Beaufort County. A day-care center is located at the depot. Adult educational services are provided by the education office at the depot and include testing and counseling, as well as college courses on and off the base.

Personal Services. A commissary and a Marine Corps exchange with a variety of concessions are available at the depot. There are also a bank and Navy Federal Credit Union, a Pizza Hut, and a food court. Although there are branch medical and dental clinics at Parris Island, dependents are seen there only on an emergency basis. Definitive medical care is provided by Beaufort Naval Hospital, located on 127 acres along the Beaufort River on Ribaut Road, about halfway between Beaufort Marine Corps Air Station and Parris Island.

Recreation. Recreational activities include an 18-hole golf course; a 20-lane bowling center; four swimming pools; a library; a theater; a fitness center; ceramics, woodworking, and auto hobby shops; a marina; and a museum.

The Local Area. The countryside around Parris Island is rich in history. Port Royal, across Battery Creek, between the depot main gate and the town of Beaufort, was first visited by the Spanish in the year 1525 and permanently settled by English immigrants in 1670. It was the site of an American Revolutionary battle in February 1779 and eventually became a Loyalist stronghold after British occupation in 1782.

The town of Beaufort, five miles north of the depot, combines the graceful architecture of preRevolutionary and Civil War America with the convenience of modern living. Beaufort is not a particularly rich town in a material sense, but it is a place where family pride runs deep. Before the Civil War, it was a cultured and affluent place and a seething cauldron of radical anti-Union sentiment; the Ordinance of Secession was drawn up there, and the town was one of the first in the South to be seized and occupied by Union forces.

Savannah, Georgia, is only 46 miles to the south of the depot, and Charleston is a 70-mile drive to the north. Hunting and fishing are varied in this area, and the mild climate permits outdoor activities year-round.

For more information, write to Public Affairs Office, P.O. Box 5059, Marine Corps Recruit Depot, Parris Island, SC 29905-9001, or call (843) 525-2111. Home page: *www.parrisisland.com.*

Navy

BEAUFORT NAVAL HOSPITAL

As the primary military health-care facility servicing both Parris Island Marine Corps Recruit Depot and the Beaufort Marine Corps Air Station, Beaufort Naval Hospital treats about 30,000 outpatients per year. The hospital is an ultramodern, twenty-bed facility staffed by 440 active-duty personnel and 190 civilian employees.

Housing, Schools, and Personal Services. The hospital operates a total of 53 family quarters—eight for officers and 45 for enlisted personnel. Bachelor accommodations are provided on the installation for enlisted personnel. Children attend area schools. There is no commissary at the hospital, but there are a minimart, a service station, an optical shop, a snack bar, a library, a branch of the Navy Federal Credit Union, and a barber and beauty shop. The hospital is located halfway between the air station and the recruit depot, and hospital personnel may take full advantage of all the facilities provided by those sprawling installations.

Recreation. Recreational facilities include a swimming pool, tennis courts, and the Heritage Consolidated Club, with its lounge, snack bar, catering service, and ticket and tour office. The morale and recreation department also operates a fitness trail, ball fields, and an equipment rental service.

For more information, write to Commanding Officer, Naval Hospital, Attention: Public Affairs, 1 Pinckney Boulevard, Beaufort, SC 29902-6148, or call (843) 525-5600.

SOUTH DAKOTA

Air Force

ELLSWORTH AIR FORCE BASE

The name Black Hills of South Dakota conjures up an image of gold, Sioux Indians, enormous buffalo herds, and the Dakota prairie. The fact is, not too long ago, all those images would have been typical of the region where today the B-1B aircraft of the 28th Bomb Wing roam the skies above the ranges where buffalo still graze.

History. Named in honor of Brig. Gen. Richard Ellsworth, who died in the crash of an RB-36 aircraft in Newfoundland in 1953, the base began its existence as an Army airfield in September 1942. Today it is home of the 28th Bomb Wing. Ellsworth's population of over 10,000 includes over 3,000 military personnel, their 3,900 family members, and 600 civilian employees.

Housing and Schools. There are over 2,000 units of family housing at Ellsworth. Guest accommodations for incoming families are also available on a reserved basis; all others are accepted on a space-available basis only. The family quarters are located in eight separate housing developments. There is a child-development center at the base, and school-age dependent children attend the Douglas School System in Box Elder, South Dakota.

The base education office offers a number of college programs for adults. These courses are available from the Black Hills State University, Embry-Riddle Aeronautical University, National College, the University of South Dakota, and South Dakota State University.

Personal Services and Recreation. The 15-bed USAF Hospital at Ellsworth is an excellent inpatient and outpatient facility. Other personal support facilities at the base include a well-stocked commissary and base exchange complex, a consolidated officers and NCO club, a convenience store, and a consolidated beverage store.

Recreational facilities include a 16-lane bowling center, a nine-hole golf course, a recreation center, a base theater, a riding club, and auto and wood hobby shops. Outdoor recreational facilities include large pavilions for picnicking, equipment rentals, a trap and skeet range, and a family camp with water, sewer, and electricity hookups.

The Local Area. Ellsworth AFB is located ten miles east of Rapid City, which has a population of over 55,000. Just to the southeast of Rapid City are Buffalo Gap National Grassland and Badlands National Monument. Due south of the city are Mount Rushmore National Monument, Custer State Park, and Wind Cave National Park; to the west is the famous Black Hills National Forest. This area offers camping and magnificent sightseeing.

For more information, write to Public Affairs Officer, 28th BW, 1958 Scott Drive, Suite 1, Ellsworth AFB, SD 57706-4710, or call (605) 385-1000. Home page: *www.ellsworth.af.mil.*

TENNESSEE

Air Force

ARNOLD AIR FORCE BASE

Arnold Air Force Base is home for the Air Force Materiel Command's Arnold Engineering Development Center. The center conducts aerospace testing in its wind tunnels, jet and rocket engine altitude test cells, space chambers, and ballistic ranges for the Department of Defense, NASA, other federal agencies, civilian educational institutions, and commercial aerospace companies. Both full-size hardware and scale models are tested there under conditions simulating altitudes up to 1,000 miles and velocities up to 23 times the speed of sound (17,500 mph).

History. Named after pioneer aviator and five-star general of the Air Force Henry H. ("Hap") Arnold, the base occupies 40,000 acres in the middle of the state of Tennessee, about halfway between Nashville and Chattanooga. Testing began there in 1953.

Arnold Air Force Base is a small, tightly knit community that supports approximately 100 active-duty Air Force personnel, 200 Air Force civilian employees, and 2,700 civilian contract personnel. Due to the type of work done at the station, entry into the work areas is strictly controlled.

Housing and Schools. Arnold operates only 40 housing units—23 for officers and 17 for enlisted personnel. Guest housing consists of forty-five rooms. Dependent schooling is available off base. No child-care facilities are available at Arnold AFB. Motlow State Community College is located nearby at Tullahoma. Middle Tennessee State University is situated at Murfreesboro, and the University of the South is at Sewanee; both are less than an hour's drive from the base. The University of Tennessee Space Institute is located about six miles from the industrial area of the base, on the shore of Woods Reservoir.

Personal Services. A small commissary and exchange offer a wide choice of items to personnel at the base. There is a medical aid station there too, but a full-time physician is not assigned to it. Most of the services normally furnished for active-duty personnel are available only at Redstone Arsenal, Alabama, approximately 60 miles to the south.

Recreation. Recreational facilities on the base include a nine-hole golf course, a skeet range, a rifle range, ball and tennis courts, a combined-ranks club, and miles of nature trails. A family camp with 22 trailer spaces is available also. A consolidated hobby shop is situated in Arnold Village, the family housing area. There are waterfront picnic areas, two beaches, and boat ramps located at points along the Woods Reservoir shore, a 4,000-acre body of water offering water sports and fishing. The Arnold special services office maintains a fleet of two fishing boats, three ski boats, two pontoon boats, and a sailboat, all of which are rented to service personnel at a minimal fee.

Hunting is a popular activity on the base. Under the control of the Tennessee Wildlife Resources Agency, the Arnold game management area offers deer, duck, turkey, and small-game hunting.

The Local Area. Arnold Air Force Base is situated approximately 65 miles south of Nashville and 65 miles northwest of Chattanooga, on Interstate 24 at Exit 117, among the cities of Tullahoma, Manchester, and Winchester. The countryside there is beautiful, well wooded and well watered, and dotted with many fine state parks. The famous Jack Daniels Distillery is located nearby, near Lynchburg.

For more information, write to Public Affairs Office, 100 Kindel Drive, Suite B-213, Arnold AFB, TN 37389-2213, or call (931) 454-7821. Home page: *www.arnold.af.mil.*

Navy

NAVAL SUPPORT ACTIVITY MID-SOUTH

History. NSA Mid-South sprawls over more than 3,400 acres near the town of Millington, Tennessee. The station complement is approximately 2,000 active-duty personnel, their 5,800 family members, 1,600 reservists, and 2,000 civilian personnel.

Originally commissioned as a Naval Reserve Air Base in September 1942, the base became Memphis Naval Air Station in January 1943. Under the Base Realignment and Closure Act of 1993, it became Naval Support Activity (NAVSUPPACT) Memphis on 30 September of that year. It assumed its present designation effective on 1 October 1998. The mission of the base today is to maintain and operate facilities providing administrative and logistic support to tenant activities. Some of those tenant activities include the Navy Personnel Command, Naval Recruiting Command, Navy Manpower Analysis, and other activities. NSA Mid-South also supports over 50,000 military retirees living in the area.

Housing and Schools. The station has over 800 family housing units for eligible personnel, as well as a Navy Lodge. Lodge reservations are accepted only from personnel arriving or departing the station on permanent-change-of-station orders. A limited number of mobile home spaces are available onboard, on a first-come, first-served basis.

There is a large day-care center onboard the station. School-age children attend local public schools in the immediate vicinity. The Navy Campus for Achievement offers a number of on-base programs during off-duty hours with the cooperation of the University of Memphis, the University of Arkansas, Embry-Riddle Aeronautical University, Southern Illinois University, and others. Professional guidance and counseling and assistance in course enrollment are available through the Navy Campus for active-duty, dependent, and civilian personnel.

Personal Services and Recreation. A commissary store and a Navy exchange with a number of concessions are located at the station. Medical care is provided by the 230-bed naval hospital. A full range of indoor and outdoor recreational activities is available on base, including a golf course, a riding stable, and an area with 14 picnic areas and about 30 acres of lakes where fishing is permitted.

The Local Area. NAS Mid-South, in Millington, is located approximately fifteen miles north of Memphis, along U.S. Highway 51 North. Seven miles west of Millington are the Mississippi River Bluffs and Shelby Forest State Park, containing thousands of acres of woodlands, walking and riding trails, picnic areas, and boat and cottage rentals. Memphis is a bustling city with all the conveniences of modern life. The city is situated on Chickasaw Bluffs in the southwest corner of the state and borders Mississippi and Arkansas. Winters in this area can be quite cold, and the summers are hot and humid.

For more information, write to Public Affairs Office, NSA Mid-South, Memphis, 7800 Third Avenue, Millington, TN 38054-5045, or call (901) 874-5507.

TEXAS

Air Force

BROOKS AIR FORCE BASE

History. Since originally opening over 80 years ago, Brooks Air Force Base has gone from a base for the crude flying machines of World War I to a sophisticated aerospace medical research and training facility.

Named after Cadet Sidney Brooks, Jr., the first native San Antonian to die in World War I, Brooks AFB lies in the southeastern area of the city of San Antonio. The base is home to 1,600 military personnel, their 2,400 family members, and 1,600 civilian employees, who work at Brooks organizations such as the 311th Human Systems Wing, Armstrong Laboratory, and the U.S. Air Force School of Aerospace Medicine. These organizations ensure that Air Force systems and operations are designed with human capabilities in mind; that weapon systems and the people operating them are compatible; that medical personnel are trained in aerospace medicine; and that the Air Force has the capability to handle all aspects of environmental cleanup, planning, and compliance.

Housing and Schools. There are only 170 units of family housing at Brooks. The waiting period for these quarters may vary from sixteen to eighteen months, depending on the size of the sponsor's family and category of housing required. Temporary quarters are provided at the guest house for newcomers and visitors, where eight units are available, and reservations are accepted on a first-come, first-served basis.

Dependent children attend local schools. There is a day-care center at the base, and the base education office offers a wide range of programs for military and civilian personnel and their dependents.

Personal Services. Services at Brooks include a base exchange, a commissary, a bank and credit union, and a medical clinic for treatment of routine medical problems; definitive care is available at Lackland Air Force Base or Brooke Army Medical Center, both conveniently nearby.

Recreation. Recreational facilities include officers and NCO clubs, a sports and fitness center, a rod and gun club, garden plots for airmen and their families, a riding stable, softball fields, swimming and wading pools, a nine-hole golf course, a picnic area, and a family camping area. A variety of youth programs is also available at Brooks.

Personnel stationed at Brooks may also use the 51-acre Randolph Recreation Area at Canyon Lake, on the Guadalupe River, about 17 miles west of New Braunfels, and the Fort Sam Houston Recreation Area, near Canyon City.

For more information, write to Public Affairs Office, 2510 Kennedy Drive, Suite 1, Brooks AFB, TX 78235-5120, or call (210) 536-1110. Home page: *www.brooks.af.mil.*

DYESS AIR FORCE BASE

Set in the middle of Texas Big Country, the very name Abilene elicits reminiscences of the Old West, cowboys, cattle drives, and gunfights. All that is gone now, if indeed it ever existed in quite the way we have come to think of it, and today the countryside surrounding Dyess Air Force Base is well integrated into the twentieth century. Home of the B-1B, Dyess also houses 27 vintage aircraft.

History. The base is named in honor of Lt. Col. William Edwin Dyess, an extraordinary hero of World War II fame who died in a crash in California in 1943, after surviving some of the most harrowing experiences in combat. The base was first established in 1956 and today occupies over 6,400 acres about six miles southwest of Abilene. It is the home to about 5,000 military personnel assigned to the 7th Bomb Wing, the 317th Airlift Group, and various associate units. The base is also home to about 6,700 military family members and over 700 civilian employees.

Housing and Schools. There are over 1,000 units of family housing at Dyess in one of the finest housing areas to be found on any Air Force base. As of press time, the waiting period for occupancy of these quarters was running at about six months. The base does have 40 temporary lodging units, as well as 175 rooms for visitors and nearly 1,000 rooms for unaccompanied airmen.

Educational opportunities for children and adults living at Dyess are excellent. The Abilene Independent School District has two high schools, five junior high schools, and 19 elementary schools, as well as excellent parochial and private schools. Adult education is offered by Abilene Christian University, Hardin-Simmons University, and McMurry College.

Personal Services. Base services include a base exchange complex and a 51,000-square-foot commissary with over 18,000 square feet of sales space. Medical care is provided by a 20-bed hospital center.

Recreation. A recreation center, a ten-lane bowling center, an 18-hole golf course, tennis courts, a gymnasium, two swimming pools, and arts and crafts and auto hobby shops are available on the base. The Air Force family camp is located at Possum Kingdom, a beautiful resort area nearby.

The Local Area. The climate at Dyess is temperate, with annual temperature averages of around 64° F. The relative humidity stays at around 40 percent in the summer, which keeps the heat from becoming too oppressive. The average annual rainfall is about twenty-five inches.

Abilene is approximately 250 miles north of San Antonio and 175 miles west of Dallas. Much culture and outdoor recreation can be enjoyed in Abilene, from the Philharmonic Orchestra, Community Band, and Fine Arts Museum to the Abilene State Park, 19 miles south of town. Fort Phantom Hill, Nelson Park Zoo, Lake Fort Phantom, Lake Hubbard, Lake Abilene, and Lake Kirby are also attractions. The city boasts many fine shops and restaurants, a 69-acre city park, three eighteen-hole golf courses, hunting and fishing, and outdoor sports in the outlying areas.

For more information, write to Public Affairs Office, 650 2nd St., Dyess AFB, TX 79607-1960, or call (915) 696-0212. Home page: *www.dyess.af.mil.*

GOODFELLOW AIR FORCE BASE

Goodfellow Air Force Base is home of the Air Force's intelligence training mission and an integral component of the Air Education and Training Command. Each year, thousands of Air Force, Army, Navy, and Marine students go there to learn the secrets and complexities of the latest intelligence skills. In today's fast-moving technological world, every graduate is assured of a job after completing training.

History. Named after Lt. John J. Goodfellow, Jr., a resident of the nearby town of San Angelo who was killed when his plane crashed in France in 1918, the base opened in February 1941. Throughout World War II and for more than a decade afterward, Goodfellow's mission consisted of training pilots. Its flying mission ended in October 1958. Since 1985, the base has been the Air Force's center for intelligence training under the aegis of the 17th Training Wing. The Army's 344th Military Intelligence Battalion is also a tenant unit at Goodfellow, along with Navy and Marine detachments. Today Goodfellow is home to over 3,000 active-duty personnel, their 4,600 family members, and nearly 1,000 civilian employees.

Housing and Schools. There are 296 units of family quarters at Goodfellow. Dormitories for enlisted and officer personnel and a transient family quarters complex are available for newly assigned personnel and their guests on a space-available basis. Dependent children attend schools in the San Angelo Independent School District. A child-care center for over 150 children is operated on base, and the base education services center provides counseling and information pertaining to local programs conducted on the base and at the campuses of Angelo State University, Howard College, Park College, and Southern Illinois University.

Personal Services. A 52,000-square-foot commissary offers over 9,000 items to shoppers, and the base exchange, with a number of concessions in its minimall, offers a wide variety of shopping bargains. Medical care at Goodfellow is provided by the 17th Medical Group, with most services dispensed on an appointment basis. Referrals are made to a regional medical center in San Angelo, as well as to several smaller hospitals. Some military patients are referred to Wilford Hall Medical Center at Lackland Air Force Base in San Antonio or Dyess Air Force Base in Abilene.

Recreation. Recreational facilities include an arts and crafts center, a woodworking center, an auto hobby shop, a recreation center, two gymnasiums, two swimming pools, an eight-lane bowling center, and Lake Nasworthy Recreation Camp, about ten miles southwest of the base. The area has fishing, boating, sailing, and outdoor sports. A spacious NCO club and an officers club serve as the hub of Goodfellow's social life. Of special note to gourmets of Texas cooking, each September Goodfellow hosts the annual Armed Forces International Chili Cook-Off at the Lake Nasworthy Recreation Camp. The winner receives an invitation to the prestigious chili championship at Terlingua, Texas. Unreconstructed Yankees and other dudes must bring their own bicarbonate of soda.

The Local Area. Goodfellow AFB is adjacent to the town of San Angelo. The climate in this part of Texas is semiarid, with average temperatures ranging between 46 and 88° F throughout the year. Rain averages about seventeen inches a year, and snowfall is very light.

San Angelo grew up around Fort Concho, which was established there in 1867 to protect settlers. Today, the Fort Concho Museum is a 40-acre national historic landmark and tourist spot. The Concho River flows through the town of San Angelo, so water sports abound in the vicinity. There are also three lakes within a 30-minute drive of the town: O. C. Fisher Reservoir; Twin Buttes Reservoir, with over 180,000 acre-feet of water; and Lake Nasworthy. Local celebrations worth the visitor's attention are the Lamblast, a world-championship lamb cookoff, and the Fiesta del Concho in June, which includes a river parade, street dancing, and other activities. The San Angelo Coliseum, capable of seating over 5,000 people, hosts many public activities, from rodeos and stock shows to symphony concerts.

For more information, write to Public Affairs Office, 184 Forth Lancaster Avenue, Suite 11, Goodfellow AFB, TX 76908-4410, or call (915) 654-3231. Home page: *www.goodfellow.af.mil.*

LACKLAND AIR FORCE BASE

For those who enlist in the Air Force, Lackland is where it all begins. The "Gateway to the Air Force" provides basic military training for all enlisted people entering the Air Force, Air Force Reserve, and Air National Guard. The 37th Training Wing is the largest training wing in the Air Force, graduating more than 70,000 students annually. Its four primary training functions—the 737th Training Group, the 37th Training Group, the Defense Language Institute English Language Center, and the Inter-American Air Forces Academy—conduct

Air Force Recruits on Parade at Lackland Air Force Base, Texas
USAF PHOTO

basic military, technical, professional, and English language training for the Air Force, other military services, government agencies, and allies. Other tenants include the Air Logistics Center, which transferred here when Kelly AFB closed, the 59th Medical Wing (Wilford Hall Medical Center), Headquarters Air Force Security Forces Center, and the 37th Support Group, the largest support group in the continental United States.

History. Lackland was named in honor of Brig. Gen. Frank D. Lackland, an early commandant of Kelly Field Flying School who died in 1943. Lackland today covers 6,726 acres, including almost 4,000 acres at the Lackland Training Annex. The base has a population of 8,300 military personnel, 1,500 family members, 3,200 civilian employees, and over 9,000 students on any given day of the week.

Housing and Schools. More than 720 units of family housing are available at Lackland, but there is a substantial waiting time. Local houses rent for $800 a month and up. Rentals for unfurnished one- and two-bedroom apartments start at $575 and $650 a month, respectively. Lackland has 157 temporary living facilities for families on permanent-change-of-station orders; more than 1,600 rooms and 3,000 bed spaces are available for temporary-duty personnel.

The Lackland Independent School District, located on base, offers schooling for military families from prekindergarten through high school. The base also operates a child-development center with a capacity for 108 children, and seventy homes on base are certified home day-care facilities. College-level courses are offered on base through Palo Alto, St. Philip's, San Antonio, and Park Colleges and Wayland Baptist and Webster Universities.

Personal Services. Medical care at Lackland is provided by Wilford Hall Medical Center, a 285-bed facility that is a major referral medical center. Lackland also offers a commissary, a main exchange, four minimarts, a convenience store, a garden shop, and a 24-hour shopette that includes a package liquor store and a ten-pump gas station.

Recreation. Recreational facilities include two picnic areas, a cinema theater, four recreational centers, a skills development center, an auto skills development center, a rod and gun club, 14 tennis courts, four swimming pools, three fitness centers, a bowling alley, and an 18-hole golf course. A colocated club housing both officers and enlisted clubs was opened in January 1997.

The Local Area. Lackland is located eight miles southwest of downtown San Antonio. Other military installations in the area include Randolph and Brooks Air Force Bases and the Army's Fort Sam Houston.

San Antonio is a tourist mecca. As the cradle of Texas independence, the Alamo is a prime feature, but San Antonio also offers other attractions, such as the River Walk, Sea World, Fiesta Texas, the Institute of Texan Cultures, Japanese tea gardens, and botanical gardens. San Antonio is also home of the NBA Spurs and the minor league's Missions.

For more information, write to Public Affairs Office, 1701 Kenly Avenue, Suite 4, Lackland AFB, TX 78236-5110, or call (808) 671-1110. Home page: *www.lackland.af.mil.*

LAUGHLIN AIR FORCE BASE

Laughlin Air Force Base is one of several "undergraduate" pilot training bases operated by the Air Force's Air Education Training Command. It sits six miles east of the border town of Del Rio, Texas, adjacent to U.S. 90.

History. Named after 1st Lt. Jack Thomas Laughlin, the first Del Rioan pilot casualty of World War II, the base became operational in July 1942 under the Army Air Corps as part of the Central Flying Training Command. Today Laughlin's 47th Flying Training Wing (AETC) trains USAF students, plus a small number of foreign students. The base has a population of over 1,300 military personnel, their 1,200 family members, and 1,900 civilian employees.

Housing and Schools. The USAF maintains over 550 units of family housing and a 20-space mobile-home park. Laughlin has 22 temporary living facilities for the families of personnel on permanent-change-of-station orders. Others may be accommodated, but on a space-available basis only. The base offers a child-care center, but children attend public schools in the surrounding community.

Personal Services and Recreation. Medical services are available at Laughlin's clinic, with referrals to San Antonio and Wilford Hall at Lackland for patients with conditions beyond the base clinic's capabilities. Other services include a commissary, a base exchange with numerous concessions, banking and credit facilities, and a colocated officers and enlisted club.

Recreation facilities include a skeet and trap range, picnic areas with playground facilities, a nine-hole golf course, a gymnasium, a ten-lane bowling center, a riding stable, tennis courts, and two swimming pools. A marina is located 23 miles northwest of the base. Many different types of watercraft, as well as campers and water skis, are available for rent there.

The Local Area. The climate around Del Rio, a town of about 30,000 people, is semiarid, with average winter temperatures of 50° F and summer averages near 90° F. Del Rio sits just to the southeast of the Amistad National Recreation Area, formed by Amistad Lake, one of the cleanest lakes in the nation and the largest in the state for water storage—5,660,000 acre-feet. The lake is 85 miles long. Striped bass weighing as much as 60 pounds can be caught in its waters. Hunting is also a popular sport in the area, and three hunting sites are located on base.

One of the major attractions in the Del Rio area is Ciudad Acuna, across the border in Coahuila, Mexico. Acuna is the sister city of Del Rio, and its quaint charms attract many tourists every year. One noted visitor was Pancho Villa. Twenty-five miles east of Laughlin, along U.S. 90 in Brackettville, is Alamo Village, a reproduction of San Antonio's famous Alamo, constructed for the purpose of filming John Wayne's epic movie, *The Alamo.* It is one of the most authentic motion picture sets ever built.

The town of San Angelo lies 150 miles north of Del Rio, along Highway 277. Uvalde is 70 miles east of Del Rio, and San Antonio lies another 80 miles east of there, along U.S. 90.

For more information, write to Public Affairs Division, 47th Flying Training Wing (AETC), 561 Liberty Drive, Suite 3, Laughlin AFB, TX 78843-5227, or call (830) 298-3511. Home page: *www.laughlin.af.mil.*

RANDOLPH AIR FORCE BASE

The "Taj Mahal" soars 147 feet into the air over Randolph, its intricate white spires pointing to a small blue and gold mosaic tile dome. The structure is covered with ornamental precast concrete, and the elegantly landscaped grounds surrounding its octagonal form lend to it an exotic Eastern atmosphere that reminded someone years ago of Shah Jahan's monument of Agra, and so it was named the Taj Mahal. The building's tower houses a 500,000-gallon water tank.

History. Named in honor of Capt. William M. Randolph, who was killed taking off from Gorham Field, Texas, Randolph Air Force Base was dedicated on 20 June 1930. Today, the base is home to the 5,900 active-duty personnel of the Air Force's Air Education and Training Command; Headquarters, Air Force Personnel Center; Headquarters, Air Force Recruiting Service; 12th Flying

Training Wing; and other tenant commands. More than 3,000 family members and 3,000 civilians live and work at Randolph.

Housing and Schools. Randolph operates over 1,000 units of family housing, consisting of Wherry units and permanent Spanish-style structures. The Wherry quarters are two- and three-bedroom units restricted to enlisted personnel. Other enlisted quarters consist of two- and three-bedroom town houses and four-bedroom NCO duplexes. Officers quarters are four-bedroom duplexes and two- and three-bedroom town-house units. Waiting periods last from six to twenty-six months. Some guest housing is available, but reservations are taken only for personnel on official orders.

A child-care center is operated on the base, as well as dependent schools accommodating students from kindergarten through twelfth grade. The education services center offers more than 250 courses each year leading to associate's, bachelor's, and master's degrees. Undergraduate institutions operating on base include Texas Lutheran College, Southwest Texas State University, San Antonio College, St. Philip's College, Incarnate Word College, and Embry-Riddle Aeronautical University. Graduate degrees are offered by St. Mary's and Southwest Texas State Universities.

Personal Services. The commissary at Randolph is a modern facility offering a variety of grocery, meat, and produce items, with seventeen checkout lanes. The base exchange is a modern, solar-powered department store that offers a full range of personal and household needs.

Recreation. Recreational facilities include Eberle Park picnic area, a hunt and saddle club, an aero club, an eighteen-hole golf course, a 24-lane bowling center, an arts and crafts center, two gymnasiums, many ball parks, and nine soccer fields.

Randolph Recreation Area at Canyon Lake, 17 miles west of New Braunfels, offers more than 51 acres of heavily forested beachfront. The lake itself has 80 miles of shoreline and 8,240 acres of water area, permitting water sports and boat rentals.

For more information, write to 12th FTW Public Affairs, 1 Washington Circle, Suite 4, Randolph AFB, TX 78150-4562, or call (210) 652-1110. Home page: *www.randolph.af.mil.*

SHEPPARD AIR FORCE BASE

Great monuments do not exist only in museums. At Sheppard, some of the famous aircraft in the history of U.S. aviation are on display, restored and mounted as if caught in actual flight and set to rest against the backdrop of the limitless Texas sky. The display includes the F-100 Super Sabre, the F-105 Thunderchief, the F-104 Starfighter, and many others.

History. Named in 1948 after U.S. Senator Morris Sheppard, a former chairman of the Senate Military Affairs Committee, the base was first established in 1941 as an Army Air Corps training school. Today its 6,000 acres are home for the 9,000 military personnel, their 4,800 family members, and 1,400 civilian employees of the Sheppard Technical Training Center, one of six such centers under the control of the 82nd Training Wing. The center also houses the 80th Flying Training Wing and other tenant units.

Housing and Schools. Sheppard has over 1,300 units of family housing and 80 units of transient lodging. Only families of personnel on permanent-change-of-station orders or families of hospital patients may obtain lodging on a reserved basis; all others are taken on a space-available basis only. Sheppard also has over 2,500 rooms for visiting officers and enlisted personnel.

Children attend schools in the Burkburnett and Wichita Falls Independent School Districts. Schooling for adults interested in continuing their education is available on base from Midwestern State University, Vernon Regional Junior College, and Wayland Baptist College.

Personal Services. Services available at Sheppard include the base exchange complex and concessions, a commissary with 81,000 square feet of sales space, two service stations, several snack bars, and banking facilities. Medical care is provided by a ninety-five-bed USAF regional hospital.

Recreation. Recreational facilities include a 40,000-volume library, an 18-hole golf course, two picnic areas, a saddle club, officers and enlisted clubs, two bowling lanes, four swimming pools, a recreation center, a 1,000-seat theater, auto and hobby shops, a skeet and trap range, and a gun club. The base also operates the Lake Texoma Recreation Annex, an 89,000-acre site located about 120 miles east of the base. Fishing, boating, waterskiing, camping, and picnicking are offered there, plus 45 cabins, each accommodating four to six people, and 12 camper spaces with hookups. A small exchange is operated in the main lodge, and equipment rental is provided there.

The Local Area. Sheppard is located approximately five miles north-northeast of the town of Wichita Falls, a community of approximately 100,000 people. Wichita Falls is about 130 miles south of Oklahoma City and 130 miles northwest of Dallas–Fort Worth. The Oklahoma border town of Burkburnett, on the Red River, is 15 miles north of Wichita Falls.

The temperature in this part of Texas averages 98° F in July and 58° F in February, with an average annual rainfall of a little over 27 inches, making outdoor activities possible year-round. Waterskiing, fishing, camping, and hunting can be enjoyed within an easy drive of the base. Lake Waurika and Lake Wichita are close by; Lake Arrowhead, Lake Kemp, and Lake Nocona are located within a few dozen miles of the base. Historic Fort Sill is about 50 miles to the north of Sheppard, and the Wichita Mountain National Recreation Area is about 55 miles north.

For more information, write to Public Affairs Office, 82nd Training Wing, Sheppard AFB, TX 76311-2349, or call (940) 676-2511. Home page: *www.sheppard.af.mil.*

Army

FORT BLISS

In the 152 years since it was founded, Fort Bliss has witnessed almost the entire history of the U.S. Army in the Southwest, from Indian-fighting cavalry to sophisticated courses for missilemen and budding sergeants major.

History. Fort Bliss was first established in November 1848 as the Post of El Paso. In March 1854, it was renamed Fort Bliss in honor of William Wallace Smith Bliss, a veteran of the Florida Seminole and Mexican Wars and later adjutant general of the Army's Western Division.

Today Fort Bliss is home to the Army's 32nd Army Air and Missile Defense Command (AAMDC), whose Range Command controls over 1.1 million acres of ranges and maneuver areas. The installation is also home to the 11th and 108th Air Defense Artillery Brigades and the U.S. Army Sergeants Major Academy, the "capstone" school in the Army's Noncommissioned Officer Education System, making the post home to over 12,000 active-duty personnel, 14,000 family members, and 6,300 civilian employees.

Housing and Schools. Fort Bliss offers every possible facility to today's soldiers and their families. The post operates nearly 3,000 sets of family quarters for enlisted and officer personnel. Ordinarily, these units are available from three to nine months after making application for them. The inn at Fort Bliss is the official on-post, 150-room guest facility, and it is available to active-duty and retired military service families and their guests.

There are three elementary schools on post, as well as two day-care centers and an in-home day-care program; high schools are available in El Paso. The education center provides an ever-expanding program of academic, technical, and vocational subjects, from improvement of basic skills to graduate degrees, without the student having to leave the post.

Personal Services and Recreation. Excellent medical and health-care services are provided by William Beaumont Army Medical Center, a twelve-story, 500-bed ultramodern facility serving a population estimated at more than 106,000 active-duty servicemembers, retired personnel, and their families. A large commissary and a main exchange with 20 concessions are also available.

The post offers varied forms of outdoor and indoor recreation programs and facilities, from museums, music, and theater to camping equipment rental facilities and saddle, flying, and rod and gun clubs. Due to the dry and sunny climate (average rainfall is only 7.7 inches annually), outdoor activities are possible year-round.

The Local Area. El Paso, situated at the tip of western Texas on the borders of Mexico and New Mexico, is the fourth-largest city in Texas, with a population of approximately 600,000. El Paso is a city of contrasts in culture, design, geography, and climate. At an elevation of over 3,600 feet, the air is dry, with virtually no humidity. Just across the border is Ciudad Juarez, the largest

Mexican city on the United States–Mexico border. El Paso is a very convenient starting place for many exciting and interesting trips to the natural wonders and historical sites that abound throughout western Texas and New Mexico.

For more information, write to Commander, 32nd AAMDC, Attention: Public Affairs, Fort Bliss, TX 79916-6816, or call (915) 568-2121. Home page: *www.bliss.army.mil.*

FORT HOOD

Fort Hood is the largest armored post, occupying 335 square miles (214,351 acres) of central Texas real estate. It is the only post in the United States capable of supporting two full-armored divisions and training them. Fort Hood is home to over 40,000 men and women of the III Corps, the 1st Cavalry Division ("First Team"), the 4th Infantry Division ("Ironhorse Division"), and several other tenant units. There are about 17,000 family members that live on post, and more than 4,500 Department of the Army civilian employees work on the installation. Fort Hood also has an extraordinary volunteer workforce that numbers over 3,500.

History. Named for Confederate general John Bell Hood, Fort Hood was constructed in 1942 and served as the Army's Tank Destroyer Center throughout World War II. Today the post has earned its reputation as being "The Great Place."

Housing and Schools. There are 13 on-post housing areas containing over 5,900 sets of family quarters at Fort Hood. The post also has two guest-house facilities: the 75-room Poxon Guest House, open to all military personnel and their family members, and the 48-room Junior Guest Quarters enlisted quarters. First priority is given to personnel in ranks specialist/corporal and below with families.

Elementary schools are provided on post for dependent children, and the Fort Hood education centers provide complete educational services for military personnel, from enhancement of basic military skills to preseparation counseling. College-level courses are available from local programs and enrollment in selected programs. College-level courses are available from local institutions such as Central Texas College, Tarleton State University, University of Mary Hardin–Baylor, Texas A & M University, Prairie View A & M University, and St. Mary's University of San Antonio, Texas.

Personal Services. Fort Hood, which supports 200,000 active-duty and retired personnel and their families, has every type of service facility used by soldiers in the modern Army.

Recreation. Fort Hood offers all types of indoor and outdoor recreation, including hunting and fishing in designated areas on the reservation. The morale, welfare, and recreation division maintains a boat dock on Belton Lake year-round, where boats and motors are available for rent for a nominal fee. A floating fishing marina, open year-round and heated during the winter season, can accommodate 50 fishermen on the inside deck and 100 fishermen on the outside deck. The 2,000-acre Belton Lake Outdoor Recreation Area is 14 miles northeast of the post and has 64 camper spaces with hookups. There are 165 ponds on the post, all suitable for fishing. In addition, Fort Hood has 12 lakes of its own.

The Local Area. Located in the beautiful "hill and lake" country of central Texas, Fort Hood's main post is about 60 miles northeast of the capital city of Austin and 50 miles south of Waco. Fort Hood is bordered on the north by the community of Gatesville and on the south by Killeen. To the west are Copperas Cove and Lampasas. Harker Heights and Temple are east of the installation. With average temperatures ranging from 38° to 94° F year-round, Fort Hood is particularly suited to all types of outdoor recreational activities.

For more information, write to Headquarters, 3rd Corps and Fort Hood Public Affairs Office, Building 1001, Room W105, Fort Hood, Texas 76544-5005, or call (254) 287-1110. Home page: *www.hood-pao.army.mil.*

FORT SAM HOUSTON

History. In its 124-year history, Fort Sam Houston has been host to notable winners and losers. The great Apache warrior Geronimo, enroute to prison in Florida, stayed there for a month in 1886. And at 9:30 A.M. on 2 March 1910, Lt. Benjamin D. Foulois became this country's first military aviator by making a solo flight in a Wright Type-A biplane at Arthur MacArthur Field. He soared to a height of 100 feet, and his aircraft attained a speed of fifty miles per hour.

Named after the great Texas soldier and first president of the Republic of Texas, Samuel Houston, Fort Sam Houston began life as the Military Post of San Antonio in 1876; its name was officially changed to Fort Sam Houston in 1890. Today the post is home to Headquarters, 5th U.S. Army; the Army Medical Command; Brooke Army Medical Center; and the Army Medical Department Center and School. It comprises some 3,200 acres on the main post and another 27,000 acres of maneuver areas and firing ranges at Camp Bullis (a training area twenty miles to the northwest of San Antonio). The post is home to over 6,900 active-duty personnel, their 2,500 family members, and more than 7,300 civilian employees.

Housing and Schools. Over 900 units of family housing are available. A 110-room guest house offers accommodations for visitors; over 1,900 rooms are also available for unaccompanied personnel. Dependent children on the post may attend a school with grades kindergarten through twelfth. Two child-care centers are also available. The Army education center offers a full range of courses and classes for military personnel, off and on duty, from MOS proficiency improvement to advanced academic degree completion programs.

Personal Services. Medical care is provided by the 450-bed Brooke Army Medical Center, one of the largest military health-care facilities in the world. The hospital is noted as one of the country's leading centers for the treatment of burn victims. Fort Sam has a commissary with over 102,000 square feet of sales space, two convenience food stores, a large main exchange, a four-seasons store, a toy store, and a shopette.

Recreation. Fort Sam offers a 36-hole golf course; a 24-lane bowling alley; two swimming pools; a riding stable; a movie theater; craft and hobby shops; handball, racquetball, and squash courts; and even a dinner theater and playhouse. The post also offers various athletic and recreational facilities and programs. Fort Sam Houston operates the Canyon Lake Recreation Area 50 miles north of the post. The area offers 32 three-bedroom house trailers, 32 water and electric hookups for recreational vehicles, and numerous camping and picnicking sites. Personnel assigned to Fort Sam Houston may make reservations up to 30 days in advance; others, seven days in advance. Camp Bullis, approximately 20 miles northwest of Fort Sam Houston, offers a variety of programs geared toward the shooting sports, such as hunting in season and archery and rifle ranges. Sand volleyball areas, horseshoe pits, and softball fields are also available.

The Local Area. The city of San Antonio, which was first settled by the Spanish in 1718, offers a delightful combination of the old and the new. The Alamo—the shrine to Texas liberty—and the Paseo del Rio, a beautiful riverfront promenade set in the heart of the city, offer pleasant contrasts to the city's modern skyline, punctuated by the ultramodern HemisFair Tower and other impressive buildings. During the annual four-day "Night in Old San Antonio," a festival celebrating the city's Spanish–Mexican–American heritage, visitors have been known to consume up to 45,000 miles of tamales!

For more information, write to Public Affairs Office, Attention: AFZG-PO, Fort Sam Houston, TX 78234-5000, or call (210) 221-1211. Home page: *www.fshtx.army.mil.*

Navy

CORPUS CHRISTI NAVAL AIR STATION

History. Corpus Christi Naval Air Station lies along the south shore of Corpus Christi Bay, not far from the Gulf of Mexico, on land that was once crawling with snakes among the mesquite brush. That was back in 1941. Today the station is headquarters for the Navy's Chief of Naval Air Training, Training Air Wing 4, the Mine Warfare Command, and various support and tenant commands. The station is home to more than 2,100 active-duty personnel, their 3,900 dependents, and 1,200 civilian employees.

Housing and Schools. The station has over 500 units of family housing. Billets are available for 500 unaccompanied enlisted personnel, as are 300 more for visitors. The Navy exchange also operates an 18-unit Navy Lodge for transients, as well as for active-duty and retired visitors and their families. A preschool and child-care center are operated on the station, but dependent schooling is conducted in the Independent School District of Flour Bluff. The

Navy Campus for Achievement assists active-duty personnel and their dependents in the pursuit of off-duty higher education. Courses are available from Corpus Christi State University, Del Mar College, and Embry-Riddle Aeronautical University.

Personal Services. The station offers a full range of morale and welfare support activities, including a Navy exchange, a commissary store, and a fifty-bed naval hospital that provides medical and surgical services to nearly 40,000 eligible personnel in the vicinity of Corpus Christi.

Recreation. Recreational activities are more than adequate and include three swimming pools, six lighted tennis courts, a skeet and trap range, a 14-lane bowling alley, an 18-hole golf course, a gymnasium, and a hobby craft center. There is also a picnic ground with camper hookups and sailboat rentals at Sunfish Beach during the summer months. The warm and sunny climate permits year-round enjoyment of outdoor activities.

The Local Area. Corpus Christi is a sparkling jewel of a city of 260,000 people. It is one of the cleanest cities in the nation and one of the fastest growing. The port there is the eighth largest in the United States. The community also offers much to do in the way of sightseeing and recreation, from the Corpus Christi Symphony to the Bayfront Plaza and Ocean Drive, a very scenic route that runs right up to the naval air station.

Corpus Christi lies about 210 miles southwest of Houston, on the same parallel as Tampa, Florida, and about 160 miles north of Brownsville, Texas, and Matamoros, Mexico. The Gulf Coast of Texas offers many attractions, from hunting and fishing to sailing, bird watching, and various local celebrations, including Corpus Christi's Buccaneer Days in April, Bayfest in September, and the Airshow/Open House Festival held at the air station in May for the benefit of the Navy Relief Society. The Shrimporee held in nearby Aransas Pass in October is a must for seafood lovers.

For more information, write to Public Affairs Office, Building 2, Corpus Christi NAS, Corpus Christi, TX 78419-5000, or call (361) 961-2811.

FORT WORTH NAVAL AIR STATION JOINT RESERVE BASE

On 1 October 1994, the U.S. Navy established NAS Fort Worth on the site of the former Carswell Field, seven miles northwest of Fort Worth. NAS Fort Worth is headquarters for the Fleet Logistics Support Wing, Marine Air Group 1, the 301st Fighter Wing of the Air Reserve Command, and other tenant units. It is a joint defense facility that plays a pivotal role in training and equipping air crews and aviation ground support personnel. Approximately 3,100 active-duty personnel, their 1,000 family members, 11,000 reservists, and about 500 civilian employees call the base home.

Housing and Schools. The base operates only 83 units of family housing and, as of press time, the wait for occupancy of these quarters was from 18 to 24 months. A total of only 126 units are available for temporary lodging. While there are no schools for dependent children on base, schooling is provided by Fort Worth's Arlington Independent School District. Currently, there are no child-care facilities on the base. Columbia College, Embry-Riddle Aeronautical University, and Northwood University provide on-site college-level programs for adults.

Personal Services and Recreation. NAS Fort Worth has both commissary and exchange facilities, as well as an AAFES Plaza that contains a credit union, clothing sales, a shoppette, a class six store, Anthony's Pizza, Frank's Franks, Sweet Reflections, and an optical shop. Also available is the Carswell Club, an auto hobby shop, a bowling center, and a library.

The Local Area. Founded in 1849, Fort Worth derives its name from Gen. William J. Worth, a veteran of the Mexican War. Today Fort Worth boasts a population of over 447,000, making Tarrant County, where Fort Worth is situated, the fourth largest in the state of Texas. Originally a "cow town" (cattle are still an important industry in this part of Texas), *Money* magazine listed Fort Worth number one on its 1998 list of the South's most livable places. In 1995, Fort Worth ranked in the top five cities of the nation for new and expanding business opportunities. Today the exuberant patrons of traditional honkytonks mix naturally on the streets with high-pressure businessmen in three-piece suits, but the cowpoke heritage of the city still lives on.

For more information, write to: Family Service Center, NAS JRB, Fort Worth, 3175 Vandenberg Avenue, Fort Worth, TX 76127-3175, or call (817) 782-5000. Home page: *www.nasft.cnrf.nola.navy.mil.*

INGLESIDE NAVAL STATION

Dedicated on 6 July 1992, Ingleside Naval Station is one of our newest naval facilities. Home port for mine countermeasures ships and coastal mine hunters, the station and its tenant commands are responsible for meeting the operational, logistical, and administrative needs of the U.S. Atlantic Fleet.

History. Groundbreaking for Ingleside began on 20 February 1988. The South Texas Coastal Bend area was chosen as the location for the station because of its quick access to the deep waters of the Gulf of Mexico, the well-protected waters inside the barrier island, the existence of sufficient land, and the area's great potential for growth. The first vessel to arrive at Ingleside, in June 1992, was the mine countermeasures ship *USS Scout*—the first U.S. Navy ship to be home-ported in Texas since World War II. Ingleside has a complement of 4,700 active-duty personnel, 235 civilian employees, and about 5,200 family members.

Housing, Schools, and Personal Services. Ingleside families live in Corpus Christi and other communities situated in San Patricio and Nueces Counties. Likewise, Ingleside children attend schools off base. The station has a bachelor enlisted facility that can accommodate 250 personnel. Health care is provided by small medical and dental clinics, with referrals to local hospitals or the naval hospital located at the Corpus Christi Naval Air Station. Although there is no commissary at Ingleside, there are a Navy exchange, a galley, a full fitness center with a swimming pool, tennis courts, and outdoor athletic fields.

For more information, write to Public Affairs Office, 1455 Ticonderoga, Suite W123, Naval Station Ingleside, Ingleside, TX 78362-5001, or call (361) 776-4200.

KINGSVILLE NAVAL AIR STATION

Kingsville Naval Air Station occupies 4,000 acres virtually on the doorstep of the King Ranch, one of the larger ranches in the world. It is home and workplace for approximately 840 active-duty personnel, their 1,200 family members, and 350 civilian employees belonging to the Training Air Wing 2. The wing performs the primary mission of training Navy aviators and turns out approximately 200 pilots every year. The station was commissioned on 4 July 1942 and was officially designated Naval Air Station, Kingsville, in 1968.

Housing and Schools. Family housing (Texas Terrace) is tight at Kingsville, with accommodations for only 244 families. Housing is situated at Texas Terrace, about two miles from the station. Ten units of transient housing are available on the station. Unaccompanied personnel live in 48 officer and 362 enlisted units.

Although there is no dependent schooling at the station, a child-care facility for 32 children is available. Many of the personnel stationed at Kingsville attend courses at Texas A & I University on the west side of town, eight miles from the station. With a student enrollment of 7,000 and a faculty of 250 members, the university offers bachelor's and master's degrees in many areas. While schools are reputedly excellent, there is only one high school, King High.

Personal Services. A Navy exchange and a commissary store are located on base. A medical clinic is also available, with referrals to Corpus Christi Naval Hospital (fifty-one miles from the station) and San Antonio. The station also has a consolidated package store, a service station, barber and beauty shops, and a minimart.

Recreation. Recreational facilities include a boat barn with equipment checkout, a bowling center, a ceramic shop, a gymnasium, a swimming pool, a youth center, a racquetball court, a skeet and trap range, and boarding for privately owned horses—even limited veterinary services. Also check out the Escondido Ranch in the heart of south Texas brush country, with almost 7,000 acres of outdoor activities.

The Local Area. The climate in this part of Texas is hot and humid, with the temperature averaging 84° F during the summer months; yearly rainfall is about 24 inches.

The town of Kingsville has a population of over 25,000. The major attraction there is the vast King Ranch, which begins only three miles from downtown Kingsville and covers an expanse of 860,000 acres. The town itself is situated along U.S. 77 a few miles inland from the Gulf of Mexico and Padre Island National Seashore. Corpus Christi is 40 miles to the north of Kingsville, and Brownsville/Matamoros is on the Gulf Coast, 94 miles south of Kingsville.

For more information, write to Public Affairs Officer, Naval Air Station, Kingsville, TX 78363-5000, or call (361) 516-6136.

Home page: *www.nask.navy.mil/index.html.*

UTAH

Air Force

HILL AIR FORCE BASE

A few miles to the west of Hill Air Force Base is the Great Salt Lake, a vast inland body of water that sits 4,200 feet above sea level. Several miles to the east are the Wasatch Mountains and Wasatch National Forest. The base sits at the heart of Utah's population center, with Salt Lake City about thirty miles to the south and Ogden about eight miles to the north. And the skies belong to the U.S. Air Force.

History. Named in honor of Maj. Ployer P. Hill, who died in the crash of the first B-17 aircraft at Wright-Patterson AFB in 1935, the base was activated in 1940. During World War II, Hill AFB provided rehabilitation, repair, and maintenance services for fighter and bomber aircraft. Today it occupies 6,698 acres and manages the 692,000 acres of the nearby Utah Test and Training Range. Its 5,700 active-duty personnel, 1,200 reservists, and 10,000 civilian employees staff the Ogden Air Logistics Center (ALC), the 88th and 419th (Reserve) Fighter Wings, and tenant units. The ALC provides support for a number of Air Force weapons systems, including the F-16, the F-4, and all of the intercontinental ballistic missile fleet. There are also 4,500 family members associated with Hill.

Housing and Schools. Hill AFB has 1,145 units of family housing and 260 rooms for visitors and guests. Plenty of excellent elementary, secondary, and high schools, as well as colleges and universities, are available in the area. A child-development center is located on the base.

Personal Services. The USAF hospital provides a 16-bed composite medical facility for active-duty and retired personnel and their families. Personal services include a commissary and base exchange with a wide variety of concessions, such as a service station, a barber shop, and base bus service.

Recreation. Recreational activities include an 18-hole golf course, a modern gymnasium, a 20-lane bowling center, a theater, a library, a recreation center,

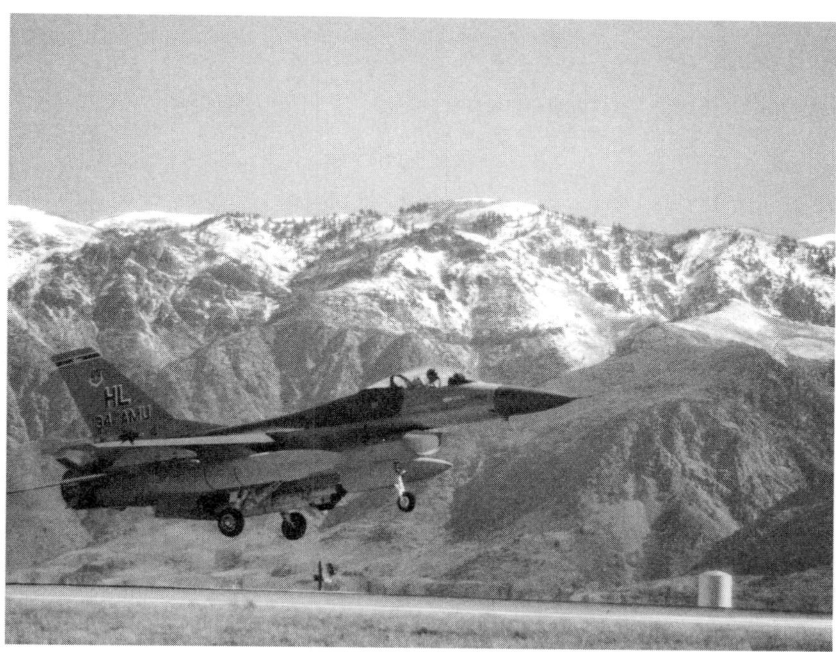

Air Force Fighter Jet at Hill Air Force Base, Utah USAF PHOTO

hobby shops, one indoor and two outdoor swimming pools, indoor and outdoor tennis courts, a rod and gun club, and fifteen restaurants and snack bars. A family camp features 14 trailer pads with hookups, camping, swimming, picnicking, and playground facilities. Hill also offers two elegant clubs for those sophisticates who enjoy an occasional evening discussing the writings of Albert Camus over gourmet food in the company of delightful and charming conversationalists.

Off-base Air Force-operated recreation facilities are the Hillhaus Mountain Lodge and a site at Carter Creek. Hillhaus, about 30 miles east of the base, is part of the Ogden Recreation Area. Carter Creek, 120 miles east of Hill in the Uinta Mountains, is used in the summer for camping and in the winter for cross-country skiing and snowmobiling. It has six cabins and eight trailer spaces, plus camping, hunting, fishing, hiking, and equipment rentals.

The Local Area. Salt Lake City, a metropolis of over 720,000, is a center of culture, as well as the international headquarters of the Church of Jesus Christ of Latter Day Saints (Mormons). Ogden is also a thriving city with many excellent cultural attractions and historic sites. The Great Salt Lake dominates the area, stretching 75 miles north to south and 25 miles wide. Its saltiness allows swimmers to float on its waters.

For more information, write to Public Affairs Office, Ogden Air Logistics Center, Hill AFB, UT 84056-5000, or call (801) 777-7221. Home page: *www.hill.af.mil.*

Army

DUGWAY PROVING GROUND

At 778,855 acres, it is larger than the state of Rhode Island. Dugway Proving Ground (DPG) is located in the west-central part of Utah, about 67 air miles southwest of Salt Lake City. The name Dugway is taken from the method used by the early pioneers to move their Conestoga wagons through the mountains, by digging a trench or grade through the passes and then using oxen to haul the wagons up by the "dug way." Among its expansive plains and salt flats, one can become lost in mind or while wandering through the deceiving terrain, so be wary when traveling in this part of the world.

History. Dugway Proving Ground was officially established on 12 February 1942. Few buildings are still in use from this period, as considerable expansion and renovation have taken place since then. Today Dugway's mission is to test Army equipment in order to provide protection for military personnel in the field against chemical and biological agents. DPG also tests battlefield smoke and obscurants and conducts production qualification testing for mortar and artillery munitions. Dugway is home to approximately 90 permanent-party military personnel. The civilian workforce numbers about 1,300 employees.

Housing and Schools. Military personnel are required to live on post at Dugway. DPG has over 400 units of family housing available, and there is no waiting period for this housing. Accommodations are available for soldiers and families, arriving or departing, and for their guests. Rooms are available for transients at the Antelope Inn, which as of February 2000 cost $21 per night for a private room for up to six months; three-bedroom homes at Dugway rent for $51 per night. Housing rentals in Tooele range from $336 a month for a one-bedroom apartment to as much as $1,200 a month for a four-bedroom home. Modern, well-equipped elementary and high schools are located on post for the children of military and civilian personnel assigned there. The schools are operated as part of the Tooele County School System. Dugway also offers a $3 million day-care center built in 1990. Adult education is available through the education center, which offers high school courses and academic college courses from Utah State University and Salt Lake City Community College.

Personal Services. There is a health clinic on the installation, but the nearest military hospital is at Hill Air Force Base, 110 miles northeast of Dugway. The nearest civilian hospital is in Tooele, about 40 miles northeast of the post.

A commissary, a post exchange, a bank, a credit union, a video rental service, a snack bar at the bowling center, a beauty and barber shop, a laundry and dry cleaner, a gas station, and a community club are available at Dugway. Note that the commissary makes a run to Hill AFB once a week to stock up on items not normally carried there.

Recreation. Recreational facilities include a library, an all-ranks community club, a sports and fitness center that opened in 1994, a nine-hole, 3,028-yard golf course, a swimming pool, tennis courts, and an outdoor recreation center offering a variety of outdoor recreation programs, including trips to nearby ski resorts and fishing spots. Recreational equipment is available for rent through the outdoor recreation office.

The Local Area. Summers at Dugway are moderately hot and very dry. Spring and fall are cool, and the winters are moderately cold, with short storms and some snow. About seven inches of precipitation fall in the area annually. The surrounding country is high in elevation, and Dugway itself is 4,300 feet above sea level. There are only two urban areas in the vicinity: Tooele, with a population of 16,000, and Grantsville, with a population of 4,500. The population density in Tooele County has an average of fifteen people to the square kilometer. The road connecting Dugway with Tooele passes over the Onaqui Mountain Range, where, passing through 105 curves, it reaches an elevation of over 6,000 feet.

For more information, write to Commanding Officer, 388th Range Squadron, 1010 Avery Road, Dugway, UT 84022, or call (435) 831-5343.

VIRGINIA

Air Force

LANGLEY AIR FORCE BASE

History. Langley Air Force Base is the oldest continuously used base in the U.S. Air Force. This is particularly fitting because Langley is situated in a part of the United States that is intimately associated with American history.

Langley Field, named in honor of Samuel Pierpont Langley, a pioneer of American aviation and former secretary of the Smithsonian Institution, was first opened in June 1917, when the 5th Aviation School, Army Signal Corps, was formed there. Today Langley hosts the Air Combat Command's headquarters, the 1st Fighter Wing, and a number of other tenant units. It is home to more than 8,800 active-duty personnel, 10,000 family members, and 1,500 civilian employees. Langley sees action on a continuous basis—for instance, it picked up Operation Northern Watch in February 2000, based out of Incirlik, Turkey.

Housing and Schools. Langley has more than 1,300 units of family housing, some located on the base itself and some in Bethel Manor, about five miles from the installation. Temporary-lodging facilities at Langley are always tight, although there are over 300 quarters available for visiting and transient personnel.

A child-care center is operated on the base and at Bethel Manor. Dependent schoolchildren attend public schools operated by the city of Hampton and York County. For adults wishing to pursue higher education, on-base courses are conducted by Christopher Newport University, George Washington University, Thomas Nelson Community College, Embry-Riddle Aeronautical University, Old Dominion University, and Hampton University.

Personal Services. The Langley Hospital is a 50-bed medical facility with over 216,000 outpatient visits and 4,700 admissions annually. It serves a local population of around 60,000 active-duty and retired personnel and their families. Other services include a base exchange with a 76,000-square-foot shopping area and eight concessions and a commissary that serves approximately 80,000 customers a month.

Recreation. Recreational facilities include two 18-hole golf courses; a 24-lane bowling center; auto and wood hobby shops; a marina with slips (both dry and wet) for over 120 private boats; and yacht, scuba, aero, saddle, and skeet clubs. In addition, there are four swimming pools, a gym, and a recreation center. Big Bethel Recreation Area, adjacent to Bethel Manor housing area, is available for picnicking and fishing. The newly renovated fitness center has state-of-the-art equipment. A juice bar offers nutritional shakes and snacks.

The Local Area. Langley is located three miles north of Hampton in an area that has many major military installations: Fort Monroe, Fort Eustis, Oceana Naval Air Station, Norfolk Naval Base, and Yorktown Naval Weapons Station.

The Hampton–Norfolk–Newport News–Virginia Beach area is rich in things to do and interesting places to see. The area is a fisherman's paradise, with plenty of freshwater and deep-sea fishing. Historic Fort Monroe, Hampton Roads, Williamsburg, Jamestown, Yorktown Victory Center, Petersburg, Busch Gardens, Water Country USA, and Richmond are all within easy commuting distance.

For more information, write to 1st FW Public Affairs, 159 Sweeney Boulevard, Suite 100, Langley AFB, VA 23655-2292, or call (757) 764-9990. Home page: *www.langley.af.mil/public.html.*

Army

FORT A. P. HILL

Located 26 miles south of Fredericksburg in Caroline County, Virginia, Fort A. P. Hill encompasses about 77,000 acres, making it the sixth-largest military installation on the East Coast. Named in honor of Lt. Gen. Ambrose Powell Hill, Confederate general and native son of Virginia, the installation was established by the War Department in 1941, when it served as a staging and maneuver area for troops during World War II.

Today, as a subinstallation of Fort Belvoir, Fort A. P. Hill is still training military personnel of all services—more than 150,000 a year in eleven campsites. The post offers the latest in live-fire ranges, handling weapons from small arms to artillery and aviation gunnery. The post has eleven acres along the Rappahannock River for floating-bridge training. Every four years, Fort A. P. Hill hosts the National Boy Scout Jamboree at Camp Openchancanough, a 200-acre site on Hearns Pond, where more than 35,000 scouts participate in the two-week event. The next jamboree is scheduled for the summer of 2001. The event usually draws 250,000 visitors. The post has a total daytime population of around 100 active-duty military personnel and approximately 350 civilian employees.

Personal Services. Fort Hill has a small post exchange with 9,000 square feet of sales space. Full-service commissary and exchange facilities, as well as definitive medical care, are available at the Naval Surface Warehouse Center Dahlgren, Quantico Marine Base, or Fort Belvoir.

Recreation. A lodge and four cabins are available for recreational purposes, as is a 48-space trailer park with hookups for water, sewage, and electricity. There are a physical fitness center, a community club, a lighted softball field, a tennis court, a multipurpose court for tennis and basketball, and an outdoor swimming pool located on the post. Fort A. P. Hill boasts 619 acres of water surface areas in twenty lakes and beaver ponds and a 200-acre wildlife refuge.

The Local Area. Fort A. P. Hill is bordered on the north by U.S. 17; the small towns of Bowling Green and Milford are just to the south, along State Route 207. U.S. 301 cuts right through Fort Hill on a north-south axis. This is Civil War history country. Fredericksburg National Battlefield Park, Chancellorsville, Spotsylvania Courthouse, and the Wilderness battlefields lie just to the northwest, a short drive from the main post. Richmond is about 35 miles south along Interstate 95.

For more information, write to Public Affairs and Protocol Office, Fort A. P. Hill, Bowling Green, VA 22427-5000, or call (804) 633-8120. Home page: *www.belvoir.army.mil/fortaphill.*

FORT BELVOIR

When Col. George William Fairfax erected his manor house in 1741, he called it Belvoir, meaning "beautiful to see." In later years, George William Fairfax, the colonel's eldest son, and his good friend and neighbor, George Washington, frequently rode over the acres of the Belvoir estate together. The manor was partially burned in 1783, and in 1814, the British demolished the remaining walls. But George Washington's graceful home, Mount Vernon, still stands above the banks of the Potomac a few miles from Belvoir, and the area is still very "beautiful to see." The ruins of Belvoir and the Fairfax family graves may still be seen on a bluff overlooking the Potomac, behind the officer housing area.

History. What is now Fort Belvoir was originally part of the old Fairfax estate. The post was designated Camp A. A. Humphreys in 1917 but renamed Fort Belvoir in 1935. Today Fort Belvoir's 8,600 acres are an installation of the Military District of Washington and home to more than one hundred tenants. Among these are the Army Information Systems Command, the Intelligence and Security Command, and other tenant units. The post has a daytime population of 8,700 active-duty military personnel, their 5,000 family members, and over 10,000 civilian workers.

Housing and Schools. Fort Belvoir is a completely modern installation that possesses all the benefits, services, and facilities available to military personnel. There are over 2,000 sets of family quarters on post, ranging from detached housing for senior officers and NCOs to two-story, row-type housing for junior officers and enlisted personnel. The waiting list varies, depending on grade and family requirements. Limited guest accommodations are available for all ranks. Single life on post is excellent, too. Over 900 enlisted soldiers live in McCree Barracks in two-person rooms with wall-to-wall carpeting and private baths.

Dependent children may attend on-post school from kindergarten through grade six; grades seven through twelve are available at the nearby Hayfield Intermediate and High School. Two child-care facilities are operated on the post. The post education center operates a program offering many opportunities. Both on- and off-post college-level courses are available from the University of Virginia, the University of Maryland, and Catholic, George Washington, Howard, and George Mason Universities.

Personal Services. With its large post exchange, well-stocked commissary, and a full range of medical-care services available at the 129-bed DeWitt Army Hospital, military personnel at Fort Belvoir are assured gracious and healthy living.

Recreation. Fort Belvoir has a marina, indoor shooting ranges, and NCO and officers clubs. The Sosa Community Center provides a wide variety of social activities for all ages. Licensed fishing is permitted in the base's ponds and on the Potomac River. There is a wildlife and wetlands refuge providing more than seven miles of hiking trails, and bow hunting is permitted during deer season. The Pohick Loop Trail, a hard-surfaced, quarter-mile trail, allows access to the wildlife refuge by handicapped users. This is the first trail of its kind on any military installation, and it is open to the public.

The Local Area. Fort Belvoir is located in historic northern Virginia, the site of many of the most famous events that have occurred in this nation's development. Washington, D.C., is only 12 miles away, and two major Civil War battlefields, Manassas and Fredericksburg, as well as Richmond, Colonial Williamsburg, and Yorktown, are within easy driving distance. Gettysburg, Pennsylvania, is somewhat farther away but still close enough for a weekend's touring pleasure.

For more information, write to Public Affairs Office, 9820 Flagler Road, Suite 201, Fort Belvoir, VA 22060-5932, or call (703) 545-6700. Home page: *www.belvoir.army.mil.*

FORT EUSTIS

Fort Eustis is situated on a historical crossroads that unites some of the most momentous of the Republic's yesterdays with its technology-based tomorrows. John Smith, famous as the savior of Jamestown (and the last English husband of Pocahontas), visited there in 1610, and its first prominent settler, John Rolfe (first English husband of Pocahontas), built his home there, near the site of the present-day golf course. Composed of former plantations of wealthy Virginia tobacco growers, this site of over 9,000 acres is now the training facility of the U.S. Army Transportation Center and Fort Eustis. Fort Eustis is also the home of the only flying saucer in captivity and a ship that is in use all the time but never goes anywhere.

History. Named in honor of Brevet Brig. Gen. Abraham Eustis (military service from 1808 to 1843), the first commandant of the Artillery School of

Practice at Fort Monroe, Fort Eustis was established in March 1918 as an artillery training area. In 1946, it became the principal training post for the Army Transportation Corps. Today it is home to the Army Transportation Center and School, the Army Aviation Logistics School, the 7th Transportation Group, and other commands (see entry for Fort Story, below—Fort Story is a subinstallation of Fort Eustis). The "ship that never sails" is a land ship, built into a pier and used to conduct classes in cargo-handling operations. Personnel assigned to the post train thousands of officers and enlisted soldiers every year in aviation maintenance, harborcraft operations and maintenance, and rail and line haul motor transport. The post is also responsible for an over-the-shore training subinstallation near Virginia Beach, where Army personnel learn about amphibious logistical operations.

Today Fort Eustis is home to around 5,200 active-duty personnel, 2,500 family members, and a civilian workforce of more than 4,200.

Housing and Schools. Fort Eustis has more than 1,000 sets of family quarters of many different basic designs, from two-story multiple units to detached homes for senior officers. Fort Eustis has 64 mobile-home spaces and also offers guest accommodations for personnel on temporary-duty or permanent-change-of-station orders.

There are no on-post schools at Eustis for dependent children, but plenty of excellent schooling is available in the local community. There is a day-care center on post, as well as an in-home day-care program. The education center hosts a variety of on-post college courses run by fully accredited institutions offering associate's to postgraduate degrees in many subjects; off-post college courses are available at the College of William and Mary at Williamsburg.

Personal Services and Recreation. Fort Eustis has both a large post exchange and a commissary. Medical care is provided by a 57-bed hospital, and additional medical care is available at nearby Langley Air Force Base.

Recreational facilities include a bowling alley; a swimming pool; handball, racquetball, and tennis courts; chapels; an 18-hole golf course; an auto shop; a post movie theater; a skeet range; and boating, hunting, and fishing areas.

The Local Area. Fort Eustis is situated on the western neck of a peninsula formed on the west by the James River and Hampton Roads and on the east by the York River and the Chesapeake Bay. It is one of the most significant historic areas in the United States: Jamestown and Williamsburg are only a few miles to the north; Yorktown is just across the peninsula on the York River; and Fort Monroe is at the tip of the peninsula, at Hampton. Across from Hampton, via the Hampton Roads Bridge and Tunnel, are Norfolk and Virginia Beach, a famous resort area. North of Virginia Beach, along the Atlantic coast, is the Cape Henry Memorial, marking the first landing place of the Jamestown settlers in 1607. And from Norfolk, one may take the famous Chesapeake Bay Bridge and Tunnel some 20 miles north across the bay to Virginia's famed Eastern Shore resort and fishing paradise.

Ah, yes, you're wondering about the captive flying saucer comment above! Well, in reality, it's one of two aero-cars built as an experimental step in the development of the vertical take-off and landing craft. It was first tested in California in 1960 and flew no higher than four feet. Today, looking more like a huge doughnut than a spacecraft, it is permanently elevated about seven feet above the ground in an outdoor display at Fort Eustis.

For more information, write to Community Services Office, U.S. Army Transportation Center and Fort Eustis, Fort Eustis, VA 23604-5000, or call (757) 878-1212. Home page: *www.eustis.army.mil.*

FORT LEE

If, as Napoleon is supposed to have said, an Army travels on its stomach, and if logistics are the "sinews" of war, then Fort Lee is truly one of our most important military installations.

The U.S. Army Combined Arms Support Command (CASCOM) and Fort Lee occupy 5,574 acres three miles east of Petersburg on State Route 36. The installation has a military population of over 3,000 and a civilian complement of 2,800 personnel. The post supports 4,900 family members and an estimated 18,000 retirees living in the area. The CASCOM is responsible for training the personnel who provide logistical support to soldiers and units Army-wide.

History. Named in honor of Gen. Robert E. Lee, the installation came to life in July 1917 as Camp Lee and was used as a mobilization and division training center. It closed after World War I but reopened in 1940, and quartermaster training operations began there in 1941. In 1950, the post was given official recognition and permanent status and designated Fort Lee.

Housing and Schools. There are over 1,300 sets of family quarters on post, the oldest having been constructed in 1950; guest-house accommodations are also available and reservations are accepted. Dependents of military personnel at Fort Lee attend the Prince George County Public School System. Military personnel may take advantage of an extensive adult education program operated at the post. John Tyler Community College, a state-supported two-year college, offers seven degree programs. Central Texas College, Florida Institute of Technology, Saint Leo College, and Virginia State University also offer on-post programs.

Personal Services and Recreation. Fort Lee offers a wide spectrum of support and morale facilities, including a post exchange, a commissary, a medical clinic, and dental care facilities.

Recreational facilities include an eighteen-hole golf course, a swimming pool, a bowling alley, an auto shop, a gymnasium, and tennis courts.

The Local Area. The city of Petersburg is located just three miles from Fort Lee. The Petersburg National Battlefield Monument marks the site of the longest siege of the Civil War. The Siege Museum in Petersburg depicts the everyday life in the city both before the war and during the ten months the siege lasted. Richmond, former capital of the Confederacy and Virginia's leading city today, is only a few miles to the north of the post, off Interstate 95. It was at Richmond's Saint John's Church that Patrick Henry made his famous "Liberty or Death" speech.

With its relatively mild winters and long summers, Virginia is an ideal place for camping, fishing, hunting, backpacking, boating, and other outdoor activities. Add to this the rich historical heritage of the Old Dominion State, and a visit to Fort Lee can be immensely rewarding professionally and personally.

For more information, write to Public Affairs Office, USA CASCOM and Fort Lee, Fort Lee, VA 23801-5009, or call (804) 765-3000. Home page: *www.lee.army.mil.*

FORT MONROE

For hundreds of years, there has been some kind of fortification on the site of present-day Fort Monroe. Two of its predecessors were destroyed by hurricanes in 1667 and again in 1749. Today things are much calmer and safer there.

History. The present structure was begun in 1819 and received its first garrison in July 1823. Originally named Fortress Monroe, in honor of James Monroe, our fifth president, it was designated Fort Monroe by the secretary of war in 1832. Today it is the home of the Training and Doctrine Command (TRADOC), the architect of the future Army, which develops doctrine, weapon systems, equipment, organizations, and training. Fort Monroe is also headquarters for the Army's Cadet Command and the Joint Warfighting Center. Interestingly, and perhaps a comfort to some slated for this assignment, there are no deployable units on the installation. Fort Monroe has a population of over 600 active-duty personnel, their 890 family members, and 2,200 civilian employees.

Housing and Schools. Government quarters are limited to about 190 units at Fort Monroe. There is some privately owned Wherry housing on the post to which assignments are made; rent for these units is very reasonable. Bachelor enlisted quarters are also available. Additionally, transient quarters are available and reservations are accepted for families in transition and for employees, military and civilian, traveling on official orders; others are accepted on a space-available basis only.

School-age dependent children attend school primarily within the city of Hampton. Child-care facilities are located on post. The post education center offers a variety of undergraduate and graduate courses, as well as educational counseling.

Personal Services and Recreation. A commissary, a post exchange, a medical and dental clinic, and a full range of morale and support facilities are available.

Recreational facilities and programs at Fort Monroe include the Casemate Museum, at which one can see the cell where Jefferson Davis was imprisoned following the War Between the States. Exhibits covering the site's nearly 400-year history are on display. There is also the Historical and Archeological Society, which conducts a variety of projects and features guest speakers at its meetings. The facility's unique location—jutting into the Chesapeake Bay and Hampton Roads—affords Fort Monroe personnel an excellent opportunity to participate in sailing, powerboating, and water sports in general. There is a marina on post, and fishing and boating equipment is available. Fort Monroe also offers bowling, tennis, hobby shops, a swimming pool, three racquetball courts, a fitness center, and a movie theater.

The Local Area. A major attraction at Fort Monroe is the rich historical tradition, which accounts for the lion's share of the thriving tourist industry in this area. Just across Hampton Roads via bridge and tunnel are Norfolk and Virginia Beach, both renowned vacation spots. Colonial Williamsburg, Jamestown, and Yorktown are situated within easy driving distance to the north of Hampton. Richmond, the capital of Virginia, and even Washington, D.C., are not too far away, easily accessible by a system of well-maintained interstate highways and rail service.

For more information, write to Army Community Services, Headquarters, Fort Monroe, ATZG-PA-HC-21, Building 36, Fort Monroe, VA 23651-6130, or call (757) 727-2000. Home page: *www-tradoc.monroe.army.mil/monroe/.*

FORT MYER

The air at Fort Myer is constantly punctuated by martial music, whether the shrill piping of the U.S. Army Fife and Drum Corps playing for a review on Summerall Field or the mournful dirge of a funeral march as a soldier is escorted to his last resting place in nearby Arlington National Cemetery. Fort Myer is truly one of the Army's finest showplaces, and the primary mission of the major units stationed there—the 3rd U.S. Infantry ("The Old Guard") and the U.S. Army Band ("Pershing's Own")—is ceremonial.

History. Originally established as a bastion in the defenses of Washington during the Civil War, the post was known as Fort Whipple until February 1881, when it was renamed in honor of Brig. Gen. Albert J. Myer, the first chief of the Army Signal Corps. Military aviation was born at Fort Myer with the flight of a Wright flying machine there on 3 September 1908, when the craft managed to stay aloft for one minute and eleven seconds; the first air fatality occurred there when Lt. Thomas Selfridge was killed in the crash of a Wright flying machine, also in 1908. Today Fort Myer is home to 2,400 active-duty personnel, 450 family members, and 900 civilian employees.

Housing and Schools. There are only 180 units of family housing at Fort Myer. Key Department of the Army staff officers, including the chief of staff of the Army and the chairman of the Joint Chiefs of Staff, occupy quarters on the post; a small number of brick duplexes are available to certain senior NCOs,

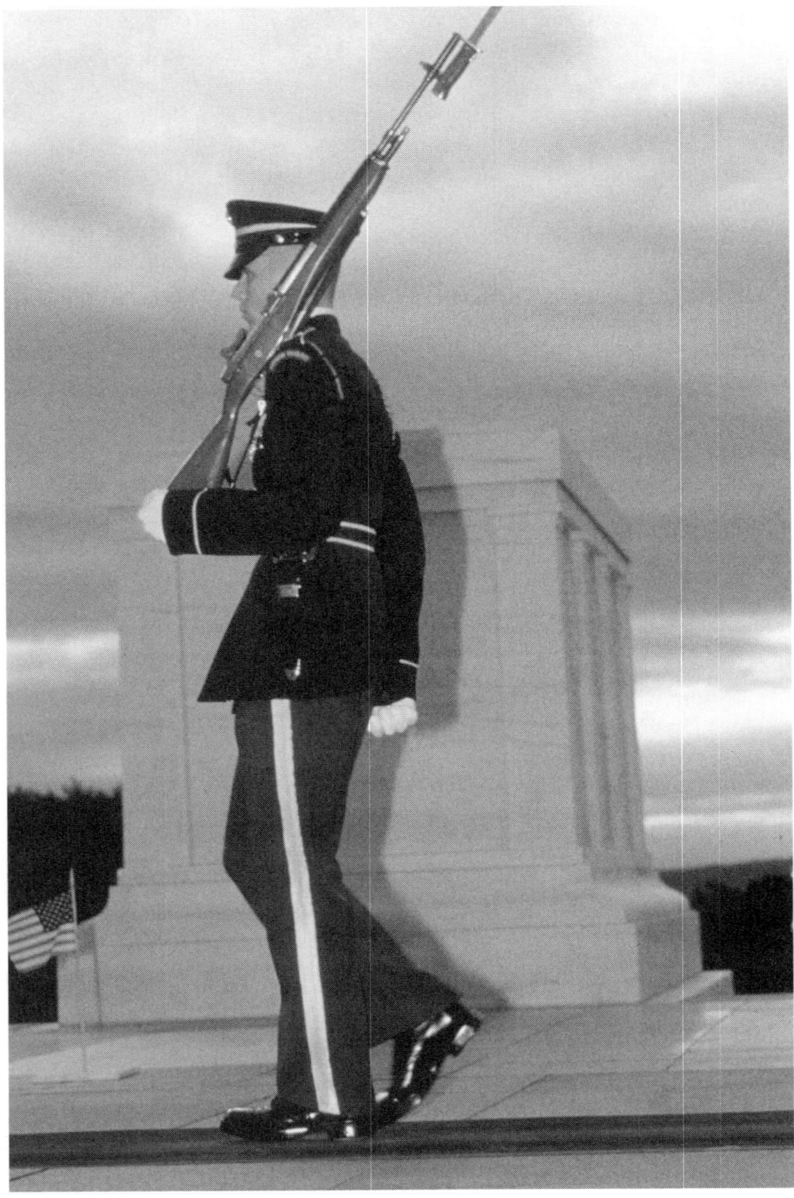

Guarding the Tomb of America's Unknown Soldier at Arlington National Cemetery, Fort Myer, Virginia U.S. ARMY PHOTO

and there is a modern high-rise for other enlisted ranks, but the waiting list for these quarters is very long.

Troop housing (for 2,400 soldiers) at Fort Myer is plentiful, and much of it is very modern. Most Army personnel on duty in the Washington metropolitan area are assigned to units at Fort Myer, and the post also provides billets and other support to members of the Navy and the Air Force on a limited basis.

Dependent children of service personnel stationed at Fort Myer attend schools in Arlington. A day-care center is available on post. Fort Myer is ideally situated for personnel who wish to continue their education. A number of renowned universities and colleges, such as Georgetown and Howard, are located in the area, and most government installations in the area, including Fort Myer, host off-duty college classes for military and civilian personnel.

Personal Services and Recreation. Fort Myer is a small post, but it does have the basic morale and service facilities found on most military installations. A new post exchange/community service center is provided, and Andrew Rader Army Health Clinic (a satellite facility of Walter Reed Army Medical Center) offers outpatient medical care. A large and well-stocked commissary, a shoppette, a bank, and a full-service gasoline station are available.

Recreational facilities include a fitness center, spacious officers and NCO clubs, a 20-lane bowling alley, a post library, two outdoor swimming pools, tennis and racquetball courts, and a gymnasium.

The Local Area. The Fort Myer area has four distinct seasons, but the general climate is mild and snowfall is usually light. Summers are very warm and humid, but the spring and fall, although generally short, are delightful.

Fort Myer is situated along a high bluff just west of the city of Washington, D.C., directly across the Potomac River and contiguous to the western boundary of Arlington National Cemetery in Arlington County, Virginia. The area is well known for its tourist attractions, not only within the city of Washington itself (the post is within walking distance of the Lincoln Memorial and the Pentagon) but also elsewhere in the surrounding area. Many Civil War battlefields are a short drive from the post. Mount Vernon is a few miles down the Potomac, and the great natural beauty of Virginia and Maryland abounds everywhere.

For more information, write to Public Affairs Office, Headquarters, U.S. Army Garrison, 204 Lee Avenue, Fort Myer, VA 22211-5050, or call (703) 696-6700. Home page: *www.fmmc.army.mil.*

FORT STORY

Located at historic Cape Henry, three miles north of Virginia Beach, Fort Story looks out onto the Atlantic Ocean to the east, the Chesapeake Bay to the north, and Seashore State Park to the west.

History. Fort Story was established in 1914 and is named after Maj. Gen. John Patton Story, a noted artilleryman. The first troops to occupy the area, two Coast Artillery Corps companies, moved in in February 1917.

Known today as "Home of the Amphibians," Fort Story's 343 acres provide space, facilities, and administrative and logistical services for the Army's amphibian operations, logistical-over-the-shore (LOTS) operations, and amphibious test and evaluation activities. The major Army units at Fort Story are the 11th Transportation Battalion (Terminal) and the 7th Transportation Group. Both officer and enlisted personnel are trained in all aspects of transportation, aviation maintenance, logistics, and deployment doctrine and research. Altogether, 1,200 active-duty personnel, 800 reservists, 160 civilian employees, and 400 dependents call Fort Story home.

Housing and Services. There are 164 units of family housing at Fort Story and guest accommodations for 23 visiting officers and enlisted personnel. The post has a small commissary and exchange. There is also a day-care facility for 60 children. There is a medical and dental clinic on post, and definitive medical care is available from local hospitals or Portsmouth Naval Hospital.

Recreation. Of course, there is swimming on the beaches along the Atlantic coast in season, but Fort Story also offers a full range of both indoor and outdoor sports and recreation, including a library, a movie theater, an auto craft shop, a gymnasium, a bowling alley, and an intramural sports program.

The Local Area. Fort Story is located in one of the most historical regions of the United States. The Cape Henry Memorial Cross on the tip of Cape Henry marks the spot where the Jamestown settlers started Virginia's first real estate boom when they landed there on 26 April 1607. The Battle of the Virginia Capes Monument commemorates the victory of French admiral Francoise de Grasse over the British fleet sent to relieve Cornwallis's army at Yorktown on 5 September 1781. The first lighthouse authorized by the federal government is also situated at Fort Story: It first cast its beams out to sea in 1792 and remained in operation until 1881.

For more information, write to HQ, Fort Story, Attention: Public Affairs Office, Fort Story, VA 23459-5000, or call (757) 422-7305. Home page: *www.eustis.army.mil/fort_story.*

Marine Corps

QUANTICO COMBAT DEVELOPMENT COMMAND

Quantico has often been called the "Crossroads of the Corps": It is at Quantico that Marine officers undergo their initial training, and they keep returning there to attend other schools, all the way up to the Command and Staff College.

History. First established in 1917, Quantico takes its name from an Indian word meaning "by the large stream." The "stream" is the Potomac River, which borders the eastern fringes of the reservation. From its beginnings as a training camp in World War I, Quantico is still in the military education business, more so than ever before. Today it is the headquarters for the Marine Corps Combat Development Command, which operates the Officer Candidate School, the basic school for officers, the Amphibious Warfare School, and the Command and Staff College, as well as schools in communications, computer sciences, and management and a course for staff NCOs. Quantico is home to 6,500 active-duty personnel, 3,300 family members, and 2,200 civilian employees. At any given time, there may be upwards of 1,200 students attending courses at Quantico.

Housing and Schools. There are more than 1,500 units of family quarters at the base. Waiting times vary, according to rank. Temporary accommodations are offered in the 34-room hostess house, located near the Potomac River. Sixty trailer sites are also available to enlisted personnel who own mobile homes.

Dependent children attend schools on base, but area schools in Stafford and Prince William Counties are highly rated. A day-care center is also located on the base. Several colleges and universities, including the University of Southern California, Averett College, Park College, and Northern Virginia Community College, provide on-base courses for interested adults.

Personal Services. Medical care is provided by the Naval Medical Clinic, which sees as many as 13,000 patients a month. Serious cases or cases requiring specialized treatment are referred to DeWitt Army Hospital, about thirty miles north of the base, at Fort Belvoir. Dental service for dependents is not available at Quantico.

A commissary store and a main exchange with several branches are available on the base, as are a check-cashing facility, a service station, a newsstand, and a cafeteria/snack bar.

Recreation. Recreational facilities are excellent at Quantico and include a sixteen-lane bowling center, a gymnasium, a movie theater, a swimming pool, tennis courts, an 18-hole golf course, a riding stable, and a rifle and pistol club. In addition, there are varsity and intramural sports.

Excellent outdoor recreational facilities are located on the base at the Lunga Reservoir Recreational Area. Reservations are required two weeks in advance to use the campers, which are available from April to October. The site offers 36 camper spaces (with water and electricity), 80 tent sites, picnic facilities, a playground, a golf course, stables, swimming pools, and boat docks. Motorboats, sailboats, canoes, rowboats, paddleboats, and horses and stables can be rented. The Quantico Marina at the end of Potomac Avenue offers overnight berthing and slip rentals for boats up to forty feet in length.

Hunting and fishing are also allowed on base in an 800-acre tract that has five miles of trout streams. Deer, squirrel, rabbit, quail, and dove can be hunted there. Trout, bass, catfish, bluegill, and pickerel can be caught in the streams.

The Local Area. Quantico is situated about 35 miles south of Washington, D.C., along Interstate 95. Because Quantico lies so near the nation's capital, there are many attractions in the area, most of them discussed elsewhere in this book. The immediate area around Quantico is one of small towns and much forestland. Prince William Forest, with hiking and picnic areas, lies only about a mile from the main gate, through the little town of Triangle. The town of Quantico itself lies surrounded on three sides by the base; on the fourth side is the Potomac River. The town of Quantico is a rail stop for the Virginia Rail Express and Amtrak. Fredericksburg is twenty-three miles south of the base.

For further information, write to Public Affairs Office, CO58, 3098 Range Road, Quantico, VA 22134-5126, or call (703) 784-2121. Home page: *www.quantico.usmc.mil.*

Navy

DAHLGREN DIVISION, NAVAL SURFACE WARFARE CENTER

Located 55 miles south of Washington, D.C., on the Potomac River and 28 miles west of historic Fredericksburg, Virginia, the Dahlgren Laboratory is divided into two separate areas: Mainside, which consists of 2,678 acres adjacent to the town of Dahlgren; and Pumpkin Neck, an isolated weapons-testing area occupying 1,641 acres between Machodoc Creek on the north and west and the Potomac on the east.

History. Naval ordnance testing got its start at Dahlgren in April 1918, when Congress voted to buy land in Virginia's Northern Neck area to establish a proving ground. The first piece of ordnance fired there, a seven-inch, 45-caliber tractor-mounted cannon, was set off on 16 October 1918. Dahlgren's mission today is to provide research, development, test and evaluation, engineering, and fleet support for surface warfare systems, surface ship combat systems, ordnance, mines, amphibious warfare systems, mine countermeasures, special warfare systems, and strategic systems. To accomplish this mission, Dahlgren maintains an extensive range of facilities, including a 25-mile-long by five-mile-wide downriver test range. Dahlgren is home to almost 900 military personnel, their 1,200 family members, and a civilian workforce of 3,000 personnel.

Housing and Schools. Dahlgren provides 250 units of family housing, plus billeting for 35 bachelor officers and 260 unaccompanied enlisted personnel. Dependent children in kindergarten through eighth grade may attend schools on base. A day-care facility at Dahlgren can accommodate up to 80 children.

Personal Services. Dahlgren has a small commissary and Navy exchange. Medical care is provided by branch medical and dental clinics. Long-term and definitive health care are available locally in Fredericksburg or at the National Naval Medical Center in Bethesda.

Recreation. Dahlgren offers a full range of recreational facilities, including an all-hands club, a gym, a marina, outdoor intramural sports, and arts and crafts shops. But one of the largest recreational attractions at Dahlgren is the outdoors itself. The center is about 50 percent wooded and offers 2,300 acres for hunting, 84 acres of lakes and ponds for fishing, and 8 miles of stream and shoreline for fishing.

For more information, write to Public Affairs Office, NSWCDD, Dahlgren, VA 22448-5100, or call (540) 653-8531.

Home page: *www.nswc.navy.mil.*

DAM NECK FLEET COMBAT TRAINING CENTER

Established in December 1941 as a live-fire range for the Anti-Aircraft Training and Test Center, the Atlantic Fleet Combat Training Center's 1,100-acre site along the Atlantic coast in Virginia Beach, just south of Oceana Naval Air Station, is home today to the Naval Surface Warfare Center, Tactical Training Group Atlantic, Navy and Marine Corps Intelligence Training Center, and other commands. The center's complement consists of 2,400 active-duty personnel and their families and about 600 civilian employees.

Housing, Schools, and Personal Services. Dam Neck operates 19 sets of family quarters, 3,200 bachelor enlisted units, and 230 bachelor officer quarters. There are also about 2,500 rooms for visitors and transient personnel.

Children attend local schools, but a day-care center at Dam Neck can accommodate over 100 children. A Navy campus at the base attends to the educational needs of adults.

Medical and dental services at Dam Neck are provided by small branch clinics, with definitive or referral care available at nearby Oceana or local hospitals. There is no commissary at Dam Neck, but there is a small exchange that operates a service station, a shopette, a barber shop, a dry cleaner, and a coin laundry. Personnel at Dam Neck can take advantage of the full range of services available at nearby Oceana Naval Air Station.

Recreation. Dam Neck offers a bowling alley, a gym, a recreation center, a fitness center, and an auto shop for indoor recreation. A pool, tennis and racquetball courts, and softball and football fields are available. Fishing and hunting are permitted in the wide variety of highlands, forest, wetlands, coastal beaches, and sand dunes that constitute Dam Neck.

For more information, write to Public Affairs Office, Fleet Combat Training Center, Atlantic, Attention: Code O1P/Building 27, 1912 Regulus Avenue, Virginia Beach, VA 23461-2098, or call (757) 492-6234. Home page: *www.damneck.navy.mil.*

NORFOLK NAVAL BASE

History. Make no mistake about it, Norfolk is a Navy town. Commissioned in July 1917, Norfolk Naval Base is the largest naval installation in the world. Norfolk is home to 81,000 active-duty naval personnel assigned to shore-based and fleet units. Add to this a total of 29,000 civilian employees and 112,000 family members, and you have a Navy community larger than most cities.

Norfolk is also host to the 6,000 military personnel who operate Little Creek Naval Amphibious Base, home to Amphibious Group 2 and other commands.

Housing and Schools. There are more than 4,400 government family quarters in the Norfolk area. There is a 200-unit Navy Lodge onboard the base, and another 90 units are available at the Little Creek Naval Amphibious Base. Over 4,000 rooms are available at Norfolk for unaccompanied married personnel.

Public schooling is provided for dependent children, and adult education programs proliferate throughout the area. The Navy campus at the naval station coordinates an active program of college-level courses designed to enable active-duty personnel to take advantage of instruction offered by sixteen academic institutions.

Personal Services. Navy exchanges and commissaries are provided in several places in the Norfolk area: at the base, at the naval air station, at the Portsmouth Naval Shipyard, and at the Yorktown Naval Weapons Station. Exchange stores are available at Fort Eustis, Fort Monroe, and Langley Air Force Base. The Naval Regional Medical Center in Portsmouth, with a military complement of more than 3,900 personnel supported by a staff of 900 civilian employees, operates a total of seventeen medical facilities in the area. The hospital itself is a 500-bed facility.

Recreation. Three Navy recreational areas are available to personnel stationed at Norfolk: Driver Point at the Naval Radio Transmitter Facility; Stewart Memorial Campgrounds at the Naval Security Group Activity, Northwest, Chesapeake; and Naval Weapons Station Camp at Yorktown Naval Weapons Station. These areas provide camper spaces and outdoor activities and are generally open during the spring, summer, and fall.

At the naval base itself are six swimming pools; three gymnasiums; two movie theaters, one of which is a ten-theater complex; two golf courses; three picnic areas; hobby and craft shops; and three bowling alleys.

The Local Area. The Norfolk–Virginia Beach–Williamsburg–Richmond area is one of the richest in historic points of interest and recreation attractions in the country. The North Carolina coast, Washington, D.C., and the Pennsylvania Dutch country are all within fairly easy driving distance of the Norfolk area. Closer are Colonial Williamsburg, Yorktown, and Revolutionary War and Civil War battlefields. Fishing, boating, swimming, hunting, and outdoor sports are available in this area year-round. Stables, skeet and trap ranges, swimming pools, picnic areas, and beaches abound. Many of these activities are available at the military installations in the area.

For more information, write to Public Affairs Office, 1530 Gilbert Street, Suite 200, Naval Base, Norfolk, VA 23511-2797, or call (757) 564-0000. Home page: *www.naval-station.norfolk.va.us.*

NORFOLK NAVAL SHIPYARD

The Norfolk Naval Shipyard (NNSY) in Portsmouth, Virginia, is one of the largest shipyards in the world, specializing in repairing, overhauling, and modernizing warships. NNSY annually does about $650 million in work on U.S. Atlantic Fleet's aircraft carriers, guided missile cruisers, and submarines.

History. Founded in 1767, NNSY is the Navy's oldest shipyard. It was here that the Confederate ironclad *CSS Virginia* was built from the frigate *USS Merrimack* during the Civil War. The Navy's first aircraft carrier, *USS Langley,* was built at NNSY.

Today NNSY is a 1,200-acre complex with four miles of waterfront, thirty miles of paved streets, and about nineteen miles of railroad track. It has a complement of 100 active-duty personnel, as well as some 5,000 shipboard personnel in port on vessels undergoing repair and a civilian workforce of about 7,000. It has its own police and fire departments, generates electricity and steam by burning trash, and operates about 400 cranes. NNSY employs about 7,000 civilian personnel.

Housing, Schools, and Personal Services. NNSY operates 125 enlisted family housing units, 80 units for unaccompanied officers, and 1,300 units for enlisted personnel. Children attend schools in Portsmouth, but NNSY operates a day-care center that can accommodate fifty-seven children. College courses are available from a number of local institutions, including Tidewater Community College, Norfolk State University, Old Dominion University, and Regent University. Medical care is provided by a branch clinic, with referral and inpatient care available at Portsmouth Naval Hospital. There is a small Navy exchange at NNSY, as well as a medium-size commissary store. The facilities at the Norfolk Naval Base, Oceana Naval Air Station, and Little Creek Naval Amphibious Base are also available to personnel stationed at NNSY.

Recreation. A bowling alley, a gym, a recreation center, a swimming pool, a softball field, and tennis, handball, racquetball, and basketball courts are available onboard the installation.

For more information, write to Public Affairs Office, Code 1160, Norfolk Naval Shipyard, Portsmouth, VA 23709-5000, or call (757) 396-3000.

NORTHWEST NAVAL SECURITY GROUP ACTIVITY

Located on top of the North Carolina border with Virginia and a few miles east of Virginia's Great Dismal Swamp National Wildlife Refuge, the Northwest Naval Security Group Activity (NSGA), Chesapeake, occupies 3,700 acres of wooded farm- and swamplands in one of the most historic regions of Virginia.

NSGA operates facilities and systems necessary to provide cryptologic communications support for the Department of the Navy and the Defense Communications System. Additional missions include direction-finding assistance to navigational aid and air-sea rescue missions. Due to the nature of the highly classified and sensitive work that goes on at NSGA, security is very high. The NSGA has a complement of 650 military personnel, 750 family members, and about 230 civilian employees, as well as tenant command personnel. NSGA is host to the Naval Satellite Communications Facility, U.S. Coast Guard Communications Area Master Station Atlantic, Marine Corps Security Force Training Company, and several other activities.

Housing and Schools. NSGA maintains 125 units of family housing, as well as quarters for about 140 bachelor enlisted personnel. Average rental property in the Chesapeake area is from $650 to $750 a month. Members can also live in Virginia Beach, Norfolk, Portsmouth, or Elizabeth City, North Carolina. Transient accommodations are also available. Dependent schooling is available in the local area, as are courses offered by Chesapeake Campus of Tidewater Community College. There is a Navy Family Services Center, home-provided child care, and an award-winning child-development center on base.

Personal Services. Active-duty medical and dental care is available at NSGA Northwest. It is provided by staff of Portsmouth Naval Hospital. Although there is no commissary at NSGA, the installation has a small Navy exchange that supports a total of 1,800 Navy, Marine, and Coast Guard personnel. There is no specific mess set aside for the enlisted or petty officers on this base. Those services NSGA does not offer, nearby Norfolk Naval Station does provide.

Recreation. The base has excellent recreation facilities for hunting, fishing, boating, and camping enthusiasts, as well as an outdoor swimming pool, ball fields, tennis and racquetball courts, a bowling alley, and a fitness center and gym, complete with a weight room. There are also auto and woodworking hobby shops.

Virginia Beach, Seashore State Park, and Back Bay National Wildlife Refuge, on the Atlantic coast, are only minutes away from NSGA, as are Portsmouth and Norfolk. Newport News, historic Jamestown, and the restored colonial village of Williamsburg are only a bit farther away.

For more information, write to Commanding Officer, Naval Security Group Activity, Attention: Public Affairs, 1320 Northwest Boulevard, Suite 100, Chesapeake, VA 23322-4094, or call (757) 421-8000. Home page: *www.nsganw.navy.mil.*

OCEANA NAVAL AIR STATION

Oceana Naval Air Station is a complex of over seven miles of runways with the latest equipment to serve military air traffic on the East Coast, supporting nine squadrons of F-14 Tomcat and A-6 Intruder aircraft. This is one of the busiest air stations in the Navy—an aircraft takes off or lands at Oceana approximately every two minutes.

History. What started as 328 acres of swampland 50 years ago has grown to over 5,000 acres today and is home to over 8,600 active-duty personnel, 14,000 family members, and 1,770 civilian employees. There are 15,000 registered automobiles at Oceana, and the station's annual payroll amounts to $286 million.

Housing and Schools. Oceana has 635 units of family housing and 3,500 units for unaccompanied personnel. There are also about 250 units available for visitors.

Excellent off-base schooling is available for dependent children, and the station's Navy campus operates an active series of off-duty educational programs that include courses offered by Tidewater Junior College and Golden Gate, George Washington, Old Dominion, Troy State, Embry-Riddle Aeronautical, Saint Leo State, and Norfolk State Universities.

Personal Services and Recreation. The station also has a complete array of support services, including a Navy exchange mall with specialty shops, a food court, and an adjoining commissary store and gas station, all located off base. A complete officers, CPO, and enlisted club system is located on the station. The station boasts an excellent recreational program that includes both indoor and outdoor activities, such as an 18-hole golf course, riding stables, a bowling alley, swimming pools, tennis courts, and three large picnic areas. Also available are seven skeet and four trap ranges, a clubhouse, and a retail sporting goods facility.

The Local Area. Oceana is located within the city limits of the world's largest resort city, Virginia Beach. The leading summer attraction is the six miles of sandy beach lined by a boardwalk. With hot summers and cold but usually snowless winters, Oceana offers some kind of activity year-round. The Norfolk–Hampton–Newport News area is just to the north, with its vast complex of naval and military installations, and Washington, D.C., is within an easy day's drive.

The history buff will find Oceana a pure delight. Nearby Fort Story is where the first permanent settlers from England landed in 1607; almost every spot in the state is near some kind of historic landmark, a Revolutionary or Civil War battlefield, or some place famous in the colonial history of this country.

For more information, write to Public Affairs Officer, Naval Air Station, Oceana, Virginia Beach, VA 23460-5120, or call (757) 433-2366. Home page: *www.oceana-navy.mil.*

YORKTOWN NAVAL WEAPONS STATION

History. The oldest structure onboard the Yorktown Naval Weapons Station is the Lee House, built around 1649, where many generations of the family lived out their lives before the property was acquired by the U.S. government. Long before the world ever conceived of such things as the testing and evaluation that now go on at the weapons station, the infantry of the American Revolution and the Civil War slogged along the Old Williamsburg Road, where today it runs through the station.

The site of the weapons station was acquired by the Navy in August 1918 and was at the time the largest naval reservation in the world, with a land area covering about twenty square miles. Over the years, the growth and expansion of the Navy's technical requirements and responsibilities have been reflected by corresponding developments at the station to support the Atlantic Fleet. Based at the station are the Naval Mine Warfare Engineering Activity, the Naval Ophthalmic Support and Training Activity, and the Marine Corps Security Force Company. Today the station is home to about 1,000 civilians, 1,000 military personnel, and 3,200 family members.

Housing and Schools. There are 450 sets of family quarters on the station, plus sites and facilities for 40 mobile homes. Guest accommodations are very limited. The station is not an open facility, and visitors must obtain proper identification and passes.

There are no dependent schools at the station, but a child-care facility is available there; older children attend the public-school system in nearby Newport News and York County.

Personal Services and Recreation. Medical care is provided by a branch medical clinic. Definitive medical care is available at Fort Eustis. A commissary and Navy exchange, a convenience store, a credit union, and an enlisted and officers club system are provided at the station.

The Japanese Gardens camping and picnic area offers space for ten campers, as well as showers, toilet facilities, and a laundry with washers and dryers. The Wright Circle Picnic Area, also on the station, provides charcoal grills, sheltered tables, and excellent recreational facilities. Fishing is permitted in various freshwater ponds at the station and off the station's fishing pier. Other recreational activities include a ten-hole golf course, a six-lane bowling alley, a gymnasium, handball/racquetball courts, a hobby shop, two swimming pools, two tennis courts, and a theater. Tours to the Yorktown Battlefield and Colonial Williamsburg and Jamestown are available at discounts through the special services office at the station.

The Local Area. The station is situated along the west bank of the York River, just above Yorktown and off Interstate 64. Yorktown, Williamsburg, Fort Eustis, and Newport News are all within twenty miles of the station. The great naval complex of Norfolk is just to the south, accessible via Interstate 64, and Richmond is somewhat farther to the north, also accessible on the interstate. Washington, D.C., is only a several hours' drive to the north on Interstate 95, and a weekend outing from the station could easily take in points as far north as Gettysburg, Pennsylvania.

For more information, write to Public Affairs Office, P.O. Drawer 160, NWS, Yorktown, VA 23691-0160, or call (757) 887-4141. Home page: *www.nwsy.navy.mil.*

Coast Guard

U.S. COAST GUARD TRAINING CENTER YORKTOWN

Nestled between the historic triangle of American history (Jamestown, Yorktown, and Williamsburg), this Coast Guard training center is one of the best the service has to offer. The training center stands off a small, scenic peninsula formed by Wormley Creek and the York River. Every year, thousands of personnel from other armed services, state and federal agencies, and allied nations converge at this important training site for both basic and advanced courses.

Housing and Schools. The Hampton Roads area is comprised of the towns of Norfolk, Portsmouth, Virginia Beach, Chesapeake, and Suffolk, with Hampton and Newport News on the Peninsula. Generally, these are the communities that most Coast Guard personnel prefer to reside in. The availability of rental property in the Hampton Roads area is plentiful and can be easily found within a one-hour commute. Rental rates are moderate to high. The rent for a one-bedroom apartment ranges from $500 to $600 per month. Most apartments are spacious and have full amenities. Homes available for purchase are plentiful. New construction is available. Prices are reasonable to high, ranging from $60,000 to $200,000, depending on location and number of bedrooms. Four-bedroom homes are available but limited. Five-bedroom homes are scarce. Government-leased housing is available for eligible Coast Guard personnel. The center housing office accepts applications for military housing and maintains a list of referrals for civilian housing. The Navy Housing Welcome Center can be contacted toll free at (800) 628-7510 for more details.

Personal Services and Recreation. Definitive medical care is "Tri-Service Coordinated" between the military hospital commanders of the McDonald Army Community Hospital at Fort Eustis, Portsmouth Naval Hospital, and the 1st Medical Group Hospital at Langley Air Force Base with referrals to local civilian facilities. Contact the Portsmouth Tricare Service Center for more detailed information at (757) 677-6000. Recreation facilities include the Holly Oaks Golf course, City Limits Recreation, a gym, and both wood and hobby shops. Summer heat can be cooled via water activities of all descriptions at Huntington and Newport News Park and Buckroe Beach in Hampton. Those interested in fishing can pack poles, bait, and snacks and head for piers or the surf or put out their boats on a host of lakes, rivers, the Chesapeake Bay, or, of course, the Atlantic Ocean. Busch Gardens theme park is in the area and features thrilling rides, entertainment, shopping, and restaurants in nine authentic European hamlets. Historic Williamsburg is only three miles away from the park.

The Local Area. "The Peninsula" is a name that fits many geographical areas. In Virginia, the name describes a close-knit group of cities and counties which share a rich heritage, going back to colonial times, and an equally rich vision for the 21st century. The peninsula area consists of the cities of Hampton, Newport News, Poquoson, and Williamsburg, along with the counties of Gloucester, James City, and York.

For more information, write to Yorktown Coast Guard Reserve Training Center, Commander, USCG Reserve Training Center, Attention: Public Affairs, Yorktown, VA 23690-5000, or call (757) 898-2222. Home page: *www.uscg.mil/hq/rtc.*

WASHINGTON

Air Force

FAIRCHILD AIR FORCE BASE

If installations can be considered offspring, Fairchild is indeed among the fairest of the Air Force's children. It is also the darling of the Spokane business community, infusing the area with jobs and the concomitant income that improves the quality of life for all.

History. The base was opened as Spokane Army Air Depot in March 1942. In 1950, it was renamed Fairchild Air Force Base after Gen. Muir S. Fairchild, a native of Bellingham, Washington, and vice chief of staff for air. Today it is home for the 92nd Air Refueling Wing, the 366th Training Group, and other units. Fairchild Air Force Base occupies over 6,000 acres approximately twelve miles west of Spokane on Highway 2. As is the case with many other sites where military bases are located, the people of Spokane donated the land for Fairchild to the U.S. government. The government accepted, partly because the weather in Spokane is better suited for air operations than in other parts of the state and partly because the base is located 300 miles from the ocean, with a mountain range intervening. This latter point was very important then because we were at war with Japan.

Fairchild is home to 3,400 active-duty personnel, their 3,400 dependents, and a civilian workforce of 1,100.

Housing and Schools. Fairchild offers nearly 1,300 government housing units, some of them located off the base up to 16 miles away. Guest housing is available, but reservations are accepted only for personnel on official business; all others are accepted on a first-come, first-served basis only.

Dependent children of military personnel stationed at Fairchild attend local public or private schools. The base education office operates programs for adults that range from pre–high school through graduate level. Participating institutions include Eastern Washington University, Gonzaga University, Spokane Falls Community College, Washington Community College District No. 17, and Washington State College District No. 17.

Personal Services. Personal services include the 25-bed USAF hospital, a child-development center, a commissary that carries 2,000 line items in stock, and a base exchange that offers a number of concessions.

Recreation. Recreational facilities include an indoor miniature golf course, a gymnasium, a 25-meter indoor swimming pool, an auto hobby shop, a bowling center, arts and crafts and wood hobby shops, and a well-equipped recreation center. Also available is the thirty-five-acre Clear Lake Resort Area, about 12 miles south of the base, which has a beach with swimming, boat docks, cabins, trailer and camper sites, and other facilities.

The Local Area. The climate in eastern Washington has four distinct seasons. The Spokane area is generally dry and mild in the summer and cold and humid in the winter. About 70 percent of the total precipitation falls between the first of October and the end of March, and about half of what falls as snow. Subzero temperatures and traffic-stopping snowfalls are infrequent; however, there is an average snowfall of 46 inches a year.

Spokane is a modern, progressive community that is a trade and service center for more than one million people over an 80,000-square-mile area. It was selected as the site for the 1974 World's Fair, and many of the structures built for the occasion are still major attractions. A unique and fascinating aspect of the city is the Skywalk Network, which connects a ten-block area by an intricate system of elevated walkways and malls, all indoors, and offers a large number of shops and restaurants for shoppers and strollers.

This part of Washington is often referred to as "the Inland Empire," and the people living there take outdoor life seriously. There are ten national parks, fifteen national forests, and more than 100 public and private campgrounds in this area. Hunting and fishing, snow skiing, hiking—almost every sport except surfing—are available here.

For more information, write to Public Affairs Office, 1 E. Bong Street, Suite 103, Fairchild AFB, WA 99011-9664, or call (509) 247-1212. Home page: *www.fairchild.af.mil.*

MCCHORD AIR FORCE BASE

Majestic, snow-covered Mount Rainier's 14,410-foot peak dominates the southeastern skyline at McChord AFB, as Puget Sound dominates the land to the west of the base. In Washington, appropriately named the "Evergreen State," nature dominates everything.

History. Named in honor of Col. William C. McChord, who died in an aircraft crash near Richmond, Virginia, in 1937, McChord Air Force Base was established in July 1940 as a bomber base. Today it is home for the men and women of the 62nd Military Airlift Wing, the 446th Military Airlift Wing (Reserve), and various tenant support units. McChord is home to more than 7,200 military personnel, their 4,500 family members, and 1,200 civilian employees.

Housing and Schools. There are over 970 sets of family quarters at McChord. Temporary lodging is available for families permanently changing station, but on a space-available basis only. The Evergreen Inn offers 360 rooms for visiting officers and airmen. Off-base rentals average from $400 a month for a one-bedroom apartment to as much as $900 a month for a four-bedroom house.

Excellent educational opportunities are available for children and adults at McChord. For children, the Sunshine Preschool and two elementary schools are located on base, and junior and senior high schools are nearby. The base education center offers 950 undergraduate college courses and 70 graduate courses each year. These are given in cooperation with Saint Martin's College, Southern Illinois University, Chapman College, and Pierce College.

Personal Services. Personal services include the McChord medical and dental clinics and Madigan Army Medical Center, three miles south of McChord. McChord also offers an excellent commissary and base exchange.

Recreation. Recreational activities include a variety of clubs, such as aero and officers and NCO wives clubs, as well as a consolidated arts and crafts center; an auto hobby shop; a 20-lane bowling center; an 18-hole, par-72 golf course; a recreation center; a base gymnasium; and swimming pools. Holiday Park is an on-base recreation area that offers eighteen trailer sites, picnic areas, playground facilities, a softball diamond, and horseshoe pits. In addition, there are a lake, a stream, and a pond on base where fishing is permitted.

The Local Area. McChord Air Force Base is sandwiched between the southern outskirts of the city of Tacoma and the vast expanse of Fort Lewis. Tacoma is Washington's third-largest city, with a population of over 156,000. The Tacoma area has one of the nicest climates to be found anywhere in the Northwest. Summer temperatures seldom exceed the 80s, and daytime winter temperatures average in the 40s. Snow usually melts before it can accumulate.

The state of Washington offers much in the way of recreation, with 250 miles of Pacific Ocean coastline and over 2,500 miles of saltwater shoreline on Puget Sound and the adjacent waterways. Because of the proximity of so much water, fishing and water sports are popular year-round. Golf is played year-round on Washington courses, and the mountains offer twenty ski areas.

For more information, write to 62nd Airlift Wing Public Affairs Office, 100 Main Street, McChord AFB, WA 98438-1109, or call (253) 984-1910. Home page: *www.mcchord.af.mil.*

Army

FORT LEWIS

On a clear day, you can see Mount Rainier looming on the horizon to the east of Fort Lewis, towering at over 14,000 feet high above the other noble peaks of the Cascade Range. From the forest-clad mountains to the inland sea waters of

Puget Sound, this is a region of great natural beauty, and Fort Lewis is at the heart of it all.

History. Named after Capt. Meriwether Lewis, leader of the historic Lewis and Clark Expedition of 1803, Camp Lewis was founded in 1917. In 1927, it was designated as a permanent Army post, and its name was changed to Fort Lewis. Together with Yakima Training Center, east of the Cascades, Fort Lewis's 260,000 acres of training, maneuver, and firing areas make it one of the largest military posts in the United States. Today it is home to the I Corps, 1st Special Forces Group, Madigan Medical Center, 3rd Brigade, 2nd Infantry Division, and 1st Brigade, 25th Infantry Division.

Fort Lewis is home to more than 20,000 soldiers, their 24,000 dependents, and a civilian workforce of 4,500.

Housing and Schools. There are over 3,800 sets of family quarters at Fort Lewis, more than 2,700 for enlisted personnel alone. Guest accommodations are available for personnel of all ranks, but only those on permanent change-of-station orders may make reservations; all others are accepted on a space-available basis. These facilities include the Fort Lewis Lodge, with 149 guest rooms; the Clark House (for enlisted families), with 5 suites and 3 single rooms; and 6 cabins for officer families.

On-post education facilities include elementary and high schools. An education center offers counseling, testing, registration, and instruction for military personnel, from remedial training and high school through advanced college degrees.

Personal Services. Madigan Army Medical Center at Fort Lewis offers a complete array of inpatient, outpatient, and specialty care for an active-duty and retired military population of more than 85,000 personnel and their dependents. Post exchange and commissary facilities at Fort Lewis are excellent, and many concessionaires offer a full range of goods and services on the post.

Recreation. Recreation centers offer activities that include parties, stage shows, dances, and tournaments, and the sports branch of the morale, welfare, and recreation office conducts a complete athletic program for both men and women. The Fort Lewis flying, hunting and fishing, and parachute clubs offer exciting outdoor activities for all. The Fort Lewis Travel Camp, located on the installation at the southern end of Puget Sound, and boating from the beach at American Lake offer further opportunities for outdoor fun and adventure.

The Local Area. Nearby communities include Tacoma, just to the north of the post, a city of about 157,000, and Seattle, forty-five miles northwest, the largest city in the Pacific Northwest, with a population of over 500,000. Seattle offers a wide variety of attractions, from Seattle Center on the World's Fair grounds to the Woodland Park Zoological Gardens. The Tacoma area abounds with scenic and natural points of interest, including Wright's Park Botanical Observatory and Point Defiance Park, 640 acres of woodland roads and trails, and a restored outpost of the Hudson Bay Company.

Farther afield are attractions such as Mount Rainier National Park and Lake Chelan, a 50-mile-long body of water that flows into the Columbia River and has been compared to the fjords of Norway.

For more information, write to Army Community Services Office, Headquarters, I Corps and Fort Lewis, Attention: AFZH-PO, Fort Lewis, WA 94833-5000, or call (253) 967-4646. Home page: *www.lewis.army.mil.*

Navy

BANGOR NAVAL SUBMARINE BASE

Occupying 7,000 acres on the east bank of the Hood Canal, just southwest of the town of Poulsbo and thirteen miles north of Bremerton, Bangor Naval Submarine Base is the home port for a squadron of Trident submarines, part of the nation's nuclear deterrent Triad, which also includes land- and air-based systems.

The Trident program can be broken down into three components: the submarine, the missile, and the base. The submarine is the 560-foot Ohio-class sub, which has 24 missile tubes and four torpedo tubes, displaces 18,700 tons of water, and costs approximately $1.2 billion. The missile is the thirty-four-foot Trident I, or C-4, which weighs 71,000 pounds, has a range of 4,000 nautical miles (1,500 miles greater than the Polaris), and costs about $17 million.

History. The base began its history in 1942, when it was purchased for use as an ammunition depot. In 1973, it was selected as home port for the Trident subs. In 1977, Bangor Naval Submarine Base was commissioned. In 1981, Commander, Submarine Group 9, and Commander, Submarine Squadron 17, were activated, and in 1982, the first Trident sub, *USS Ohio* (SSBN 726), arrived at the base. The base is 155 nautical miles from the Pacific Ocean, with access through the Strait of Juan de Fuca. Approximately 4,500 active-duty personnel, their 8,000 family members, and 1,500 civilian employees are stationed at Bangor.

Housing and Schools. Over 1,300 units of modern family housing are available on base, in the southeast and southwest sectors near the main gate. A Navy Lodge opened in the spring of 1992.

Although there is no dependent schooling on the base, a child-care center is available. The Navy campus offers programs ranging from high school completion to master's degree courses from such institutions as Olympic and Chapman Colleges, Central Washington and Southern Illinois Universities, and the Universities of Southern California and Puget Sound.

Personal Services. Medical care is provided at the Bremerton Naval Regional Medical Center, eight miles south of the base. The hospital has 170 beds and offers a full range of services. A large Navy exchange and commissary and a variety of other support facilities are available on base.

Submarine from the U.S. Navy Submarine Base, Bangor, Washington
U.S. NAVY PHOTO

Recreation. Recreational facilities include a recreation complex with a gymnasium, saunas, exercise rooms, a swimming pool, indoor handball and squash courts, a bowling alley, hobby and craft shops, tennis courts, a theater, three on-base lakes for fishing, an archery range, and a boat ramp and boat rentals.

The Local Area. Outdoor recreational activities are also important factors in the lives of Navy personnel, as they are for Washingtonians in general: Hunting, trapping, fishing, camping, boating, and snow and water skiing are all available within the Puget Sound region. Just to the west of the base, across Hood Canal, is the Olympic National Forest, open all year. Many of the mountain peaks there exceed 7,000 feet, and visitors may enjoy the pristine beauty of the forests that climb their majestic slopes.

A relatively short distance to the east of the base, across Puget Sound, is Seattle, a major deepwater port and cultural, industrial, and agricultural center of the Northwest. Somewhat farther north, but still easily accessible, are the vast expanses of the Canadian Northwest.

For more information, write to Family Services Center, Naval Submarine Base, Bangor, Bremerton, WA 98315-5000, or call (360) 396-4840. Home page: *www.bangor.navy.mil.*

BREMERTON NAVAL HOSPITAL

Situated on the western side of Puget Sound in a wooded site overlooking Ostrich Bay, Bremerton Naval Hospital is the principal naval health-care facility in the Pacific Northwest. It sits just off State Route 3, a mile from Bremerton, Washington, between the old Puget Sound Naval Shipyard five miles to the south and Bangor Naval Submarine Base ten miles to the north. The hospital provides 60 beds and definitive medical services to more than 60,000 military personnel and their families residing within its area of responsibility.

The hospital has an active-duty complement of over 700 personnel, supported by a professional staff of 460 civilians.

Housing, Schools, and Personal Services. Although there is a small Navy exchange at the hospital itself, all other services are provided by the nearby submarine base or local community. Family housing facilities are available at the nearby Bangor Naval Submarine Base or in the local community. Schools are supported through the submarine base and its resources.

The main hospital building, a 60-bed, seven-story structure, sits on a 49-acre campus. In August 1999, construction began on a three-story, $24 million, 55,000-square-foot wing complete with a 250-car parking garage. The wing is scheduled to be ready in September 2002 and will replace the portable trailers that were set up in 1995 to handle an increasing population.

The hospital operates branch clinics throughout the Pacific Northwest at the Puget Sound Naval Shipyard; Bangor Naval Submarine Base; Everett Naval Station, the Naval Undersea Warfare Center, Keyport, Washington; and Port Hadlock. In July 1999, construction began on a 23,000-square-foot, $6 million branch clinic at Everett Naval Station.

For more information, write to Public Affairs, Naval Hospital Bremerton, HP01 Boone Road, Bremerton, WA 98312-1898, or call (800) 422-1383. Home page: *www.nh_bremerton.med.navy.mil.*

EVERETT NAVAL STATION

Groundbreaking began at Everett Naval Station on 9 November 1987, and its $56 million carrier pier was formally opened in June 1992. In 1994, personnel from the Puget Sound Naval Station began moving to Everett. In September 1994, the Oliver Hazard Perry class–guided missile frigates *USS Ingraham* and *USS Ford* arrived there, followed by the destroyer *USS Paul F. Foster;* the carrier *USS Abraham Lincoln* arrived in December 1996. Today Everett's 4,700 active-duty personnel and 400 civilian employees operate and maintain the facilities needed to support a carrier battle group, as well as numerous tenant activities.

Housing and Schools. Everett Naval Station maintains 220 units of family housing at four locations off the station. Local rentals are available and range from as much as $650 a month for a one-bedroom apartment to $1,300 a month for a four-bedroom unit. Utilities, depending on the size of the unit, can range from $50 to $150 a month. A 50-unit Navy Lodge is available at the Marysville Complex, just north of Everett.

Schooling for children is available in Everett and nearby Marysville. Child care is available from certified providers. The Navy campus offers adults associate's and baccalaureate degrees through Everett Community College and Columbia College, respectively.

Personal Services. Medical care is provided by a branch clinic operated by Bremerton Naval Hospital. The Family Support Complex, a 52-acre facility located in Marysville, offers a main exchange and country store, a commissary, a bank, an education office, and other facilities.

Recreation. The Family Support Complex has an auto hobby shop, Craftech for hobbyists, and a full array of outdoor sports. On the station itself is a fitness center, the Boiler Room club, and a 90-slip marina with direct access to Puget Sound. The Pacific Beach Recreation, Training and Conference Center on the coast, 176 miles southwest of Everett, is a private getaway for station personnel. Three- and four-bedroom ocean-view houses are offered there, along with RV spaces and tenting areas, the Windjammer Bar and Lounge, a gym and fitness area, a sauna, and bowling lanes.

The Local Area. Situated on Gardner Bay, only 26 miles north of Seattle, Everett is a city of over 60,000. Everett started out as a lumber port a century ago, and today Boeing assembles 747s and 767s at its Everett complex. Many of the mansions built by the lumber barons still stand, and the Marina Village, along the bay, re-creates the 1890s-style waterfront, complete with shops and restaurants. There is also a large casino in Marysville operated by the Tulalip Indian tribe, which boasts the largest poker room in the state of Washington.

For more information, write to Public Affairs Office, 2000 West Marine View Drive, Naval Station Everett, Everett, WA 98207-5001, or call (425) 304-3000. Home page: *www.everett.navy.mil.*

WHIDBEY ISLAND NAVAL AIR STATION

Whidbey Island sits like a huge stopper in the mouth of Puget Sound, its north end jutting into the Strait of Juan de Fuca and its southern end pointing directly toward Seattle. At 64 miles long, Whidbey is the largest island in the continental United States, and Whidbey Naval Air Station is the largest Navy installation in the Northwest.

History. Commissioned in 1942, Whidbey Island NAS is home today for all Navy electronic warfare squadrons flying the EA-6B "Prowler" tactical jamming aircraft, as well as the P-3 Orion. There are approximately 7,500 active-duty personnel, 12,000 family members, and 2,000 civilian employees onboard the station.

Whidbey Island NAS is actually composed of two bases five miles apart: the seaplane base and the naval air station (Ault Field). Located on the western shore of the island, the air station contains most of the military activities. The seaplane base is on the eastern shore, at the edge of the town of Oak Harbor. It houses the family services center, the commissary, the exchange, and some of the family housing units.

Housing and Schools. There are 1,506 sets of family quarters for personnel stationed at Whidbey. A Navy Lodge is also available.

There is no dependent schooling at Whidbey, but day-care services are available. The Navy College Office offers college-level courses from Embry-Riddle Aeronautical University, Chapman College, Skagit Valley College, and Western Washington University in programs leading to bachelor's and master's degrees.

Personal Services. The Navy exchange operates outlets and concessions at both the station and the seaplane base, while the commissary store provides approximately 12,000 line items for sale. A twenty-five-bed medical-surgical hospital, staffed by approximately 200 personnel, provides medical care for a population of approximately 38,000 eligible active-duty, retired, and dependent personnel.

Recreation. Extensive indoor and outdoor recreation facilities are available to Navy personnel at Whidbey, including two outdoor recreation areas on the base, a 32-lane bowling alley, and an 18-hole golf course. Hunting, fishing, camping, hiking, and boating are all offered and avidly pursued by the residents of Washington. Just ten miles north of Oak Harbor is Deception Pass State Park, which is visited each year by more people than any other park in the state. The San Juan Islands, north of Whidbey Island and between the Straits of Georgia, are another very popular outdoor spot. For those who like the big city, Seattle, with a metropolitan population of 1.8 million, and nearby Tacoma are within easy commuting distance.

For more information, write to Public Affairs Office, Naval Air Station, Whidbey Island, Oak Harbor, WA 98278-5000, or call (360) 257-2211. Home page: *www.naswi.navy.mil.*

WISCONSIN

Army

FORT MCCOY

The only active U.S. Army installation in the state of Wisconsin, Fort McCoy, named after Maj. Gen. Robert Bruce McCoy, a veteran of the Spanish-American War and World War I, is situated on 60,000 acres between the towns of Sparta and Tomah, 105 miles northwest of the city of Madison and 35 miles east of LaCrosse. The Army has used the area for training troops since 1909. Named in 1910 for General McCoy's father, Civil War veteran and local landowner Bruce E. McCoy, the post was redesignated in honor of the general in 1926.

Today Fort McCoy has a permanent active-duty population of 300 personnel and 600 family members, as well as a civilian workforce of about 1,300. It is a regional training center that annually supports year-round training for approximately 105,000 active-duty and reserve component personnel.

Housing and Schools. Fort McCoy operates 90 sets of family quarters and a sixteen-unit trailer park. There is also a small guest house. Another 630 sets of quarters are available for transient personnel. Schooling for children is conducted by the public-school systems in Tomah and Sparta. There is a day-care center at Fort McCoy that can accommodate 52 children.

Personal Services. Medical and dental care are provided by the Fort McCoy Medical Department Activity. Full commissary and post exchange services are available. The commissary store stocks 8,800 line items in its 12,000 square feet of sales space. A gas station, a self-service car wash, and a convenience store are also on post.

Recreation. The recreational scene at Fort McCoy is dominated by the Pine View and Whitetail Ridge recreation areas. Pine View is a 200-acre park with 135 campsites. Of these, 105 are RV sites with electric hookups. All sites have ground grills and picnic tables. The campground has three shower stations. A variety of outdoor activities are available there, including boating, fishing, swimming, miniature golf, picnicking, and hiking. There is also a snack bar. Whitetail Ridge is open from December through March and serves as both a recreation and a training area. It has both downhill and cross-country ski courses, a tubing slope with rope tow, and a chalet where food and beverages are sold. The recreational facilities at both sites are open to the public. The Rumpel Fitness Center on the main post has weight-training rooms, basketball and racquetball courts, saunas, and an Olympic-size indoor swimming pool. The post recreation equipment rental facility has a wide variety of equipment for rent. A recreation center and community theater round out the picture.

The Local Area. Tomah and Sparta are thriving little communities, each of about 8,010 people. Tomah was named after a Menominee Indian chief, Thomas Carron ("Tomah" is the French pronunciation of Thomas), because he was so friendly to the early settlers. Sparta is far from Spartan: More than 60,000 people go there every year to use the Sparta State Bike Trail's thirty-two-mile course. The town is also proud of its 18-hole municipal golf course, one of the finest in the state.

For more information, write to Public Affairs Office, Attention: Community Relations, 100 E. Headquarters Road, Fort McCoy, WI 54656-5263, or call (608) 388-2222. Home page: *www.mccoy.army.mil.*

WYOMING

Air Force

F. E. WARREN AIR FORCE BASE

History. If the buildings and grounds at Warren Air Force Base could speak, they would tell a fascinating story, because they have seen everything from the Army's horse cavalry to the Peacekeeper ICBM. There has been some kind of military activity going on at the site of present-day Warren AFB since the winter of 1867 to 1868, when troops of the U.S. Cavalry established Fort D. A. Russell on the site. Troops from the fort participated in the Sioux Campaign of 1876, the same campaign that saw Custer's 7th Cavalry Regiment decimated at the Little Bighorn.

In 1930, the name of the post was changed to Fort Francis E. Warren, in honor of the first governor of Wyoming, a Medal of Honor winner in the Civil War. Then, in 1947, the post was ceded to the U.S. Air Force, becoming Francis E. Warren Air Force Base. Today it is home to the 3,700 military personnel, 4,200 family members, and 400 civilians of the 90th Missile Wing. Warren is an Air Force base without a single fixed-wing aircraft and no runway. What it does have, however, are 150 Minuteman III and 50 Peacekeeper missiles.

Housing and Schools. There are over 800 units of family housing at Warren, 156 of them brick two-story dwellings that were built between 1885 and 1930. Personnel often wait up to one year for quarters at Warren. Guest housing is available, but reservations may be made only by incoming or outgoing permanently assigned personnel.

There are plenty of educational opportunities at Warren. Courses are offered there by the University of Wyoming, the University of Northern Colorado, Colorado State University, Chapman College, Southern Illinois University, Lesley College, and Laramie County Community College.

Personal Services. Personal services include a commissary, a base exchange, a service station, and the USAF hospital, a 30-bed facility that provides dental and medical care.

Recreation. Recreational facilities at Warren are excellent. The base museum contains many artifacts and memorabilia of the Old West and the Old Army. Also available are a rod and gun club, a roller skating rink, auto and arts and crafts hobby shops, an 18-hole golf course, a 12-lane bowling alley, stables, a gymnasium, a swimming pool, officers and NCO clubs, and a family camp featuring picnicking and camping spaces with hookups for 24 campers.

The base itself is a great attraction for most Air Force personnel because it offers a unique opportunity for them to live and work amid reminders of the daily life of a frontier Army garrison: The child-care center building went up in 1885 as an enlisted barracks; the education center was also built in 1885, as enlisted quarters; the indoor track and fitness facility was built as a cavalry drill hall in 1907. In 1975, the base was designated a national historic landmark.

The Local Area. Warren AFB is on the plains at an altitude of over 6,000 feet, which makes breathing difficult for newcomers. The weather changes rapidly there and may go from a -25° F windchill factor to 40° F very quickly. Winters are cold and the wind blows hard; summers are dry and mild, and it seldom gets hot enough to use air-conditioning.

Warren lies in the northwestern quadrant of the city of Cheyenne, a metropolis that, for its size, has perhaps the cleanest air in the United States. The city boasts four golf courses, three bowling centers, a symphony and choral society, and no traffic jams. To the west and north is Medicine Bow National Forest. Fort Collins, Colorado, is 50 miles south of Cheyenne, and Denver is 100 miles south. Laramie is 50 miles west.

For more information, write to Public Affairs Division, 5305 Randall Avenue, F. E. Warren AFB, WY 82005-2266, or call (307) 773-1110. Home page: *www.warren.af.mil.*

PART TWO

Overseas Installations

AZORES

Air Force

LAJES FIELD

It is said that there are no horizontal spaces at Lajes Field, unless you find them in bed. The people who live in the Azores are as rugged as their country. In 1581, they repelled an invading Spanish army by unleashing a herd of cattle on it, and some believe the Azoreans may even have visited the New World before Columbus.

History. Lajes Field, or Portuguese Air Base No. 4, was activated in 1943 by the British, and the first U.S. military personnel arrived there the same year. In 1953, the 1605th Air Base Wing of the Military Airlift Command, now the 65th Air Base Wing (ACC), was established there. Today Lajes is home to about 3,000 Americans: military personnel, family members, and civilian employees.

Housing and Schools. There are 489 sets of government quarters at Lajes. One hundred twenty-nine cottages on or immediately adjacent to the base are available for purchase by married personnel under the base-supported leasehold housing program. These dwellings are prorated among eligible personnel, with price and disposition strictly prescribed and controlled by base regulations. Prices range from as little as $500 to as much as $16,000, with the local credit union giving signature loans up to $2,500. These cottages are erected on Portuguese land and held on assignable land leases that give full reversionary rights to the landowner upon termination of the land lease. Furnishings are provided by base housing, and utilities are also furnished by the base at established monthly rates. Off-base housing is limited, and the types of units available are small by U.S. standards.

Schooling for dependent children from kindergarten through grade twelve is provided at Lajes Field. A child-development center offers a full range of services for the families stationed at Lajes Field for children from six months to ten years of age. College-level courses from the University of Maryland, Troy

State University, and the City Colleges of Chicago are available for adults through the base education center.

Personal Services. Medical care at Lajes is provided by the seven-bed USAF hospital. Dental care is limited, however. Patients requiring special care beyond the local health-care professionals' capabilities are evacuated to Wiesbaden, Germany, or to the United States.

The commissary carries about 4,000 items, and the base exchange, besides operating a main retail store, offers a family shopping center, a toy store, an outdoor-living store, a cafeteria, a service station, and other concessions.

Recreation. One of the premier recreational attractions at Lajes is the 18-hole golf course located in a mountain valley approximately ten miles from the base. The course is playable most of the year. Other recreational facilities include ceramics, wood, and auto hobby shops; a skating rink; a gymnasium; two tennis courts; a swimming pool; a 16-lane bowling alley; a base library; a recreation center; and a youth center. Officers and NCO clubs are also available.

The Local Area. The Azores Archipelago consists of nine inhabited islands in the North Atlantic, about 2,300 miles east of Washington, D.C., and 900 miles west of Lisbon, Portugal. They have a total land mass of 888 square miles, and about 230,000 people live on them. Lajes Field is located on the northeast tip of Terceira Island, which measures roughly 10 by 20 miles. The town of Angra do Heroismo, the central district's capital city, is approximately 13 miles from the base and has a population of 15,000. Praia da Vitoria is about 3 miles from the base and has about 7,000 inhabitants. Terceira is almost totally bordered by high cliffs, and many of its roads are narrow, winding, and made of dirt.

The Azores' climate is semitropical. There is little rain in the summer, but the temperatures are ideal, with a daily low of 65° F and a high of about 75° F. In the winter season (October through May), it can be damp and chilly, and during this period there are frequent rains and high winds, and the mountains are generally covered by clouds that often descend into the valleys as thick fog or mist.

Agriculture and fishing are the primary vocations in the Azores. Portuguese is the official language of the islands, although the dialect spoken there is different from that in Brazil or continental Portugal. The people are hardy, independent, and fun-loving.

For more information, write to Public Affairs, 65ABW (ACC), Unit 7710, APO AE 09720.

BAHRAIN

Navy

NAVAL SUPPORT ACTIVITY BAHRAIN

NSA Bahrain claims to cover the world's busiest 60 acres. Located in the "middle of the Middle East," support is provided to ships at sea, remote sites throughout the region, and military and civilian personnel living in Bahrain. NSA is currently undergoing a new construction and renovation project that will greatly increase facilities and services. NSA Bahrain supports Navy, Army, and Air Force members in its mission for the Commander, U.S. Fifth Fleet, deployed assets, military and Department of Defense civilian personnel, and families in Bahrain.

History. The British Navy established a naval installation known as HMS JUFFAIR on 13 April 1935 in the area where NSA is located today. In 1950, the United States Navy leased office space aboard HMS JUFFAIR from the British. In 1971, after their treaty expired, the British left Bahrain, granting the island total independence. The United States, through agreement with the Bahraini government, took over part of HMS JUFFAIR, renaming it Administrative Support Unit Bahrain. The command title was changed to Administrative Support Unit, Southwest Asia (ASU SWA), in 1992 to reflect the new mission to support ships and remote sites throughout the COMUSNAVCENT Area of Responsibility. In 1999, ASU SWA became NSA Bahrain. The major commands supported include U.S. Naval Forces, Central Command; Logistics Forces, U.S. Naval Forces Central Command (CTF-53); Naval Support Activity, Bahrain (NSA Bahrain); and Destroyer Squadron 50 (COMDESRON 50). NAS Bahrain also reaches out to the remote sites of Fujairah, United Arab Emirates (UAE); Jebel Ali, UAE; Hurghada, Egypt; Port Liaison Element, Abu Dhabi, UAE; Patrol Squadron (VP); Jeddah, Saudi Arabia; Logistics Support Station Doha; and Qatar Navy Regional Contracting Center (NRCC), Dubai, UAE. Multiple tenant commands support on-going Middle East operations.

Housing and Schools. If accompanied, one can expect temporary lodging for up to 60 days. Depending on the size of your family and whether or not you have pets, you will stay in off-base quarters usually at a local hotel. Interestingly, arrivals receive temporary lodging allowance (TLA), which must be reapplied for every ten days. Transient personnel (not permanent-change-of-station personnel) coming to Bahrain will usually stay in transient quarters. All personnel will live on the local economy, except for a very few special-assignment personnel. Rent is paid in Bahrain dinars (BD). There is usually a three-month advance payment of rent required, which can be requested as advance overseas housing allowance (OHA). Electricity tends to be expensive and is billed monthly. Telephones are also expensive. The phone company requires an advance deposit of 100 BD ($265). As phones are mandatory for recall purposes, an advance may be obtained for the phone deposit once housing is secured. Most electrical appliances can be used here with a transformer, but most unconverted washers, dryers, and refrigerators will be inoperable in Bahrain.

A Department of Defense Dependents School is located adjacent to NSA Bahrain for grades kindergarten through twelve. Navy PACE provides accredited college courses for service members. On-site University of Maryland and City Colleges of Chicago offer courses for associate's and bachelor's degrees. Local private schools and universities are available, but they are quite expensive for non-Bahrainis.

Recently, the Navy policy changed to pay 100 percent tuition for active-duty military members. For those who are interested, a tour of duty in Bahrain can be a true learning experience. The Navy College offers a variety of exams, including CLEPS and DANTES. Tuition assistance for family members is available. Family members can participate at a small cost in any of the DANTES examinations/tests.

Personal Services. There is only one military medical and dental treatment facility in Bahrain, which is always busy. Its motto is "quality care for quality people," and its goal is to provide the highest quality care possible anywhere. Offered are outpatient services, with no emergency service capability, with reliance on the local host nation assets for these services. By special arrangement with host nation health-care facilities, NAS Bahrain coordinates specialty care and hospitalization for all Navy and Marine Corps personnel throughout southwest Asia. Health-care services in Bahrain are considered very good but more limited in some respects than in the United States.

Immunizations are a must and administered on a rigid schedule.

Recreation. Tremendous effort has been put into making the morale, welfare, and recreation department in Bahrain one of the best in the Department of Defense. Recreation, food, entertainment, activities, athletics, child and teen programs, trips and tours in and around Bahrain, as well as concessionaire services, are offered. These include a full-service gymnasium with a gear issue office, an aerobic center, and a weight room with the latest in free weights, treadmills, stairmasters, rowing machines, and life circuit machines. Racquetball, martial arts, step aerobics, ballet, jazz, ballroom dancing, and intramural sports are also offered. There is a bowling center, a recreation center, a library, the Desert Dome, the Dunes Officers Club, restaurants, two swimming pools, a theater (all movies are free), a laundromat, a tailor, a hair-cutting salon, a shoe shop, a laundry and dry cleaner, and much more.

The Local Area. In addition to high temperatures, humidity tends to be very high during summer months. As a result, the apparent temperature may be 10° to 20° F greater than the actual temperature. There have been three- to five-day periods of temperatures above 120° F in July and August. November through March brings beautiful weather. The climate is quite pleasant, occasionally even chilly from December to March, with temperatures ranging from 40° (4.4° C) to 76° F (24° C). Temperatures are coolest from December to March, when winds blow from the north and northwest. In July, August, and September, temperatures average 96° F (36° C), and the shallow waters of the Gulf make for high humidity. Still, the summer climate is often tempered by northwesterly Al-Barah winds. The annual average rainfall, during December through February, is approximately three inches. Bahrain abounds with history, ancient cultures, modern museum facilities, on-going restoration activities, and large and small shopping areas. Attractions include a wildlife park, bargain shopping opportunities for gold and jewelry, a national museum, mosques, and ancient forts.

For more information, write to PSC 451, Box FSC, FPO AE 09834. Home page: *www.asuswa.com.*

THE BALKANS AND HUNGARY

Bosnia–Herzegovina (B-H)

The "Balkans" is a geographic term for the countries in southeastern Europe: Greece, Albania, Bulgaria, Romania, and several countries that formerly were part of Yugoslavia—the now-independent Croatia, Bosnia–Herzegovina, and Macedonia, and the still-federated Yugoslav republics of Montenegro and Serbia.

History. The state of Bosnia first appeared in the tenth century A.D. It came under Turkish rule in 1463 and under Austro-Hungarian rule in 1878. In 1918, the region became a province of Yugoslavia when that country was created following World War I. Bosnia is somewhat unique in that its population consists of Muslims, Roman Catholics, Orthodox Christians, and Jews.

The political-military problems today in the Balkans are due to the breakup of the Serb-dominated Yugoslavia, which resulted in Serbia invading Croatia when Croatia declared its independence in 1991; Serbia, and later Croatia, invaded parts of Bosnia–Herzegovina when Bosnia declared its independence in 1992. The brutal, interethnic atrocities, known as ethnic cleansing, lead to NATO intervention in December 1995 in the form of air patrols and the dispatch of a 14,000-man peacekeeping force, under United Nations auspices, which was known as the Stabilization Force (SFOR), with the operation titled Joint Endeavor, Joint Guard, and now Joint Forge.

International military forces in Bosnia consists of military units from Estonia, Latvia, Finland, Poland, Denmark, Lithuania, Norway, Iceland, Sweden, Russia, Turkey, and the United States, which are organized into a unit called Multinational Division (North) (MND-(N)). U.S. forces participating in MND-(N) are known as Task Force Eagle.

Army active-duty and reserve component forces rotate in and out of Task Force Eagle about every six months, and plans have been published to continue unit rotations for the next several years. Army units consist of infantry, armor, artillery, engineers, military police, civil affairs, special forces, and military intelligence, as well as the supporting logistics troops.

The six-month tours of duty are unaccompanied.

Soldiers assigned to duty in B-H are entitled to $150 a month Imminent Danger Pay, $100 a month Family Separation Allowance, and Foreign Duty Pay (enlisted personnel only based on grade from $8–$22.50 a month). Mail from the United States takes 7–10 days to reach units in BH. Soldiers there are allowed to make one 15-minute telephone call home per week. Calls to and from stateside military installations are free; calls to commercial numbers are not. Home Page: *www.tfeagle.army.mil.*

Facilities. Task Force Eagle operates out of four camps in Bosnia: Eagle Base in Tuzla, Camp Dobol, Camp Comanche, and Camp McGovern. Over the past five years, Army engineers and Logistics Civil Augmentation Program (LOGCAP) contractors have worked tirelessly to make these "temporary" bases livable. Most bases in Bosnia now have wooden barracks, mess halls, and recreation facilities. Some elements at Tuzla have fixed facilities.

CAMP COMANCHE

Aviators based at Camp Comanche enjoy a fitness center offering all the amenities of any similar-size stateside facility as well as a fest tent with live concerts, pool, games, and karaoke; a video theater; a paperback lending library; and a cyber hut.

CAMP DOBOL

Located southeast of Tuzla, Dobol offers the soldiers stationed there facilities that "are better than any soldier could dream about in a field environment, and the dining facility is so good that it is hard to stay trim," according to a source who knows. To support that statement, soldiers based at Dobol can enjoy the Thunderdome morale, welfare, and recreation services fest tent, a 24-hour facility that offers live concerts, basketball, indoor soccer, and volleyball. There is also a state-of-the-art fitness center at Dobol, a ping-golf complex, a recreation center, a library, and a cyber hut. Dobol is expected to close in 2001.

CAMP MCGOVERN

The infantrymen assigned to Camp McGovern enjoy recreational facilities similar to those at the other Task Force Eagle bases, but to round out the picture, McGovern also has the Rose Garden, an outdoor concert site, and the ZOS Café Recreation Center with a cappuccino bar, DJ booth, and karaoke.

EAGLE BASE

Eagle Base, near Tuzla, offers a wide variety of morale and welfare facilities and activities, ranging from an ice-cream parlor to a mile-long outdoor running trail. The indoor recreational activities available at Eagle include Alma's Juice Bar Recreation Center and library, which is open around the clock; a recreation center featuring Baskin-Robbins, a deli, a 52-inch TV screen and pool tables (also open 24 hours); Triggers, a soldiers' club with a food concession and other diversions; a video theater where first-run videos are shown seven days a week (the popcorn is free); and a state-of-the-art fitness center. Outdoor recreation at Eagle Base includes a softball field, a running trail, a soccer and football field, and Minue Park, a picnic area which also has two volleyball courts. This picture is rounded out with a cyber hut, which offers computer terminals and free Internet access. The Red Cross has representatives permanently stationed at Eagle Base.

Hungary

TASZAR AIR BASE/SUPPORT BASE

Hungary, of course, is not a Balkan country. It is one of NATO's newest members. Taszar Air Base is located approximately 110 miles southwest of Budapest, Hungary, and is an active MiG-21 base of the Hungarian air force. U.S. operations have been run by the men and women of the USAF's 4400th Operations Squadron and the U.S. National Support Element (NSE), primarily an Army outfit. Practically all U. S. Army supplies convoyed south into Bosnia-Herzegovina are flown into Taszar. The Air Force's C-5 Galaxys, C-17 Globemaster IIIs, C-130 Hercules and C-141 Starlifters have ferried thousands of tons of equipment and supplies into Taszar and thousands of replacements for the Army units deployed in Bosnia–Herzegovina.

Taszar was selected as the site of the initial staging base for a variety of reasons. The area is a multimodal transportation hub where road, rail, and air transport converge. There is also a robust road network in all directions, and the area offers multiple railheads. Perhaps most significantly, Taszar offers the closest airfield to Bosnia and Croatia capable of landing strategic aircraft such as C-5 Galaxies and Boeing 747s.

Today the NSE and the Taszar Support Base serve as far more than a deployment center. TSB provides base operations support for Department of Defense forces and civilians deployed in Hungary, Croatia, and Bosnia (less MND-(N)). It coordinates all host national support with Hungary in support of Operation Joint Forge; provides for the reception, staging, and onward-movement back-up of units and individuals deploying or redeploying in the area. It serves as a transportation node on the theater line of communication by providing a 1,500-bed transient facility.

Servicemembers stationed at Taszar live, for the most part, in fixed facilities and contractor-provided buildings.

Home page: *www.af.mil/news/airman/hungary* and *www.hqusareur.army.mil*

Kosovo and Macedonia

Serb atrocities in its formerly autonomous province of Kosovo in 1999 were caused by the Serbian leadership's attempt to expel the 90%-majority ethnic Albanian population from Kosovo. U.S. military forces, primarily Army, have been assigned to the U.N./NATO-sponsored Kosovo Force (KFOR), also known as Multinational Division (East), since mid-1999. U.S. Army forces are collectively known by the name Task Force Falcon. The mission of these forces is to keep the peace between the majority ethnic Albanian population and the small ethnic Serbian population.

Tours of duty with KFOR are of six months' duration, with most rotations occurring on a unit basis. About 7,000 soldiers rotate in and out of Kosovo and the related support base in the adjoining Republic of Macedonia about every six months. The Army recently published a multiyear plan of rotations, which will include active-duty and reserve component forces. Because of the newness of the camps established there, facilities are less well-developed.

TASK FORCE FALCON

Task Force Falcon was formed to support the military mission in Kosovo by providing humanitarian assistance to the inhabitants of the region and support to the multinational effort to restore civil government in the region. Under the operational control an Army combat brigade, American forces in Kosovo consist of armor, infantry, artillery, aviation, military police, military intelligence, transportation, public affairs, psychological operations, personnel services, and air defense artillery units—more than 7,000 U.S. military personnel in all.

Task Force Falcon operates out of two bases in Kosovo, Camp Monteith and Camp Bondsteel, and one camp in Macedonia, Camp Able Sentry.

Camp Monteith is named in honor of 1st Lt. Jimmie W. Monteith, Jr., who won the Medal of Honor with the 1st Infantry Division on Normandy beach, 6 June 1944. Camp Bondsteel is named in honor of Staff Sgt. James L. Bondsteel who won the Medal of Honor as a soldier with the 1st Infantry Division in Vietnam. Camp Able Sentry was established in 1992 to support the U.N. observation mission along the border between Yugoslavia and Macedonia. It operates today as Task Force Falcon-Rear and is the temporary home for various finance, engineer, quartermaster, military police and other support units.

Facilities. The morale and recreation facilities available to the soldiers of Task Force Falcon vary from excellent to adequate. At Camp Bondsteel, for instance, the brand-new South Side Fitness Center that opened in December 2000 offers a wide variety of exercise equipment, including treadmills, cross-trainers, stationary bicycles, stairmasters, and free weights. Indoor and outdoor basketball and volleyball courts and a built-in musical system complete the picture. At more remote mountain stations such as Patrol Base Tango 16, the Eagle's Nest, as it's called by the soldiers of armored company based there, the mess hall doubles as a combination movie theater, reading room, conference room, and foyer to their billets, which have one shower for 20 men. The men wash four or five at a time, each group for no more than ten minutes, otherwise the 25-gallon water heater would run out. For soldiers who may have served in Korea and Vietnam, the Eagle's Nest brings back poignant memories. The men fill their off-duty time watching videotapes and DVDs, lifting weights, and playing pool on the full-size table that was installed just before press time. R&R for these men consists of weekly visits to Camp Monteith.

Soldiers stationed with Task Force Falcon receive the same additional pay as do soldiers in Bosnia. Home page: *www.tffalcon.army.mil.*

BELGIUM

SUPREME HEADQUARTERS ALLIED POWERS EUROPE (SHAPE)

SHAPE is the military headquarters of Allied Command Europe. The Supreme Allied Commander Europe (SACEUR) coordinates the defense of Europe throughout an area that stretches north to south from Norway to the Mediterranean and west to east from the Atlantic Ocean to the Caucasus Mountains in Turkey—an area of two million square kilometers.

SHAPE is located near Mons, about thirty miles from Brussels, where it moved from Paris after France withdrew from the military component of NATO. SHAPE began operations at Mons on 31 March 1967.

The international SHAPE staff consists of 749 officers, 1,249 other ranks, and 370 civilians. With the addition of locally employed civilians and 7,700 dependents, the SHAPE community consists of over 12,000 personnel. The national breakdown of the staff consists of 22 percent American, 16 percent from the United Kingdom, 13 percent German, 5 percent Belgian, 5 percent from the Netherlands, 6 percent Italian, and the remaining 33 percent from other nations.

Housing and Schools. The 498-acre SHAPE complex consists of 253 buildings and 600 apartments and houses, 264 for officers and other personnel. The SHAPE International School provides international and national kindergartens and elementary schools, with an international and an American high school.

Personal Services. Medical and dental care are provided by the SHAPE Healthcare Facility, a polyclinic staffed by physicians from the various SHAPE nations under U.S. leadership.

Recreation. Among the numerous recreational facilities available are fields, pitches, and courts for virtually every type of sport, including soccer, football, rugby, cricket, baseball, tennis (indoor and all-weather), squash, racquetball, and basketball. There are also an all-weather athletic track, an indoor swimming pool, and Nautilus exercise equipment. An arts and crafts center provides wood-

Supreme Headquarters Allied Powers Europe (SHAPE) at Mons, Belgium NATO PHOTO

working, photography, ceramics, and other hobby facilities, as well as a theater that presents six productions a year, ranging from musicals to dramas.

The Local Area. The city of Mons is over 1,000 years old and today is the capital of the province of Hainaut. It is situated on a ridge between the Trouille and Haine Rivers. Mons has witnessed many major events in European history. In the seventeenth and eighteenth centuries, Mons suffered a series of sieges conducted by French, Spanish, Dutch, and Austrian forces contending for control of the region. On 23 August 1914, it was the site of the Battle of Mons, the first engagement of British and German troops in World War I. This was once a vast coal-mining region. The Borinage coalfields just to the west of Mons were part of an industry that stretched from northern France to the Ruhr in Germany.

For more information, write to Public Information Office, B-7010 SHAPE Belgium, CMR 450, Box 7500, APO AE 09705.

CUBA

Navy

GUANTANAMO BAY NAVAL BASE

Guantanamo Bay Naval Base is the only U.S. military installation located in an unfriendly communist country. Situated in the southeast corner of the Republic of Cuba, Guantanamo is the oldest U.S. overseas base, originally leased from the Republic of Cuba in 1903 as a coaling station for Navy ships. In 1934, the original lease agreement was formalized by a treaty signed as part of President Franklin Roosevelt's Good Neighbor policy. Approximately 7,000 military personnel, their dependents, Cuban exiles, and foreign nationals now live on the base.

Housing and Schools. The base has 906 housing units. There are an elementary school and a high school at Guantanamo, along with adult education programs that offer courses from City Colleges of Chicago, Troy State University, and Central Texas College.

Personal Services and Recreation. The base has a Navy commissary/exchange mall with a pizza shop, a minimart, a laundry facility, a tailor shop, a bakery, and a Baskin Robbins ice cream parlor. Other facilities include officers and enlisted clubs and a 100-bed hospital. Recreation facilities include a new gym with modern weight-lifting equipment and boat, bike, and golf and fishing equipment rentals. The base has a corral, a veterinarian, Spanish and English religious services, three galleys, and numerous clubs. With the tropical climate, outdoor recreation is possible year-round.

The Local Area. Located approximately 525 air miles from Miami, Guantanamo is a closed base with access by air only. Access is strictly controlled, and only official travelers and relatives of naval base personnel are permitted entry, with the approval of the base commander. A ferry crosses the bay to the naval air station located on the leeward, or western, side of the bay. On an average day, the ferry transports more than 700 people. There is no entry into Communist

Cuba from the base except for a small group of Cuban nationals still employed by the U.S. government.

For more information, write to Public Affairs Officer, U.S. Naval Station, Box 25-505, FPO AE 09593-1000, or call 011-53-99-4502. Home page: *www.nsgtmo.navy.mil.*

DIEGO GARCIA

Navy

DIEGO GARCIA U.S. NAVY SUPPORT FACILITY

When they start calling the Navy exchange the "Ship's Store," either you're far, far from land or you're on land that is far, far from land. Even in the geography of the Indian Ocean, noted for its remote islands, Diego Garcia is far from civilization. The nearest port is Colombo, Sri Lanka, 960 nautical miles (a nautical mile is 1,852 meters) to the north-northeast. Duty on Diego Garcia entitles each sailor to a daily dose of beautiful weather.

History. The station was commissioned on 20 March 1973, and following the crises in Yemen in 1979 and Iran–Afghanistan the following year, the strategic importance of the island became apparent. Much money has since been spent there to expand its facilities to meet future operational needs in the Indian Ocean and Middle East.

About 3,500 personnel live on Diego Garcia, made up of U.S. and British military and civilian personnel and 1,400 contract personnel from Mauritius and the Philippines. Because it is a remote site, service personnel are authorized thirty days of environmental and morale leave after the first three months of each twelve-month tour. Popular leave destinations include the United States, the Philippines, Singapore, Japan, Hawaii, Spain, and Italy.

Housing and Schools. Dependents are not authorized on Diego Garcia. Bachelor living facilities are spacious. There are 18 permanent living facilities available to enlisted personnel on the Indian Ocean side of the island. Officers are accommodated in nine units on the lagoon side of the island just behind the snorkeling reef. Officers, chief petty officers, and first-class petty officers are all afforded their own living quarters. All other ranks are two to a room. Each bachelor quarters is centrally air-conditioned, with E-7 and above having small kitchens.

With the isolation comes enough free time to offer everyone plenty of opportunity to pursue educational goals while on duty there. Correspondence courses are available from a variety of colleges and universities, in addition to the Central Texas College courses offered on the island at the Navy College Office.

Personal Services. The island medical center is designed to meet the medical and dental needs of both fleet and island personnel and includes the equipment necessary to respond to emergencies. The facility includes an operating room, ward space to accommodate eight holding beds, and two treatment areas for sick call. A dental lab, an operatory, and hygiene rooms are also located within.

The ship's store is authorized a $2 million inventory. Health and comfort items, plus a limited amount of luxury items, such as TV sets, stereo components, and cameras, are available. Additionally, a catalog corner allows customers to order from a variety of stateside sources for items not carried to accommodate individual tastes. The island also has a local, cash-banking facility and a branch of the Navy Federal Credit Union.

Recreation. One thing Diego Garcia has is places to eat. Besides an officers club that offers a spectacular view of the Indian Ocean and a CPO club that overlooks the island's lagoon, there is the Seamen's Club and the 61 Club, which cater to the island's inhabitants. The Peacekeeper's Inn is an all-hands restaurant with an à la carte menu and an order service. Also, there are the Diego Burger fast-food restaurant, the passenger terminal snack bar, and the Burgers-n-Bytes, a computer-café-restaurant allowing Internet access while you lounge. And to top it all off, there is the $5 million combined dining facility, with a menu loaded with all sorts of dishes prepared by contract civilians.

In the realm of recreation, Diego Garcia is not to be outdone. There are sports leagues ranging from basketball and softball to bowling and golf. There is an Olympic-size swimming pool, a gymnasium complex, a four-lane bowling alley, a marina with motorboats, a golf range and golf course, eight outdoor tennis courts, two outdoor racquetball courts, and lots of swimming and fishing areas. (Watch out for the variety of sea life which inhabits the waters.) Movies are shown nightly (sometimes double features) at the main outdoor theaters, as well as in the clubs and bachelors quarters lounges. The island also offers an extensive 8,000-volume library.

The Local Area. Diego Garcia is a part of the British Indian Ocean Territory (BIOT) dependency since 1965. It was formed from territory formerly belonging to Mauritius and the Seychelles. The island is only one of 56 in the Chagos Archipelago, which extends over 10,000 square miles of ocean. The island is shaped like a horseshoe and consists of a narrow coral atoll with a land area of about 11 square miles nearly enclosing a lagoon. Diego Garcia stretches 37 miles from tip to tip. Shallow reefs surround it on the ocean side, as well as within the lagoon. Most of the landfill used in construction there is blasted from the outer reefs and then crushed to the required size. Diego Garcia poses no threat to anyone suffering from acrophobia: It's only four feet above sea level.

The climate on Diego Garcia is tropical, and island plant life is lush. No dangerous wildlife exists there, but there are donkeys whose ancestors worked the Capra plantations that once flourished there.

Diego Garcia is on year-round Daylight Savings Time, so from October through April, when it is 6 P.M. there, it's 7 A.M. in Washington, D.C.; 6 A.M. in Gulfport, Mississippi; 5 A.M. in Denver, Colorado; and 4 A.M. in San Francisco, California. From April through October, advance the stateside times one hour.

For more information, write to Commanding Officer, U.S. Naval Support Facility, Diego Garcia, PSC 466, Box 2, FPO AP 96595-0002. Home page: *www.dg.navy.mil.*

ENGLAND

Air Force

RAF LAKENHEATH

One of the first things you see upon arriving at Lakenheath is the Statue of Liberty. This is a bronze replica of the famous statue, dedicated 25 November 1981 to commemorate the fortieth anniversary of RAF Lakenheath and the 48th Fighter Wing, "the Liberty Wing" (after its insignia). With the cooperation of the Bartholdi Museum in Colmar, France, the Lakenheath statue was cast from an original first-step model of the famous Statue of Liberty, which French sculptor F. A. Bartholdi created for the American people in 1884.

History. Lakenheath was established in 1940 as a Royal Air Force Base. British fliers conducted nearly 2,250 wartime sorties from the base against targets in Europe. The U.S. Air Force began regular basing of its aircraft there in 1949, and the British government turned over operational control of the base to the USAF in 1951. Today Lakenheath's just over 2,000-acre expanse is home to two squadrons of F-15E Strike Eagle all-weather fighters and one squadron of F-15C Eagle air superiority fighters of the 48th Fighter Wing, an all-time winner of the Air Force Outstanding Unit Award. In 1974, the RAF field at Feltwell came under Lakenheath's control, and today more than 7,000 military and civilian personnel work there, accomplishing the wing's mission as part of the U.S. Air Force, Europe (USAFE).

Housing and Schools. Lakenheath controls over 2,369 units of family housing, which it shares with RAF Mildenhall. This includes about 1,065 leased units. Temporary lodging is available for families in the base visiting officers' and visiting airmen's quarters, with up to a sixty-day reservation, depending upon mission requirements.

Dependent schools on base include kindergarten through twelfth grade, with a middle school at Feltwell. Free transportation is provided for students living within a twenty-five-mile radius of the base. A child-care facility is also available. Off-duty adult educational opportunities are plentiful. The base education center offers courses at Lakenheath and Mildenhall from Embry-Riddle Aeronautical University, the University of Maryland, and the University of Oklahoma.

Personal Services. Lakenheath has the largest medical facility in the U.S. Air Force, Europe. The hospital was renovated in 1993. Medical care at Lakenheath is complete, but dental care for family members is limited and depends on whether time and space are available.

The Lakenheath commissary, which opened in 1986, serves more than 20,000 customers, including personnel from nearby RAF Mildenhall. It carries more than 7,000 line items. The base exchange at RAF Lakenheath carries a full range of department store items. The base also has dry-cleaning services, a service station, and banking facilities. RAF Mildenhall houses a Four Seasons and a toy store, as well as a food court and a 24-hour service station. RAF Feltwell even has a furniture store.

Recreation. Recreational facilities include a gymnasium, a 20,000-volume library, a recreation center, and officers and enlisted clubs. The local rod and gun club offers four skeet ranges and a trap range and leases a 4,500-acre hunting preserve for the exclusive use of its membership. An Olympic-size, heated indoor swimming pool, the only indoor pool in USAFE, is open year-round. Lakenheath also has the only USAF golf course in the United Kingdom, a nine-hole course that also has a pro shop and a steak house. A 24-lane bowling center and hobby shops are also available at the base.

The Local Area. RAF Lakenheath is located in East Anglia, West Suffolk County. East Anglia sticks out into the North Sea and is composed of small market and farming villages. Lakenheath itself is situated in farming and cattle-raising country and boasts a population of around 4,300. The town lies just over the western boundary of the base and consists of only a few shops, a couple of pubs and gas stations, and a magnificent old church. The nearest train stop is Lakenheath Halt, five miles to the north. Thetford, about 12 miles northeast of the base, is a thriving metropolis of 15,700 people. It is chiefly notable as the birthplace of Thomas Paine. The town of Bury Saint Edmunds (population 28,000) lies about 16 miles southeast of the base and is noted for the ancient ruins of the abbey built there to honor the martyred king of the East Angles, Edmund, who was beheaded by the Danes about a thousand years ago.

Newmarket, 15 miles south of the base, has about 14,500 residents, and the beautiful city of Ely is to the west, in the counties of Cambridgeshire and Ely. Ely was a religious center, founded by Saint Etheldreda in 673 A.D., and in 1973, the town celebrated the 1,300th anniversary of its beautiful cathedral.

For more information, write to 48th FW Public Affairs Office, Unit 5210, Box 215, APO AE 09464-0215. Home page: *www.lakenheath.af.mil.*

RAF MILDENHALL

RAF Mildenhall, "Gateway to the United Kingdom," is the aerial port of entry for the majority of U.S. military personnel and their families assigned to the United Kingdom. This is a first-class assignment, with all of the extras and comforts associated with Air Force installations. RAF Mildenhall is also home to the 100th Air Refueling Wing (USAFE), flying 13 KC-135R Stratotankers.

History. RAF Mildenhall was established in 1934. Within six hours of the time England declared war on Germany on 3 September 1939, three Wellington bombers left the field to bomb German battleships. Americans first came to the base in July 1950. Today it is home of the 3rd Air Force, four major Air Force commands, and a U.S. naval flight facility. The base covers about 1,200 acres and has a permanent U.S. military population of about 4,700 personnel. Added to that are 6,000 military dependents, 215 U.S. government employees, and 550 British employees. And at any time there may be as many as 500 military personnel passing through the base on temporary duty.

Housing and Schools. RAF Mildenhall has only 76 family housing units for enlisted members and 42 for officers, but there are an additional 2,178 family housing units in the local area, serving both RAF Mildenhall and RAF Lakenheath. Single enlisted airmen live in the 576 on-base dormitory spaces. There are also 40 temporary-lodging facilities for families.

There are no dependent schools at Mildenhall. Dependent schooling is offered at RAF Lakenheath for children in kindergarten through fifth grade and high school and at RAF Feltwell for grades six through eight. Government transportation is provided for families living within twenty-five miles of the base. The Lakenheath-Mildenhall education center offers a wide selection of courses for adults, from high school completion to postgraduate degrees. Courses are offered from City Colleges of Chicago, Embry-Riddle Aeronautical University, the University of Maryland, Troy State University, and Central Texas College.

Personal Services. Only active-duty personnel may be treated for routine medical problems at the RAF Mildenhall Medical Clinic. Dependent medical care and specialized medical care for active-duty personnel are available at the sixty-bed 48th Medical Group hospital at RAF Lakenheath.

Personnel stationed at Mildenhall use the Lakenheath commissary store, which serves a total of 20,000 people in the area. There are a mini-commissary and a convenience store at Mildenhall, as well as a package liquor store, a doughnut shop, a four-seasons store, a Stars and Stripes bookstore, and some AAFES concessions, such as a service station, a barber and beauty shop, and a laundry and dry cleaner.

Recreation. Recreation facilities at Mildenhall include officers and NCO clubs, a 12-lane bowling alley, a base theater, youth and recreation centers, a physical fitness center, a hobby shop complex, and a three-quarter-mile jogging track/par course. Lakenheath has a nine-hole golf course and a rod and gun club with a 4,500-acre leased preserve for hunting pheasant, partridge, and deer. Lakenheath also offers an Olympic-size indoor swimming pool.

The Local Area. Mildenhall is located in the western part of Suffolk County, which is in the eastern part of England. The town of Mildenhall lies just beyond the southeast corner of the airfield and boasts a population of 10,500. (It's the biggest town within 15 miles of the base.) Adjacent to the north side of the base is Beck Row, a small village with about 3,000 inhabitants. West Row stretches for about a mile along a winding road southwest of the airfield. Mildenhall is close enough to London for those who want big-city life, but it's far enough out in the country to satisfy the person who wants to get away from urban sprawl. To the south and east of the base are low, rolling hills with farms growing barley, sugar beets, wheat, and cattle. Across these hills, some forty miles away, is the North Sea.

For more information, write to Public Affairs Office, 100th Air Refueling Wing (USAFE), Unit 4890, Box 190, APO AE 09459-5000.

THE TRI-BASE COMPLEX, RAF MOLESWORTH

The principal activity at the Tri-Base Complex is the European Command's Joint Analysis Center (JAC). The JAC mission is to analyze, process, and produce intelligence for NATO. The JAC's area of responsibility includes more than 77 countries spread across Europe, Africa, and the Middle East. Its work supports mission planning and operations by U.S., Allied, and NATO commanders during peacetime, crisis situations, and actual war. The host unit providing support to the men and women of the JAC is the 423rd Air Base Squadron (ABS). The 423rd supports a population of 1,400 active-duty personnel, their 2,400 family members, 665 civilian employees, and a retired population of more than 1,300 personnel.

RAF Alconbury is located three miles northeast of the town of Huntingdon and 60 miles north of London. RAF Alconbury was established as a Royal Air Force base in 1938. Various Army Air Corps units utilized the base during World War II. Between the end of the war and the present time, the base was home to selected U.S. Air Force units. The 423rd ABS was commissioned there on 12 July 1995.

RAF Alconbury contains many of the support units and recreational facilities for the complex, such as the family support center, housing office, commissary, base exchange, concessionaires, theater, dependent schooling, and some family housing. These facilities include an elementary, junior high, and high school; an arts and crafts center; an auto craft center; a 12-lane, fully automatic bowling center; a consolidated club, the Stukeley Inn, and a pub/restaurant, the Mole and Newt; a fitness and sports center; a video club; a library; and an outdoor recreation center. The latter offers ski trips, horseback riding tours, whitewater rafting trips, camping, and a well-stocked retail shop.

The Alconbury commissary offers more than 7,500 line items for sale and a fresh bakery and a delicatessen. Note that a ration card is required to purchase tobacco items. The base exchange at Alconbury has a shoppette that carries necessities, such as milk, bread, soda, and some groceries. There is also a frozen food department and a video rental section, as well as a Class Six store. Other services available include a service station, Anthony's Pizza, a Burger King, the ethereal delights of a Baskin Robbins ice cream shop, a beauty and barber shop, and a laundry and dry-cleaning facility.

RAF Molesworth is located 14 miles west of RAF Alconbury and 11 miles northwest of Huntingdon. Hosted are the 423rd ABS command section and orderly room, the JAC, Defense Reutilization and Marketing Office (DRMO), National Imaging and Mapping Agency (NIMA), and other organizational units. supporting U.S. Air Force, Europe, and United States European Command (USEUCOM). Originally established as a bomber base for the Royal Air Force, it was first occupied by the Royal Australian Air Force. The first U.S. units arrived there in 1942. More recently, Molesworth was home to a U.S. tactical missile wing equipped with the cruise missile. Some of the facilities still remaining at Molesworth are subject to inspection under international treaty until well into the year 2001.

RAF Upwood is located to the southwest of the town of Ramsey, about 14 miles from RAF Alconbury. Upwood is a multi-million-dollar complex housing medical outpatient care facilities for authorized users in the Tri-Base Complex area. Most standard medical care is available there. Definitive care is available at RAF Lakenheath, about 48 miles east of RAF Alconbury. RAF Upwood also has housing for enlisted families.

For more information, write to Public Affairs Office, 423 ABS/DPF Unit 5585, Box 100, APO AE 09470, call 011-44-1480-823557 or fax 011-44-1480-823581. Home page: *http://www.famnet.com/usaf/alconbury.*

GERMANY

Air Force

RAMSTEIN AIR BASE

Ramstein Air Base (AB) is one of the six main U.S. air bases in Europe. It is located approximately two miles west of Landstuhl, one and a half miles east of the city of Ramstein, and seven miles west of the city of Kaiserslautern. The base is in the German state of Rheinland-Pfalz.

Ramstein AB is part of the Kaiserslautern Military Community (KMC). The 86th Airlift Wing is the host unit at Ramstein, and the wing commander dually serves as KMC commander. The wing supports four other smaller Air Force installations: Kapaun Air Station, Einsiedlerhof Air Station, Sembach Air Base, and the Vogelweh military complex, which are part of KMC. In addition, Ramstein is the home of Headquarters, U.S. Air Force, Europe; Headquarters, Allied Air Forces Central Europe; and a NATO headquarters, as well as European headquarters elements of Air Mobility Command and Air Education and Training Command.

There are more than 7,600 military members and 1,300 Department of Defense civilians assigned to the base, bringing with them more than 11,000 family members. Ramstein's population also comprises Canadian, German, British, Belgian, and Netherlands forces.

For details on housing, schools, recreation facilities, and personal services, see Kaiserslautern Military Community on page 320. Home page: *www.usafe.mil/bases/ramstein.*

SPANGDAHLEM AIR BASE

History. Spangdahlem Air Base is located in the famous Eifel Region of west-central Germany, an area that has seen war since the days of Attila the Hun. The most recent warrior to visit there was none other than Gen. George S. Patton, "Old Blood and Guts" himself. The Germans staged their Battle of the Bulge offensive from there; the region is also the birthplace of Karl Marx.

Spangdahlem is home to the 52nd Fighter Wing, U.S. Air Force, Europe's largest fighter command. The 52nd has the mission of supporting NATO and

U.S. Forces. The 22nd and 23rd Fighter Squadrons fly the F-16 Fighting Falcon, the 43rd flies the F-15 Eagle, and the 81st flies the A-10 Thunderbolt II.

Housing and Schools. There are 2,196 units of family housing at Spangdahlem—569 units on base, 1,127 units at the Bitburg Annex, and 500 units of leased housing. Waiting time for these quarters can range from immediate occupancy up to two years, depending on the size of the family that requires housing. Transient accommodations for families are available at the temporary-lodging facility at the Bitburg Annex. Local rents vary from $300 a month for one-bedroom apartments to as much as $700 a month for larger units.

Elementary and middle schools are located on Spangdahlem and at the Bitburg Annex, with high school classes also held at the annex. The annex is about nine miles away. Government transportation is provided. Two child-care centers are also available. The base education office offers a number of college courses under the auspices of the Universities of Maryland and Oklahoma, Troy State University, Embry-Riddle Aeronautical University, City Colleges of Chicago, Central Texas College, and the Community College of the Air Force.

Personal Services. The Army and Air Force Exchange Services operates base exchanges at both Spangdahlem and the Bitburg Annex, as well as a number of concessions, including a Burger King and Popeye's. There are also commissaries at both Spangdahlem and Bitburg, carrying some 5,000 line items. NCO and officers clubs are also available.

Recreation. Recreational facilities include a nine-hole golf course, an 18-lane bowling center, hobby and craft shops, a community activities center, and several athletic facilities, including a gym. There is also an outdoor recreation facility with a winter ski club.

The Local Area. One of the most centrally located of all U.S. bases in Europe, Spangdahlem is only a 30-minute drive from Luxembourg, 45 minutes from Belgium, an hour from the French border, and an hour and a half from the Netherlands. The town of Bitburg began as a stopover place for Roman legionnaires 2,000 years ago. At nearby Fliessen is a partly restored Roman villa with well-preserved mosaics. Bitburg was first mentioned as a fortified city known as Bedense in 414 A.D. In 1239, Luxembourg acquired Bitburg and kept it for the next 500 years.

For more information, write to Public Affairs Office, 52nd Fighter Wing, Unit 3680, Box 220, APO AE 09126-0220.

Home page: *www.spangdahlem.af.mil.*

Army

ANSBACH MILITARY COMMUNITY

Ansbach's connection with the Americans began in 1777, when two regiments of soldiers raised there were hired out to Great Britain to fight in the American Revolution. The proceeds of this arrangement went to pay off the city's debts.

Today the 8,000 members of the Ansbach Military Community (AMC) form a potent armed force dedicated to protecting their country's commitment to the NATO Alliance. They occupy several stations in and around Ansbach: the 235th Base Support Battalion at Barton Barracks; the Headquarters of the 1st Infantry Division's 4th Aviation Brigade at Katterbach Kaserne; air defense artillery at Shipton Barracks; and elements of the V Corps' 12th Aviation Brigade at Storck Barracks. Also in the area is "Gruss Gott," as they say in northern Bavaria, and "Willkommen zum Illesheim" (Welcome to Illesheim). The town of Illesheim is a small German town in the state of Franconia with a population of about 4,000 people. It is located about 45 minutes from the historic city of Nurnberg and two hours from Frankfurt. Storck Barracks is named in honor of Colonel Louis J. Storck, U.S. Army. Currently, Storck Barracks serves as the Headquarters for the 11th Aviation Regiment. The 11th aviation mission is to provide support to V Corps. Major units stationed here are the 2nd and 6th Battalions, 6th Cavalry and Headquarters, Headquarters Detachment, and A Company 7th Battalion, 159th Aviation Regiments.

Housing and Schools. There are 1,189 units of family housing available in the AMC, plus 150 government rental units. As of January 1996, there was a thirty-day waiting period for occupancy of these quarters, and soldiers were not authorized housing off post. Children in the AMC attend Department of Defense schools—Ansbach Elementary School in the Katterbach housing area, Rainbow Elementary at Barton Barracks, and Ansbach Junior/Senior High, also in the Katterbach housing area. There is also a child-development center at Katterbach. College courses are available through the Katterbach education center from the University of Maryland, Central Texas College, Embry-Riddle Aeronautical University, and the City Colleges of Chicago.

Personal Services. Medical care is provided by the Katterbach health clinic. Inpatient and specialty treatment are available at Wurzburg Army Hospital, approximately fifty miles from Ansbach. Shuttle-bus transportation is available twice daily. The Katterbach dental clinic offers general dental services and orthodontics. There is a full-service commissary at Katterbach, and just across the street at Bismarck Kaserne is the post exchange. The exchange also operates an auto parts store, a shopette, a four-seasons store at Barton and Shipton Kasernes, a South of the Border Mexican restaurant, an Anthony's Pizza, a Baskin Robbins ice cream shop, and a Burger King at Katterbach Kaserne. A German restaurant is located across the street at Bismarck Kaserne, and at Barton Barracks there is a burger bar open for breakfast and lunch. There is also a post exchange facility at Storck Barracks, as well as a shopette, a restaurant, and a Baskin Robbins.

Recreation. The Katterbach Club and the Von Steuben Club on Bismarck Kaserne are open to all members of the AMC, as is the Fort Apache Club at Storck Barracks. Katterbach and Bismarck Kasernes have a physical fitness center, a bowling alley, and a movie theater. Barton Barracks has an auto craft shop, an outdoor recreation center, an arts and crafts shop, and a physical fitness center.

The Local Area. A city of about 40,000 inhabitants, Ansbach is located in the northern part of the German state of Bavaria and is the capital of Franconia. The area is mentioned in old records as far back as 700 A.D., when it was first settled by a man named Onold, who established himself in the Rezat Valley. Ansbach became a town by 1221 A.D. and was linked to the Hohenzollern Dynasty for almost 500 years. During the latter part of the fifteenth century, it was noted for the magnificent jousts held there during the reign of Albrecht Achilles. The historic core of the city was spared destruction during the Allied bombings of World War II.

For more information, write to Public Affairs Officer, 235th Base Support Battalion, Unit 28614, APO AE 09177. Home page: *www.ansbach.army.mil.*

BAD AIBLING STATION

Nestled in southeastern Germany, 35 miles southeast of Munich, Bad Aibling Station unobtrusively carries on operations underwritten by a long and colorful military tradition. The main mission is intelligence work conducted through Intelligence and Security Command (INSCOM). Operations include rapid radio relay and secure communications, high frequency and satellite operations, communications research and testing, and evaluation of the latest communications equipment.

History. Bad Aibling airfield was intended to support airfields for Hitler's military aggression in the 1930s. Plans for the camp were drawn up in February 1936. Highly skilled architects were selected from all over Germany to collaborate on these plans. (An indication of their importance is the fact that actual construction was begun in May 1936, only three months after planning commenced.) Although the last buildings were not finished until the spring of 1941, the first troops arrived in February 1937 and the first planes were delivered in July 1937. The "peacetime" strength of the camp, as defined in that turbulent era, was 1,000 officers and men. This figure was tripled when the large-scale actual war began in 1939. The famed Messerschmidt fighter (ME-109) was based here at first, giving the camp the nickname of "Jaegerplatz" (Hunter's Place). An interesting historical sidelight is the fact that during the initial stages of excavation, graves were found that dated back to the 30 Years War with Sweden in 1618. This created an appreciable furor in historical and archaeological circles. The field was strafed and bombed in the latter stages of the war, but no damage was done to the camp proper. After the war ended, the camp was utilized as a prisoner of war camp. The majority of the prisoners were from the German southern Army group in Italy, plus local political prisoners. This number was increased when several German generals came from northern Germany to avoid capture by the Russians. After this period, it was utilized by the United Nations Relief and Rehabilitation Agency (UNRRA), the International Refugee Organization (IRO), and as a combination displaced persons camp and orphanage. The U.S. Army took over the camp in 1952; the Department of Defense assumed control from 1972 to 1994. In 1994, the U.S. Army once again assumed control. Today the station is home to 746 military personnel and 900 family members.

Housing and Schools. Government housing is available for active-duty military and their family members. There is a waiting period of ten to twenty days for on-base housing, depending on the bedroom authorization required for the family. There are two, three, and four bedrooms available for government housing. For single servicemembers, there is no waiting period for on-base housing. E-5s and below must live in unaccompanied personnel housing (UPH). E-6s have the choice of living in UPH or living off base. E-7s and above have the choice of living in the senior enlisted quarters or to live off post.

College classes in the United States usually take 16 weeks to complete. In Germany, classes are only eight weeks long. Two- and four-year degrees are offered. For students who cannot fit the traditional programs into their schedule, video and distance (e-mail) education courses are offered. The Department of Defense Dependents Schools provide schooling for command-sponsored students in full-day kindergarten, elementary, middle, and high schools. Bad Aibling has one school for all grades, due to the small enrollment of students. During the 1999 school year, there were approximately 150 elementary students, 45 middle school students, and 40 students in grades nine through twelve. High school classes range in size from five to thirteen, while the elementary students average near 18 students per class.

Personal Services. The Bad Aibling health clinic is not intended for the treatment of life-threatening or serious emergencies. The Bad Aibling clinic is supported by an American physician and by other German- and English-speaking local national physicians who provide excellent quality medical care.

Bad Aibling Station does not have a dental facility. The closest dental facility is Garmisch, which is two hours away. There is a dental van that comes to Bad Aibling quarterly.

Recreation. While small, there are amenities that include an auto hobby and wood shop, a six-lane bowling alley, arcades, a fitness and outdoor recreation center, a full-service restaurant, a library, and a crafts and photo shop. There is no officers or enlisted club.

The Local Area. Bad Aibling, a picturesque resort, is an ancient town with a compelling history. In 1844, Aibling became the first mud bath resort in Bavaria. It was in the Ludwigsbad Hotel that Dr. Desiderius Beck founded the first salt and mud bath establishment, with himself as proprietor. Today Bad Aibling is not only known for its peat baths but also for its central location. Bad Aibling is a great place to live, especially if you like to travel. Nearby cities include Munich, Salzburg, and Venice. For more information, write to Bad Aibling Station, CMR 407, HOC 718MI, APO AE 09098.

BAD KREUZNACH MILITARY COMMUNITY

If you suffer from rheumatism, gout, spinal troubles, circulatory problems, lung trouble, female disorders, or all of the above, Bad Kreuznach might be just the place for you. Since 1817, when a young doctor discovered that the springs in the area had healing properties, the noble and the rich have visited the town seeking a cure for all of those ailments.

History. The U.S. Army first came to Bad Kreuznach in 1945, when it took over Hindenburg Kaserne from the German Army. In July 1945, the French relieved the Americans and renamed their headquarters Marshal Foch Kaserne. In July 1951, the U.S. 2nd Armored Division took over the kaserne and renamed it Maurice Rose Kaserne, in honor of Maj. Gen. Maurice Rose, a hero of World War II. From December 1957 to 17 January 1991, it was the home of the 8th Infantry Division. On that January date, the 8th Infantry Division was inactivated and redesignated the 1st Armored Division, the current occupant of the kaserne.

Today Bad Kreuznach Military Community, 410th Base Support Battalion (BSB), is part of the 53rd Area Support Group. The BSB and the headquarters of the Division Engineer Brigade are at Marshall Kaserne; the headquarters of the 1st Armored Division and the 141st Signal Battalion occupy Rose Kaserne; and the headquarters of the 53rd Area Support Group, the 9th General Hospital, the 766th Dental Detachment, and the high school are located at Hospital Kaserne. The 123rd Support Battalion and the 501st Military Intelligence Battalion are situated at Anderson Barracks, near the small town of Dexheim.

Housing and Schools. There are 950 family housing units in the Bad Kreuznach-Dexheim community, almost all of them government owned, and 216 more in Dexheim. There are 34 rooms available as transient quarters in Bad Kreuznach. The 410th BSB has a high school, an elementary school, and two child-care centers in Bad Kreuznach and an elementary school and a child-care center at Dexheim. A variety of college courses is offered through the education office.

Personal Services. A full range of support facilities is available in the community. Army and Air Force Exchange Service facilities include a post exchange, cafeterias, a convenience store, an auto garage, a gas station, and a coin laundry, located near the dependent housing areas at Bad Kreuznach and Dexheim, and a commissary at Dexheim. The nearby communities of Wiesbaden, Kaiserslautern, and Frankfurt offer similar facilities.

Recreation. Recreational activities and programs here are among the best available anywhere in Europe. Two bowling centers are operated in the community, a ten-lane center in Bad Kreuznach and a four-lane center in Dexheim. Dexheim is also home to the Rheinlander Club, open to personnel of all ranks, as well as civilians. The Nahe Club, on the edge of Bad Kreuznach near the bachelor officer quarters, is open to officers, enlisted personnel in the senior grades, and civilians; the Century Club, located near Rose Barracks, is open to all enlisted personnel. Dexheim also has its own recreation facilities and a library. An auto hobby shop, a library, and a tour office and travel section are located at Rose Barracks.

The primary outdoor recreation facility at Bad Kreuznach is the Kuhberg Recreational Complex, almost three miles southeast of Rose Barracks. The complex has 26 paved camping pads, numerous primitive tent sites, large picnic sites with tables and grills, two pavilions, a miniature golf course, an archery range, and a playground. The complex is open year-round.

The Local Area. The climate in this part of Germany is characterized by an early spring and a long-lasting fall, with relatively mild winters and cool summers.

The city of Bad Kreuznach dates back to about 839 A.D., when it was first mentioned in old records, although excavations have revealed Roman ruins dating from much earlier. The city is nestled at the foot of the Hunsruck Mountains on the winding Nahe River. Bad Kreuznach has a resident population of 43,000, which swells temporarily during the summer, as thousands of tourists and health seekers come to visit the springs and baths.

There are a number of excellent restaurants in the city, among them Fausthaus, supposedly the residence of the legendary Dr. Faust, whom the poet Johann Wolfgang von Goethe immortalized in his poem Faust. Another attraction is the ruins of Kauzenburg Castle, originally built in 1206 on a hill overlooking the valley. In its dungeon, visitors can enjoy a "knight's meal." Among the city's most famous landmarks are the so-called fifteenth-century bridge houses, built on a 700-year-old bridge that spans the Nahe. The location is also noted for its wine, which can be favorably compared to the more famous vintages from the Rhein and Mosel areas. Every year, on the first full weekend following 15 August, Bad Kreuznach holds its Jahrmarkt, a five-day festival akin to a state fair. The Rhine River is only nine miles from Bad Kreuznach and offers many historic castles, camping sites, and wine fests.

For more information, write to HQ, 410th BSB, Attention: PAO, Unit 23408, APO AE 09252.

BAMBERG MILITARY COMMUNITY

Bamberg, like Rome, is built on seven hills. The Regnitz River cuts a path through the valley, dividing the city into two sections, the Bishop's Town and the Burgher's Town. The civic center of the town is the small islet formed by the two arms of the river. This area is reserved for pedestrians, small shops, and open-air markets; across the river, on the surrounding hills, are the spires of the churches that dominate the high ground in the "ecclesiastical" section of the city. Because the city was not bombed during the war, Bamberg is one place where you can see what Germany looked like before the war, and it is an experience you'll never forget.

The principal installation in the Bamberg Military Community (BMC) is Warner Barracks, named in honor of Pfc. Henry F. Warner, who was killed in action near there in 1945. The principal units are the 7th Corps Support Group and the 71st Combat Support Battalion. Altogether, approximately 8,500 military personnel, family members, and Department of the Army civilians live and work in the community.

Housing and Schools. There are 747 family housing units available in the BMC. Two school facilities for dependents are operated in the community—one elementary school and one high school. The BMC also has two child-care centers. The education center offers a number of services, including college-level programs.

Personal Services. Medical care is provided by the 188th General Dispensary and a dental clinic. Both facilities offer a number of specialty clinics for outpatient treatment. Inpatient services are available at the Bamberg city clinic or the U.S. hospital at Wurzburg. The BMC has a post exchange that operates several concessions, including a Burger King, a shopette, a snack bar, an auto parts store, a beauty shop, and a service station. There are also a commissary and a club system.

Recreation. Recreational facilities include a bowling alley, a gymnasium, a recreation center, an arts and crafts shop, an entertainment center, a teen center, a movie theater, a rod and gun club with its own fishing lake, and a nine-hole golf course. Hunting facilities are available in state-owned forests. Excursion trips are offered to places such as the Armed Forces Recreation Center in Garmisch.

The Local Area. The city of Bamberg today has a population of more than 72,000 people, although the number of inhabitants was presumably much smaller when invading Franks established a castle, the Altenberg, on the site in 531 A.D. In 1007, Emperor Henry II gained control of the city. The center of the town is its magnificent cathedral, built in the late thirteenth century, which contains numerous art treasures of medieval times, including the "Bamberger Rider." An example of virtually every style of architecture since the Romanesque period can be seen in this city.

For more information, write to Public Affairs Office, 279th BSB, Unit 27535, APO AE 09139. Home page: *www.bamberg.army.mil.*

BAUMHOLDER MILITARY COMMUNITY

Known as the "Home of Champions," Baumholder's 222nd Base Support Battalion is stationed in the wooded hills of the Western Palatinate in the German federal state of Rheinland-Pfalz, only 30 miles from the French and Luxembourg borders.

History. The German army came to Baumholder in 1938; here German and Austrian units trained for service on the various fronts of World War II. The training area was bombed extensively by the Allies in 1944. In 1945, the post surrendered without a fight, and between 1945 and 1951, it was occupied by the French. In 1951, American forces took over most of the area. Today Baumholder's H. D. Smith Barracks is home to the 12,000 soldiers, civilians, and family members of the 1st Armored Division's 2nd Brigade and Division Artillery.

Housing and Schools. There are over 2,000 sets of family quarters available to personnel stationed at Baumholder, as well as 488 government-leased quarters. Waiting periods for occupancy for two-bedroom units, as of the summer of 2000, ranged from 10 to 60 days. Temporary quarters and guest accommodations are available on post. Schooling is provided for children in kindergarten through twelfth grade through the Wetzel Elementary School and Baumholder High School, operated by the Department of Defense Dependents Schools. College courses for adults are available through the University of Maryland, Central Texas College, and the City Colleges of Chicago.

Personal Services. Medical care is provided by the U.S. Army Health Clinic, Baumholder, a full-service medical facility. Specialized and long-term medical care is available at the Landstuhl Regional Medical Center, about a 45-minute drive from Baumholder. Free shuttle-bus service is available daily. There are a commissary and post exchange, plus various concessions, such as a Book Mark, a car sales outlet, a garage, a gas station, two barber shops, a beauty shop, a four-seasons shop, a flower shop, a coin laundry, and shopettes in the Smith and Wetzel housing areas.

Recreation. Recreational facilities include a family activity center with an indoor pool, outdoor recreation, arts and crafts, a campground, and a golf course. Baumholder also has a rod and gun club, two gyms, a video rental and video arcade, a bowling alley, a Burger King, a Baskin Robbins, an Anthony's Pizza, a movie theater, a post library, and all major outdoor sports.

The Local Area. The first recorded mention of Baumholder is found in a document dated 1156. Portions of the original town wall, the funeral gate, and the "thick tower" date from the 1500s, which is comparatively recent in this area. The history of this region dates as far back as 5000 B.C., when a Celtic tribe known as the Treverians lived there. The Romans took over in 52 B.C. In the fourth and fifth centuries A.D., the Germanic tribes migrated into the area. The Franks settled the region around 500 A.D.

Baumholder is located in a rural, hilly area reached via narrow, winding roads. Kaiserslautern, the Mosel River, and the French border are all within a 50-mile radius of Baumholder. Baumholder is at an elevation of about 1,800 feet and enjoys a climate comparable to the Pacific Northwest. The summers are mild and short, and the winters are cold and damp. In summer, the highs average around 75° F, and in winter, the lows average around 25° F. The nearest town to Baumholder, Idar-Oberstein, is twelve miles to the north.

For more information, write to Public Affairs Office, 222nd Base Support Battalion, Unit 23746, Box 32, APO AE 09034. Home page: *www.baumholder.army.mil.*

FRIEDBERG/GIESSEN DEPOT

Elvis Presley slept here! Germany was considered the crossroads of Europe, and even the king of rock 'n' roll rolled through this area. Soldiers assigned to First Brigade will be stationed at Ray Barracks, Friedberg, or Giessen Depot, Giessen. Here the action centers on the M1A1 tank and the M2A2 Bradley. When you come here, be prepared to assist in conducting the many peacekeeping operations that have kept U.S. forces engaged in European affairs during the 1990s.

History. Friedberg is a town with a history that goes back to 11 B.C. Friedberg's history as a garrison town dates back to 1645, when a company was formed there to guard the castle. Ray Barracks, known as Wattrum Kaserne, was originally built in 1900 and used during World Wars I and II. During World War I, captured Russian, French, and English officers were confined to the kaserne. During World War II, the kaserne was occupied by two German infantry battalions. Giessen, the capital of the former province of Upper Hessen, lies in the confluence of the Wieseck and Lahn Rivers. The Lahn River valley is bounded by the foothills of the Taunus and Vogelsberg Mountains. Friedberg's history dates back to 11 B.C., when it was a boundry outpost for the Roman Empire. Bad Nauheim housing area, located 15 minutes from Ray Barracks in the Usa River valley at the foot of Johannisberg Hill, has been colonized for several thousand years. Precious salt water from the springs bubbling up through the ground has drawn people to this area for a long time. Excavation findings from the stone age, bronze age, iron age, and from Celtic and Germanic settlements, as well as from Roman and Franconian cultures, were found throughout the area. The first American units occupied the kaserne in 1945. Various commands used the barracks until Combat Command C moved in on 13 February 1953. The barracks were named in honor of 1st Lt. Bernard J. Ray, Company I, 8th Infantry Regiment, who was awarded the Medal of Honor after his death. And yes, among the more notable personages who have served at Ray Barracks is the late Elvis Presley!

Housing and Schools. Current waiting periods for family housing depends on rank, with enlisted persons waiting one to three months and officers from zero to two months. The approximate waiting time for temporary quarters is two to four weeks. Most soldiers will be given temporary quarters in Giessen, which will create transportation difficulties if your car has not arrived. All elementary and high school education resources that serve the 284th BSB are Department of Defense Dependent Schools. For information on adult education, the Ray Barracks and Giessen Depot education centers provide education services to active-duty military personnel, Department of Defense civilians, and family members. Undergraduate and graduate-level college programs and proficiency and military testing services are among the many programs offered. The centers offer information and testing for the general education degree (GED).

Kindergarteners must be five years old on or before 31 October the year they enter school. Students in grades one through six attend either Bad Nauheim Elementary School, Butzbach Elementary School, or Giessen Elementary School. Students in grades seven through twelve attend the Giessen High School, approximately 45 minutes by bus from Friedberg. For any additional information, contact the schools' liaison office at 0641-402-7047.

Personal Services. Active-duty members have first priority for medical services and are entitled to complete and qualified treatment. Family members are second priority and are entitled to medical services. This service depends upon space availability and facilities. Retired members and their family members, as well as the family members of deceased retirees, are provided service on a space-available basis. Care for Department of Defense civilian employees is provided on a space-available fee basis. Care can be obtained through the two major Army hospitals located in Heidelberg and Landstuhl or in one of the area clinics or dispensaries. Individuals can also be referred to medical care on the economy. The nearest commissary serving the Giessen Community is located in Giessen. The nearest full-service post exchange is located at Pendleton Barracks, just a few blocks from Giessen Depot. There is a large commissary and exchange complex at Wolfgang Kaserne, Hanau, approximately 45 minutes from Friedberg and one hour and fifteen minutes from Giessen. AAFES has facilities throughout the 104th Area Support Group area, which include retail stores, service stations, shoppettes, book stores, military clothing sales, a four-seasons shop, Class Six and beverage shops, and Power Zones. Other AAFES facilities include barber and beauty shops, a Burger King, a Popeye's, other food concessions and clubs, laundromats, alteration shops, and movie theaters.

Recreation. Available are arts and crafts centers, bowling centers, libraries, sports and fitness centers, outdoor recreation centers, and more. The military clubs feature fine dining and a variety of evening entertainment. Special events, such as Monte Carlo night, bingo, Sunday brunch, and live bands, are often available. The sports and fitness centers provide opportunities for both individual and team sports. Among activities available are aerobics, weight training, basketball, racquetball, volleyball, boxing, flag football, softball, and other programs.

The Local Area. In this small area, there are 10,492 active-duty troops with 5,296 family members, 4,300 retirees, and 442 civilian employees, both providing and using service and support. It is an engaging and educational experience for those living here. The largest (interior measurements) remaining castle in Germany is located in Friedberg and invites visitors to experience a taste of medieval history. Central Germany lies at the same latitude as southern Canada, a fact that says more about daylight hours in the country than it does about weather. Summer days in Germany are long, from approximately 4:30 A.M. to 9 P.M. hours; winter days are short, at their shortest getting light about 8:30 A.M. and getting dark about 4:30 P.M. hours. But weather? Well, it's similar to the weather in the northwestern United States. There's plenty of rain. In the summer, the temperature can get into the 90s, but seldom for more than a couple of weeks. In winter, the temperature is often below freezing. The coldest weather (obviously) is in the Alps; Germany's warmest area is the Upper Rhine Valley, in the southwest.

For more information, write to Public Affairs Office, HQ, 7th Army Training Command, Unit 28130, APO AE 09114-5412.

GRAFENWOEHR TRAINING CENTER

A lot of unpleasant comments have been made about "Graf" over the years, no doubt inspired by the post's isolation (60 miles east of Nurnberg), its unpredictable weather (the temperature dipped to freezing there one day in August 1987), and the rigors of the military training that goes on there almost year-round. But residents know Graf as one of the cleanest and most picturesque areas in Germany, and though sunbathing days are scarce during the summer months, the climate is invigorating and a long stay there will endear you to the post and its charming rural environs.

History. Grafenwoehr Training Center's history began in 1907, when it was selected as the training site for the Bavarian III Corps Artillery. Construction began in 1908, and the first artillery round was fired there in 1910. The training area was expanded in the 1930s to accommodate the growing Wehrmacht, and during World War II, thousands of Allied prisoners of war were interned there.

The U.S. Army came to Grafenwoehr in 1945, and in 1958, the 7th Army Training Center was established there. In July 1976, the site was redesignated the 7th Army Training Command. Today Grafenwoehr's 56,615 acres are home to Headquarters, 7th Army Training Command; the 100th Area Support Group; and a number of tenant units, with over 2,500 soldiers and family members and 3,100 German and American civilian employees.

Housing and Schools. Grafenwoehr has 554 units of family housing. Waiting periods vary, depending upon the size and category of unit needed. A limited number of transient billets are reserved for arriving and departing families. Reservations are accepted ninety days in advance.

An elementary school with a student enrollment of over 400 is operated on post. There are intermediate and high schools in Vilseck, about 15 miles from the Grafenwoehr main post. Day-care and preschool facilities are also available.

Personal Services and Recreation. Medical care is provided by a general-health clinic on the main post. Inpatient and specialized outpatient care is available at Nurnberg. The Grafenwoehr dental clinic is a 12-chair facility staffed with three dental officers and a hygienist.

The post offers a full range of personal services and recreational facilities, including a commissary, a post exchange, clubs, a theater, a golf course, a 24-lane bowling alley, craft shops, a rod and gun club, and a recreation center. A Burger King and a Chi Chi's restaurant on the main post are sure to tickle the tastebuds of all newcomers. The field house is one of the best in Germany, featuring saunas, cardiovascular and weight machines, Nautilus equipment, racquetball courts, and qualified instructors for a variety of sports.

The Local Area. The Grafenwoehr Training Center is located fifty-five miles north of Nurnberg, in the heart of the "Franconian Alps," a land of rolling, thickly forested hills stretching from the city of Nurnberg to the Czechoslovakian border, which is about 30 miles due east of the main post area. Hunting, fishing, and hiking are the major sporting activities in the area. The major local industry is farming. Traveling along the area's backcountry roads on an early summer morning is one of the finest and rarest pleasures to be found in Germany, and the food offered in the local gasthauses (not to mention the German beer!) is delectable.

The climate in this part of Germany is temperate, with many cool, wet days throughout the year. Heavy fog is common in all seasons. Summer temperatures average 75° F, and winter temperatures often dip below freezing; heavy snow is rare.

For more information, write to Public Affairs Office, HQ, 7th Army Training Command, Unit 28130, APO AE 09114-5412.

HANAU MILITARY COMMUNITY

Located about 20 miles southeast of Frankfurt, Germany, the Hanau Military Community is home to approximately 12,000 military and civilian personnel and their families. The Hanau Military Community consists of 17 individual kasernes located in four cities: Hanau, Erlensee, Buedingen, and Gelnhausen. The Hanau Military Community is home to numerous units with a variety of missions. The largest units include the 4th Brigade of the 1st Armored Division and the 709th Military Police Battalion on Fliegerhorst Kaserne in Erlensee; the 130th Engineer Brigade on Pioneer Kaserne; the 18th Corps Support Group on Hutier Kaserne; the 1-1 Cavalry Squadron on Armstrong Kaserne in Buedingen; and the 5/7 Air Defense Artillery Battalion on Underwood Kaserne. The 414th Base Support Battalion, whose higher headquarters, 104th Area Support Group, is also located in Hanau, maintains the Hanau Military Community's activities and upkeep.

Housing. There are approximately 1,800 sets of family quarters available throughout the 414th BSB. As of October 1999, the average waiting period for occupancy for all grades was four months. A one-bedroom, unfurnished apartment on the local economy rented for about $550, plus an estimated $150 a month for utilities. Guest housing is available at the New Argonner and Pioneer Inns in Hanau and at the Coppertop Inn in Gelnhausen. For billeting reservations, call 011-49-6181-88-1700 (from the United States).

Schools. Children attend Department of Defense Dependents Schools (kindergarten through twelfth grade) in the local area. There are three elementary schools, one middle school, and one high school. College-level courses are available through the education center from the University of Maryland, University of Oklahoma, Embry-Riddle Aeronautical University, City Colleges of Chicago, and Cameron University.

Personal Services and Recreation. Medical and dental care are provided by the Hanau health clinic on New Argonner Kaserne and the Buedingen health clinic on Armstrong Kaserne. Inpatient and emergency care are provided by local German hospitals, located no more than ten minutes from any housing area. The nearest U.S. military hospital is in Heidelberg, a two-hour drive from Hanau.

A commissary and post exchange are located at Wolfgang Shopping Complex in Hanau. This complex also offers a garden center and toyland, a Class Six store, a Book Mark, a service mart, barber and beauty shops, military clothing sales, a thrift shop, photo processing and banking facilities, German and U.S. postal offices, a car wash center, video rentals, a Burger King, a Frank's Franks, a Baskin Robbins, and a Popeye's. Recreational facilities at Wolfgang include a bowling center, a roller rink, an arts and crafts center, a music center, a sports store, and an outdoor store. Pioneer Kaserne offers video rental, a service mart, a shoppette, a movie theater, a burger bar, a launderette, the Flood Zone club, a library, a gym, a chapel, and an AAFES gas station and auto repair facility. Fliegerhorst Kaserne in Erlensee offers a video rental, a shoppette, the Modernaire Club, a community bank, a gym, a launderette, and a chapel. Coleman Housing in Gelnhausen offers a commissary and a video rental. Armstrong Kaserne in Buedingen offers a commissary, a post exchange, a shoppette, a gym, a chapel, a library, the Blackhawk Club, a bowling center, and a thrift shop.

For more information, write to Relocation Program Manager at Army Community Service, 414th BSB, ATTN: ACS-Relocation, Unit 20193, Box 0006, APO AE 09165. Home pages: *www.dmdc.osd.mil/sites* (choose Hanau) and *www.hanau.army.mil;* e-mail: *SITE1615@414bsbexch.hanau.army.mil.*

HEIDELBERG MILITARY COMMUNITY

Heidelberg holds a half-million years of human history, beginning with the Heidelberg Man, whose jawbone was discovered there in 1907, and continuing through the Romans down to the present time. Today Heidelberg is a city of about 150,000, including the student body at Heidelberg University, founded in 1386.

The personnel assigned to the Heidelberg Military Community (HMC) comprise the staff of Headquarters, U.S. Army Europe and 7th Army; HQ V Corps; the 7th Medical Command; Allied Land Forces Central Europe (LANDCENT); the 1st Personnel Command; and various support groups. The total U.S. population in the HMC, civilian and military, is 18,000.

History. The first U.S. troops entered Heidelberg on Good Friday 1945. The HMC today comprises nineteen separate installations, or *kasernes* (German for "barracks"), most originally built between 1890 and 1939. Most of these survived the war intact, since Heidelberg was largely spared the devastating air raids of World War II.

On the south side of the city are Campbell Barracks and the family housing area known as Mark Twain Village. Just south of Campbell Barracks in Nachtrichten Kaserne is the Heidelberg Hospital and Headquarters, 7th Medical Command. To the northwest of Campbell Barracks is Patton Barracks, headquarters for the HMC and the site of troop barracks. To the west of Campbell, across the autobahn, is Patrick Henry Village, a 250-acre complex built in the 1950s and home to more than 3,500 American troops and their families. Other areas include the Heidelberg Army Airfield, a forty-five-acre complex in the southwest corner of the city, and the Koenigstuhl Relay Station.

The shopping center, across Czernyring from the Heidelberg Main Railway Station, houses the commissary, the main post exchange, and other exchange outlets.

In nearby Schwetzingen are Kilbourne and Tompkins Barracks, where troop housing and the 1st Personnel Command headquarters are located. Stem Kaserne, between Mannheim and Heidelberg, is home to the Criminal Investigation Command's Second Region.

Housing and Schools. More than 2,000 units of government housing are available to eligible soldiers—those serving a thirty-six-month accompanied tour with command-sponsored families.

Dependent schooling is available throughout the HMC: a high school at Mark Twain Village; elementary and middle schools at Patrick Henry Village; and child-care centers at Mark Twain and Patrick Henry Villages and the Heidelberg Hospital Kaserne. Adult education programs are available through centers located at Campbell, Tompkins, and Patton Barracks and Patrick Henry Village.

Personal Services. Medical and dental services are provided by the 130th Station Hospital. Full commissary and post exchange services are available at the downtown shopping center complex. Also available there are a liquor store, a garage, an auto parts store, a recreational equipment rental service, a bank and credit union, an optical shop, a bookstore, an audio store, a snack bar, and other facilities.

Recreation. The HMC offers a variety of military clubs for entertainment and dining: the Recovery Room at Nachrichten Kaserne and the Village Pavilion club and Lexington's at Patrick Henry Village. The Heidelberg Rod and Gun Club offers rifle, pistol, and shotgun ranges; archery; a sports equipment store; a picnic area; and a restaurant and bar that serves a variety of German and American food at reasonable prices. Library facilities are available at Patrick Henry Village and Campbell Barracks. Baseball fields, basketball and tennis courts, gymnasiums, a movie theater at Patrick Henry Village, and an 18-hole golf course round out the recreational picture.

The Local Area. Heidelberg is nestled on the Neckar River in south-central Germany, between Stuttgart to the south and Frankfurt to the north. Many of the city's ancient buildings, some dating from the twelfth century, are still standing. Visitors can enjoy tours along the Neckar, and the German Grand Prix is held at the Hockenheim Race Track, about seven miles from the city. Heidelberg is only ninety minutes from the Black Forest.

For more information, write to Commander, 26th Area Support Group, Attention: PAO, Unit 29237, APO AE 09102.

HOHENFELS COMBAT MANEUVER TRAINING CENTER

The Hohenfels Combat Maneuver Training Center is part of the 7th Army Training Command. Located in the state of Bavaria, Hohenfels is the largest maneuver area (as opposed to live-fire area) for the U.S. Army, Europe. Approximately 2,000 soldiers train there each month.

History. The training area takes its name from the rural town of Hohenfels (population 2,200), located one mile east of the center's boundary. Known history in these parts dates back to about 50 B.C., when Julius Caesar led his army in the conquest of the Celtic and Gallic tribes in that area. In 946 A.D., the count of Hohenfels built a castle on a steep rock above the valley. Part of the castle still stands in the center of town.

In 1938, the German army established a training area north of the town. After the collapse of the Third Reich, the camp served as a reception area for displaced persons. In 1951, U.S. forces claimed the area for military training. Today it covers a total area of some 40,000 acres and is home to the 1st Battalion, 4th Infantry Regiment, which acts as the opposing force for all units training at Hohenfels. Other units stationed at Hohenfels include the 282nd Base Support Battalion and A Company, 94th Engineers, a heavy-construction unit. Altogether, over 5,900 military and civilian personnel call Hohenfels home.

Housing and Schools. There are 539 sets of government-owned and built-to-lease family quarters located both on and off post. Guest housing is available, but limited. On-post schools for dependent children in kindergarten through high school, as well as preschool and day-care facilities, are available, as are a number of college-level courses.

Personal Services and Recreation. Definitive medical care is provided by local German hospitals and the U.S. Army hospital in Wurzburg, about 120 miles from Hohenfels. The 731st General Dispensary and the 561st Medical Detachment provide medical and dental treatment, respectively.

Hohenfels has a new commissary, a new post exchange, a cafeteria, two shopettes, and several clubs. Recreational facilities include a new theater, a gym with an annex, a bowling alley, a recreation center, and automotive, photo, ceramics, and leather craft shops. Two swimming pools are available in the town of Parsberg (eight miles away), and there is a golf course in the town of Schmidmuhlen (12 miles away).

The Local Area. The climate in the Hohenfels area is generally mild, but the weather can be unpredictable. Winter occasionally brings snow, and roads are sometimes covered by freezing rain, particularly in the morning and evening hours. Temperatures in winter dip occasionally into the 20s. Summers are generally cool, with temperatures sometimes rising into the 80s. The area is quite picturesque and is among the environmentally cleanest in Germany. The nearest big cities are Nurnberg (sixty miles away) and Regensburg (thirty miles away).

For more information, write to Commander, 282nd BSB, Attention: SB-PTMS-PAO, Unit 28216, APO AE 09173.

KAISERSLAUTERN MILITARY COMMUNITY

Kaiserslautern earned its name because it was once the favorite hunting retreat of Kaiser (Emperor) Frederick I, known as Barbarossa ("Red Beard"), who ruled the Holy Roman Empire from 1155 to 1190. When Barbarossa built his castle there between 1152 and 1160, the Lauter River was an important stream that actually formed the center of the town into an island, and today the remains of Barbarossa's castle can still be seen in front of the city hall (Rathaus). In fact, the shield of the city depicts an open-mouthed carp on it, and it is said that this fish was the emperor's favorite dish, but that may again be nothing more than a fish story.

History. Americans came to Kaiserslautern in March 1945. Today the Kaiserslautern Military Community (KMC) includes a number of installations: Ramstein, seven miles west of the city; Landstuhl (see separate entry); Miesau; and Pirmasens. The Army's 415th Base Support Battalion at Kleber Kaserne provides support to the community. Other units include the Headquarters of the 21st Theater Area Command at Panzer Kaserne; Headquarters, 37th Transportation Command at Kleber; the 29th Area Support Group at Daenner and Pulaski Kasernes; the 119th Ordnance Battalion at Miesau Arms Depot; and other units.

Kleber Kaserne has been occupied by troops since 1913, when it was called the Twenty-third Kaserne, after the 23rd Bavarian Regiment, which built it. After World War I, it was temporarily occupied by French troops, including Vietnamese motorized support troops. After World War II, the French again occupied the post and renamed it in honor of Gen. Jean Baptist Kleber, a famous general under Napoleon. In the early 1950s, the U.S. Army moved in and rebuilt much of the kaserne.

On the western side of town are the Vogelweh Complex, the Pulaski Barracks, and the Rhine Ordnance Barracks (home for the 39th Transportation Battalion and a battery of the 7th Air Defense Artillery). The Vogelweh Complex includes the largest family housing area in Europe. The westernmost installation is the Landstuhl Regional Medical Center.

Housing and Schools. The 35,000 Americans who live and work in the KMC constitute one of the largest American communities outside the United States. There are 593 housing units for officers and 4,928 for enlisted personnel. The housing office is operated by the 86th Airlift Wing at Ramstein Air Base and serves both Army and Air Force personnel. The waiting period for occupancy depends on grade and the size of quarters needed.

The KMC operates eleven separate schools for dependent children, with an approximate enrollment of 7,500 students. There are an elementary, middle, and high school at Kaiserslautern; an elementary school at Vogelweh; two elementary schools and a junior high at Ramstein; an elementary/middle school at Landstuhl; an elementary/middle school at Sembach; and an elementary school at Pirmasens. Child-development centers are available at Kleber Kaserne, Landstuhl, Miesau, Pirmasens, Ramstein, Sembach, and Vogelweh. Transportation to and from these schools is provided by government contract buses.

Adult education is offered through the education centers at Kleber Kaserne, Rhine Ordnance Barracks, Miesau, Pirmasens, Ramstein, Sembach, and Vogelweh and consists of extension courses from Central Texas College, City Colleges of Chicago, Embry-Riddle Aeronautical University, and the University of Maryland.

Personal Services. The major medical facility in the area is the Landstuhl Regional Medical Center, the largest U.S. medical facility in Europe. There are branch health and dental clinics at Kleber Kaserne, Vogelweh, and Ramstein.

The KMC has commissary stores at Pirmasens, Ramstein, Sembach, and Vogelweh. Exchanges are located at Pirmasens, Ramstein, and Vogelweh. Shopettes are available at Kleber Kaserne, Panzer Kaserne, Rhine Ordnance Barracks, Landstuhl, Miesau, Ramstein, Sembach, and Vogelweh.

The club system in the KMC is extensive, with the Landstuhl Combined Community Club, Miesau Combined Club, Ramstein Enlisted Club, Ramstein Officers Club, Sembach Officers Club, Sembach All-ranks Club, Vogelweh Kazabra All-ranks Club, and Armstrong's at Vogelweh.

KMC also offers ten barber shops, six beauty shops, four bookstores, three car washes, five Class VI stores, three flower shops, three four-seasons stores/toylands, three garages, four gas stations, five laundries, six libraries, three optical shops, and eleven snack bars and food malls, including complexes at Ramstein and Vogelweh. The Ramstein food mall offers a Baskin Robbins, La Casa de Amigos Mexican food, Robin Hood Sandwiches and Salads, Frank's Franks, Anthony's Pizza, Sweet Reflections, a doughnut shop, the German Kanteen, Burger King, Popeye's, and a delicatessen. The Vogelweh complex is similar to Ramstein's, except that it has a fish and chips and a potato bar and offers pizza delivery.

Recreation. The recreational picture in the KMC is bright. There are three arts and crafts centers, seven auto craft and hobby centers, three auto parts stores, seven bowling centers, a golf course at Ramstein, ten gyms, six movie theaters, four outdoor recreational equipment checkouts, three recreation centers, the Vogelweh Rod and Gun Club, the Vogelweh roller rink, three sports shops, seven tennis courts, and video rentals at Pirmasens, Ramstein, Sembach, and Vogelweh. In addition, the USOs at Kleber Kaserne, Landstuhl, Miesau, Ramstein, and Vogelweh offer a series of inexpensive one-day tours to such places as Paris, Holland, Heidelberg, Frankfurt, the Verdun battlefield, and the Rhine River.

For those who enjoy the outdoors, there is the 42-mile Barbarossa Hiking Trail (Barbarossa-Wanderweg) around Kaiserslautern. This is a part of the West Pfalz Hiking Network and takes about four days to walk. Bookings include overnights, breakfasts, and baggage transfer.

The Local Area. Over 60 percent of Kaiserslautern was destroyed during World War II, but since then it has been totally rebuilt and now has a population of 160,000. Ramstein has a population of about 18,000, and Landstuhl has a population of 10,000. The weather in this part of Germany is moderate, with lots of rain and occasionally some fog. Measurable rainfall is recorded on an average of 149 days a year. Winters are generally not too severe, with morning lows around 15° F and afternoon highs averaging between 30 and 45° F.

People have been living in this area since at least as early as 800 B.C., as evidenced by some Celtic tombs uncovered in the Miesau area. By 250 B.C., the Romans occupied the area. In the fourth and sixth centuries A.D., a German tribe known as the Franconians settled in the area. The first fortress or castle was built here in 622 A.D. The oldest church in Kaiserslautern was constructed from 1250 to 1350; Saint Martin's Kirche was built from 1300 to 1350, and in part of the church's rear yard, a section of the original city wall still stands.

For more information, write to Commander, 415th Base Support Battalion, Attention: AEUSG-K-ACS, Unit 21352, APO AE 09227. Home page: *www.hqusareur.army.mil.*

KITZINGEN MILITARY COMMUNITY

In the year 745 A.D., the countess of Schwanberg, according to legend, lost her bejeweled scarf while walking along the battlements of her castle, high above the Main River valley where the town of Kitzingen now stands. She promised to build a cloister on the spot where the scarf was found. When a shepherd named Kitz found it, she kept her word, built the cloister, and named it Kitzingen.

History. At the end of World War II, 1,200 years after the countess lost her legendary scarf, the U.S. forces came to Kitzingen. Today the major administrative unit in the Kitzingen area is the 98th Army Support Group's 417th Base Support Battalion. The 417th provides support to the Army units within its area of responsibility. These include Headquarters and Headquarters Company, 1st Infantry Division at Leighton Kaserne in Wurzburg; the 701st Maintenance Support Battalion at Harvey Barracks in Kitzingen; 4th Battalion, 3rd Air Defense Artillery and 121st Signal Battalion at Larson Barracks, Kitzingen; and Army aviation, air defense, and weather units at Giebelstadt Army Airfield.

Harvey Barracks was used by the German air force during both world wars. It was named in 1951 after Capt. James R. Harvey, Company E, 359th Infantry Regiment, who was killed during the invasion of Normandy. Larson Barracks was established in 1936 for training antiaircraft gunners. In 1962, it was named in honor of Capt. Stanley I. Larson, Company C, 10th Engineer Battalion, who was killed clearing a minefield under enemy fire at Anzio beachhead on 23 May 1944. Leighton Barracks at Wurzburg is named in honor of Capt. John A. Leighton, Company G, 10th Armored Infantry Battalion, 4th Armored Division, who was killed in action 18 July 1944.

Housing and Schools. On-post and government-leased housing is available to families in the Kitzingen Military Community (KMC). There is none at Giebelstadt, however, and sponsors assigned there must apply for quarters at Wurzburg. Waiting times vary from eight to twelve months at Kitzingen and two to twelve months at Wurzburg.

Children attend schools in the KMC: the Kitzingen elementary school and its annex located at Marshall Heights, Wurzburg elementary at Leighton Kaserne, the Wurzburg Middle School, and the Wurzburg American High School. College extension courses, offered by the University of Maryland, Central Texas College, the University of Oklahoma, and City Colleges of Chicago, are available from the Army education centers at Kitzingen and Wurzburg.

Personal Services and Recreation. At Kitzingen's Harvey Barracks, about twelve miles southeast of Wurzburg, there are a health clinic, a commissary, a barber shop, a bookstore, a food mall, a garage, an auto parts store, a gas station, a fitness center, a post exchange, a tailor shop, a movie theater, and the Woodland Inn (rod and gun shop). At Larson Barracks, there are an auto craft shop, a barber shop, a bookstore, a Burger King, a library, a fitness center, a post exchange and shopette, a tailor shop, and a theater.

At Giebelstadt, about ten miles south of Wurzburg and Leighton Barracks, there are a health and dental clinic, an auto craft shop, a barber shop, a bookstore, a bowling center, a Class VI store, a commissary, a food mall, a physical fitness center, a coin laundry, an NCO club, a post exchange and shopette, a tailor shop, and a movie theater. At Wurzburg's Leighton Barracks, there are a commissary, barber and beauty shops, a garage and auto parts shop, a bookstore, a Burger King, a gift shop, a flower shop, a food mall, a library, NCO and enlisted clubs, a fitness center, a post exchange and shopette, a sight and sound shop, a sports shop, a theater, and the Top of the Marne Club.

The Local Area. The histories of Kitzingen and Wurzburg are closely entwined. Kitzingen became a free imperial city around the year 1000, but over the next 600 years it was often sold to various buyers to refill the coffers of the bishops of Wurzburg. Situated on the Main River, the city today has a population of about 22,000 and is known for its fine wines. During World War II, much of the city was destroyed by Allied bombers, but today it has recovered completely.

Wurzburg first appeared in the news in 689 A.D., when three Scotch-Irish missionaries were murdered in the duke's court there. In 740, the name Wurzburg—"Castellum Virteburch"—was first recorded. Today Wurzburg, a city of 130,000, is the capital of Lower Franconia. Like Kitzingen, Wurzburg is known for its vineyards.

For more information, write to Public Affairs Office, 417th Base Support Battalion, Unit 2612, APO AE 09031.

Home page: *www.8\98asg.wuerzburg.army.mil/417.*

LANDSTUHL REGIONAL MEDICAL CENTER

Landstuhl Regional Medical Center (LRMC) occupies over 470 acres atop Kirchberg Hill, overlooking the small town of Landstuhl, which has been inhabited at least since Roman times. Just to the east is the city of Kaiserslautern, and a bit farther west is Saarbrucken. Luxembourg and Belgium are also within easy driving distance.

History. The 18 large stone buildings constituting the lower post area of LRMC were originally built by the German army in 1938 and served first as home for a battalion of infantry, then as a reserve field hospital, and from 1944 to 1945 as a field hospital for the Waffen SS. The area was captured by U.S. forces on 19 March 1945. From 1945 through 1947, the French occupied the site; the 320th General Hospital, predecessor to the 2nd General Hospital, arrived there in 1951. Landstuhl Regional Medical Center was established in 1952.

The buildings standing today on the higher slopes of Kirchberg Hill are known as Wilson Barracks, in honor of Tech. 5th Grade Alfred Wilson, a medic with the 26th Infantry Division who was awarded the Medal of Honor for action in Europe during World War II. These buildings were originally known as the Hitler School and were built for use by the Hitler Youth Movement.

Today Landstuhl Post comprises 726 acres spread across Kirchberg Hill, predominantly occupied by medical units.

LRMC is a 213-bed, fully-accredited medical facility with the capability to expand to a 500-bed capacity in an emergency. It is staffed by 110 doctors, 250 nurses, 40 Medical Service Corps officers, 700 enlisted personnel, and 500 civilian employees. Each day, the hospital averages 30 admissions and 23,000 outpatient visits per month. It serves a local population of 60,000 personnel and 250,000 personnel referred from the European Theater.

Housing, Personal Services, and Recreation. Landstuhl controls 290 units of family housing. An elementary school and a day-care center are operated on post. Full post exchange and commissary facilities are available in nearby Kaiserslautern; a post exchange/snack bar facility is located right at Landstuhl. Recreational facilities on post include a gymnasium, a handball and racquetball court, and a bowling center.

For more information, write to Public Affairs, Landstuhl Regional Medical Center, CMR 402, APO AE 09180. Home page: *www.lrmc.amedd.army.mil.*

SCHWEINFURT MILITARY COMMUNITY

The city of Schweinfurt, like the legendary phoenix, has twice risen from its own ashes, both times better than it was before. The first occasion was in 1554 and the second was after World War II, when 75 percent of the city was left in ruins by Allied bombing attacks. An October 1943 attack was mounted by the U.S. 8th Air Force and involved a force of 228 heavy bombers, 62 of which were lost along with their ten-man crews and 138 others damaged. The removal of the rubble took three years after the war finally ended in 1945.

Schweinfurt is home to a number of combat and combat-support units. At Ledward Barracks are the headquarters of the 280th Base Support Battalion, elements of the 15th Infantry, 10th Field Artillery, 10th Engineers, and support units. At Conn Barracks are the HQ, 1st Brigade, 3rd Infantry Division, 3rd Squadron, and the 4th Cavalry, as well as elements of the 15th Infantry, the 3rd Support Battalion, and the 64th Armor. The 280th BSB has approximately 12,000 military personnel, family members, and Department of the Army civilians.

Housing and Schools. Family housing is situated at York Town Village, a complex consisting of single-family quadruplexes for enlisted personnel. A middle school is adjacent to York Town Village, and elementary schools are located at Askren Manor and Bad Kissingen housing area.

Personal Services. Health care for personnel living in the BSB is provided by the 24th Medical Detachment's U.S. Army health clinic. Patients requiring hospitalization or extensive specialist treatment are referred to the U.S. Army hospital in Wurzburg. The commissary is located at Askren Manor housing area and sells a variety of foods and meat cuts, which can be special-ordered twenty-four hours in advance. The post exchange facility is located at Ledward Barracks.

Recreation. Recreational facilities include three bowling alleys, one of which is a 24-lane, fully computerized facility. There are theaters at both Conn and Ledward Barracks, and automotive, ceramics, and photo craft shops are also available. Gymnasiums are located at Ledward and Conn Barracks; the Kessler Fitness Center offers a sauna, a weight room, and racquetball and tennis courts. A community club is located at Conn Barracks. The Community Recreation Division also supports a vigorous sports program open to all who are interested.

The Local Area. Schweinfurt is located in Bavaria, about 66 miles east of Frankfurt on the Main River. The first mention of the city occurs in old records dating from about 714 A.D., when it was little more than a fishing village. Despite the damage done to the city during the war, some of the older buildings are still standing, most of them dating from the sixteenth and seventeenth centuries. The surrounding countryside, which is very scenic, includes the ancient Mainberg, Bad Sennfeld, and Werneck Castles, as well as the cliffs of the Steigerwalt, the Hasseberge Hills, and the oak forests in the countryside of the Rhoen and Spessart region.

For more information, write to Army Community Service, 280th BSB, CMR No. 457, APO AE 09033-2012. Home page: *www.schweinfurt.army.mil.*

STUTTGART MILITARY COMMUNITY

The Stuttgart Military Community (SMC) is known as a "Purple Community" (that is, no particular uniform dominates) because it supports all branches of the military services, including reserve and National Guard units. The 6th Area Support Group is the host unit to the U.S. forces based in Stuttgart. Its mission is to provide command, control, communications, and base operations to those forces and their associated units, which include Headquarters, United States European Command, the 52nd Signal Battalion, 510th Personnel Service Battalion, elements of the 10th Special Forces Battalion, and Marine Forces Europe.

Five primary installations comprise the SMC: Patch Barracks, Kelly Barracks, Robinson Barracks, Panzer Kaserne, and the Stuttgart Army Airfield, all within thirty to forty minutes of each other.

Housing and Schools. The SMC maintains 1,100 units of enlisted and 530 of officer family housing. Also available are 43 temporary and 54 transient units for enlisted families and 176 units for bachelor enlisted and officer personnel. Housing is also available for rent on the local economy. As of the summer of 2000, rents averaged from $900 a month to as high as $2,425 a month for apartments. Temporary lodging for visitors is available on post at the Kelley Community Club, Panzer Community Club, the Schwabian Inn at Patch Barracks, and Robinson Hill Top Hotel.

There are four Department of Defense Dependents Schools in the SMC: Patch Elementary, Patch Middle/High School, Robinson Elementary, and Boblingen Elementary. For adults, associate's, bachelor's, and master's degree programs are offered from a variety of universities and colleges, which can be arranged through the education center.

Personal Services. The U.S. Army Hospital in Heidelberg, two hours north of Stuttgart, provides definitive medical care for the SMC. Landstuhl Regional Medical Center is also a referral facility and it lies about three hours from Stuttgart. The Stuttgart Medical Clinic is available for routine medical care. There are commissaries at all four locations within the SMC. A combined exchange and commissary is available at Robinson Barracks. A large post exchange is available at Patch Barracks, while Kelley Barracks and Panzer Kaserne each have shoppettes. An Anthony's Pizza, a Baskin Robbins, a Burger King, and a Taco Bell are located at Patch, while both Patch and Robinson offer a bakery and deli.

A full range of recreational facilities and activities is available to the residents of the SMC.

The Local Area. Stuttgart is located in the state of Baden-Wuerttemberg, an area of rolling hills and forests about the size of Switzerland with a population of nearly ten million. Stuttgart takes its name from "Stuten garten," or "stud farm," after the horse-breeding facility established there by Duke Luitolf von Schwaben around the year 950 A.D. A town called "Stutkarten" grew up around the locality, which finally became known as Stuttgart when first mentioned in a deed from the year 1229.

Stuttgart is best known as the manufacturing site of Mercedes and Porsche motor cars. The city's population is more than 600,000, 1.5 million if the adjacent suburbs are included. As befits a modern European city, Stuttgart's cultural

Family Housing, Vilseck, Germany U.S. ARMY PHOTO

and shopping opportunities are virtually unlimited. Near Panzer Kaserne is a shopping mall very much like any we have in the States.

For more information, write to Army Community Services, 6th ASG, Unit 30401 Box 4010, APO AE 09131.

VILSECK COMBINED ARMS TRAINING CENTER

The Vilseck Subcommunity is home of the 409th Base Support Battalion; the 3rd Brigade, 3rd Infantry Division; the 94th Engineer Battalion; the Combined Arms Training Center (CATC); and other units. Vilseck is located in a beautiful area of Bavaria known as the Oberpfaelzer Jura, where many ridges and hills and steep valleys and gorges dot the countryside.

History. U.S. forces first came to Vilseck when a training center was established there in 1947. The post consists of Rose Barracks, named after Maj. Gen. Maurice Rose, commander of the 3rd Armored Division, who was killed in action on 30 March 1945. The garrison consists of approximately 5,000 military personnel and 5,000 family members.

Housing and Schools. There are approximately 1,100 sets of family quarters at Vilseck. Waiting times vary according to rank and the size of housing unit needed. As of fall 2000, soldiers were waiting, depending on grade and size of unit required, from two to ten months for quarters. Guest housing is available at Vilseck. On-post dependent schooling, kindergarten through high school, is provided, as well as preschool and day-care facilities. The education center at Rose Barracks offers a number of college-level courses, and courses are also available at nearby Grafenwoehr.

Personal Services. Definitive medical care is provided by the 12th General Dispensary. Dental care is provided by the 561st Medical Company (DS). Vilseck has a large commissary and post exchange with a food mall, a cafeteria, a shopette/liquor store, a Book Mark bookstore, a community bank, a federal credit union, a coin laundry, a furniture store, a Burger King, and beauty, barber, tailor, and flower shops.

Recreation. Recreational facilities include a newly renovated theater; automotive, photo, ceramics, wood, and leather crafts shops; two gyms; a twenty-four-lane bowling alley; and recreation, youth, and outdoor recreation centers. There are also an outdoor swimming pool in the town of Vilseck (about 2.5 miles from the post), a golf course, and a rod and gun club at Grafenwoehr.

The Local Area. The climate in the Vilseck area is generally mild year-round. Winter seldom brings much snow, but it is damp and cold, with the temperatures occasionally dipping into the 20s. The summers are generally cool, with temperatures sometimes rising into the 80s.

Founded about 1000 A.D., Vilseck was granted city status in 1332. Today the town's population is about 5,500. Most of its citizens farm in the fields of the surrounding countryside.

Eating out in Vilseck is affordable, and the local specialties are worth tasting. Try the Bauernseufzer, smoke-fired sausage with Blechtrommel, "tin drum," and coffee, or Bratwurstl süss-sauer, fried sausages in a sweet-and-sour sauce with onions.

For more information, write to Public Affairs Officer, HQ 409 BSB, Unit 28130, APO AE 09112. Home page: *www.vilseck.army.mil.*

WIESBADEN-MAINZ COMMUNITY

History. Wiesbaden Air Base, the primary facility in the Wiesbaden geographical area, is known to have been used since at least as early as 1184, not for flying but as a fairgrounds, and it is said that Emperor Friedrich I knighted his sons on the field there. Today Wiesbaden AB is home to the 3rd Corps Support Command (COSCOM).

The Wiesbaden-Mainz Community (WMC) is commanded and serviced by the 221st Base Support Battalion. It consists of over 21,000 people, of whom more than 3,800 belong to the 3rd COSCOM. Other installations in the community include the Mainz facilities and McCully Barracks in Mainz-Wackernheim and the Mainz-Kastel Storage Station.

Housing and Schools. There are over 3,000 units of family housing in the WMC. Hainerberg in Wiesbaden and Martin Luther King (MLK) Village in Mainz are the two largest, but seven smaller housing areas are situated within the community.

More than 3,200 school-age dependent children live in the WMC; they attend one of three elementary schools, a middle school, and a high school. Child-development services are available at the Hainerberg Housing Area, MLK Village, and Wiesbaden Air Base. Various education centers about the community offer college courses from Big Bend Community College, Central Texas College, City Colleges of Chicago, the University of Southern California, Boston University, Troy State University, Embry-Riddle Aeronautical University, and the University of Maryland.

Personal Services. Medical services are provided by a troop medical and dental clinic at the air base. The 97th General Hospital, Frankfurt, is used for inpatient services. Local German hospitals provide emergency-room care and other services.

Shopping facilities include a commissary in the Hainerberg housing area and an annex in the MLK Village. One of the larger exchanges in Europe is in the Hainerberg section. It includes two theaters and several concessions. There is also a large shopping facility at the Mainz-Kastel storage station and a post exchange shopette in Mainz.

Recreation. Recreational facilities include gymnasiums, the Rheinblick Golf Course, a rod and gun club range, arts and crafts shops, and a recreation center. An outdoor recreation rental facility provides equipment and services.

The Local Area. Wiesbaden is the capital of the German state of Hesse, which contains Frankfurt, Darmstadt, Offenbach, Hanau, and a dozen smaller cities that cluster together in a complex of industry, commerce, and culture. Still, one-quarter of the area is covered in woods and parks. Wiesbaden itself is located between the Taunus Mountains and the Rhine River, in the Rheingau wine-producing area, and is frequently the center of festivals and celebrations. Many Roman archaeological sites are situated in and around Wiesbaden, and some of the Rhine's most picturesque castles are nearby, along the Rhine River.

For more information, write to HQ 221st BSB, Public Affairs Office, Unit 29623, APO AE 09096.

Armed Forces Recreation Center–Europe

GARMISCH AND CHIEMSEE

The Armed Forces Recreation Center–Europe (AFRC-E) at Garmisch and Chiemsee is a unique, wonderful, and exciting place where military personnel, Department of Defense civilian employees, retirees, and their families can enjoy, at very modest expense, one of the finest outdoor recreation areas in the world.

AFRC-E offers excellent American and European cuisine, skiing, hiking, camping, hang gliding, para-gliding, windsurfing, and exciting sightseeing opportunities—more than 30 programs and activities year-round. The center has a total of 327 guest rooms, five apartments and suites, and even a conference facility for those who wish to bring their work with them.

Garmisch lies at the foot of the Zugspitze, the highest mountain in Germany at 9,720 feet. The town of Garmisch was made famous in 1936 when the Winter Olympics were held there. It still retains much of its Old World charm. Approximately 50 miles south-southwest of Munich, Garmisch is within easy driving distance of Italy and Austria.

Accommodations at Garmisch consist of the General Von Steuben Hotel with 76 rooms, five apartments, five suites, and a restaurant and a lounge, and the General Patton Hotel, with ninety-five rooms and a lounge. In addition, the Keans Lodge offers open-bay lodging for large groups. Conference facilities are available at Garmisch in the Abrams Complex, which also houses headquarters facilities and employee housing. The Hausberg Ski Lodge offers summer and winter equipment issue plus a cafeteria and a bar; the nine-hole golf course has a restaurant and a pro shop. Of course, no winter holiday would be complete without pizza, and that is available at the swanky touch-of-home called the Trattoria de Marco. A travel camp is also available at Garmisch. To round out this mountain wonderland picture is the "Just for Kids" mini-Bavarian tour for children ages five to twelve—just the thing to get the little dears off mom and dad's back long enough to enjoy some uninterrupted grown-up stuff.

Chiemsee, about 40 miles east-southeast of Munich, at 31 square miles in circumference, is the largest lake in Bavaria. It is situated 1,699 feet above sea level and contains three islands. Many different types of water sports are available there during the appropriate season.

Accommodations at Chiemsee consist of the Lake Hotel, with 83 rooms, two restaurants, a lounge and conference facilities, and the Park Hotel, boasting 73 rooms, conference facilities, and a "Just for Kids" program similar to the one operated at Garmisch. Of course, the private beaches at Chiemsee are a big attraction, and paddleboats, canoes, windsurfing, and sail boating are available. There is also a travel camp, prepared for tents and overflow camping, a miniature golf course, and an Armed Forces Exchange Service shoppette and laundromat.

Rates are based on grade. As of press time, they were as follows: Room rates at Garmisch and the Lake Hotel at Chiemsee for one night ranged from $61 for personnel E-1 to E-5 up to $86 per night for flag officers. At Garmisch, a small suite costs $115 a night and a large suite costs $125, while at the Lake Hotel those rates were $105 and $115, respectively. The nightly rate at the Chiemsee's Park Hotel ranged from $57 to $82. Daily rates at the travel camps ranged from $15 to $25 at gravel sites with electricity; $13 to $19 at gravel sites without electricity; $10 to $15 per tent in the tent areas; $135 per night for deluxe cabins; and $57 per night for rustic cabins. Monthly rates ranged from $300 to $449.

For more information, write to AFRC–Europe, Vacation Planning Center, Unit 24501, APO AE 09053, or call 011-49-8821-3942 (civilian) or 4402-575 (DSN). Home page: *vacation@afrc.garmisch.army.mil.*

GUAM

Air Force

ANDERSEN AIR FORCE BASE

At the site of the old 8th Air Force headquarters building at Andersen Air Force Base, located at the north end of the island of Guam, is the final resting place for "Old 100," one of the last B-52 aircraft to bomb North Vietnam and a machine that flew over 5,000 hours in the air war over Southeast Asia. The bomber gets its nickname from its tail number, 55-0100. "Old 100" is part of the Arc Light Memorial at Andersen, dedicated to the seventy-five men who lost their lives flying B-52 missions against the Communist forces in Vietnam.

History. Named in honor of Brig. Gen. James Roy Andersen, who was lost at sea in a flight that originated on Guam in February 1945, the base today is home to the 36th Air Base Wing of the Pacific Air Forces, which is responsible for host support of all assigned and tenant units, including the 13th Air Force, the 634th Air Mobility Support Squadron (AMC), and the U.S. Navy's Helicopter Combat Support Squadron Five (HC-5).

Housing and Schools. There are 1,389 family quarters at Andersen in the Fleming Heights, Capehart, Roberts Terrace, and Wilson Homes housing areas. Dependent education is handled through the government of Guam's department of education. The Andersen child-development center offers day-care and preschool services for children at reasonable rates. Adult on-base education is offered by Troy State University and the Universities of Maryland and Oklahoma.

Personal Services. The USAF clinic at Andersen provides outpatient care along with a variety of medical services. Specialty and inpatient services are available at the U.S. Naval Regional Medical Center, Agana, about 45 minutes south of Andersen.

The base exchange at Andersen offers a number of facilities, including a camera shop, a furniture mart, an audio center, a china shop, a four-seasons shop, a toy store, and a garage. A number of exchange food services are operated on base, including the Latte Stone Restaurant and the Hafa Adai Inn, which is open 24 hours a day in the passenger terminal. Andersen also has a newly renovated and expanded commissary.

Recreation. Recreational facilities include an auto hobby shop, a theater, a twelve-lane bowling center, a youth center, a base gymnasium, a library, arts and crafts shops, and a Burger King, Anthony's Pizza, Robin Hood Deli, and Baskin Robbins ice cream parlor in the Latte Stone Restaurant. Outdoor recreation facilities include the eighteen-hole, 6,242-yard Palm Tree Golf Course, two swimming pools, and three beaches—Tarague, Sirena, and Pati Point. At Tarague Beach, a natural cave has been set aside for use by picnickers, and the other beaches have acres for picnicking and leisure-time activities, which include camping, hiking, shell gathering, fishing, swimming, snorkeling, and scuba diving.

For more information, write to Public Affairs Office, 36th Air Base Wing, Unit 14003, Box 25, APO AP 96543-4003. Home page: *www.andersen.af.mil.*

Navy

U.S. NAVAL FORCES GUAM

Guam is 205 square miles of lush and rugged hills, colorful reefs, luxuriant waterfalls, warm blue waters, and sandy beaches inhabited by some of the most beautiful and friendly people on earth. It is also sometimes referred to as being in the middle of nowhere, 6,000 miles west of San Francisco, 3,340 miles beyond Honolulu, and 1,500 miles east of Manila, in the northwest corner of three million square miles of ocean expanse dotted with the islands of Micronesia.

History. The U.S. Navy first came to Guam in 1898, when Capt. Henry Glass captured the island by firing a volley over the rooftops of Agana from the *USS Charleston.* For many years thereafter, the island was administered by the U.S. Navy until 1950, when it became an organized unincorporated territory of the United States. Today the citizens of the territory elect their own governor and send a delegate to the U.S. Congress.

More than 6,300 naval personnel and their 6,300 dependents are stationed on Guam, assigned to a number of commands. West of Agana, the capital city, overlooking Apra Harbor, is Commander, U.S. Naval Forces Marianas, who provides support to the operating forces of the U.S. Navy and shore facilities on Guam, Australia, and New Zealand. The Naval Computer and Telecommunications Area Master Station (NCTAMS) Western Pacific occupies about 4,800 acres of land on the northwest side of the island and is home for 1,200 naval personnel. In the south-central part of the island, isolated from populated areas, is the U.S. Naval Activities Ordnance Annex, sitting upon 8,800 acres. Other commands include the naval regional medical center, the naval supply depot, and a ship repair facility.

Housing and Schools. U.S. government housing is available to Navy personnel in 16 areas throughout the island. The quarters are built in a number of styles. The housing referral office also maintains a listing of approved off-base apartments available for rent.

Dependent education is carried out in the Guamanian public-school system. Location of schools attended is determined by the housing area in which the children live. Child-care and nursery facilities are available at Naval Activities, NCTAMS, and the naval hospital. Adult education is carried on through the Navy campus, and college classes off base may be attended at either the University of Guam or Guam Community College, both of which are located on the eastern coast of the island in the village of Mangilao.

Personal Services. Medical care is provided by the naval hospital in Agana Heights. The hospital operates four dispensaries around the island. Navy exchange and commissary facilities on the island are modern and well stocked. All stations have a retail store and concessions, which range from a Baskin Robbins to watch-repair shops. The Naval Activities commissary is well stocked and carries almost 3,800 line items, including meat items from the United States, Australia, and New Zealand.

Recreation. The recreational facilities for service personnel on Guam are among the best offered anywhere. The Nimitz Golf Course, located at the naval air station, is an 18-hole championship course. Four bowling centers, seven swimming pools, six beaches and picnic areas, 28 tennis courts, three hobby centers, and gymnasiums are available to military personnel on the island.

The Local Area. Guam has a tropical climate, with annual temperatures averaging between 75° F and 85° F. About 85 inches of rain fall on the island in a year. March is the driest month, with about two and a half inches of precipitation. Typhoons sometimes come ashore on Guam. The worst in recent times was Karen in 1962. Karen carried maximum winds of 150 knots; Pamela, in 1976, reached winds of 120 knots. The island is about thirty miles long. At its narrowest point, it is about four miles across. At its widest, it is about 12 miles.

The highest point of Guam is Mount Lamlam in the south, which soars to an elevation of 1,334 feet. The northern part of the island reaches an elevation of 600 feet at Ritidian Point, which is a limestone plateau about eight miles across. Today approximately 120,000 people live on Guam.

Europeans first came to Guam in 1531, when explorer Ferdinand Magellan claimed the island for Spain, although Spanish colonists did not actually take possession until 1668. The Spanish conquered the island by killing off most of the native Chamorros men and marrying their women. Today the local population shows a strong mixture of Filipino and Mexican-Spanish intermarriage.

For more information, write to Navy Family Service Center PSC 455, Box 157, FPO AP 96540-1157. E-mail: *nO2fscpa@guam.navy.mil.*

ICELAND

Navy

KEFLAVIK NAVAL AIR STATION

Iceland is known as the "Land of Fire and Ice." Mount Hekla, the largest of Iceland's volcanoes, was once believed to be the mouth of hell; its last eruption occurred on 17 August 1980. In contrast to this, 13 percent of Iceland is still covered by glacial ice, including Vatnajokull, larger than all of Europe's glaciers combined.

History. American forces first came to Iceland during World War II, but after the war they departed, and an arrangement was made with the Icelandic government so that U.S. planes could be refueled at Keflavik Airport. The U.S. military role expanded in Iceland during the fifties, and in 1961, the Navy assumed host command status from the Air Force. Today Keflavik NAS provides services and materiel in support of the 2,200 military personnel and 2,300 family members of the Navy and other services in Iceland.

Housing and Schools. There are over 900 family housing units on the station. A well-furnished Navy Lodge is also available, with 31 rooms that can be reserved for up to 14 days, but because the Icelandic government requires all personnel to live on base, space there is very tight. Dependent schooling, kindergarten through high school, is provided on the base. Adult education courses, through the Navy campus, include instruction from the University of Maryland, City Colleges of Chicago, Central Texas College, and the University of Oklahoma.

Personal Services. Medical and dental care are provided by a station hospital and a dental clinic. Medical and dental treatment are also available in Reykjavik and Keflavik, and personnel requiring specialty care and hospitalization are sometimes evacuated to hospitals in the United States. A Navy exchange, a commissary, a minimart, a service station, and a cafeteria are available at the station.

Recreation. Recreation facilities include a 500-seat movie theater, a gymnasium, a pool, an 18-lane bowling alley, a community center, and various hobby and craft shops. The Hvitarbakki Lodge, a recreation facility leased by the Navy in the Borgarfjordur Valley, about 100 miles northeast of Keflavik, provides camping, lodging, swimming, horseback riding, hunting, and fishing.

The Local Area. Although its northern tip nearly touches the Arctic Circle, Iceland has a climate moderated by a current of the Gulf Stream. But Keflavik's exposed position, surrounded by ocean on three sides, results in rainy, windy, and cloudy winters and cool, windy, and cloudy summers. Temperatures average 32° F in January and only 52° F in August! Prolonged snow rarely occurs at Keflavik. During the months from May to July, the sun never sets, which permits extensive outdoor activities during that time.

Eighty percent of Iceland is uninhabited, and of the island's 260,000 people, fully 90 percent of them live in towns and cities. Reykjavik, the capital, is its cultural and population center, with a total of 100,000 inhabitants. Icelanders are very independent and well-educated people. In fact, more books are published per capita in Iceland than in any other country in the world. Iceland has the oldest existing parliament in the world, the *Althing,* which was established in 930 A.D. Norse influence is strong in Iceland, and schoolchildren today can read ancient Norse sagas as they were originally written, because their language has changed very little in the past 1,000 years. Icelanders, with a per capita income of $15,000, enjoy one of the highest standards of living in Europe, so buying things off base can be expensive. Civilian clothing is required off base.

For more information, write to Commander, Iceland Defense Force, PSC 1003, Box 45, FPO AE 09728-0301. Home page: *www.nctskef.navy.mil/nas.*

ITALY

Air Force

AVIANO AIR BASE

Aviano Air Base is located in the extreme northeast corner of Italy, at the foot of the Pre-Alps. It is in a beautiful setting with excellent recreation and travel opportunities.

History. Aeroporto Pagliana e Gori was established in 1911 as Aviano Airfield. During World War II, the Germans used the base, and the USAF came there in 1954. Today it is the home of the 31st Fighter Wing and 16th Air Force, which have 3,165 military personnel, 3,800 dependents, and more than 800 civilian employees. In addition, there are about 100 USAF personnel at Ghedi Air Base in the Po Valley. The 31st Fighter Wing also controls an ammunition supply squadron at Camp Darby.

Housing and Schools. There is no on-base family housing at Aviano. All single and unaccompanied officers also live off the base. Generally, newly arrived personnel find housing within thirty days of their arrival. Dependent schooling is conducted in four American elementary schools and the Aviano High School. A child-care center is available at the base. The Aviano education center offers college courses from the City Colleges of Chicago, the University of Maryland, Embry-Riddle Aeronautical University, and Central Texas College.

Personal Services. Medical services are provided by the USAF Clinic Aviano, where routine medical and dental treatment are available. Patients with serious conditions are referred to hospitals at Vicenza, nearby Pordenone, or Germany.

There are a base exchange with 13,000 square feet of display space; a commissary, with 13,000 square feet of space and more than 6,200 line items for sale, adequate for the population served; a foodland with four-seasons and toy stores; and a consolidated open mess that serves both officers and enlisted personnel.

Recreation. Recreational facilities include a base gymnasium; a nine-hole golf course; an Olympic-size outdoor swimming pool; a twelve-lane bowling center; a sports center where a wide variety of sporting, camping, backpacking, and ski equipment can be rented; and a newly renovated recreation center. There are also wood and auto hobby shops.

The Local Area. The weather in this part of Italy is generally cold, foggy, and wet in winter and moderate the rest of the year, with four distinct seasons.

Aviano is an agricultural town with a population of over 8,000. The base areas nestle at the foot of the Alps, and Mount Cavallo, the highest peak, looms 7,000 feet above the village. Southward, the terrain flattens out. The city of Pordenone, provincial capital, is eight miles south of the flight-line area and inhabited by about 50,000 people. The closest major city, Udine, is 30 miles east. Udine is an alpine city, and the Germanic influence is very strong there. Venice, on the Adriatic Sea, is only 50 miles to the southwest.

For more information, write to Public Affairs Office, 31st FW (USAFE), Unit 6125, Box 45 APO AE 09601-0100. Home page: *http://www.setaf.army.mil* or *www.aviano.af.mil.*

Army

VICENZA AND LIVORNO

The army communities situated in Vicenza and Livorno, Italy, are administered by the 22nd Area Support Group (ASG). The two installations are 164 miles apart, and travel between them, from Vicenza in the northeast corner of Italy to Livorno or Camp Darby on the shores of the Tyrrhenian Sea, takes about three and a half hours. Formed in 1985, the 22nd ASG is headquartered at Caserma Ederle in the southeastern corner of the city of Vicenza. The 22nd ASG mission is primarily to support soldiers, family members, and civilians of the Southern European Task Force and to provide support for U.S. personnel stationed at the NATO headquarters in Verona, Italy.

The major units at Vicenza are HQ, Southern European Task Force (SETAF), the 22nd Area Support Group, the SETAF Infantry Brigade, 3rd Battalion, 325th Infantry Regiment (Airborne Combat Team), and the 14th Transportation Battalion. At Livorno are the Area Support Team, Leghorn Army Depot Activity, and the Defense Fuel Region, Europe. With approximately 9,000 soldiers, family members, and civilian employees, the 22nd covers an area in northern Italy about the size of Massachusetts.

Housing and Schools. Temporary lodging is available at the Ederle Inn, a modern, 54-room hotel. Each room has a private bath, microwave, sink, and refrigerator. The Casa Toscana at Livorno offers clean, well-appointed accommodations. Arrangements for family housing can be made through the family housing offices located at both Vicenza and Livorno. The Department of Defense Dependents School System operates facilities at both Vicenza and

Livorno. Adult education consists of courses available from the University of Maryland, City Colleges of Chicago, and Troy State University, all of which have extension programs in both communities.

Personal Services. The Vicenza Medical Department Activity provides medical care for the Vicenza and Livorno communities with its 20-bed hospital. In October 1995, the facility became a full-service health clinic. There is also a health clinic at Livorno. Serious cases or referrals are treated at local hospitals or the Army Regional Medical Center in Landstuhl, Germany. Both communities boast well-staffed, modern dental facilities.

The magnet mall at Caserma Ederle is the largest facility of its kind in the European theater. The Army and Air Force Exchange Service provides a full range of facilities at both communities, including shopettes, beauty and barber shops, coin laundries, and movie theaters. Each community also has an AAFES bookstore and a full-service commissary. Additional facilities include auto parts stores, garages, four-seasons stores, sight and sound stores, optical shops, and video rental outlets.

Recreation. Both communities offer a full range of sports and recreational facilities. Each has a well-equipped gym complete with Universal, Nautilus, and free-weight equipment, as well as aerobics classes and indoor racquetball and basketball. Tennis courts and bowling are also available. Each has swimming pools open throughout the summer.

The crown jewel of the 22nd ASG recreational scene is the American Beach in Tierrenia, near Camp Darby. The beach offers water sports, equipment rental, beach chairs, umbrellas, and food and retail outlets. A campground at Camp Darby has spaces for trailers and tents, as well as a number of camper trailers on pads. Sea Pines Lodge on Camp Darby offers clean, reasonably priced lodging for soldiers and their families vacationing in the area. Ski trips to the Italian Alps and the Armed Forces Recreation Centers in Germany are offered at reasonable prices through the Vicenza Outdoor Recreation Center.

The Local Area. Vicenza, a bustling city of 110,000 inhabitants, lies at the foot of the Italian Alps, only a 45-minute drive west of Venice. Vicenza was home of the Renaissance architect Andrea Palladio, and two of his famous monuments, the Teatro Olimpico and the Basilica, still stand downtown. Weekend excursions to Venice, the city of canals and gondolas, are a favorite pastime of soldiers stationed at Vicenza.

Livorno is only a 20-minute drive south of the city of Pisa, home of the Leaning Tower, and a ten-minute drive from the Tyrrhenian Sea. Camp Darby is a one-hour train or car ride from the city of Florence, home of the Uffizzi Gallery and Michelangelo's statue of David. Florence also boasts hundreds of fountains, art museums, and historic sites, all of which make it one of the most interesting cities in northern Italy.

For more information, write to Public Affairs Office, 22nd Area Support Group, Unit 31401, Box 80, APO AE 09630. Home page: *www.setaf.army.mil.*

Navy

LA MADDALENA NAVAL BASE

La Maddalena is a small island that sits just off the north coast of the island of Sardinia (or Sardegna, in Italian). La Maddalena is actually the largest island in an archipelago of seven islands and some 14 islets. The island is a tourist resort with a permanent population of 16,000 (of which 3,000 are Navy personnel, Department of Defense employees, and their dependents). During the tourist season, La Maddalena's population swells to as many as 50,000 people. But Navy personnel get the benefits of living in a tourist attraction year-round, absolutely free.

On the southern side of La Maddalena is the rocky and uncultivated island of Santo Stefano, where there is a NATO facility that is the home port of the U.S. Navy submarine tender *USS Simon Lake,* aboard which Commander Submarine Squadron 22 is embarked.

Housing and Schools. Government housing is very tight at La Maddalena, with 262 units available, most of which are allotted to enlisted personnel. Cost of local rental housing varies between $500 and $1,400 a month. Bachelor housing consists of two bachelor enlisted quarters; one in La Maddalena and the other on Santo Stefano. There are no transient accommodations.

Dependent schools at La Maddalena operate classes for kindergarten through eighth grade. High school students attend an American school in England or Rome. Limited nursery and day-care facilities are available at La Maddalena. Limited off-duty adult education is provided by the University of Maryland and Central Texas College.

Personal Services. Medical and dental facilities are limited. The clinic is staffed by two family practice medical officers, two nurses, a dental officer, three dental technicians, one clinical social worker, and ten hospital corpsmen. More extensive care is available at the Naval Regional Medical Center in Naples or Rota, Spain. La Maddalena is considered an isolated station, and personnel with medical conditions cannot be sent there. A combination commissary and Navy exchange facility is housed on the island of La Maddalena.

Recreation. Navy facilities are located primarily on the islands of Santo Stefano and La Maddalena, with a recreation center and small exchange in the town of Palau, the nearest city to the base on the northern Sardinian mainland. On La Maddalena, there are limited athletic facilities and a recreation center, a hobby and craft shop, a marina, and a movie theater.

The Local Area. The local area is an ideal location for most water sports, including swimming, sailing, boating, windsurfing, diving, and fishing. There are many beautiful beaches with crystal-clear water in the La Maddalena and northern Sardinia area. La Maddalena may be reached from the port city of Palau by a 20-minute ferry ride.

The climate on Sardinia offers hot, dry summers and cool winters. The island itself, the second largest in the Mediterranean, averages more than 2,000 hours of sunshine per year, but winds are strong and constant there. There are the northwesterly wind, known as the maestrale, the tramontana from the north, the scirocco from the southeast, and the ponente from the west. The maestrale is violent in the winter and actually bends trees toward the southeast. The scirocco is a warm, humid wind that sometimes brings dust from North Africa.

La Maddalena as an inhabited island has a history stretching back only to 1767, but Sardinia, an autonomous province of Italy, has been inhabited for thousands of years. An ancient people who lived on the island built a number of tombs and other structures that are still standing. The Phoenicians began colonizing the island in 900 to 800 B.C., and since then the area has seen the Carthaginians, the Romans, the Pisans, the Genovese, the Aragonese, and the French.

For more information, write to Public Affairs, Naval Support Activity, PSC 816, Box 1795, FPO AE 09612.

SIGONELLA NAVAL AIR STATION

Sicily is the largest island in the Mediterranean, with nearly five million inhabitants and more than 9,900 square miles of land, which makes it about the size of Maryland. A large number of Sicilians make their living farming and observe the customs and traditions of their forefathers, and although many Americans have their roots in Sicily, it's still a very different country.

History. Sigonella bills itself as the "Fastest Growing Naval Air Station in the World." Sigonella and its many tenant commands have a population of over 7,000 military personnel, civilian employees, and their dependents. Over 350 personnel deploy to Sigonella with patrol squadrons that come to the base on six-month rotations. In addition, VRC-40, a cargo squadron that supports a deployed carrier battle group, rotates almost 100 personnel to Sigonella with each battle group. Sigonella's airfield and port liaison operations have greatly increased over the past years, and the station is now an important staging and resupply point for the U.S. military and NATO forces in the Mediterranean.

There are two main parts to the station: NAS I, the support base, and NAS II, the airfield, eight miles away. Sigonella itself is located about ten miles southwest of Catania, Sicily.

Housing and Schools. On-station housing consists of about 98 units for military families, plus 205 units that are leased near NAS I and another 104 leased at Costanzo, just north of the city of Catania. Rentals on the local economy run from $400 to $900 a month, depending on currency exchange rates. An elementary school, junior-senior high school, and an education center are located in the NAS I area. There is also a child-development center with a capacity of 200 children.

Personal Services. Medical and dental care are provided by a full-service hospital. The Navy exchange offers a limited range of services and merchandise, including a retail store, a food-service department with two cafeterias, a beverage store, and some personal services, such as barber and beauty shops. The commissary supplies about 2,300 items. About 16,000 pounds of frozen meats are purchased there each month, most of which are shipped from Iceland.

Recreation. Recreational facilities include tennis courts, a gymnasium, a swimming pool, a ten-lane bowling alley, a movie theater, and a library at NAS I. At NAS II are an auto hobby shop, a gymnasium, athletic fields, four tennis courts, a weight-lifting room, and an Olympic-size swimming pool and diving pool.

The Local Area. The climate in the Sigonella region is similar to that of the Gulf Coast but without the high humidity. The temperatures during the coldest month, January, average between 40 and 50° F. During the warmest months, the temperatures sometimes exceed 100° F, when the hot scirocco winds blow in from the African desert. The summer months are dry and dusty, and rain occurs seasonally from October through February.

This beautiful coastal area offers sun, azure seas, and white, sandy beaches. During the winter and early spring, skiing can be enjoyed on the slopes of nearby Mount Etna.

For more information, write to Public Affairs Office, U.S. NAS Sigonella, PSC 812, Box 2650, FPO AE 09627. Home page: *www.sicily.navy.mil/nassig.*

U.S. NAVAL SUPPORT ACTIVITY, NAPLES

Naval Support Activity (NAVSUPPACT) Naples provides administrative support to U.S. personnel stationed in the Naples area and to the forces of the Sixth Fleet. The U.S. community includes about 10,000 people. This includes about 2,000 Navy personnel and their families living in the coastal town of Gaeta, homeport of the Sixth Fleet flagship. Sixth Fleet forces are composed of about 40 ships, 175 aircraft, and 21,000 support personnel. NAVSUPPACT Naples supports more than 106 activities that range from support of the U.S. Embassy in Rome to administration of the U.S. automobile licensing program for all of Italy.

Housing and Schools. The military community is in the midst of a transitional phase. As a result of the Naples Improvement Initiative (NII), a five-year construction project, personnel will enjoy all newly constructed facilities when the project is complete in 2003. The initial phase of construction has provided new administrative buildings and 500 units of government housing at the Gricignano Support Site, a 20-minute drive from the main military base in Capodichino. Housing alternatives are government-leased apartments or local economy rentals throughout the Naples area. Naples offers temporary quarters at the local Navy Lodge or commercial hotels while awaiting housing availability. Naples also enjoys a newly constructed high school and elementary school at the support site. The Department of Defense Schools System also operates a school, kindergarten through eighth grade, in Gaeta. High school-age students living in Gaeta are bused to the Naples High School daily. Both Naples and Gaeta offer child-development services. Navy College in Naples offers both undergraduate and graduate programs for assigned personnel.

Personal Services. With the completion of the NII, all current support activities will move into new facilities at the support site. Naval Hospital, Naples, currently overlooks the Agnano complex and provides primary medical care with priority for visiting operating forces and assigned active-duty military personnel. Patients with complex medical conditions and those requiring extended hospitalization are evacuated to facilities in Germany or the United States. Dental care is provided at clinics located in the hospital or at Capodichino. Dental services include a mobile dental van to provide follow-up care to elementary and high school students.

The Agnano complex houses both the navy exchange and commissary. Navy exchange vendors cover a wide range of products and services, from Subway and Baskin Robbins to currency exchange and photo services. The NATO Allied Forces, Southern Europe (AFSOUTH) complex in Bagnoli, a five-minute drive from Agnano, offers additional shopping for military personnel.

Recreation. Naples area recreation facilities are extensive. Admiral Carney Recreation Park, just outside of Naples, offers a nine-hole golf course, softball diamonds, tennis courts, football/soccer fields, volleyball and basketball courts, fitness trails, and camping/picnic facilities. Capodichino offers one of the Navy's best-equiped fitness centers in the FitZone, which includes basketball and raquetball courts, aerobics classes, exercise equipment, and an indoor pool. Also at Capodichino are a theater, an all-hands club, and a family-style restaurant.

The Local Area. The Naples area enjoys a mild climate—wet winters and warm, dry summers. Naples usually receives 4.5 inches of rain between October and January, with July being the year's driest month. Just south of Naples lies Mount Vesuvius and the excavated ruins of Pompeii and Herculaneum, buried by volcanic ash in 79 A.D. Further south are Sorrento and the Almalfi coast, reached by a coastal roadway offering one of Europe's most breathtaking drives. Local Information, Tours and Travel (ITT) and USO offices offer frequent tours in the local area, as well as throughout Europe. France, Austria, Switzerland, and Germany are easily accessible by train or automobile.

For more information, write to NAS, Naples, PSC 810, Box 53, FPO AE 09619. Home page: *http://www.nsa.naples.navy.mil.*

JAPAN

Air Force

MISAWA AIR BASE

What do the cities of Misawa, Japan, and Wenatchee, Washington, have in common? Almost nothing, but there is a link. The first nonstop flight across the Pacific originated at Misawa in October 1931 when American pilots Clyde Pangborn and Hugh Herndon flew from Misawa to Wenatchee in 41 hours and ten minutes. The Misawans are proud of this accomplishment, and today a memorial to the American fliers stands at Sabishiro Beach, near the spot where the aircraft, Miss Veedol, took off on its historic flight.

History. Built in 1942 as an air facility for the Japanese Naval Air Force, Misawa Air Base first saw Americans on 2 September 1945. Today, the base is home to the 35th Fighter Wing, which supports a base population of more than 15,000. This includes over 3,200 members of the Japan Air Self-Defense Force at the base. The 35th Fighter Wing provides tactical airpower in both air-to-air and air-to-ground missions in support of U.S. forces and our allies throughout the Pacific Theater. It performs these roles with two squadrons of F-16 C/D aircraft. All four U.S. armed services are represented at Misawa, including Naval Air Facility Misawa, the U.S. Army's 750th Military Intelligence Detachment, and Company E Marine Support Battalion, along with the 3rd Space Surveillance Squadron and the 35th Fighter Wing.

Housing and Schools. On-base family housing consists of over 2,200 units built by the Japanese government. There are 51 temporary family quarters and 115 transient quarters on the base.

Misawa has two elementary schools and a high school, which enroll an average of 1,900 students. Preschool facilities are also available. Adult education is provided through the base education center and consists of college courses offered by the University of Maryland, Central Texas College, and the University of Oklahoma.

Personal Services. Misawa has a state-of-the-art hospital, completed in 1994, which provides both inpatient and outpatient services. Dental service is available to all members of the military community, including dependents. The base offers an excellent exchange and commissary store. The exchange also operates a number of concessions, including a service station and a personal services arcade, as well as several fast-food restaurants.

Recreation. Recreation facilities include an 18-hole golf course; a 26-lane bowling center; a base gymnasium; a base beach on Lake Ogawara; and a ski lodge with a slope, located near Lake Ogawara. There are also arts and crafts centers, a rod and gun club, and a recreation supply office that offers equipment for checkout.

The Local Area. Misawa is located on the north tip of Honshu Island (the main island of Japan), along the Pacific coast, not far from the city of Hachinohe. Although archaeological evidence points to human inhabitation of the area more than 8,000 years ago, Misawa Hamlet was founded under the jurisdiction of Momoishi Village in 1872 and became an independent village in 1879. The area is noted for its horse breeding: In 1371, the Nambu Clan established nine horse farms in the area, and eventually between 8,000 and 10,000 animals were being bred there each year between the months of April and October. Since the 1940s, the population of Misawa has grown from about 1,200 to more than 40,000.

This part of Japan has four distinct seasons, and in this it is similar to the midwestern region of the United States. The major difference is that the area averages 121 inches of snow a year. The winters there are cold, with the temperatures averaging between 20 and 30° F.

For more information, write to 35th Public Affairs Office, Unit 5009, Box 10, APO AP 96319-5009. Home page: *www.misawa.af.mil.*

YOKOTA AIR BASE

To virtually everyone in the western world, Mount Fuji is Japan. Indeed, at more than 12,000 feet, Mount Fuji dominates the horizon from Yokota in the winter, when the air is clear, and is only a two-hour drive from the base. Downtown Tokyo is only 24 miles from Yokota. With an 11,000-foot runway, the base serves as a layover point for Air Mobility Command flights originating throughout the Far East. The aerial view of Tokyo and Mount Fuji has proven unforgettable for thousands of U.S. servicemembers and their families over the years.

History. Yokota Air Base was originally known as Tama Army Airfield, a Japanese base that opened in 1939. In August 1945, the Occupation Forces changed the name to Yokota after a small village located at the northeast corner of the base. Today Yokota is home for the 5th Air Force, whose tactical fighter and reconnaissance squadrons support our defense treaties with Japan. The base is also headquarters for a number of other units, including the host wing, the 374th Airlift Wing, the 630th Air Mobility Squadron, and Headquarters, U.S.

Forces, Japan. Yokota has a U.S. military population of 3,700 and their 4,500 family members, plus more than 3,300 civilian employees.

Housing and Schools. There are about 2,500 units of family housing at Yokota. The average wait for on-base housing is from 90 to 180 days. Temporary lodging is also available for about 296 family members. Off-base rentals are extremely expensive in Japan. A two-bedroom apartment costs $1,000 a month, not including utilities, which average $300 per month.

Yokota has two elementary schools (Yokota East and Yokota West) and a high school. There are also a variety of child-development services available at the base. On-base college courses are available from the University of Maryland, Central Texas College, the University of Oklahoma, Troy State University, and Chapman College.

Personal Services. Among the personal support facilities available at Yokota is an Air Force hospital, a modern medical facility operated by the 374th Medical Group. The commissary store offers shoppers more than 6,000 line items displayed in over 20,000 square feet of shopping space. The Japan Area Exchange (JAAX) also offers Yokota shoppers an excellent facility with well-stocked shelves and many bargains. Concessions available at Yokota include an audio-photo center, a furniture mart, a four-seasons store, a French restaurant, an ice cream parlor, a Burger King, two cafeterias, three snack bars, a full-service garage, and many other facilities.

Recreation. Yokota boasts some of the best recreational facilities in the Far East. There are a thirty-two-lane bowling center; a nine-hole, par-three golf complex; officers and enlisted clubs; craft and hobby centers; and two gymnasiums. Added to all of this is the unique Tama Hills Recreation Area, a picnic and camping ground about 15 miles southeast of Yokota. Another delightful aspect of duty at Yokota is that, as a major aerial port, flights are available there for trips to many other places in the Far East.

The Local Area. Yokota is bordered by small cities that make up part of the suburban environment of Tokyo in an area known as the Kanto Plain. The city of Fussa, considered the Yokota Air Base City, has enjoyed an excellent relationship with the base down through the years. Tokyo, with all the sights and excitement of one of the largest and most modern cities in the world, is only a one-hour trip from the base. There are many other attractions as well, such as the Imperial Palace and famous shrines.

For more information, write to Public Affairs Office, HQ 374th Airlift Wing (PACAF), Unit 5123, APO AP 96328-0000. Home page: *www.yokota.af.mil.*

Army

CAMP ZAMA

In both 1992 and 1993, Camp Zama was named the Army Communities of Excellence (Overseas) runner-up. The installation earned this honor because its commanders are dedicated to the military personnel who live there, their families, and the base's civilian workforce.

History. U.S. troops first came to what is now Camp Zama on 5 September 1945, when one battalion of the 1st Cavalry Division entered Sobudai, the Japanese equivalent of West Point, which had been moved there in 1937. In 1950, Headquarters, U.S. Army, Japan (USARJ), moved to the site and has remained there ever since. The Commander, USARJ, commands all assigned U.S. Army forces in Japan and is responsible for logistical support to Army and U.S. government agencies in Japan, as well as the maintenance of war reserves and stocks for contingencies. About 1,900 Army personnel, 3,700 family members, and 970 Department of Defense employees are assigned to duty in Japan.

Housing and Schools. Approximately 1,050 sets of family quarters are available to people assigned to Camp Zama, including a high-rise apartment building and 64 town houses that were completed in 1991. These quarters are situated in three areas: Sagamihara housing area, Sagami General Depot, and Camp Zama itself. All three are within a short commute from the headquarters. The waiting time for occupancy varies from no wait to as much as six months. Zama has 77 units for temporary lodging.

Dependent education is conducted at two Department of Defense schools: Zama American High School and Arnn Elementary School. Total enrollment as of winter 2000 was over 1,300 children. The Army academic training division offers resident credit from the University of Maryland, the University of Oklahoma, and Central Texas College.

Personal Services. Adequate medical and dental facilities are provided at the Camp Zama clinic. Specialized medical and surgical care are offered at nearby military facilities. The post exchange offers a broad selection of clothing and electronic equipment. Concessions include a Burger King, a Baskin Robbins ice cream shop, and an Anthony's Pizza.

Recreation. A full range of recreational activities, including an active Army sports program, is offered to personnel living at Zama. In addition, the Far East Network of the Armed Forces Radio and Television Services broadcasts U.S. radio programs and closed-circuit English TV programs. The outdoor recreation program operates a rental center that features camping, hiking, skin diving, and fishing gear and supplies. Tours to Tokyo Disneyland and numerous other Japanese attractions are offered on a regular basis through the base tours office. A 43,000-square-foot community club offers a formal dining room, three lounges, and a ballroom.

The Local Area. The weather in the Tokyo area is often compared to that of Washington, D.C., with warm, humid summers and rather mild winters. This is not typical of all of Japan, however. In the mountainous areas of Honshu, winters are severe, and on the western slopes of these mountains, there is frequently enough snow for long skiing seasons. This part of Japan has a feature that is reminiscent of the American West Coast—in the Tokyo area, mild earthquake tremors often can be felt.

Camp Zama is only 40 miles from Tokyo, the world's most populous city. Within its 796 square miles live more than 11 million people. The city is a blend of the East and the West. Within walking distance of the Imperial Palace is the Ginza, one of the best-known shopping centers of the city. Tokyo's modern architecture and public transportation system are the envy of many more-modern American cities.

For more information, write to Chief, Public Affairs Office, HQ USARJ, Unit 45005, APO AP 96343-0054. Home page: *www.zama.army.mil.*

Marine Corps

IWAKUNI MARINE CORPS AIR STATION

If you can imagine an ice cream parlor coexisting with the graceful and ancient shrines of Japan nestled among groves of bamboo and pine, you can imagine Iwakuni, Japan, where the very new and the very old manage to get along quite peacefully.

History. The air station at Iwakuni began originally as a Japanese airfield in 1940 and then passed to the U.S. Air Force after passing through the hands of British, Australian, and New Zealand forces. The Marines came here in 1958, and today Iwakuni is the only Marine Corps base on the mainland of Japan. MCAS Iwakuni is home for about 10,000 U.S. servicemembers, U.S. civilians, and Japanese civilians supporting Marine Aircraft Group 12's F/A-18 Hornets, AV-8B Harriers, and EA-6B Prowlers.

Housing and Schools. There are a variety of government family quarters at Iwakuni, but even so, some families must rent private dwellings on the Japanese economy. There are many private rentals within a two-mile radius of the station. Rents are from $400 to $1,300 a month, with utilities ranging from $90 to $400 per month, depending on the size of the house and family. A forty-eight-room temporary-lodging facility is available at the station.

Matthew C. Perry Elementary and High Schools have an enrollment of approximately 600 dependent children in kindergarten through grade twelve. The station also has a child-care center and preschool facilities. Off-duty education is available through the Joint Education Center and includes college courses from the University of Maryland, Central Texas College, and Troy State University.

Personal Services. Medical care at Iwakuni is provided by a branch medical clinic. Patients requiring extensive hospitalization or specialized care are flown to the naval regional medical center at Yokosuka. General dental treatment is available for military personnel at Iwakuni, as are most specialty services, but dependent care is limited.

The station has both an exchange and a commissary store with 10,000 square feet of sales space and over 5,000 brand-name items, as well as fresh fruits and vegetables and bread and bakery products. The Marine Corps exchange, besides retail sales, offers a number of concessions, including a food court. An officers club, a staff NCO club, an enlisted club, and an all-ranks restaurant are also available on the station.

Recreation. Recreational facilities include a gymnasium with basketball courts, handball courts, a sauna, and a number of tennis courts. There are also a hobby shop, a tape room, a theater, a nine-hole golf course, 14-lane and six-lane bowling centers, an Olympic-size indoor swimming pool, and a roller rink. In addition, Information, Tours and Travel, combined with a civilian travel agency in one location, offers a quick and easy way for the military or family traveler to arrange travel plans.

The Local Area. Iwakuni lies at the southeasternmost end of Yamaguchi Prefecture, facing the Seto Inland Sea on the southeast and adjoining Otake City in Hiroshima Prefecture on the north; the Ozu River flows in between. The city is backed by mountains, and its front borders the Inland Sea. The Nishiki River runs through the city of Iwakuni from east to west. The climate in this part of Japan is wet, with plenty of fog in the spring and autumn.

Iwakuni has a population of more than 100,000. It is noted for the beautiful cherry trees (over 3,000 of them) that bloom in April and the famous Kintai Bridge and Castle. The local economy is extremely expensive, compared with U.S. standards. A gallon of gasoline off station fluctuates around $5. A soft drink in town can run as much as $1.50.

For more information, write to MSC Personal Services, Dept. FSC, PSC 561, Box 1861, FPO AP 96310. Home page: *www.iwakuni.usmc.mil.*

Navy

ATSUGI NAVAL AIR FACILITY

Atsugi personnel rarely venture off base without being heavily armed—with cameras, that is—because the area abounds with so many contrasting views of Japanese culture, traditional and modern, that even the most camera-shy sailor will turn into a shutterbug after a while.

History. The U.S. Navy first came to Atsugi in October 1950, when a team of a dozen Seabees arrived there to renovate the installation after it had been abandoned by the U.S. Army. Atsugi Naval Air Facility was officially commissioned on 1 December 1950. Today, it is used jointly by the U.S. Navy and the Japan Maritime Self-Defense Force. The base provides various aviation support functions for tenant and transient commands—for instance, Marine Corps helicopter units that support operations at nearby Camp Fuji and the helicopters of HSL-51 (a light helicopter squadron) that deploys to small ships. When the *USS Independence* uses nearby Yokosuka as its home port, Atsugi has been host to the embarked air wing, which flies there as the carrier nears its home port.

Housing and Schools. There are 493 sets of family quarters at Atsugi. The waiting period for occupancy ranges from 18 to 24 months. Off-base apartment rentals range from $750 to $1,200 a month, depending on unit size. There is also a Navy Lodge with 88 rooms.

Children living at Atsugi attend the Shirley Lanham Elementary School at the air facility or Zama American Middle and High School at nearby Camp Zama. A preschool program is also available at the air facility. The Navy campus provides educational guidance and counseling to active-duty military personnel and their dependents, and courses at the college level are offered on base by the University of Maryland and Central Texas College.

Personal Services. Most medical and dental services are available on base through the naval regional medical center branch clinic. Supportive dependent dental care is of the maintenance type only, but a percentage of time is usually available for these services.

The Atsugi Navy exchange offers a broad range of outlets where articles and services may be obtained. These include a main retail store; a minimart; a furniture mart; snack bars; and a personal services arcade, which houses a flower shop, a portrait painter, and other concessions. The exchange also operates a garage that can repair most automobiles. Atsugi's commissary store offers a wide variety of goods, such as fresh fruits and vegetables, as well as many stateside products, such as frozen, canned, and packaged goods.

There is also a Japanese-American exchange that includes three dining facilities. This exchange, commonly known as the Kosei Center, offers items sold on the Japanese economy at a discount.

Recreation. Recreation facilities at Atsugi include the Trilogy enlisted club, the Skymasters CPO club, and an officers club. The facility's 18-hole golf course is used by service personnel from stations throughout the area. A rod and gun club organizes shooting, hunting, fishing, and other outdoor sports and maintains a skeet and trap range for the use of its members. There is also a pro-golf shop operated by MWR.

The Local Area. Atsugi is in nearly the same latitude as Washington, D.C., and has a similar climate. The four seasons are distinct, with warm, humid summers and chilly winters, but snow is rare. Rain is frequent and sometimes very heavy. Atsugi is not in an area of Japan often touched by typhoons, but its closeness to the sea often exposes it to heavy winds that sometimes brew rainstorms that can be quite violent.

For more information, write to Atsugi Family Services Center, PSC 477, Box 32, FPO AP 96306-1232. Home page: *www.atsugi.navy.mil.*

FLEET ACTIVITIES, SASEBO

Sasebo has been a naval city since 1 July 1889, when, as a lowly lieutenant commander, the famous Admiral Heihachiro Togo—victor over the Russian fleet at the Battle of Tsushima in 1905—visited there.

History. The land parcels around Sasebo Harbor were developed as an Imperial Japanese Navy Base in 1889, and during World War II, ships like the battleship *Musashi* operated from its facilities. U.S. forces first came to Sasebo in September 1945, and Fleet Activities was established there on 30 June 1946. The old Imperial Japanese Navy dockyard is occupied today by SSK, a commercial company and the largest employer in Sasebo.

Today Sasebo supports U.S. naval forces in four principal areas: fuel storage, ordnance storage, ship repair, and fleet liberty. The city of Sasebo, with a population of 250,000, is an ideal liberty port from the Navy's standpoint, with a clean downtown area, virtually free of crime and drugs, and many tourist attractions. During 1994, 109 ships visited Sasebo to take advantage of its facilities, which can service conventional aircraft carriers, as well as nuclear submarines. Sasebo is home to approximately 2,450 active-duty military personnel.

Housing and Schools. There are 643 housing units available at Sasebo, 155 at main base and 488 at the Hario Village, about a thirty- to forty-five-minute drive away. Nearly 400 families live at Hario. The Navy runs free bus service between the main base and the Hario Village complex. A new 32-room Navy Lodge opened in 1992.

School facilities for dependent children in kindergarten through twelfth grade are available on base. Approximately 300 children are enrolled in the Department of Defense schools at Sasebo.

Personal Services and Recreation. Medical care is provided by the U.S. naval regional medical center at Yokosuka, which maintains a branch clinic at Sasebo. Hario Village has a gym, a softball field, a golf driving range, a swimming pool, a Navy exchange and commissary, an all-hands club, a post office, a dispensary, a library, a community center, hobby and woodworking shops, and a gas station.

The Local Area. Sasebo is located on the western shore of Kyushu Island and is the second-largest city in Nagasaki Prefecture. It is about 800 miles from Tokyo, 120 miles from the Korean peninsula, and 40 miles from Nagasaki. Within a few miles of the base is the Saikai National Sea Park, a marine preserve of more than 1,500 small islands that offers excellent fishing and boating. Other sightseeing havens include the cities of Nagasaki and Fukuoka, and historic Hirado Island, the area in which the novel *Shogun* was based.

The average winter temperature in Sasebo seldom dips below 42° F, and July and August average 82 to 101° F.

For more information, write to Public Affairs Office, Fleet Activities, Sasebo, PSC 476, Box 1, FPO AP 96322-1100. Home page: *www.cfas.navh.mil.*

FLEET ACTIVITIES, YOKOSUKA

Yokosuka is a city of many faces. For example, only a five-minute walk from the bustling metropolis surrounding Chuo train station is a tranquil seaside park built around the old Imperial battleship *Mikasa.* There are also many small Japanese restaurants, where you may buy a beer to go with your dinner, which might include sushi (strips of uncooked fish atop cakes of cold cooked rice), kake soba (plain noodles served in broth), or shabu-shabu (thinly sliced meat served in boiling water).

History. Yokosuka (pronounced "yo-ko-ska") Naval Base laid the keel of its first ship in 1866, and the largest Japanese ship, the *Shinano,* a 68,000-ton aircraft carrier, was launched there in October 1944. It was sunk by a U.S. sub while in trials in Sagami Bay in November 1944, never having launched a plane or fired a shot. The base surrendered on 30 August 1945. Today Yokosuka is the largest U.S. naval shore facility in the Far East, covering approximately 500 acres. The Commander, Fleet Activities, Yokosuka (COMFLEACT), maintains and operates the base for logistic servicing of U.S. naval forces assigned to the western Pacific.

Housing and Schools. Yokosuka has housing facilities for 1,750 families at the station itself. Additional housing is available for 405 families in the Negishi Housing Area, Yokohama, 17 miles north of the base. Waiting periods for occupancy vary from 12 to 28 months, depending on grade. About 1,900 families live off base in private rental units. The Navy Lodge has 165 rooms, 110 with kitchenettes, available for transients and guests.

There are two elementary schools: Sullivan's Elementary at Yokosuka and Byrd at Negishi. Nile C. Kinnick High School at Yokosuka draws students from Yokosuka and Negishi. The fleet Navy campus provides college courses from Central Texas College and the University of Maryland.

Personal Services. Medical care is provided by Yokosuka U.S. Naval Hospital, a five-story, 110-bed facility. The Yokosuka U.S. Naval Dental Clinic provides routine dental care on a space-available basis for command-sponsored dependents.

The commissary at Yokosuka stocks 7,000 line items of food and household supplies. The Navy exchange has two major outlets in the Yokosuka area and carries a wide range of merchandise. Colocated with the main exchange is a minimart convenience store, open from 7 A.M. to 10 P.M. daily. There is also a package store that sells alcoholic beverages, soft drinks, mixers, and snacks. Other major exchange services include a contract taxi service, several fast-food emporiums (including a Pizza Inn, a Baskin Robbins, and a McDonald's), a variety of restaurants, home appliance and car rentals, a gas station, an auto hobby shop, barber and beauty shops, an optical shop (no contact lenses available, however), and a video rental shop. The fleet exchange carries electronic equipment at reasonable prices for military personnel.

Recreation. Recreational facilities include four military clubs and athletic facilities. The enlisted club, Club Alliance, is the largest club in the Navy and offers three floors of discos, bars, and dining areas. Yokosuka's other three clubs are the Admiral Arleigh A. Burke officers club, the CPO club, and the Negishi Club.

A wide range of athletic and recreational facilities is available in Yokosuka. Two large gyms offer saunas, Nautilus equipment, extensive outdoor athletic fields and tennis courts, a racquetball court complex, a pro shop, and gear issues. Negishi's gym offers a new aerobics center, a pro shop, saunas, a weight room, gear issue, and tennis, basketball, and volleyball courts. There are also four swimming pools (one fully enclosed), a 32-lane bowling center, a roller skating rink, a sailing facility that offers free lessons, two movie theaters, and a tour office that offers Navy people and their families a wide variety of shopping, special events, entertainment, and sightseeing tours to such places as Mount Fuji, Tokyo, Kyoto, Hong Kong, and even Thailand.

Yokosuka's climate has often been compared to that of Washington, D.C. Summers are hot and humid with temperatures in the 80s and 90s; winters are cold, with temperatures in the 20s and 30s but little snow accumulation.

Not more than half an hour from the base is historic Kamakura, which is accessible by rail. (It's the fifth stop from Yokosuka, known as Kita-Kamakura.) Here is the world-famous Daibutsu, the Great Buddha, cast in bronze in the year 1252. At 44 feet high, it is the largest uncovered buddha in Japan. Among the many attractions here is the Enkakuji Temple, founded in 1282; one of its features is an immense bronze bell cast in 1301.

For more information, write to COMFLEACT Family Service Center, Code 013, PSC 473, Box 1, FPO AP 96349-1100. Home page: *www.nctsfe.navh.mil.*

KOREA

Air Force

KUNSAN AIR BASE

Kunsan Air Base, home of the 8th Fighter Wing (FW), "Wolf Pack," lies seven miles from Kunsan City on the west coast of the Korean peninsula, near the Kum River estuary.

History. Originally built by the Japanese as a fighter-interceptor base in 1938, the base became home for the U.S. Military Assistance Advisory Group following World War II. In August 1950, Kunsan was captured by the North Koreans; in September of that year, U.S. forces recaptured the city and the base. The 8th FW, Kunsan's current occupant, flies the F-16 Fighting Falcon aircraft. Over 2,500 military personnel are stationed at Kunsan.

Housing and Schools. There are no family housing or child-care facilities at Kunsan. A few personnel do have their families there, but they are required to live on the local economy. For the most part, economy housing is substandard, and strict safety and hygiene rules must be met before American personnel are authorized to occupy off-base housing. There are no schools on base or in Kunsan City to serve American dependents.

Personal Services. Medical care is provided by the USAF Hospital, Kunsan. Patients requiring care beyond the capabilities of the hospital are sent to the 121st Evacuation Hospital at Yongsan, in Seoul.

The Local Area. Kunsan City is a deepwater port that can accommodate large oceangoing vessels. With a population of almost 200,000, the city lists fishing as a major industry, along with plywood and shoemaking. The city has many interesting places to see, such as parks and temples, and there are plenty of markets in which to shop. Commercial airline service to Kunsan began in December 1992.

For more information, write to Public Affairs Office, Unit 2090, 8th FW (PACAF), APO AP 96264-2090. Home page: *www.kunsan.af.mil.*

OSAN AIR BASE

The country around Osan Air Base has seen some of the most desperate fighting in the annals of American military history.

At a spot only a few miles north of the base on the road to Suwon, 408 men of Task Force Smith lost their lives in the initial action between U.S. and Communist forces in the Korean War on 5 July 1950. The task force held its position for seven hours that day against an entire North Korean division with 37 tanks supporting it. The survivors fought on for another sixteen days, delaying the North Koreans until the 24th Infantry Division could land at the port of Pusan and secure a defensive perimeter around the city.

On 7 February 1951, along the slopes of Hill 180, which today dominates Osan Air Base, Capt. Lewis L. Millett led his men in a bayonet charge against Communist Chinese forces. That action was the first company-size bayonet charge made by the U.S. Army since World War I, and for his heroic action that day Captain Millett was awarded the Medal of Honor.

History. Prior to the outbreak of the Korean War, the area now designated Osan Air Base consisted of four villages and a number of rice paddies where the runway now lies. Originally designated K-55, the base was not renamed until late 1956. Today the base covers 1,250 acres and boasts a 9,000-foot runway. It is home to the 7th Air Force Headquarters, the 51st Wing, and the air arm of the U.S. Forces, Korea, Air Combat Command. The pilots of the 36th Fighter Squadron of the 51st Wing fly F-16 C/D model aircraft, while those of the wing's 25th Fighter Squadron fly OA-10 Thunderbolt IIs. Osan is home to 6,700 U.S. military personnel, their 2,100 family members, and 300 Department of Defense civilian employees.

Housing and Schools. There are 275 units of family housing available for authorized military personnel on base at Osan's Mustang Village. Housing is also available off base but must meet required health and safety inspections. The housing referral office at Osan keeps track of acceptable housing in the area.

Single military personnel live in 5,200 dormitory rooms on base and 90 units in Air Force Village. Dorms on base include carpeting, refrigerators, and semiprivate baths. Officers and senior NCOs have private rooms, and many have cooking facilities.

Osan American School for elementary and junior high students is located next to the commissary. High school students attend classes at Seoul American School located at Yongsan Army Garrison; bus transportation is provided. A child-care facility and a preschool are also available at Osan. The base education office offers college-level courses from Central Texas College, the University of Maryland, the University of Oklahoma, and Troy State University. Osan's base library offers 35,000 volumes for the reader and researcher.

Personal Services. Medical and dental care at Osan are provided by the 51st Medical Group in a 30-bed, 92,000-square-foot hospital facility. Specialized care is available at the 121st Evacuation Hospital in Seoul or from hospitals in Japan and Hawaii.

Osan has a 20,000-square-foot commissary stocked with over 9,000 items, an exchange, a barber shop, a beauty shop, a food court, a launderette, a dry cleaner, a gas station, and a movie theater. An arcade also offers everything from custom tailoring to Korean-made furniture and sporting goods.

Recreation. For the bowler, there is a 22-lane alley at Osan; golfers will enjoy the 18-hole course there. Officers and NCO clubs, as well as an aero club, arts and crafts facilities, a 24-hour recreation facility, and a base gymnasium, round out the recreational facilities at Osan.

The Local Area. The village of Osan lies 35 miles south of Seoul and six miles from Osan-Ni, its namesake village. The climate in Korea is temperate, with generally humid weather; the hottest months are July and August and the coldest are December and January. The mean temperature at Osan is in the 80s in the summer and in the mid- to upper 30s in the winter.

For more information, write to 51st Wing Public Affairs Office, Unit 2067, APO AP 96278-2067. Home page: *www.osan.af.mil.*

Army

CAMP CARROLL

Sometimes called "Wigwam," after the nearby town of Waegwan, population 30,000, Camp Carroll lies near the Naktong River, nestled among rolling, tree-covered hills and terraced rice fields, and is only a three-hour drive from Seoul.

History. Named in honor of SFC Charles R. Carroll, who was killed in action near Waegwan, what is today called Camp Carroll was part of the famous Pusan Perimeter established in the early days of the Korean War to halt the Communist North Korean armies sweeping down on the United Nations forces from the north. It was from this contracted, defensive posture in September 1950 that the UN forces burst out upon the invading armies, in conjunction with General MacArthur's landing at Inchon, to pinch off the North Korean assault.

Today Camp Carroll, a subinstallation of Camp Henry at Taegu, is home to the 6th Ordnance Battalion, a subordinate unit of the 19th Theater Army Area Command. The battalion exercises control over six ordnance companies located throughout the Republic of Korea and is also responsible for monitoring the Chinhae Ammunition Pier (on the southeast coast, opposite Pusan) for explosive safety. The battalion's basic mission is ammunition accountability, surveillance, and maintenance supervision. Its subordinate units coordinate directly with the Republic of Korea Army units who receive, store, issue, and transport the ammunition in accordance with an international agreement established in 1974 to govern the handling and management of U.S.-titled ammunition. Also stationed at Camp Carroll is the 23rd Chemical Battalion. Authorized a wartime strength of 720 personnel, only 50 are U.S. soldiers; the remainder of the battalion's complement are Korea Service Corps personnel.

Housing and Schools. Currently, all government family quarters and schools are located in Taegu, about 15 miles southeast of Waegwan. School, work, and other shuttle buses run from 6:30 A.M. to as late as midnight on weekends to provide access to the Taegu Military Community. The education center provides complete vocational and technical programs in automotive, electrical, welding, and computer science disciplines. College courses available on post are given under the auspices of the University of Maryland. There are also a language lab and a post library.

Personal Services. Medical and dental care are available on post, although the major medical facility for soldiers and their dependents is the 121st Evacuation Hospital, in Seoul. A post exchange, a commissary, and a clothing sales store are also located on the installation.

Recreation. Camp Carroll boasts a complete range of recreational facilities. The all-ranks club, opened in 1986 at a cost of $2 million, is available to military personnel and their families; a gymnasium with a fully equipped weight room and racquetball courts opened in 1982; a music/theater entertainment center was completed in 1987; and the arts and crafts center was totally refurbished in 1986. In addition, there are a movie theater, a swimming pool, a bowling alley, a recreation center, and three snack bars.

On the weekends, there are a number of inexpensive day-long tours offered to a large number of attractions, including the Joint Security Area in Panmunjom, shopping trips to the markets of Seoul, and visits to the grounds of ancient Buddhist temples.

For more information, write to Army Community Service, Unit 15476, APO AP 96260-0546. E-mail: *trappev@usfk.Korea.army.mil.*

CAMP CASEY

Camp Casey is located only twelve miles from the 38th Parallel, which has divided the Republic of Korea from the "Workers' Paradise" of North Korea since 1953. Named after Maj. Hugh B. Casey, who died on a hill overlooking Camp Casey in January 1952, today the installation covers over twelve square miles and is home to the majority of the 2nd Infantry Division's 16,500 soldiers. The units stationed there consist of the 1st and 2nd Brigades, the Division Support Command, and several separate battalion- and company-size units. The division headquarters is located at Camp Red Cloud, just outside scenic Uijongbu, nine miles south of Camp Casey.

Housing and Schools. Because duty at Camp Casey is considered a hardship tour, family housing is not authorized there. Personnel assigned to the 2nd Infantry Division who do bring their families must find accommodations on the local economy. Landlords require a cash deposit in advance, which can range from $500 to as much as $5,000, depending on the type of dwelling. Rents vary from as little as $200 a month for an unfurnished one-bedroom apartment without modern cooking or toilet facilities to $700 a month for a modern three-bedroom unfurnished unit. Only privately operated schools are available for children.

Personal Services and Recreation. Medical care is provided by a clinic located at Casey, and definitive medical care is available from the 121st Evacuation Hospital in Seoul. There are both a commissary and a post exchange at Camp Casey, as well as a concessionaire, a barber and beauty parlor, a coin laundry, a bookstore, a Popeye's, and a Burger King. Banking and credit union facilities are also available. Recreational facilities include an arts and craft shop, a bowling alley, and a swimming pool.

The Local Area. Camp Casey is located 25 miles north of Seoul, the capital city of the Republic of Korea. Just outside the gate is the town of Tongduchon, which occupies over 50 square miles of land and has a population of 70,000. Tongduchon is renowned for its shopping and entertainment districts.

Railroad and bus services are available for transportation to and from Seoul, but most soldiers take the Myung Jin Shuttle Bus, which cost 650 won as of winter 2000. A taxi cost around $40. The trip to Seoul takes approximately one and a half hours by road.

An area of interest is Soyo Mountain, where there are beautiful Buddhist temples and waterfalls.

For more information, write to ACS, 501st Opps Support Group, Unit 15543, APO AP 96224-0453.

CAMP HIALEAH

At first glance, there appears to be nothing in common between Camp Hialeah, the Pusan Military Command's major installation, and the famous racetrack in Florida, after which it is named. But the main area of Camp Hialeah was once owned by the Cho Sun Racing Association (also known as Morning Calm Horse Racing Association). The road circling the Hialeah Heaven Club and Headquarters, 20th Support Group, was the track, and the entrance to the Pusan officers open mess was the ticket office. So hence the name—Camp Hialeah—which, under the circumstances, seems quite natural.

History. During World War II, the area now known as Camp Hialeah was used by the Japanese Imperial Army for bivouac, training, and maneuvers. U.S. troops occupied the site in 1945, the first site of allied occupation. In those days, Hialeah was in the suburbs of Pusan City, but now it is in the middle of a bustling neighborhood and home to the Army, Navy, Air Force, and Marine Corps in the southern part of Korea. After 1950 and the outbreak of the Korean Conflict, the 8,069th U.S. Replacement Depot operated from the compound and was a hub for the comings and goings of troops and materiel. After the Treaty of

Panmunjom in 1953, Hialeah housed troops of the Korean Communications Zone. Today the camp serves over 20 different commands and approximately 500 military personnel, 200 U.S. civilian employees, and 450 dependents, living and working within the 137-acre confines of Camp Hialeah.

Housing. There are 180 units of government family housing available at Camp Hialeah. Housing rental costs on the local economy range from about $750 a month for a two-bedroom duplex to as much as $1,300 a month for a four-bedroom apartment; utilities can range from $150 to $250 a month, depending on the size of the unit.

Personal Services. Camp Hialeah is a small, self-contained city that offers its residents the services available in any comparable community in the United States. The housing area contains schools, a dispensary and dental clinic, retail sales outlets in the post exchange, and various concessions, including a garage, a snack bar, and a commissary. It supports those residing in the Pusan area, including Pier 8, the Pusan Storage Facility, the Defense Reutilization Management Office, and several commands from Kimhae Airport, west of Pusan.

Recreation. Sedentary entertainment is available through the community club system. The more athletically inclined may take advantage of a bowling alley, a gymnasium, a tennis court, a swimming pool, and a lighted athletic field. The recreation center provides various craft shops, weekly tours, and many organized seasonal sporting events.

The Local Area. Pusan, the largest port city in the Republic of Korea, boasts a population of 4 million. The metropolis sprawls 18 miles east to west and 13 miles north to south; the port alone measures 14 miles in circumference.

The climate in this part of Korea is generally comfortable year-round. In July and August, the temperatures sometimes reach as high as 95° F, and rainfall during those months averages six to 12 inches. In December and January, the coldest months, the thermometer may dip to as low as 20° F, but there are only traces of snow in winter. The temperature in Pusan is generally about 10° warmer in the winter and cooler in the summer than it is in Seoul, about 200 miles to the north.

Pusan is a city of vivid contrasts, combining the hustle and bustle of a major deepwater port city with the splendid parks, museums, and ancient temples for which most Korean cities are famous. First opened to international trade in 1876, Pusan now receives approximately 45 percent of South Korea's export items and 95 percent of its container transport. Pomosa Temple, about 15 miles north of Camp Hialeah, has been a center of Buddhist ritual for more than 1,300 years. The UN cemetery in Pusan, the only one of its kind, is the final resting place for over 2,200 soldiers from sixteen nations who died fighting in the Korean War.

For more information, write to Army Community Services, Unit 15181, APO AP 96259-0270.

TAEGU MILITARY COMMUNITY

The Taegu area sits in a bowl, surrounded on all sides by a wall of steep hills. It is known as both the hottest and the coldest city in the Republic of Korea.

The Taegu Military Community (TMC) consists of four military installations—Camp Henry, Camp Walker, Camp George, and the Taegu Storage Area. The major U.S. military command in the community is the 19th Command, which plans and directs the provision of direct combat service support throughout Korea.

Housing and Schools. There are 96 units of family housing at Camp Walker and 200 at Camp George. Waiting times vary from fewer than 60 days for quarters at Camp Walker to sixty to ninety days at Camp George.

The Taegu American School serves students in all grades, from kindergarten through high school. Adult education is available from the University of Maryland, Chapman College, the University of Southern California, and Central Texas College.

Personal Services. Medical care is provided by a local health clinic, but the major medical facility for U.S. forces personnel throughout Korea is the 121st Evacuation Hospital in Seoul, with a 300-bed inpatient and an extensive outpatient clinic facility.

Recreation. Located at Camp Walker, about a 20-minute walk from Camp Henry, are a post exchange, an arcade, a commissary, a snack bar, a Burger King, a recreation center, a gymnasium, bowling lanes, a library, a chapel, officers and enlisted clubs, a nine-hole golf course, a swimming pool, and most of the troop billets. A movie theater, an NCO club, a snack bar, and some bachelor enlisted rooms are at Camp Henry.

The Local Area. Taegu is known as the "Apple Capital of Korea" and is one of the Republic's larger cities, with a population of 2.5 million. It lies 170 miles southeast of Seoul and 86 miles northwest of Pusan, in the Nakdong River valley, bounded on the north and south by the Palgong Mountains.

Taegu first appears in the historic record in 366 A.D. In 757 A.D., the city was granted its present name, which means "great hill," perhaps a reference to the mud-wall fortress that once formed the center of the ancient city.

For more information, write to Army Community Affairs, Unit 15494, Box 2093, APO AP 96218. Home page: *www.korea.army.mil.*

U.S. ARMY GARRISON, SEOUL

At one time, duty in Korea was considered the "best-kept secret" in the Army. Considered a hardship tour even today (most soldiers cannot bring their families), the fact is that a tour of duty in Korea can be one of the most pleasant and educational interludes in a soldier's enlistment or career. This is due in part to the fact that since the end of the Korean War, U.S. forces have acted as a bulwark against incursions from North Korea (Seoul is less than forty miles from the Demilitarized Zone). But more importantly, the Koreans have used the years of peace since 1954 to build for themselves one of the most modern and progressive societies in all Asia.

History. The primary U.S. Army headquarters in Korea is the 8th U.S. Army. The 2nd Infantry Division, the principal ground defense component of the 8th Army, currently occupies blocking positions north of Seoul, along the traditional invasion routes from the north. In July 1957, the Headquarters, United Nations Command, moved from Tokyo to Seoul; concurrently, Headquarters, U.S. Forces, Korea, was formed to serve as a control and planning headquarters for all U.S. ground, air, and naval elements assigned to the Republic of Korea. Yongsan is also home to the UN Command, Combined Forces Command (the Republic of Korea and United States) and U.S. Forces Korea. Yongsan compound houses the headquarters and military community support facilities.

Housing and Schools. There are more than 1,250 sets of family housing in the Seoul area, consisting of two-, three-, and four-bedroom duplex and apartment units. Priority for occupancy goes to key personnel whose positions are considered essential to the command and who are in Korea on a two-year tour; other command-sponsored military personnel are placed on a waiting list.

Seven Department of Defense schools are located throughout Korea. Families assigned to the Seoul area may send their children to the Seoul American Elementary School or the Seoul American High School. A child-care center is available at Yongsan South Post and Hannam Village, a housing area near the Han River. The Yongsan education center offers adult education in the form of college programs from several well-respected, fully accredited U.S. colleges and universities.

Personal Services and Recreation. On-post facilities in the Seoul area are excellent. The Yongsan library, for instance, is the largest Army library in Korea, with 140,000 volumes. Also located on Yongsan are a modern NCO club, a modern 32-lane bowling center, a community club, a youth activities center, a music theater, two gymnasiums, three swimming pools (including one year-round pool on the main post), and tennis courts. The Moyer Community Activities Center includes a recreation center, an arts and crafts center, and Yongsan Tour and Travel, which runs an extensive domestic and out-of-country tour program. AAFES operates a movie theater on Yongsan. The 8th Army golf club, a championship 18-hole course that serves an important role in both the U.S. and Korean communities, has been relocated to Sungnam, a suburb of Seoul, about 45 minutes from the Yongsan compound. Bus transportation is provided to players and guests.

Situated in the middle of Yongsan Compound's South Post is the Dragon Hill Lodge (DHL), a 229-room military hotel for the use of all classes of Department of Defense–affiliated personnel. An expansion begun in 1998 will soon add 100 more rooms to the facility. Rates for military personnel on leave start at $43 per night, depending on rank. All rooms are equipped with a TV, VCR, refrigerator, microwave oven, double bed, and sleeper sofa. The DHL also has four restaurants, two lounges, and a shopping arcade offering everything from Asian gift items to designer suits. There are also a banking facility, a hair-care center, and a tailor shop.

DHL's dining facilities consist of the Greenstreet offering a la carte Sunday brunch and everything else from soup and salad to T-bone steak. The Greenstreet is open from 6 A.M. to 2 P.M. for breakfast and lunch and from 5 P.M. to 10 P.M. for dinner. The Oasis offers a choice of Mexican or American food and deli items including freshly baked pastries, cakes, and a variety of hot and cold takeout food. It's open from 11 A.M. to 10 P.M. daily. Bentley's Pub provides a congenial watering spot open weekdays from 4 P.M. and weekends from 11 A.M. The Whispers Lounge, open the same hours as Bentley's, is the place to go for quiet conversation and liquid refreshment. And just added is Primo's Express, a delightful pizza and pasta restaurant for those going off their diets. This is not the Yongsan your father knew!

Rounding out the picture at DHL is The Point, a membership health club featuring a wide variety of state-of-the-art equipment and fitness programs for members and guests. This equipment includes the newest line from LifeFitness, Stairmaster, and Cybex. Aerobics, sports events, and personal exercise programs with certified trainers are also available. The locker rooms are first-class with all the amenities for personal grooming.

To make reservations from CONUS, call 011-82-2-790-0016 or fax 011-82-2-790-1576 or send an e-mail to *www.dragonhilllodge.com.*

One of the most spectacular tourist attractions in this part of Asia is Cheju Island, an hour flight from Seoul, about halfway between Japan and Korea. Fresh- and saltwater fishing are available in the many lakes, ponds, streams, and off-shore waters.

The Local Area. Seoul, the capital city of Korea, was founded in 1392. Although it was almost totally destroyed during the war (Seoul was captured twice by the Communists and recaptured by the UN forces), today Seoul is an ultramodern metropolis with a population of over 10 million. It was chosen as the site of the 1988 Summer Olympics.

Korea is a peninsula that extends 525 miles from the Asian mainland, varying in width from 100 to 130 miles. While Korea's mountains are not spectacularly high, the country is extremely rugged, with only 20 percent of its land flat enough to be cultivated. Roughly equal in size to the state of Virginia, the Republic of Korea has a population of about 43 million. The literacy rate among its people is 97 percent, and the per capita income is $8,400 per year. The climate is rarely extreme. Winters are mildly cold and dry, with little snow accumulation outside the mountainous areas. Summers are sultry with a distinct rainy season, not unlike those of Washington, D.C.

For more information, write to Public Affairs Office, 34th Support Group, Unit 15333, APO AP 96205-0010.

THE NETHERLANDS

Army

SCHINNEN

Welcome to the Netherlands, the land of windmills, wooden shoes, tulips, and dikes.

History. Schinnen, located in Limburg Province, between Germany and Belgium, is home to the 254th Base Support Battalion. Originally designated the Allied Forces Central Europe (AFCENT) Support Activity at Fountainbleu, France, this function moved to South Limburg, the Netherlands, in 1971, when France withdrew from NATO. The Schinnen military community was redesignated a base support battalion effective 1 October 1993. Schinnen takes its name from the torpedo factory that used to be there.

The peacetime mission of the 254th BSB is to provide basic quality of life support to the units within its area of responsibility. In war, the battalion would open and operate the Netherlands line of communication, receiving, processing, and deploying forces and equipment through the Netherlands, Germany, and other locations. The 254th BSB supports operations at Coevorden, in northeast Netherlands, along the German border, where the Combat Equipment Battalion Northwest (CEBN) is stationed, and the Military Traffic Management Command (MTMC), Europe, in Capelle Aan Den Ijssel, a suburb on the eastern edge of Rotterdam, just north of the Ijssel River. The CEBN mission is to receive, store, maintain, and issue prepositioned organizational material configured to unit sets (POMCUS), everything up to and including Abrams main battle tanks. The MTMC during the last few years has averaged over four million measured tons per year through the Benelux ports.

Today the 254th BSB supports a population of 5,000 active-duty U.S. personnel, 3,800 family members, over 2,000 U.S. reserve component personnel, and 620 Department of Defense employees.

Housing and Schools. There are no government-owned quarters in the Netherlands. All family quarters are leased and usually are available to incoming personnel within three to four weeks during the summer or 30 to 90 days in the winter. There are no government-leased quarters for officers. The leased housing areas are widespread throughout the local communities and are generally small, containing units accommodating from ten to 25 families. Temporary military lodging is not available. The average rent paid in this area as of January 1996 was about $915 a month.

The AFCENT international campus at Brunssum, 15 minutes from Schinnen, boasts a highly qualified staff of U.S., United Kingdom, and Canadian teachers providing schooling from kindergarten through high school for dependent children. Students are bused to and from the campus. Other schools available include Coevorden American (kindergarten through eighth grade), Saint Maartens International in Groningen (seventh through twelfth grades), American International of Rotterdam (kindergarten through eighth grade), and the American School of the Hague (kindergarten through twelfth grade). Adult education is available from the University of Maryland, Central Texas College, City Colleges of Chicago, Big Ben Community College, and Oklahoma University.

Full-day, hourly, and before- and after-school care are available for children ages six weeks to five years from the child-development center at Brunssum, with a yearly $12 registration fee per family. As of January 1996, the waiting period for enrollment was six months.

Personal Services. Medical service is provided by the Geilenkirchen health clinic at the Geilenkirchen NATO Air Base in Germany, approximately 30 minutes from Schinnen. Definitive medical care is available at U.S. military hospitals in Germany at Wurzburg, Landstuhl, or Heidelberg.

The Army and Air Force Exchange Services operates a main exchange on the Schinnen compound; there is a smaller store at AFCENT. The Schinnen commissary provides grocery items, produce, meat, plants, fresh pizza, a delicatessen, frozen foods, and special orders. A shopette, a dry cleaner, and shoe repair shops are also available.

Recreation. The colocated clubs at Brunssum, formerly the officers and NCO clubs, now known as Club 13, offer dining, private parties, meeting and reception rooms, and catering. At Schinnen, there are an outdoor recreation center, a bowling center, and a fully equipped fitness center with Nautilus equipment. At AFCENT, there are a swimming pool with a sauna, sports fields and a pavilion, arts and crafts and auto craft shops, a golf course, a gym, and a 385-seat movie theater. The library at AFCENT has over 35,000 books and 200 newspapers and magazines.

The Local Area. The village of Schinnen is located near the Geleen Valley and has been occupied since at least 54 B.C., when it was a Roman colony known as Sunici Schinkes or Scynne. Terborg Castle was built there in 1285 A.D. It has been owned by the village since 1969 and today is used for many community social activities.

The climate in the Netherlands is generally cool and wet, with the coldest months from December to March. Much of the country is below sea level, and the proximity of the sea provides cool breezes and plenty of moisture. Annual precipitation is thirty inches, and temperatures average 34° F in winter and 78° F in summer.

For more information, write to Commander, 254th BSB, Attention: PAO, Unit 21602, APO AE 09703.

OKINAWA

Air Force

KADENA AIR BASE

Okinawa is primarily a Marine Corps station, but Kadena Air Base is home to 7,400 Air Force personnel, their family members, 1,500 Department of Defense civilian employees, and 700 dependent school staffers, for a total base population of 24,000.

History. Kadena was originally built by the Japanese, who surrendered it on 7 September 1945, following the Battle of Okinawa. The fighting resulted in the death of more than 12,500 Americans, 100,000 Japanese soldiers, and about 100,000 Okinawan civilians. The surrender site memorial is located in what is now the Stearley Heights housing area. Today Kadena's 14,000 acres are home to the 18th Wing's 25 squadrons, consisting of over 100 aircraft, including F-15C/D fighters, KC-135R tankers, E-3B AWACs, and HH-60G rescue helicopters. Torrii Station is also an important partner with Kadena Air Base.

Housing and Schools. There are more than 3,500 units of family housing at Kadena, situated among eleven different housing areas; total housing assets on the island are over 8,100 units, all of which, even those on Marine Corps, Army, and Navy installations, are managed by the Air Force. Guest facilities are available through the base billeting office.

All American children on Okinawa attend Department of Defense schools. The schools have an enrollment of approximately 10,000 students. Kadena has primary, intermediate, and high schools, as well as child-development and child-care centers. Adult education is offered through the base education office and includes college courses from Michigan State University, the University of Oklahoma, University of Maryland, Troy State University, and Central Texas College.

Personal Services. Health and dental services are offered through the 18th Medical Group and dental clinics. A medical staff of about 440 doctors, dentists, nurses, and technicians attends to the many needs of Kadena's Air Force population, seeing an average of 650 patients each day. Further care is available at the U.S. Naval Hospital, Camp Lester, a medical facility with a staff of 3,500 personnel.

The Defense Commissary Agency operates four branches on the island, while diverse shopping needs are met by the Army and Air Force Exchange Services. Eating establishments abound on Kadena and Okinawa: Mexican, Italian, and Chinese restaurants; a Popeye's; a Burger King; and a sandwich fare, plus a number of other concessions. There are also officers, NCO, and airmen's clubs. In addition, there are the Tee House restaurant on the golf course, overlooking the East China Sea, and Jack's Place, offering the best Kobe beef on Okinawa.

Recreation. Recreational facilities include the Kadena Marina, just outside Gate Four, where a charter fishing boat may be reserved; an eighteen-hole golf course; a miniature golf course; a 55,000-volume base library; a 46-lane bowling center; arts and crafts centers; four swimming pools; three fitness centers, including one of the Air Force's finest athletic facilities, the Risner Athletic Complex; dozens of tennis courts and ball fields; a community activities center, and more than 100 playgrounds.

The Air Force operates the Okuma Recreation Area, an island vacation site 51 miles north of the base, which offers seven year-round air-conditioned cabanas with 64 rooms and two large campsites. Facilities include a surfside restaurant, a bar and lounge, indoor and outdoor theaters, a nine-hole golf course, tennis courts, and beautiful white sandy beaches. Swimming, fishing, and boating can also be enjoyed in the area.

For more information, write to 18th Wing Public Affairs, Unit 5141, Box 30, APO AP 96368-5141.

Marine Corps

U.S. MARINE CORPS INSTALLATIONS, OKINAWA

History. The battle for Okinawa, which commenced on 1 April 1945, was one of the longest and most bitterly fought campaigns of the war in the Pacific. But with time, even the most bitter memories fade, and in 1972, the Ryukyu Islands (there are about 140 islands in the chain, of which Okinawa is the largest) were returned to Japan after being under American administration since 1945.

Of the approximately 30,000 U.S. personnel currently based on Okinawa, fully 18,000 of them are Marines, and the U.S. Marine Corps installations occupy about 10 percent of the island's total land area. The Marine installations on Okinawa stretch from one tip of the island to the other and fall under the corporate title of Camp S. D. Butler.

Going from the southwest to the northeast is Camp Kinser on the north, or East China Sea, side of the island, home for the 3rd Force Service Support Group and the Marine Corps Air Station at Futenma, home of the helicopter and transport aircraft of the 1st Marine Air Wing. Farther north, at Camp Foster, are the headquarters of the Commander, Marine Corps Bases Japan; Commanding General, 1st Marine Aircraft Wing; and Commanding General, Marine Corps Base, Camp S. D. Butler. The naval regional medical center is at Camp Lester and borders Kadena Air Base. On the Pacific side of the island are Camp McTureous, consisting mainly of military family housing units, and Camp Courtney, site of the command elements of the 3rd Marine Expeditionary Force, 3rd Marine Division, and 31st Marine Expeditionary Unit, overlooking Kin Bay. On the other side of the bay is Camp Hansen, home for the 3rd Surveillance, Reconnaissance, Intelligence Group, and a bit farther north is Camp Schwab, headquarters for the 4th Marine Regiment. In addition, large areas in the central and northern regions of the island are used as training areas.

Housing and Schools. More than 7,200 sets of family quarters are available for Marine and Navy personnel on Okinawa. The waiting period for these quarters varies from four to 12 months. The Kuwae Lodge at Camp Lester offers 70 single rooms and 40 adjoining rooms for incoming families. Other transients may be accommodated there on a space-available basis. There are also lodges at Camp Courtney and Camp Hansen.

Dependent children attend one of ten Department of Defense schools on Okinawa. These include seven elementary, one junior high, and two high schools. There are also three preschools on the island. A number of education centers on Okinawa offer college courses at both the graduate and undergraduate levels. These include the University of Maryland, the University of Oklahoma, the University of Southern California, and Central Texas Community College.

Personal Services. The primary medical care facility for Marine and Navy personnel on Okinawa is the U.S. naval hospital at Camp Lester. There are branch clinics at Camp Kinser; MCAS, Futenma; Camp Foster; and Camp Courtney.

Commissaries are located at Camp Foster, Kadena Air Base, Camp Courtney, and Camp Kinser. Exchanges are located at Kadena, Camp Foster, Futenma, Camp Kinser, Camp Courtney, Camp Hansen, Camp Schwab, and Camp Lester. Foodlands and coin laundries are conveniently located at facilities throughout the island. There are seven service stations and ten snack bars, as well as more than thirty different kinds of exchange repair outlets, offering services from air-conditioning repair to watch repair.

Recreation. Recreational activities and facilities are plentiful on Okinawa. There are ten bowling centers available to the military community, ranging in size from the 46-lane center at Kadena Air Base to the four-lane center at White Beach. Three military golf courses are also provided, as are two driving ranges. There are two skeet and trap ranges located at Camp Courtney and Camp Hansen. Swimmers have their choice of numerous sandy, tropical island beaches and 16 pools. There are seven gymnasiums on the island and even a roller skating rink at Kadena AB.

Outdoor recreation is even better. The Okuma Rest and Recreation Center, 51 miles north of Kadena and just outside the town of Hentona, is a 120-acre complex operated by the Air Force for all the military personnel on the island. Located on the East China Sea side of the island, the complex offers 58 cabanas. There are also a base exchange and a coin laundry, a surfside restaurant, a bar and lounge, and a recreation center. Camping is permitted in specified areas. Swimming, fishing, sailing, waterskiing, windsurfing, a nine-hole golf course, and many other facilities are available there. Another beach is Oura-Wan, at Camp Schwab; this 300-foot beach has beach house facilities. Marek and Schilling Parks, Kadena AB, and Camp Lester have picnic facilities for parties ranging in size from 75 to 200 persons.

The Local Area. Okinawa is 77 miles long and from two to 16 miles wide. To the east is the Pacific Ocean, and to the west is the East China Sea. The island lies about halfway between Japan and Taiwan. Over a million Okinawans (Japanese citizens) live there. Temperatures range from the low 50s during the winter to the 90s during the summer, so outdoor activities are possible year-round. Rainfall averages about 83 inches per year. The total land area of the island is 454 square miles. Northern Okinawa is heavily forested and has some rather high mountains and a few short rivers. At the southern end of the island is a plateau with steep cliffs. The southern portion of the island is densely populated. The city of Naha (population 310,000) is the principal metropolis of the island.

The original people of Okinawa were probably a mixture of several ethnic strains. Chinese culture made an impact on the islanders when trade began with them in 1372, but the islands were conquered by a band of Japanese warriors from southern Japan in 1609 and have remained under Japanese influence since then. Today the islands are a prefecture of the Japanese home islands.

For more information, write to Community Relations Officer, Marine Corps Base, Camp Smedley D. Butler, Unit 35026, FPO AP 96373-5001. Home page: *www.mcbbutler.usmc.mil.*

PUERTO RICO

Army

FORT BUCHANAN

Fort Buchanan is the Army's only active post in Puerto Rico and the Antilles. Today it is a Forces Command installation providing administrative and logistical support to all active-duty Army and reserve elements on the island, including one of the largest Reserve Officer Training Corps programs in the nation. Fort Buchanan is located in the southwest portion of the greater San Juan area. Headquarters, U.S. Army South is also based here.

History. Fort Buchanan was named after Brig. Gen. James A. Buchanan, first commander of the Puerto Rican Regiment, U.S. Volunteers, which was formed in 1900. The post was established on a 300-acre tract along the south shore of San Juan Bay in 1923 and served as a target range and maneuver area for Army and National Guard troops. Today its 450 military personnel support reserve and guard units as a mobilization station.

Housing and Schools. There are 361 sets of government quarters at Fort Buchanan—32 for field-grade officers, 141 for company-grade and warrant officers, 91 for senior NCOs, and 97 for junior enlisted personnel. The Su Casa Guest House offers 29 air-conditioned rooms for military personnel on permanent-change-of-station orders and for visiting military and civilian personnel. The rate is $27 per night, with special rates for additional guests and children. Information or reservations may be obtained by calling (809) 792-7977.

The Antilles Consolidated School System operates four schools at Fort Buchanan: an elementary school, an intermediate school, a middle school, and a high school. In addition, there is a child-care center that can accommodate children from six months to ten years of age. This facility also offers two preschool programs. The post education center offers a full range of educational assistance.

Personal Services. Medical care is provided by the U.S. Army health clinic, a satellite of the Eisenhower Medical Center of Fort Gordon, Georgia. The clinic provides general ambulatory care, including two family practice physicians, one internal medicine officer, and one general medicine officer. Dental services for active-duty military personnel and their dependents are available on a space-available basis.

The Fort Buchanan post exchange offers a wide range of services, including a main store, a convenience store, a toy store, a new car sales outlet, a beer and soda store, a service station, barber and beauty shops, optical and watch shops, a dry cleaner, a flower shop, a TV rental and repair shop, and a cafeteria. There is also a full-service commissary on post.

Persons being stationed at Fort Buchanan should be aware that a valid Puerto Rico driver's license must be obtained within 120 days of arrival. Also, an excise tax may be imposed on motor vehicles brought into Puerto Rico if they are purchased and shipped after the date of military orders assigning an individual to Fort Buchanan. The minimum tax payable is $250.

Recreation. The morale support activities (MSA) program at Fort Buchanan offers six core programs: arts and crafts, sports, youth activities, a library, tours and travel, and outdoor recreation/supply. The sports program provides a fitness center complete with a swimming pool, a sauna, and various courts, as well as an excellent scuba program. An eighteen-lane bowling center was opened in August 1992.

The outdoor recreation/supply program makes available boats and camping and picnic equipment at no charge for active-duty personnel and for a minimal fee to other authorized users.

MSA also operates a nine-hole golf course and four picnic areas throughout the post. A fitness and nature trail is available for those who enjoy walking and getting in touch with nature.

The Fort Buchanan Community Club features a large common ballroom and separate lounges, as well as dining and private activity rooms offering a menu of select cuisine and varied entertainment.

The Local Area. Puerto Rico was discovered by Christopher Columbus on 19 November 1493, during his second voyage to the New World. He named the island San Juan Bautista. Spanish settlement began in 1508, and the city of San Juan, the second oldest in the New World, was founded in 1521. Since 1917, the people of Puerto Rico have been U.S. citizens.

Nowhere else will you find scenery so varied in such a small place as you will in Puerto Rico. The island boasts glistening, palm-fringed beaches and green mountains. The sun shines steadily there throughout the year. San Juan is a city surrounded by ancient walls and fortresses that contrast with modern buildings and hotels.

There are a number of state forests in the commonwealth of Puerto Rico, as well as Luquillo National Forest, on the slopes of El Yunque, the only tropical rain forest in the U.S. National Park System. Along its coasts and in its mountains, Puerto Rico offers a number of beautiful resorts easily accessible by paved roads. Puerto Ricans are avid sports fans, and fishing, skin diving, sailing, and surfing are among their favorite pastimes. The island has one of the

A U.S. Navy Hornet Launching from the *USS George Washington*, near Roosevelt Roads, Puerto Rico U.S. NAVY PHOTO

world's largest underground cave systems and the world's largest radio telescope, both open to the public.

For more information, write to Army Community Services, HQ, Fort Buchanan, PR 00934, or call (787) 273-3400.

Home page: *www.buchanan.army.mil.*

Navy

ROOSEVELT ROADS NAVAL STATION

The name Roosevelt Roads is the heritage of both the station's wartime mission and the man who first conceived it, Franklin D. Roosevelt. The roadstead as envisioned by the president was never completed, but the name was carried over when the base was named after him.

History. Located on the eastern tip of Puerto Rico, the U.S. Naval Operation Base, Roosevelt Roads, was commissioned in 1943. The station's airfield stretches for 11,000 feet. "Roosey" is the largest naval station in the world, with 8,000 acres on the island of Puerto Rico and another 25,000 on nearby Vieques Island. Today the Commander, Naval Forces, Caribbean, and a number of tenant activities are based there. About 3,000 military personnel and their dependents, as well as 2,500 civilians, live and work there.

Housing and Schools. The station has 1,000 family housing units consisting of Capehart housing, built in 1959, which are single-level, single-family quarters, and Turnkey housing, built in 1974, which are two-story, multifamily units. These homes are situated in four housing areas. The waiting period can exceed six months. There are accommodations for 1,300 temporary-duty personnel; there are also 12 temporary-housing units for families waiting for a housing opening, but they are booked far in advance. There is also a 72-unit Navy Lodge at the station.

There are an elementary school, a middle school, and a high school at Roosey and adult education programs that offer courses from Central Texas College, New Hampshire College, and Columbia College.

Personal Services. Medical care is provided by a Navy hospital. The station has an exchange, a commissary, and numerous concessions, including a furniture store, a deli and pizza shop, snack bars, a minimart, a package store, an auto service center, and a gas station.

Recreation. Roosey offers a nine-hole golf course, a marina, a movie theater that offers two or three movies daily, two fitness centers, outdoor equipment rentals, a flying club, and two guarded beaches for swimming and other water fun. Various clubs are available at Roosey: the Grandstand Sports Lounge, open to all hands; the Dragon Inn, which offers authentic Chinese food; the All Hands Lounge; O'Reilly's at the officers club; and the Captain's Table, also open to all hands.

The Local Area. The coldest temperature ever recorded in Puerto Rico was 40° F in Aibonito in 1911; otherwise, the averages range from 70° F in winter to 73° F in July.

The nearest towns to Roosey are Ceiba, a small village, and Farjardo, a medium-size town, both right outside the base. Luquillo, famous for its beaches, and Humacao are within a 30-minute drive, while San Juan, the largest city on the island, is only about an hour away from Roosey, on the Atlantic side of the island. There is no government transportation between Roosey and San Juan. A taxi ride will cost about $50.

Puerto Rico is 100 miles long by 30 miles wide at its widest point. The interior is quite mountainous, with Cerro de Punta reaching an elevation of 4,389 feet. The island has a population of 3.4 million people. Discovered by Columbus in 1493 and settled by Ponce de Leon in 1508, Puerto Rico was part of the Spanish empire until 1898. Since 1917, Puerto Ricans have been U.S. citizens. San Juan has been the capital city of Puerto Rico since 1521. With its tropical climate, water sports are available year-round, and every year tourists flock to the island to enjoy its many beaches. Naval personnel and their families assigned duty at Roosey get it all free.

For more information, write to Family Service Center, U.S. Naval Station, Roosevelt Roads, PSC 1008, Box 3591, FPO AA 34051. Home page: *www.nctspr.navy.mil.*

SPAIN

Navy

ROTA U.S. NAVAL STATION

Rota is located on the Atlantic coast of Spain, across the bay from the city of Cadiz in Cadiz Province, in the region of Spain known as Andalusia. The vineyards of Jerez de la Frontera, eighteen miles inland from the base, are known for the excellent and only true sherry in the world.

History. The U.S. Navy first came to Rota in September 1953. A Spanish naval base (Base Naval de Rota) covering more than 6,000 acres just outside the city walls of Rota, the naval station is also home to approximately 8,500 U.S. military personnel. The U.S. Navy controls approximately 5,200 acres at Rota. The mission of the station is to service the 6th Fleet with fuel, ammunition, and spare parts and to coordinate all U.S. naval activities in Spain, Portugal, and Gibraltar.

Housing and Schools. There are more than 800 units of government housing at Rota. The older sets were built between 1957 and 1959, while the newer ones were built in 1965. Two-bedroom units for enlisted families are usually available in eighteen months, while two-bedroom units for officers have a waiting list of nine to 12 months. The Navy Lodge offers 22 guest units suitable for families of up to five people. The Gateway Inn (phone: 011-34-956-82-1751) and the Navy Lodge (1-800-NAVYINN or 011-34-956-82-2643) handle most transient accommodations.

Education for dependent children is provided by Department of Defense schools located on the base. The Navy campus provides college courses from the City Colleges of Chicago, Embry-Riddle Aeronautical University, Rota Community College (short-term, self-improvement, noncredit courses), the University of Oklahoma, and the University of Maryland.

Personal Services. Most family and personal services are processed through the Navy Family Service Center. Medical services are provided by the U.S. naval hospital, a facility opened in 1989 that offers family-practice care as well as inpatient and outpatient care, dental facilities, and a number of specialty clinics. Extensive hospitalization or conditions beyond the capability of the local medical staff are handled by evacuating the patients either to other U.S. hospitals in Europe or to the United States.

The Navy exchange at Rota is one of the largest in the Mediterranean, offering many retail and service outlets, including furniture, appliances, hardware, small-appliance repair, a video rental shop, a service station, and a computer store. The commissary store at Rota offers shoppers more than 3,400 line items. Eggs, fruits, and vegetables are available year-round from Spain and Germany; fresh meat is available from Germany and England.

Because Rota is not a U.S. military base, military personnel on leave are not authorized use of the Navy exchange or commissary. Access to the base is strictly controlled by the Spanish Navy, but morale, welfare, and recreational facilities are available to everyone.

Recreation. Recreational facilities include a sixteen-lane bowling center, two swimming pools, 14 tennis courts, and five handball/racquetball courts. The base also has a Nautilus center; a fitness center with steam rooms, saunas, and a retail pro shop; a marina; a 360-seat movie theater; a drive-in theater; and a 200-acre, 18-hole, par-72 golf course. A woodworking shop, an auto hobby shop, an arts and crafts center, and a photo lab are also available.

The Local Area. Spain is a land of oranges, olives, horses, and sherry. It has been populated continuously for over 2,000 years. The climate in this part of Spain is sunny and warm, and the temperatures range from 75 to 90° F in summer and from 40 to 70° F in winter. Don't let the comparative mildness of the winters fool you; they can be very damp, so you will find sweaters and coats handy. The summers are very dry.

The nearby town of Puerto da Santa Maria, only 15 minutes away, offers rows of sidewalk cafes with fresh seafood and shellfish ready to eat. This is a country where you can windsurf, sail, fish, and skin-dive along the Atlantic in the morning, and ski and mountain climb in the Sierra Nevada in the afternoon—and the cost of living here is moderate. Within only a few hours' drive from Rota are the cities of Seville, Cordoba, and Granada. The region offers entertainment ranging from flamenco dancing and city fairs to bullfights and religious festivals.

For more information, write to Navy Family Service Center, PSC 819, Box 57, FPO AE 09645. Home page: *www.ntams.rota.navy.mil/nsga.*

TURKEY

Air Force

INCIRLIK AIR BASE

Hos geldiniz, as the Turks say, "Welcome" to Incirlik Air Base, the only U.S. tactical air operation between Italy and the Far East. Turkey occupies a strategic position within the NATO Alliance, sharing, as it does, borders with Syria, Iran, Georgia, Armenia, Iraq, and Greece. Turkey contributes a significant share of manpower to NATO.

History. Incirlik (pronounced "in-jur-lick") in the Turkish language means "fig orchard," which is what the land was used for before 1951, when construction on the air base began. The first U.S. unit arrived there on 10 May 1954, when the 7,216th Air Base Squadron at Wheelus Field, Libya, began transferring personnel and equipment to the installation, known in those days as Adana Air Base. It was from Incirlik, on 1 May 1960, that Francis Gary Powers began his ill-fated reconnaissance flight over the Soviet Union, where his shootdown caused international embarrassment to the United States.

Today Incirlik is home to the 39th Wing, which is responsible for preparing and conducting combat and combat support operations as directed by the U.S. Air Forces, Europe, and U.S. European Command. One of these missions is to provide support for the no-fly zone over the 36th parallel. Personnel of the 628th Air Mobility Support Squadron provide airlift service for the Mediterranean region, supporting C-5 Galaxy, C-141 Starlifter, C-130 Hercules, C-17 Globemaster, and C-9 Nightingale aircraft, moving an average of 2,390 personnel and 1,212 tons of cargo each month aboard 433 regularly scheduled flights through Incirlik. The American population at Incirlik, which is a joint-user air base (shared with the 10th Tanker Base Command, Turkish Air Force), is 5,200—approximately 2,800 military (including members deployed to support the Combined Task Force Operation Northern Watch) and 2,400 civilians (U.S. government employees and family members).

Historic Clock Tower in Izmir, Turkey USAF PHOTO

Housing and Schools. There are 900 units of family housing at Incirlik—225 single-family officer housing and 675 single-family enlisted housing. There are fifty double-occupancy unaccompanied officer houses, as well as 20 officer dormitory rooms and 622 enlisted dormitory rooms. Transient housing is available at the Hodja Inn with 344 visiting quarters and 80 temporary-living facilities. All military and Department of Defense civilians must live on base.

Incirlik has an elementary school, a middle school, and a high school for dependent children, as well as a child-care center and preschool. Adult education is available through the base education office and includes college courses from the University of Maryland and City Colleges of Chicago.

Personal Services. Medical care at Incirlik is provided by the base hospital and dental clinic. A wide range of services is available, including internal medicine, optometry, general surgery, radiology, and veterinary services.

The base exchange at Incirlik is open seven days a week and includes retail shopping needs and a catalog service. The exchange also operates a number of concessions, including a furniture store, an optical shop, a car sales outlet, a video rental club, and a food court, which provides a variety of fast-food fare, including a Baskin Robbins ice cream shop, a submarine sandwich stand, and a pizza restaurant. The exchange also operates the Oasis Theater, featuring popular stateside movies seven days a week.

The commissary at Incirlik is comparable to any stateside grocery store. The produce section features a combination of U.S. and locally purchased fresh produce; meat from the States and England is available in a variety of popular cuts.

Recreation. A wide variety of recreational facilities are available at Incirlik, including an Olympic-size swimming pool; a nine-hole golf course; an 18-lane bowling center; arts, crafts, and auto hobby shops; a gymnasium; a rod and gun club, a scuba club; a library with 20,000 books; and a consolidated officers/enlisted club system.

The Local Area. Incirlik is located in the southern part of Turkey, about eight miles east of Adana, Turkey's fourth-largest city (population over one million), and thirty miles from the Mediterranean Sea. The seasons in this part of Turkey are distinct and correspond to those we are used to in the States; the winters are cool and damp, and the late summer months (July, August, and September) are hot and dusty. The climate farther east is more severe, particularly in the winter.

Turkey is a bridge between Europe and Asia. It consists of more than 300,000 square miles and is separated from European Thrace by the Bosphorus, the Sea of Marmara, and the Dardenelles. Recorded history began in Turkey with the Hittite Empire, more than 4,000 years ago. Today Turkey is an agricultural and industrial nation, whose four major cities (Adana, Izmir, Istanbul, and Ankara) have populations of up to eight million. Turkey shares the same latitude as Philadelphia, Indianapolis, and Denver.

Turkey abounds in historic sites. Only 24 miles from Adana is Tarsus, birthplace of St. Paul and rendezvous of Antony and Cleopatra; within easy driving distance is Antakya-Antioch, where St. Peter founded the first Christian community; 66 miles southeast of Adana is the Plain of Issos, where Alexander the Great defeated Darius in 333 B.C.

The Turks are a very proud and conservative people who consider casual manners and clothing inappropriate. While Turkish men do not consider it odd to hold hands in public, they view shorts as unacceptable masculine wearing apparel. As a general rule, it is not wise for a man to strike up a conversation with a Turkish woman unless he has been formally introduced to her. Insulting the Turkish flag, armed forces, or Mustafa Kemal Ataturk, the founder of the Republic of Turkey, can land you in jail. Trafficking in narcotics will land an American in jail for a long time, a minimum of 30 years for manufacturing, exporting, or importing drugs; the penalties for possession of illegal drugs are three to five years in prison and fines ranging into the millions of Turkish lira. (There are about 470,000 lira to the dollar.) The American who can observe these cultural sensitivities will find the Turks an interesting and hospitable people, staunch allies of the United States who fought with extraordinary valor alongside our forces during the Korean War. For the American so privileged, traveling and living in Turkey can be an exceptionally rewarding experience.

For more information, write to 39th Wing Public Affairs, Unit 7090, Box 135, APO AE 09824-5000. Home page: *www.incirlik.af.mil;* e-mail: *39wg.pa@incirlik.af.mil.* (Note: Country and theater approval is needed to visit Incirlik.)

IZMIR AIR STATION

Izmir Air Station (IAS) is located in the port city of Izmir, the third-largest city in Turkey. Approximately 700 U.S. military personnel, 250 civilians, and 800 family members are assigned to the station's various units. The host unit at Izmir is the 425th Air Base Squadron, which has the mission of supporting all U.S. and NATO units in the Izmir vicinity. Additionally, the group manages U.S. support to nearby Cigli Turkish air base.

The 425th ABS is headquartered in an eight-story office building three blocks from Izmir Bay. Other group functions are housed in approximately 30 leased buildings located throughout the city.

Allied Land Forces Southeastern Europe is a NATO unit responsible for deterring all forms of aggression along the Turkish Straits, eastern Thrace, and Turkey's southern border and eastern frontier. NATO's LANDSOUTHEAST headquarters is located on Sirinyer Garrison, about 15 minutes from downtown Izmir. Also located at Sirinyer Garrison is the Sixth Allied Tactical Air Force, whose mission is to ensure full-time air defense of Turkey and the combat readiness of all assigned forces.

Housing and Schools. Izmir Air Station doesn't have a "fence line" like other military installations, and there are no dormitories or base housing. All members assigned there live on the economy. Rents range from $250 to $1,100, depending on the area. The rent for a three-bedroom apartment meeting minimum standards, with running water and electricity, averages about $590 a month. The billeting facility is in the five-star Izmir Etap Pullman Hotel. Three floors are leased strictly for air station use, and there is a billeting office in the lobby.

The Department of Defense Dependents School offers classes for about 350 students in kindergarten through twelfth grade.

Personal Services and Recreation. The Izmir Community Center features a child-development activity, a family support center, a fitness center, a recreation center, a library, a bookstore, an audiovisual sales store, a thrift shop, and the American Youth Activities Center. The nearby exchange minimall houses a base exchange, a snack bar, an ice cream shop, beauty and barber shops, a dry cleaner, a tailor shop, and various specialty shops.

Six miles from downtown is Bayrakli Park, a complete fitness and recreation complex solely for the military community. The park has a swimming and wading pool; a large playground; a picnic area; a snack bar; softball, football, and soccer fields; a running track; and tennis, basketball, and racquetball courts.

The Local Area. The metropolitan city of Izmir (population over three million) is located on a bay of the Aegean Sea on Turkey's west coast. The people of Izmir earn their living in tourism, industry, the import-export business, and agriculture. Major businesses are found in food, heavy steel, automotive, and import-export. Izmir is divided into four boroughs, each with its own mayor and subgovernor, who report to the Izmir governor.

Local water and electricity services may cause infrequent hardships on the American residents in Izmir. Tap water is generally considered nonpotable, but bottled water is readily available. Home telephone service is available but expensive. As Izmir is located in a cove, winter coal burning for heating purposes and the massive number of diesel-burning vehicles are causing an increasingly hazardous air pollution problem in the city. Public transportation is very convenient and cheap.

With a recorded history going back as far as 3000 B.C., there are many historic sites to visit in the area. Smyrna, Ephesus, and Pergamum are just a few. An ancient castle built by Alexander the Great still stands today, overlooking Izmir from Kadifekale Hill. The area is well known for its gold, copper, brass, carpets, and embroidered goods. August in Izmir presents the opportunity to visit the city's international fair, famous throughout Europe.

For more information, write to Public Affairs Division, 425th Air Base Squadron, USAFE, Unit 6870, Box 50, APO AE 09821.

PART III

Maps

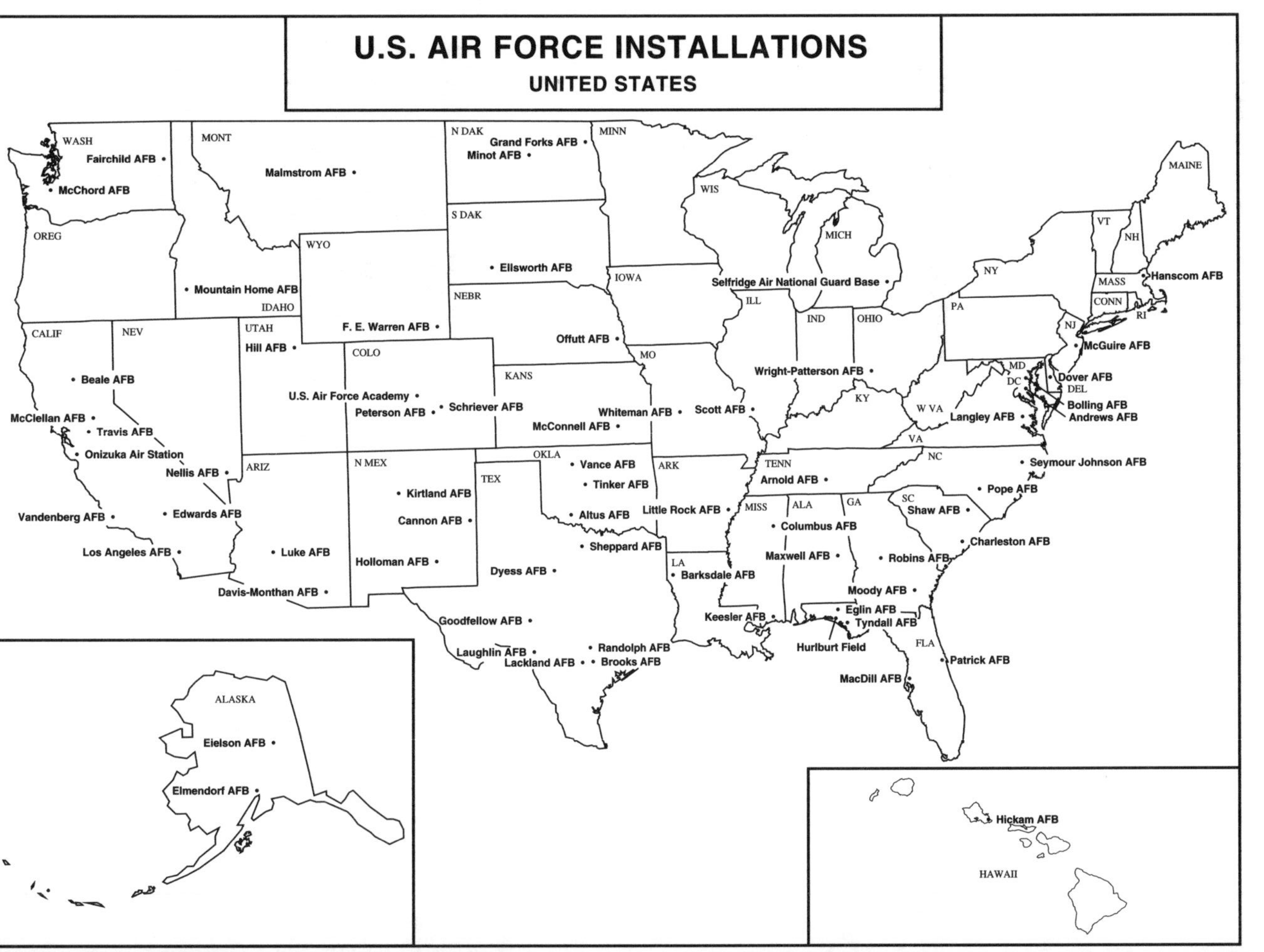
U.S. AIR FORCE INSTALLATIONS
UNITED STATES
WASH
Fairchild AFB
McChord AFB
OREG
MONT
Malmstrom AFB
N DAK
Grand Forks AFB
Minot AFB
MINN
WIS
MICH
MAINE
VT
NH
S DAK
WYO
Ellsworth AFB
IOWA
Selfridge Air National Guard Base
NY
MASS
Hanscom AFB
CONN
RI
Mountain Home AFB
IDAHO
NEBR
ILL
IND
OHIO
PA
NJ
CALIF
NEV
UTAH
F. E. Warren AFB
Hill AFB
COLO
Offutt AFB
MO
McGuire AFB
Beale AFB
KANS
Wright-Patterson AFB
MD
DC
Dover AFB
DEL
U.S. Air Force Academy
Peterson AFB
Schriever AFB
Whiteman AFB
Scott AFB
KY
W VA
Bolling AFB
Andrews AFB
McClellan AFB
Travis AFB
McConnell AFB
Langley AFB
VA
Onizuka Air Station
OKLA
Vance AFB
TENN
NC
Seymour Johnson AFB
Nellis AFB
ARIZ
N MEX
ARK
Arnold AFB
TEX
Tinker AFB
Kirtland AFB
Pope AFB
SC
Shaw AFB
Vandenberg AFB
Edwards AFB
Altus AFB
Little Rock AFB
MISS
ALA
GA
Cannon AFB
Columbus AFB
Charleston AFB
Los Angeles AFB
Luke AFB
Sheppard AFB
Holloman AFB
LA
Maxwell AFB
Robins AFB
Dyess AFB
Barksdale AFB
Davis-Monthan AFB
Moody AFB
Eglin AFB
Goodfellow AFB
Keesler AFB
Tyndall AFB
Hurlburt Field
FLA
Laughlin AFB
Randolph AFB
Lackland AFB
Brooks AFB
Patrick AFB
MacDill AFB
ALASKA
Eielson AFB
Elmendorf AFB
Hickam AFB
HAWAII

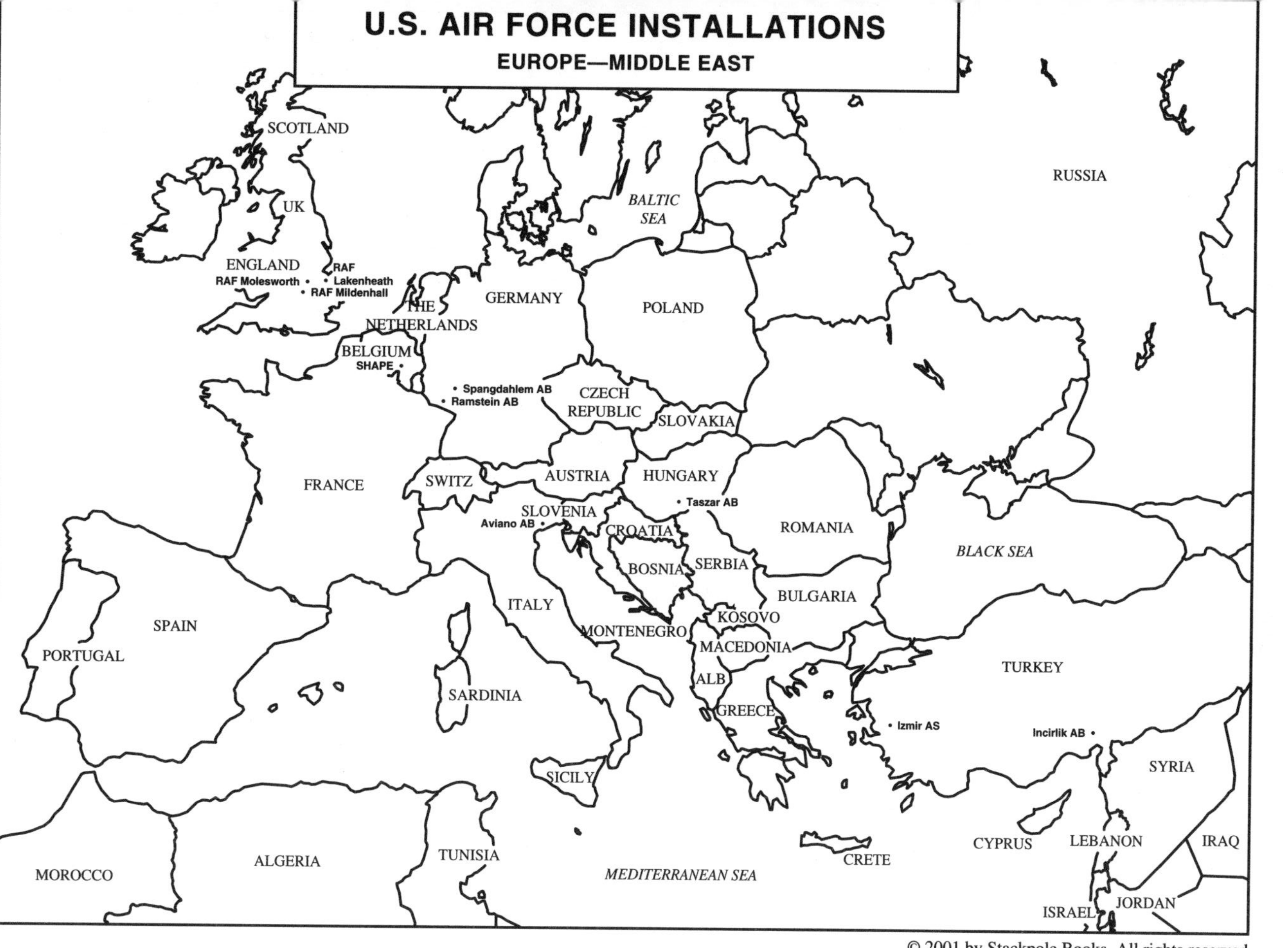
U.S. AIR FORCE INSTALLATIONS
EUROPE—MIDDLE EAST
SCOTLAND
UK
ENGLAND
RAF Molesworth
RAF Lakenheath
RAF Mildenhall
BALTIC SEA
RUSSIA
THE NETHERLANDS
BELGIUM
SHAPE
GERMANY
Spangdahlem AB
Ramstein AB
POLAND
CZECH REPUBLIC
SLOVAKIA
FRANCE
SWITZ
AUSTRIA
HUNGARY
Taszar AB
SLOVENIA
Aviano AB
CROATIA
ROMANIA
BLACK SEA
BOSNIA
SERBIA
BULGARIA
ITALY
KOSOVO
MONTENEGRO
MACEDONIA
SPAIN
PORTUGAL
TURKEY
ALB
SARDINIA
GREECE
Izmir AS
Incirlik AB
SYRIA
SICILY
CYPRUS
LEBANON
IRAQ
MOROCCO
ALGERIA
TUNISIA
MEDITERRANEAN SEA
CRETE
ISRAEL
JORDAN

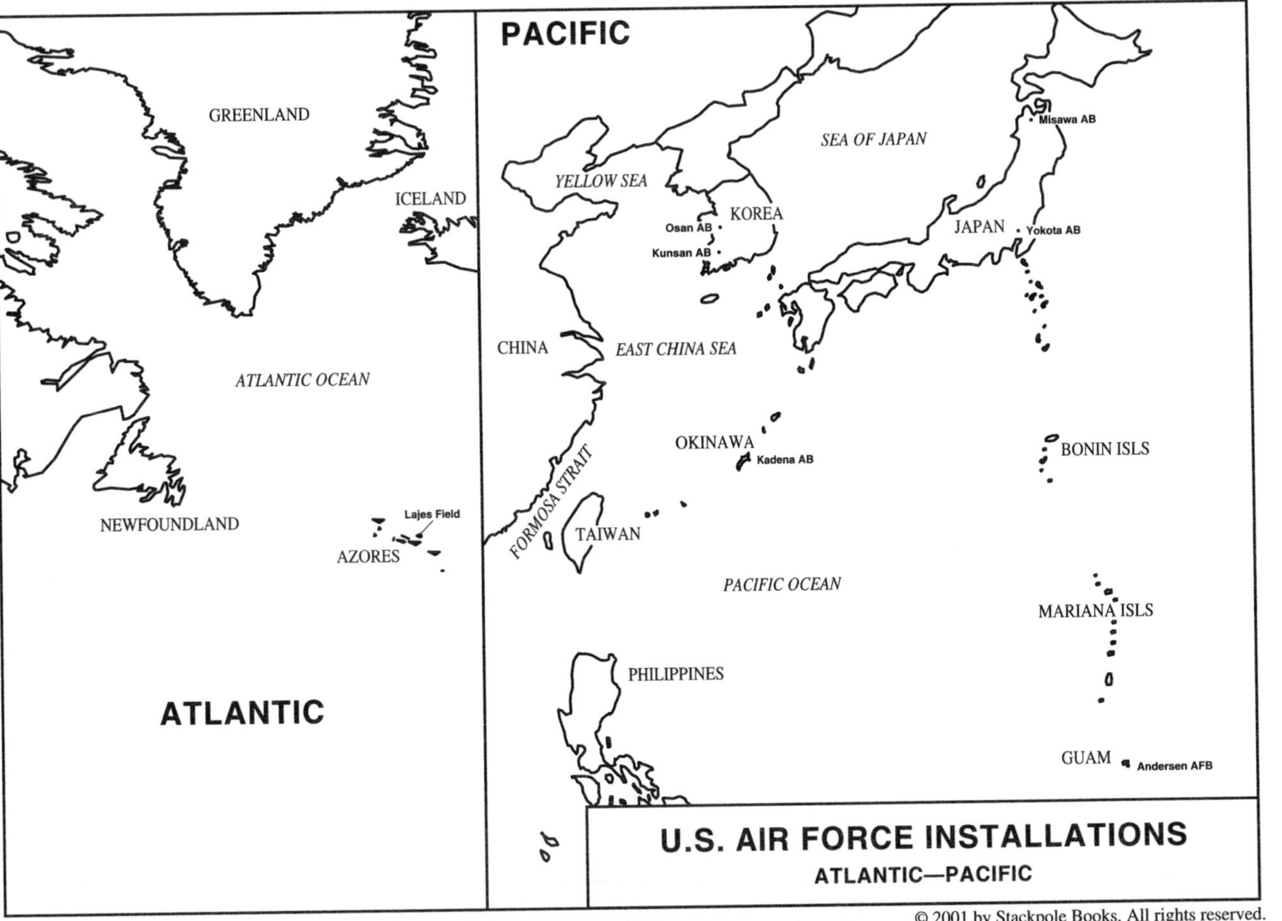
ATLANTIC
GREENLAND
ICELAND
ATLANTIC OCEAN
NEWFOUNDLAND
Lajes Field
AZORES
PACIFIC
YELLOW SEA
SEA OF JAPAN
Misawa AB
KOREA
Osan AB
Kunsan AB
JAPAN
Yokota AB
CHINA
EAST CHINA SEA
OKINAWA
Kadena AB
BONIN ISLS
FORMOSA STRAIT
TAIWAN
PACIFIC OCEAN
MARIANA ISLS
PHILIPPINES
GUAM
Andersen AFB
U.S. AIR FORCE INSTALLATIONS
ATLANTIC—PACIFIC
© 2001 by Stackpole Books. All rights reserved.

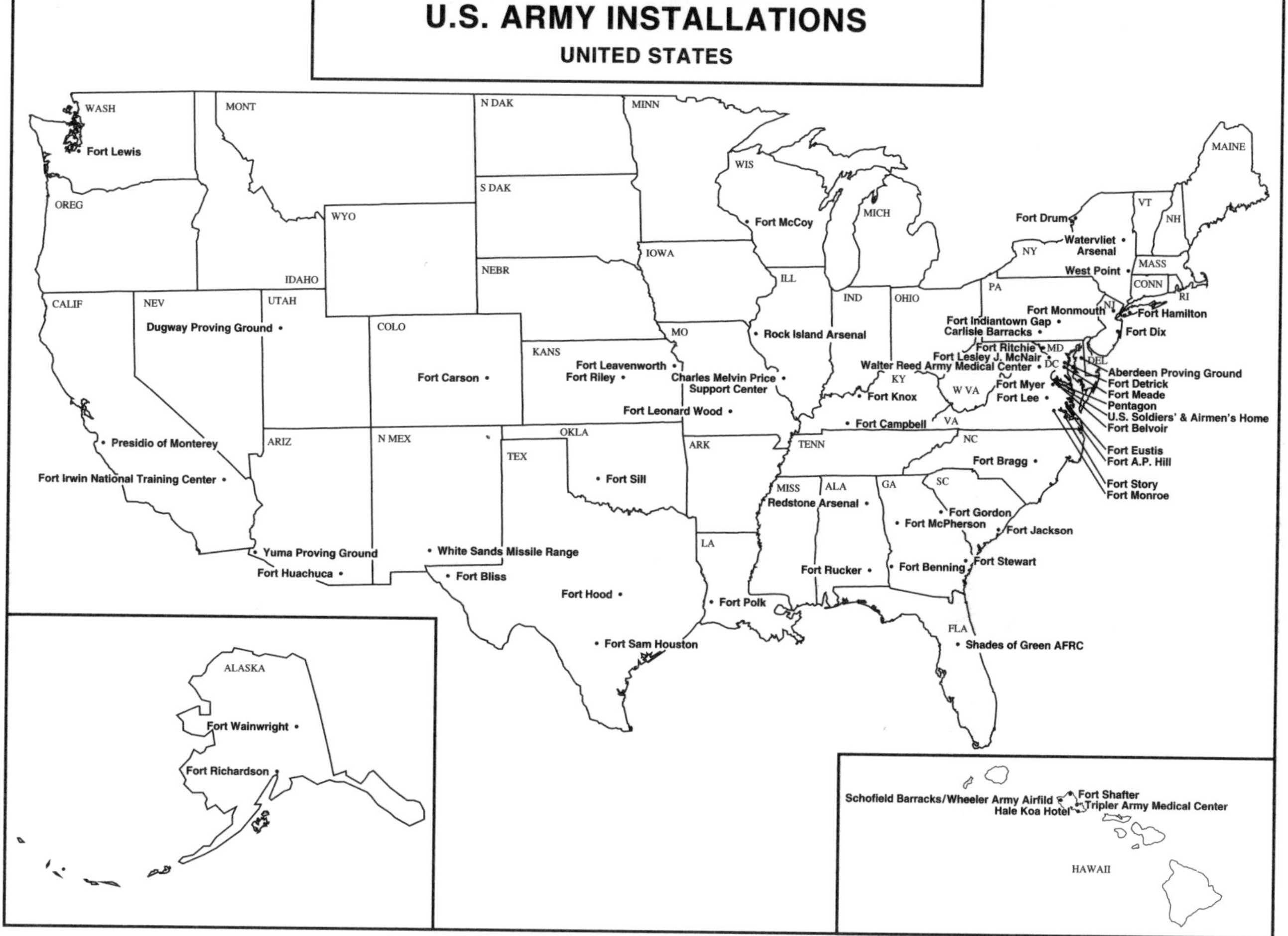
U.S. ARMY INSTALLATIONS
UNITED STATES
WASH
MONT
N DAK
MINN
OREG
S DAK
WYO
WIS
MICH
IDAHO
NEBR
IOWA
ILL
CALIF
NEV
UTAH
COLO
KANS
MO
IND
OHIO
PA
NY
VT
NH
MAINE
MASS
CONN
RI
NJ
MD
DEL
DC
KY
W VA
VA
NC
TENN
OKLA
ARK
ARIZ
N MEX
TEX
MISS
ALA
GA
SC
LA
FLA
ALASKA
HAWAII
Fort Lewis
Dugway Proving Ground
Presidio of Monterey
Fort Irwin National Training Center
Yuma Proving Ground
Fort Huachuca
White Sands Missile Range
Fort Bliss
Fort Carson
Fort Leavenworth
Fort Riley
Charles Melvin Price
Support Center
Fort Leonard Wood
Fort Sill
Fort Hood
Fort Sam Houston
Fort Polk
Fort McCoy
Rock Island Arsenal
Redstone Arsenal
Fort Rucker
Fort Knox
Fort Campbell
Fort Benning
Fort McPherson
Fort Gordon
Fort Jackson
Fort Stewart
Shades of Green AFRC
Fort Bragg
Fort Drum
Watervliet
Arsenal
West Point
Fort Monmouth
Fort Hamilton
Fort Dix
Fort Indiantown Gap
Carlisle Barracks
Fort Ritchie
Fort Lesley J. McNair
Walter Reed Army Medical Center
Fort Myer
Fort Lee
Aberdeen Proving Ground
Fort Detrick
Fort Meade
Pentagon
U.S. Soldiers' & Airmen's Home
Fort Belvoir
Fort Eustis
Fort A.P. Hill
Fort Story
Fort Monroe
Fort Wainwright
Fort Richardson
Schofield Barracks/Wheeler Army Airfild
Hale Koa Hotel
Fort Shafter
Tripler Army Medical Center

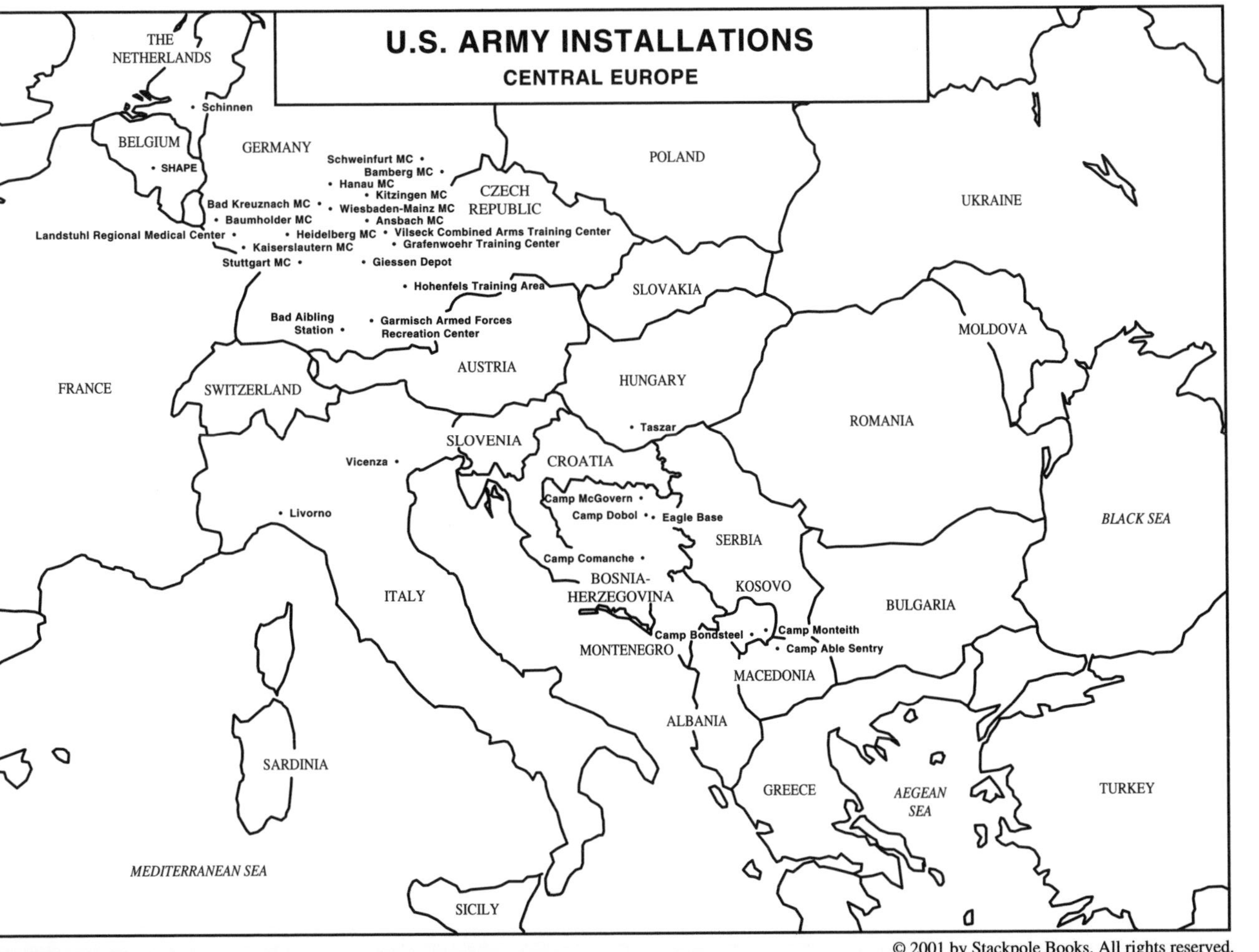

U.S. ARMY INSTALLATIONS
CENTRAL EUROPE
THE NETHERLANDS
Schinnen
BELGIUM
SHAPE
GERMANY
Schweinfurt MC
Bamberg MC
Hanau MC
Kitzingen MC
Bad Kreuznach MC
Wiesbaden-Mainz MC
Baumholder MC
Ansbach MC
Landstuhl Regional Medical Center
Heidelberg MC
Vilseck Combined Arms Training Center
Kaiserslautern MC
Grafenwoehr Training Center
Stuttgart MC
Giessen Depot
Hohenfels Training Area
Bad Aibling Station
Garmisch Armed Forces Recreation Center
CZECH REPUBLIC
POLAND
UKRAINE
SLOVAKIA
MOLDOVA
AUSTRIA
HUNGARY
FRANCE
SWITZERLAND
ROMANIA
Taszar
SLOVENIA
CROATIA
Vicenza
Camp McGovern
Livorno
Camp Dobol
Eagle Base
BLACK SEA
SERBIA
Camp Comanche
BOSNIA-HERZEGOVINA
KOSOVO
ITALY
BULGARIA
Camp Monteith
Camp Bondsteel
MONTENEGRO
Camp Able Sentry
MACEDONIA
ALBANIA
SARDINIA
GREECE
AEGEAN SEA
TURKEY
MEDITERRANEAN SEA
SICILY

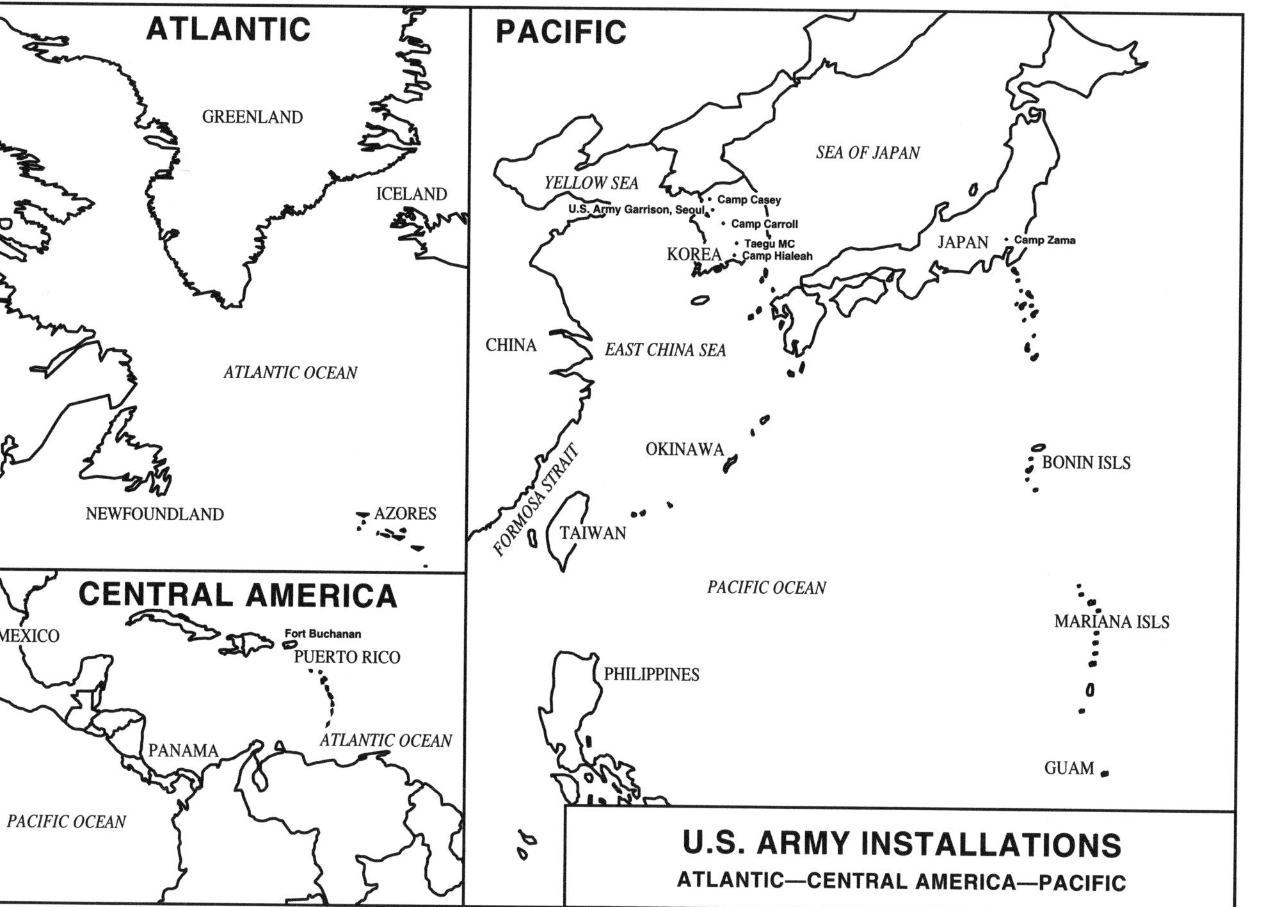
ATLANTIC
GREENLAND
ICELAND
ATLANTIC OCEAN
NEWFOUNDLAND
AZORES
CENTRAL AMERICA
MEXICO
Fort Buchanan
PUERTO RICO
PANAMA
ATLANTIC OCEAN
PACIFIC OCEAN
PACIFIC
SEA OF JAPAN
YELLOW SEA
Camp Casey
U.S. Army Garrison, Seoul
Camp Carroll
Taegu MC
Camp Hialeah
KOREA
JAPAN
Camp Zama
CHINA
EAST CHINA SEA
OKINAWA
FORMOSA STRAIT
TAIWAN
BONIN ISLS
PACIFIC OCEAN
MARIANA ISLS
PHILIPPINES
GUAM
U.S. ARMY INSTALLATIONS
ATLANTIC—CENTRAL AMERICA—PACIFIC

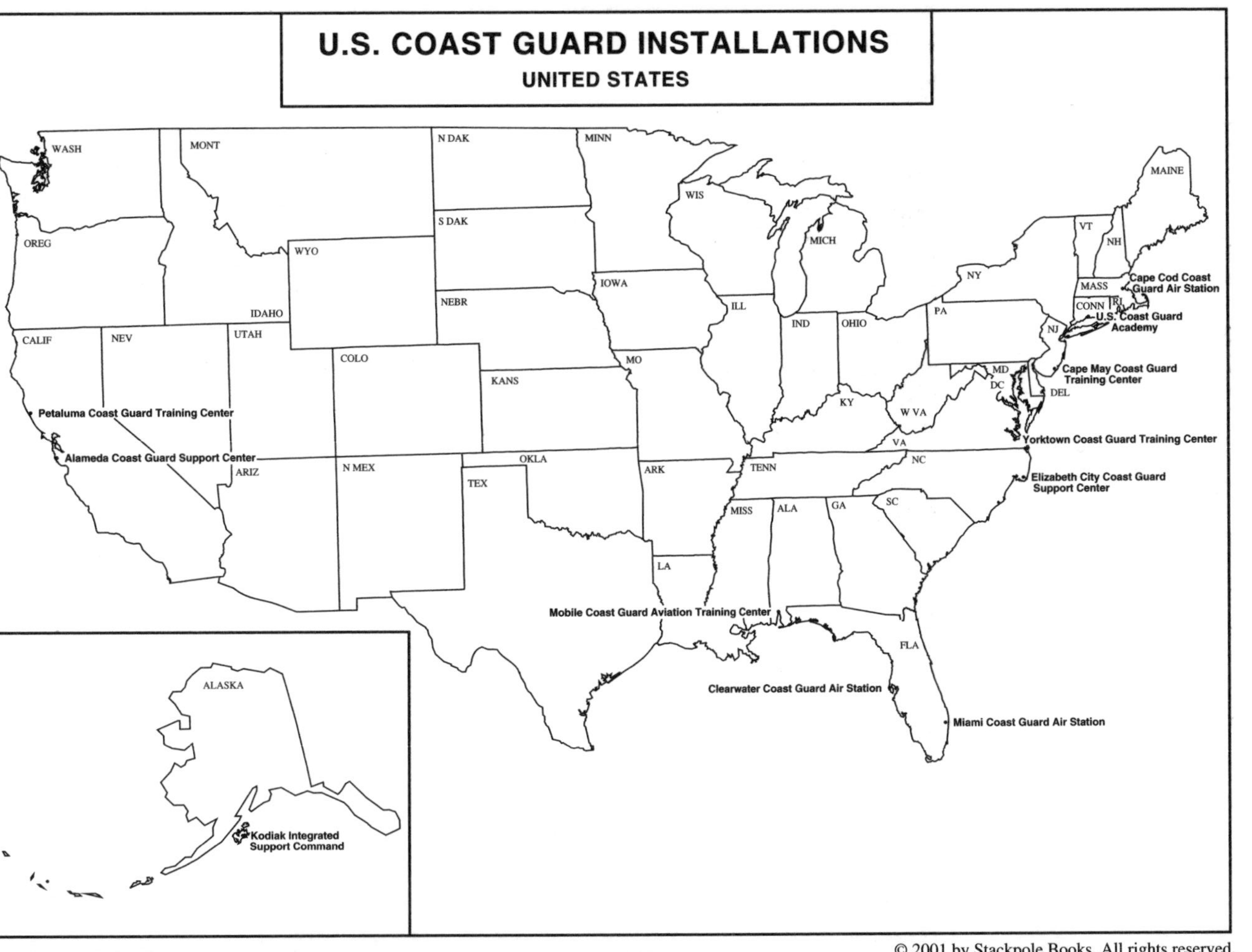
U.S. COAST GUARD INSTALLATIONS
UNITED STATES
WASH
MONT
N DAK
MINN
OREG
S DAK
WIS
MICH
WYO
IOWA
NEBR
IDAHO
ILL
IND
OHIO
PA
NY
MAINE
VT
NH
MASS
CONN
RI
NJ
Cape Cod Coast Guard Air Station
U.S. Coast Guard Academy
CALIF
NEV
UTAH
COLO
MO
KANS
KY
W VA
MD
DC
DEL
Cape May Coast Guard Training Center
Petaluma Coast Guard Training Center
Alameda Coast Guard Support Center
ARIZ
N MEX
OKLA
ARK
TENN
VA
NC
Yorktown Coast Guard Training Center
Elizabeth City Coast Guard Support Center
TEX
MISS
ALA
GA
SC
LA
Mobile Coast Guard Aviation Training Center
FLA
Clearwater Coast Guard Air Station
Miami Coast Guard Air Station
ALASKA
Kodiak Integrated Support Command

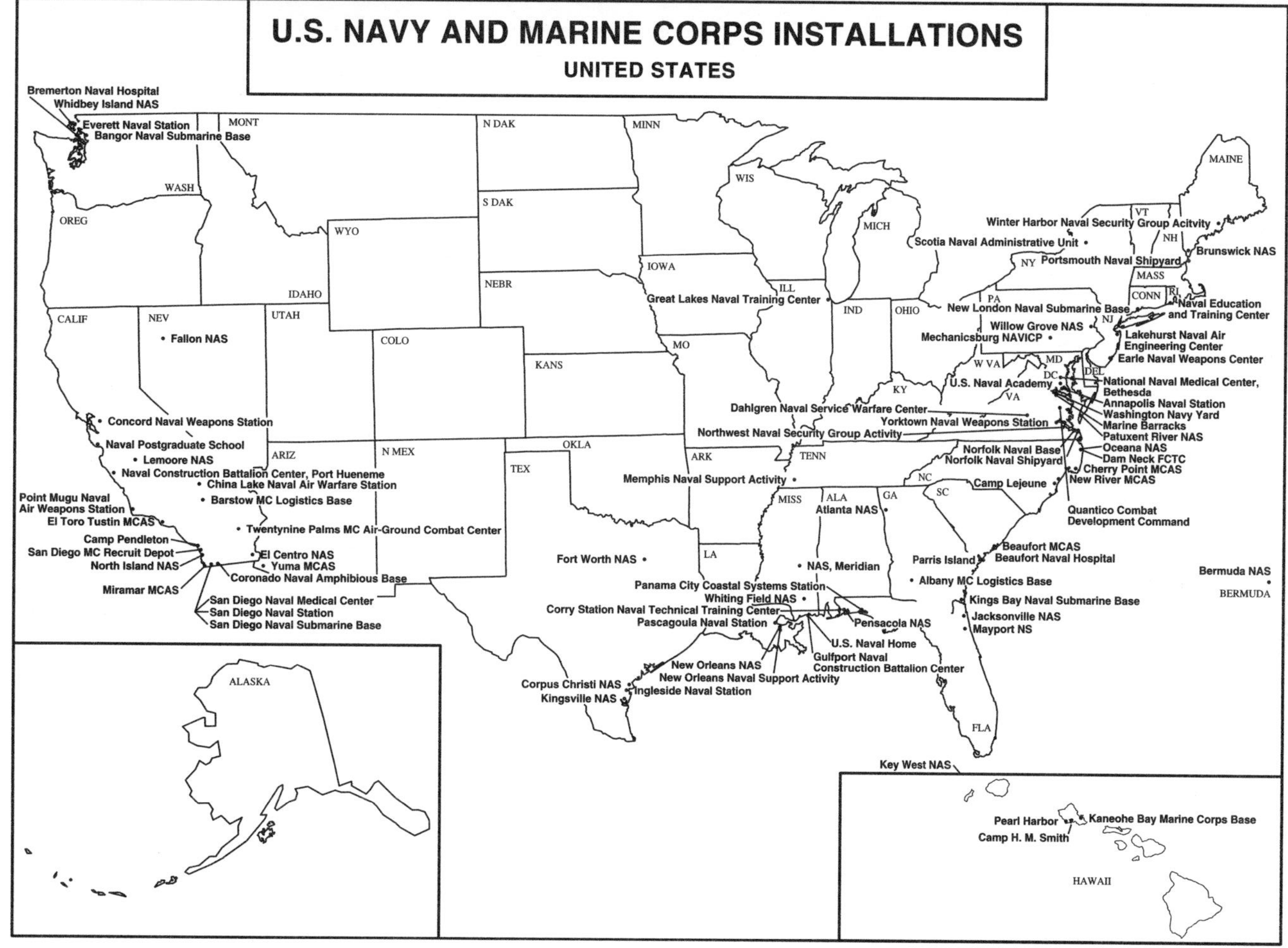
U.S. NAVY AND MARINE CORPS INSTALLATIONS
UNITED STATES
Bremerton Naval Hospital
Whidbey Island NAS
Everett Naval Station
Bangor Naval Submarine Base
Concord Naval Weapons Station
Naval Postgraduate School
Lemoore NAS
Naval Construction Battalion Center, Port Hueneme
China Lake Naval Air Warfare Station
Barstow MC Logistics Base
Fallon NAS
Point Mugu Naval Air Weapons Station
El Toro Tustin MCAS
Camp Pendleton
San Diego MC Recruit Depot
North Island NAS
Miramar MCAS
Twentynine Palms MC Air-Ground Combat Center
El Centro NAS
Yuma MCAS
Coronado Naval Amphibious Base
San Diego Naval Medical Center
San Diego Naval Station
San Diego Naval Submarine Base
Fort Worth NAS
Corpus Christi NAS
Kingsville NAS
Ingleside Naval Station
New Orleans NAS
New Orleans Naval Support Activity
Panama City Coastal Systems Station
Whiting Field NAS
Corry Station Naval Technical Training Center
Pascagoula Naval Station
Pensacola NAS
U.S. Naval Home
Gulfport Naval Construction Battalion Center
Memphis Naval Support Activity
NAS, Meridian
Atlanta NAS
Parris Island
Beaufort MCAS
Beaufort Naval Hospital
Albany MC Logistics Base
Kings Bay Naval Submarine Base
Jacksonville NAS
Mayport NS
Key West NAS
Great Lakes Naval Training Center
Dahlgren Naval Service Warfare Center
Yorktown Naval Weapons Station
Northwest Naval Security Group Activity
Norfolk Naval Base
Norfolk Naval Shipyard
Camp Lejeune
Quantico Combat Development Command
U.S. Naval Academy
Mechanicsburg NAVICP
Willow Grove NAS
New London Naval Submarine Base
Scotia Naval Administrative Unit
Portsmouth Naval Shipyard
Winter Harbor Naval Security Group Acitvity
Brunswick NAS
Naval Education and Training Center
Lakehurst Naval Air Engineering Center
Earle Naval Weapons Center
National Naval Medical Center, Bethesda
Annapolis Naval Station
Washington Navy Yard
Marine Barracks
Patuxent River NAS
Oceana NAS
Dam Neck FCTC
Cherry Point MCAS
New River MCAS
Bermuda NAS
BERMUDA
Pearl Harbor
Camp H. M. Smith
Kaneohe Bay Marine Corps Base
HAWAII
ALASKA
WASH
OREG
CALIF
NEV
IDAHO
MONT
WYO
UTAH
ARIZ
COLO
N MEX
N DAK
S DAK
NEBR
KANS
OKLA
TEX
MINN
IOWA
MO
ARK
LA
WIS
ILL
MICH
IND
OHIO
KY
TENN
MISS
ALA
GA
FLA
SC
NC
VA
W VA
PA
NY
MD
DC
DEL
NJ
CONN
RI
MASS
VT
NH
MAINE

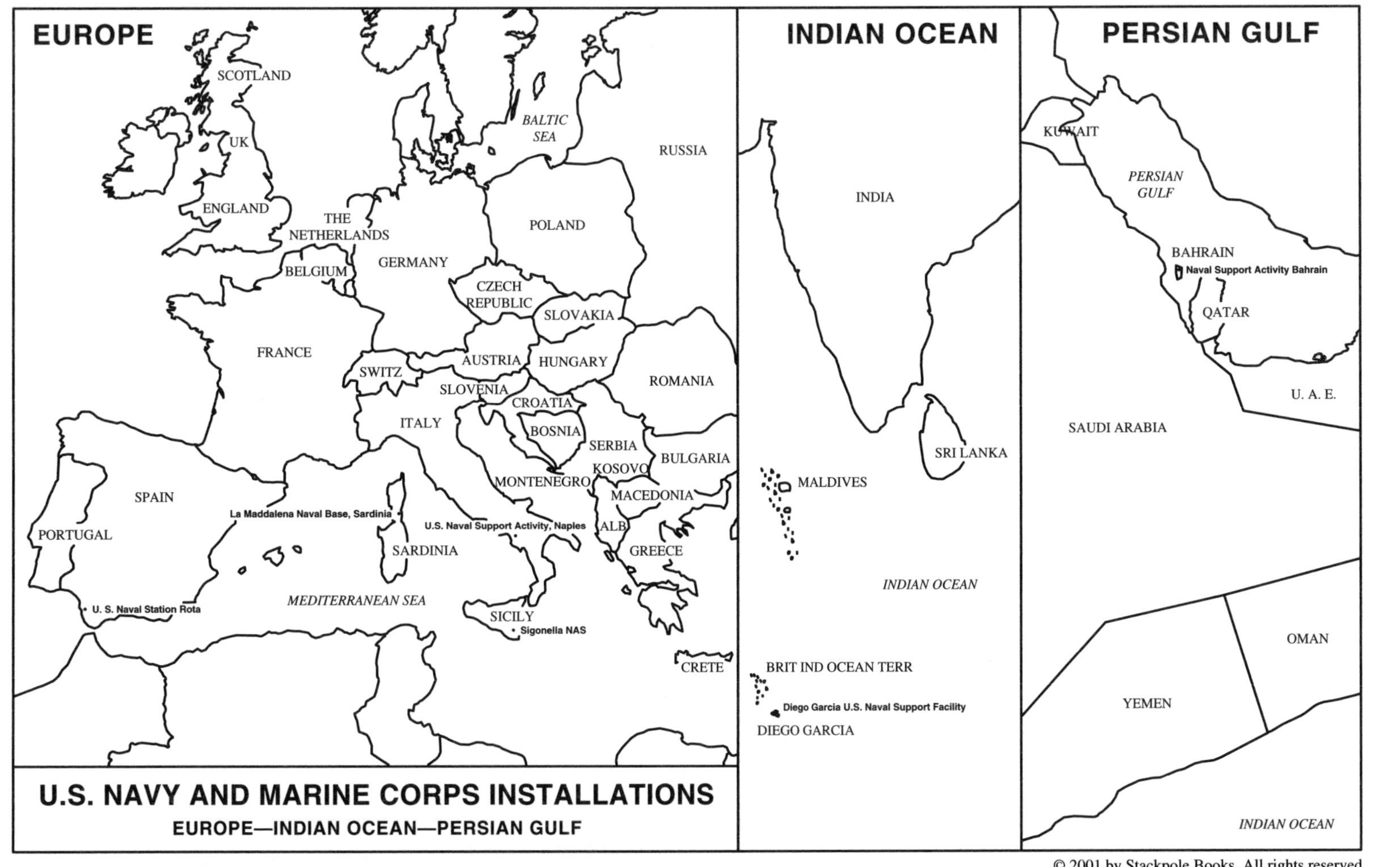

U.S. NAVY AND MARINE CORPS INSTALLATIONS

EUROPE—INDIAN OCEAN—PERSIAN GULF

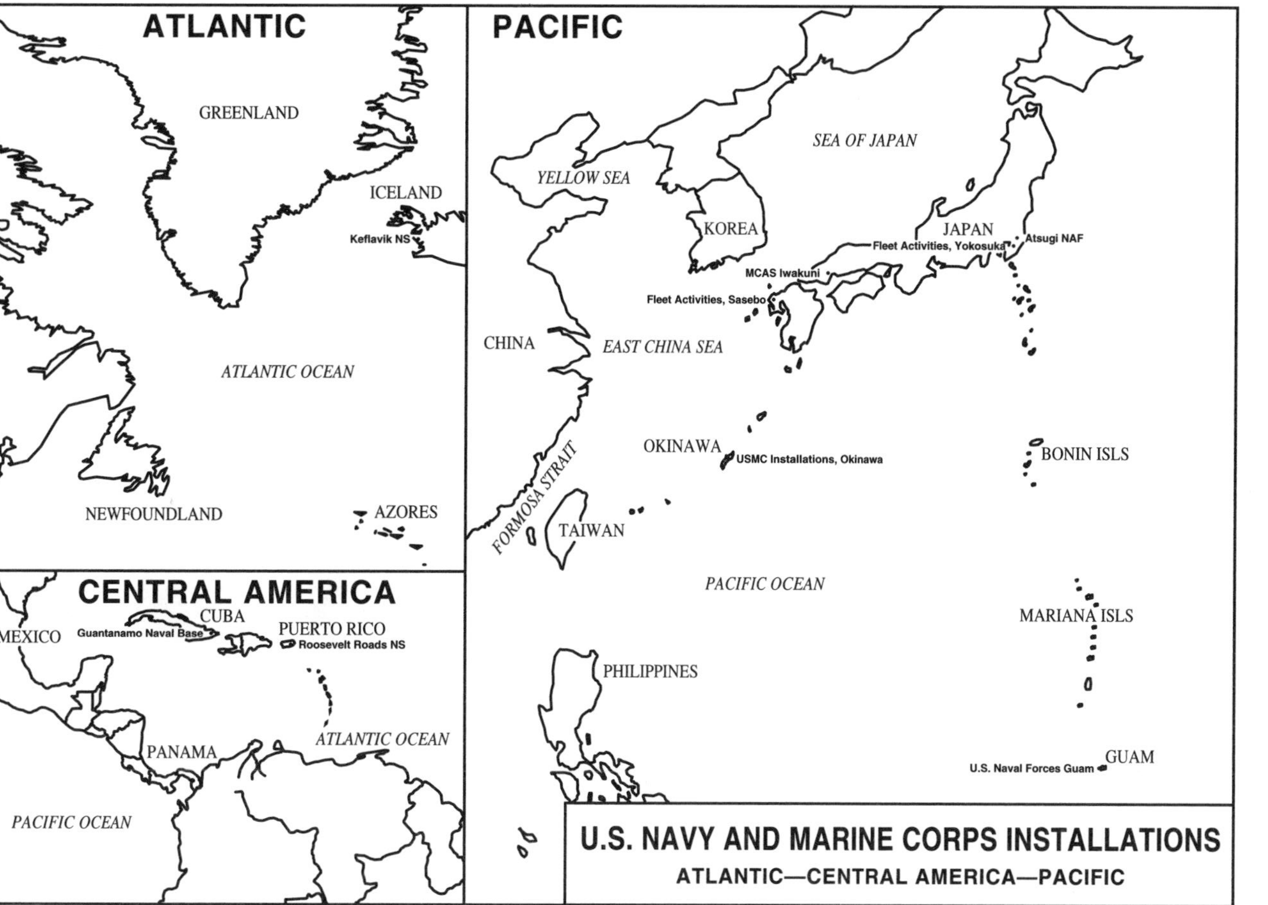
ATLANTIC
GREENLAND
ICELAND
Keflavik NS
ATLANTIC OCEAN
NEWFOUNDLAND
AZORES
CENTRAL AMERICA
MEXICO
CUBA
Guantanamo Naval Base
PUERTO RICO
Roosevelt Roads NS
PANAMA
ATLANTIC OCEAN
PACIFIC OCEAN
PACIFIC
YELLOW SEA
SEA OF JAPAN
KOREA
JAPAN
Fleet Activities, Yokosuka
Atsugi NAF
MCAS Iwakuni
Fleet Activities, Sasebo
CHINA
EAST CHINA SEA
OKINAWA
USMC Installations, Okinawa
BONIN ISLS
FORMOSA STRAIT
TAIWAN
PACIFIC OCEAN
MARIANA ISLS
PHILIPPINES
U.S. Naval Forces Guam
GUAM
U.S. NAVY AND MARINE CORPS INSTALLATIONS
ATLANTIC—CENTRAL AMERICA—PACIFIC

APPENDIX

The author and the publisher strive to make this guide as complete as possible by contacting all U. S. military installations worldwide and asking them to participate. Sometimes, through circumstances beyond anyone's control, the requested updates are never received or our queries go unanswered. As a service to our readers, addresses of installations for which insufficient information had been received as of press time are listed below.

Anniston Army Depot: 7 Frankfort Avenue, Anniston, AL 36201-4199

Augsburg, Germany: AST-Augsburg, Unit 25001, APO AE 09178

Borinquen Coast Guard Station: Commanding Officer, U.S. CG Air Station, Aguadilla, PR 00604-9999

Bremerton Naval Station: Commander, NS Bremerton, 120 S. Dewey Street, Bremerton, WA 98314-5020

Buckley Air National Guard Base: Commander, 821st Space Group, Buckley ANGB, Aurora, CO 80011-9544

Camp Beauregard: Commanding Officer, Detachment 1, HQ STARC, 409 F Street, Camp Beauregard, Pineville, LA 71360-3737

Camp Frank D. Merrill: HQ, 5th Ranger Training Battalion, Wahsega Road, Dahlonega, GA 30533-9499

Camp Grayling Training Center: Commander, Camp Grayling Maneuver and Training Center, Camp Grayling, MI 49739-0001

Camp Humphreys, Korea: Commander, USA Support Activity & Area III, Unit 15716, APO AP 96271

Camp Red Cloud (Uijongbu), Korea: Unit 15471, APO AP 96258-0003

Charleston Naval Hospital: 3600 Rivers Avenue, North Charleston, SC 29405-7769

Chevres Air Base, Belgium: Commander, 80th ASG (NSSG), CMR 451, Box 6675, SHAPE, APO AE 09708.

Cheyenne Mountain Air Station: Commander, North American Aerospace Defense Command, No. 1 Norad Road, Bldg 101, Cheyenne Mountain Air Station, CO 80914

Coast Guard Headquarters: 2100 2nd Street, SW, Washington, DC 20593-0001

Coast Guard Integrated Support Command: Commander, 14th Coast Guard District, Honolulu, HI 96819-4398

Darmstadt, Germany: Army Community Services, CMR 431, APO AE 09175

Fleet Training Center: Commander, Fleet Antisubmarine Warfare Training Center, 3975 Norman Scott Road, Suite 1, San Diego, CA 92136-5588

Fort Chaffee Training Center: Commander, Ft;. Chaffee Maneuver Training Center, Bldg. 1370, Chaffee, AR 72905-5000

Fort Gillem: Commander, HQ, First Army, Fort Gillem, Forest Park, GA 30050-5000

Geilenkirchen Air Base, Germany: Commander, 470 ABS/FSC, APO AE 09104

Giebelstadt, Germany: Commander, 417th BSB, CMR 408, APO AE 09182

Henderson Hall: HQ, U. S. Marine Corps, 1555 S. Southgate Hall, Arlington, VA 22214-5001

Kelley Air Force Base: Commander, San Antonio Air Logistics Center, Kelly AFB, TX 78241-5842

Little Creek Naval Amphibious Base: 2600 Tarawa Court, Norfolk, VA 23521-3229

Mannheim, Germany: 293rd BSB, Unit 29901, Box 25, APO AE 09086

Moron Air Base, Spain: Commander, Moron Air Base, APO AE 09643-5000

Natick Soldier Systems Command: Commander, NSSC, 15 Kansas Street, Natick, MA 01760-5012

Naval Computer Telecommunications Area Master Station, Hawaii: 500 Center Street, Wahiawa, HI 96786-3050

Pensacola Naval Hospital: 6000 W. Highway 98, Pensacola, FL 32515-0003

Pine Bluff Arsenal: 10020 Kabrich Circle, Pine Bluff, AR 71602-9500

San Juan Coast Guard Base: Commander, San Juan Coast Guard Base, PO Box S-2029, San Juan, PR 00902

Santa Clara Naval Air Reserve Center: 500 Shenandoah Plaza, PO Box 128, Moffett Field, VA 94035-0128

Souda Bay Naval Support Activity, Greece: Commander, US Naval Support Activity, Public Affairs Office, PSC 8154, Box 01, FPO AE 09865

Thule Air Base, Greenland: 12th SWS/CCF, APO AE 09704

Torii Station, Okinawa: Commander, 10th ASG, APO AP 96376

Index